Black Roots

A Beginner's Guide to
Tracing the African American
Family Tree

TONY BURROUGHS

A FIRESIDE BOOK

Published by Simon & Schuster

NEW YORK   LONDON   TORONTO   SYDNEY   SINGAPORE

FIRESIDE
Rockefeller Center
1230 Avenue of the Americas
New York, NY 10020

Copyright © 2001 by Tony Burroughs
All rights reserved,
including the right of reproduction
in whole or in part in any form.

FIRESIDE and colophon are registered trademarks
of Simon & Schuster, Inc.

Design by Stratford Publishing Services

Manufactured in the United States of America

10   9   8   7   6   5   4   3   2   1

Library of Congress Cataloging-in-Publication Data

Burroughs, Tony.
    Black roots : a beginner's guide to tracing the African American family tree / Tony Burroughs.
      p.   cm.
    Includes bibliographical references and index.
    1. Afro-Americans—Genealogy—Handbooks, manuals, etc.   I. Title.

E185.96.B94   2001
929'.1'08996073—dc21
                                           00-048462

ISBN 0-684-84704-3

The photograph on page 168 appears by courtesy of the Daniel and Jessie Lie Farber Collection of
Gravestone Photographs, American Antiquarian Society.

To my best friend, Ralph G. Moore,
for his foresight, understanding, kindness, and generosity

Acknowledgments

Without the help of many other people, this book would not be what it is. An author always needs the perspective, wisdom, consultation, advice, and support of many other people. Fortunately, I know some nice people who are very knowledgeable. They helped to make my ideas easier to understand. Others provided information or access to information necessary to finish the book.

First I'd like to thank Ralph G. Moore and the offices of RGMA, Inc. Without Ralph and RGMA, this book would not have been completed. It takes much more than a good idea and a knowledgeable writer to complete a book. If there is no support system, no project will succeed. Ralph has said he has written nary a word, but nary a word would appear in print if it weren't for Ralph G. Moore.

Next I'd like to thank my agent, Jeff Herman, who ensured this manuscript was published. I'd also like to thank my editor, Cherise Grant, and all the wonderful people at Simon & Schuster.

I'd like to thank my mentor, Jimmy Walker, who encouraged me to go through with the book many years ago and offered before he died to write an introduction.

Several individuals read versions of the manuscript or the proposal and offered invaluable comments. Thanks to Janice Bell Ollavaria; Kathy Tellengater; Helen Sclair for the cemetery chapter and hours of consultation; and my pre-editor extraordinaire, Renee Moore. Renee also gave inspiring words of encouragement when I needed them most. Thanks also go out to several friends and fellow genealogists who reviewed early versions of the manuscript and made excellent suggestions: Eva Lacey, Carol McNeely, Patricia Perkins, Eunice Pressie, Cristal Simmons, Roma Stewart, Barbara Woods, and Delores Woodtor. Patricia's insights on computer programming also helped to solve some sticky computer problems, as well as transportation problems.

For the generous use of their homes for me to get away and write a couple of times, I want to thank Dr. James and Irene Pillars, and Yemi and Payne Brown. I also want to thank Yemi and her brother Bete for their Ethiopian lineage and inspiring family stories.

Special thanks go out to Michelle Anton for her enthusiastic support and key referral; Sue Tellengater, who provided experienced insight on the publishing industry; and my good friend Charles Brewer, whose support and infinite wisdom helped many parts of this book. In our thousands of hours of conversations, I think I learned something from Charles every time we talked. He was my right arm in Washington, did hours of my research, and also connected me with numerous experts around the country.

Other genealogists helped supply documents or gave important insights on different chapters: Desmond Walls Allen for information on Arkansas death records and funeral practices; Jamie Harris for correspondence with her relative; Pat Hatcher for ideas on writing, publishing, organization, and evidence; Ron Smith and Jackie Frye, who provided access to photocopying, transportation when I had none, moral support, delicious home-cooked meals, and a lot of questions; E. Renee Ingram for information on her Stanton family cemetery; and Bell Cheatham for information on Whittaker Memorial Cemetery, midwife information, insights, and moral support.

I thank the following individuals for supplying letters of support: Peter Bunce, former director of the National Archives, Great Lakes Region; Frazine K. Taylor, head of Ready Reference at the Alabama State Archives; Frazine also helped secure a cemetery photograph and relayed the inspirational story of the Huntsville students; David Thackery, former curator of Local and Family History at the Newberry Library; Kathryn M. Harris, director of the Illinois State Historical Library; Pat Van Skaik, head of the History and Genealogy Department of the Cincinnati Public Library; and Dr. Johnnetta B. Cole, former president of Spelman College.

I'd also like to thank Peggy King-Jorde, memorialization executive of the African Burial Ground Project; Carmelene Sanders for GSA information; Kurtis Productions for the New Explorers video *Slavery's Buried Past;* Cousin Danny Barbour for consultation on funeral homes and practices; Dr. Debra Ware for information on midwives; Laurel Gabel for sharing articles on the African Burial Ground and tips for shooting gravestones; *Toledo Blade* journalist Rhonda Sewell for interviewing me and sharing her family stories; and Collette DeVerge for sharing her rich story.

No one can complete a book without knowledgeable help from reference librarians at good institutions. Leading the pack are the wonderful and knowledgeable staff at the National Archives, Great Lakes Region, as well as the staff in Washington, D.C. So much of genealogy is contingent on using records created by our federal government. I'd like to especially thank the following librarians at other institutions: Marsha Selmer, maps librarian at the University of Illinois at Chicago, for steering me to solving the Conjockta Creek mystery and giving loads of other help; Kathleen Bethel at Northwestern University; Jim Stewart at the Harold Washington Library in the Chicago Public Library System; and Archie Motley and the staff of the Chicago Historical Society.

In addition, staffs at the following libraries were very helpful: the Newberry Library, University of Illinois at Chicago; the University of Chicago; Vivian Harsh Collection of the Chicago Public Library; Chicago Public Library (various branches); the Library of Congress; the Buffalo, New York, Public Library; and the Social Security Administration Library and Historian.

I'd be remiss if I didn't thank those institutions and organizations that provided me opportunities to teach and lecture. In that category are Mary Kirk, director of the Options Program, and Chicago State University for accepting my class for ten years, permitting me to hone my teaching skills; and Jerri Conner at the Avalon Branch of the Chicago Public Library for seeking my assistance in establishing their African American Genealogy Collection and providing outreach workshops. And a special thanks to the Federation of Genealogical Societies, the National Genealogical Society, and other libraries, historical societies, and genealogical societies around the country that invited me to teach others about genealogy. This book is a direct result of those efforts. Along with the institutions go all the students who attended my classes and served as guinea pigs and the thousands of people who attended my lectures and workshops over the years, many times asking challenging and probing questions. They forced me to think about things I hadn't considered and to return with more answers. You don't know how helpful you were.

I'd like to thank members of the African-American Genealogical and Historical Society of Chicago (AAGHSC) not only for electing me president and vice-president, but for their support and camaraderie.

Other friends lent various kinds of support, including Freddie Barr, Willie Clausell, Yvette Collins, Nancy Davis, Cheryl Gaines, George Lowery, and Dan Perkins. I apologize to anyone I've missed, which unfortunately happens when you start naming names. But any errors or shortcomings in this book are solely my responsibility.

Finally, I would like to thank all my relatives and ancestors. Many of their stories and experiences are in the pages inside. Without them there would not be a need for this guide. I'd like especially to thank both my parents, who are not around to see the fruits of their labor—Mom for supporting me in all my endeavors and encouraging me to be the best at whatever I do, and Dad for challenging me to defend my positions and prove I was right. This yin and yang developed me without my knowing it.

Thank you all.

—Tony Burroughs

Contents

Preface: Why a Need for This Book?

After I had been researching my own family history for several years, people began asking me to recommend a beginner's guide to researching African American family history. No book immediately came to mind, and so I started looking for one. There are several good books on rudimentary genealogy, written for the general public, but they either don't cover Black genealogy or give it only a cursory mention. I found a few titles written specifically for African Americans, but none were step-by-step "how-to" guides. One book had not been updated in thirteen years, one was not professionally published, another was very misleading, another was out of print and couldn't be located. They concentrated on sources instead of methods, barely mentioning where to find records.

Therefore, because of my genealogical experience and expertise, I felt compelled to write a guide to help those starting to research African American family history. I've been teaching a class in introductory genealogy in the Adult Education Department at Chicago State University since 1990. Many of the methods used in that class are included in this book.

Now, eleven years after I started the book, a few new titles on African American genealogy have been published, but they still do not go into depth and detail on the fundamentals that beginners need to learn to build confidence and success. And with the growth of the Internet, it is even more imperative that beginners learn the basics and put technology into the proper perspective. Many researchers' first experience in genealogy is not through reading a good genealogy book, taking a genealogy class, or joining a genealogical society. It's through name surfing on the Internet without any guidance as to what they should be doing. The Internet has a vast number of resources and can be a very inefficient tool.

How I Got Started

The thought of searching for my family roots first occurred while I was a student at Southern Illinois University in Carbondale. I attended a lecture on February 14, 1969, given by Alex Haley for Black History Week (that was before it was turned into a month-long celebration). *The Autobiography of Malcolm X* was a bestselling book at the time, and Malcolm X had been assassinated. The Black Student Union couldn't invite Malcolm, so we thought about the next best thing. We invited his biographer.

We were expecting Haley to tell us about how he wrote *The Autobiography of Malcolm X* and about Malcolm's life and his own relationship with Malcolm. We heard none of the above. Instead, he spoke of Kunta Kinte, Kizzy, Chicken George, and other people he'd found in his search for his family tree back to Africa. Haley was a great storyteller, and I was mesmerized. I had never heard anyone talk about searching for their ancestors before, let alone listened to someone who had actually done it and, incredibly, back to Africa. At that time I said I would like someday to trace my family history.

Alex Haley's book on his own family was delayed, and I soon forgot about it. Then on Thanksgiving Day, November 27, 1975, while waiting for the relatives to come by, I saw an article in the *Chicago Sun-Times* about giving thanks to your ancestors and tracing the family history. I remembered listening to Alex Haley six years earlier when in college. The newspaper article talked of a book written by the Boy Scouts of America, called *Genealogy*. It was a "how-to" guide for tracing your family history. I figured it would be easy to read, and if it was good enough for the Boy Scouts, it was good enough for me. I am a former Boy Scout and Cub Scout.

I immediately purchased the book. I read it and started interviewing my parents, aunts, uncles, and grandmother. I was hooked from the very first day and I've been researching ever since.

On that Thanksgiving Day in 1975, a twenty-three-year odyssey began. I interviewed every relative I could meet, and I met new ones all the time. I went to the cemeteries where my ancestors were buried and the library or archives almost every day. I began reading additional books and attending seminars and lectures on genealogy.

In 1977 I attended a three-week genealogy institute sponsored by the National Archives in Washington, D.C. The National Institute of Genealogical Research is still conducted, but now it lasts only a week. Lectures were given by state archivists, librarians, and genealogical experts from around the country. We attended lectures all day and spent evenings researching our own families in the National Archives, the Library of Congress, and the DAR Library (Daughters of the American Revolution). We also took a side trip to a state archive. I went to Harrisburg, Pennsylvania, because my maternal ancestors were from Pennsylvania. My genealogical knowledge and skills expanded exponentially.

I also had the good fortune to meet James Dent Walker. He was an archivist on staff at the National Archives with about twenty-five years of experience. Being a navy veteran, he specialized in military records. He conducted the session at the institute on "Military Records

Research." I was very impressed by his knowledge and thorough coverage of the subject. Since my great-grandfather was in the military in 1882, I pestered Walker about records for him and other ancestors. He took me under his wing, showed me the ropes, and took me into the closed stacks where the archivists managed the original records. I recall walking down the aisles and him pulling items off the shelves and saying, "Look at this, look at this." Then when I finished, he sat me down and asked what I had found. He critiqued my research and offered additional suggestions. We became good friends. I learned many things from him that would have taken years to learn on my own.

Years later we renewed our friendship and he invited me to stay at his house when I came to Washington. Jimmy (as he let his friends call him) continued to consult on my research even after he retired. He had so much knowledge and experience and his library was so extensive that staying in his home was like being inside a genealogy book. I recall his wife, Barbara, saying, "Now don't be shy. I know you're not going to be here long. Ask him all the questions you want because he doesn't mind you asking and he likes to help." That was all I needed to fire away. Years later when I told him I was writing a book, he offered to write the foreword. Unfortunately, he passed away before I finished.

From there I started giving lectures and teaching classes. I established an organization called the African American Institute of Ancestry (AAIA). We had ten members. I had envisioned developing a library specializing in African American family history. I quit teaching and wanted to head the organization full time. However, I was not able to secure financing and after about a year the group disbanded. Around the same time I had started AAIA, the Afro-American Genealogical and Historical Society of Chicago (AAGHSC) was forming. They have now been in existence for twenty-one years and are progressing strongly. After I joined they discovered I had a lot of experience and I was soon asked to deliver lectures. I was elected vice-president in 1989 and eventually president in 1991, serving a two-year term.

That is how I began tracing my family history, and I have been researching, studying, and teaching genealogy ever since. I've now gone back seven generations, discovering more than a thousand ancestors. Not a day goes by that I don't either conduct genealogy research, teach or lecture on genealogy, prepare to teach or lecture on genealogy, discuss genealogy, or merely think about genealogy. I've come to the realization that family history research never ends. Each generation back doubles the number of ancestors you're searching for! Once you find a new ancestor, you always want to ask the question: "Who were *their* parents?"

Introduction

Congratulations! Welcome to the world of ancestor hunting. You have taken the first step on an exciting journey. This may be the most interesting adventure you have ever taken. If you like game shows, treasure hunting, mysteries, detective games, research, or just plain satisfying your curiosity, you'll love ancestor hunting! Once you start looking, you don't know what you'll find. Your search may lead to meeting interesting people, going to interesting places, and being involved in interesting events you never knew existed.

Speaking of ancestors, we might as well make the distinction between relatives and ancestors now. Ancestors are dead relatives that we're descended from—parents, grandparents, great-grandparents, and so on all the way back. We sometimes refer to their deceased brothers and sisters as our collateral ancestors.

How This Books Works

Black Roots is not a complete reference guide to researching African American family history. It is easy to start researching African American families, but the research can become very complex. It would take multiple volumes to present a comprehensive study. Most African American genealogy guides try to be comprehensive, covering every step from beginning to end. The only way to do that in one volume is to gloss over everything, giving very little detail. Such a book might provide the names of records, but the reader would not know what the records looked like, have no idea when to use them or how to use them successfully, and would therefore gain little understanding of important and sometimes complex documents.

By contrast, *Black Roots* is simple but detailed, designed for beginners or those who have had little or no experience researching their families. Many researchers begin by trial and error, missing many important fundamentals. So I recommend that experienced researchers also read *Black Roots*. It will undoubtedly cover methods, techniques, and sources they missed on the way to becoming experienced. *Black Roots* is limited in scope but goes into depth and detail explaining records, sources, and methods beginners encounter in African American genealogy.

The objective of *Black Roots* is not only to teach the fundamentals of African American genealogy; it's to help you successfully go back through the twentieth century. That's a hundred years of research. So try to start at the beginning of the book (I guess you have if you have started here). Each chapter is developed in a progressive fashion to build upon skills learned in the previous chapter.

Takes a Step-by-Step Approach

Black Roots is not about my family history (hopefully, that will come later), although it does show examples from my family. This book is a step-by-step "how-to" guide on how *you* can trace *your* African American family history. It concentrates on methods and techniques instead of sources. It also includes experiences from other genealogists around the country, as well as from professional genealogists and historians.

Black Roots is designed to start readers from the beginning and progress step by step to success in researching their African American family. As you progress through the book, you'll learn how to locate a record and how the information contained in the record can logically lead to another record. *Black Roots* also deals with sources but puts them into a logical sequence.

The sequence of researching records is extremely important as you proceed from one source to the next. Research should be prioritized. Just because you think an ancestor was a slave does not mean you should run out and research slave documents. That is one of the biggest traps beginners (and even intermediates) fall into—not prioritizing research and getting into certain records prematurely. If strong foundations are not built, genealogical scaffolding collapses.

Emphasizes Method

Many books on African American genealogy are like a dictionary of sources, providing very little methodology other than the author's limited experience. *Black Roots* does get into sources, but there is much more to genealogy than knowing about sources. I am a firm believer that if you learn methods, you can uncover sources. You can have directories of all the sources in the world, but if you don't know why, when, and how to apply them to solve individual problems of locating your ancestors, the sources will not do you a bit of good. That's the main problem I see with many books and articles on African American genealogy. They mention tons of sources but provide little direction on why, when, and how to use them.

Many people don't like to start at the beginning or do things in a planned, organized way. For some reason, they are ashamed to call themselves beginners. It's OK if you have success that way. But I have found that successful family history research follows a very logical, methodological pattern. If you understand the logic and the fundamentals, you can better determine how to focus your research and know where to look next.

Gives Real-Life Examples

Few books provide examples of using records to solve genealogical problems. Few even describe some of the problems that will be encountered along the way. I've even seen sources listed that authors obviously haven't used, and others that are not even useful for genealogy. Just because a record is historical and perhaps mentions African Americans, it does not necessarily qualify as being useful for genealogical research or for solving specific genealogical problems.

This book is not the result of artificial case studies or a college term paper. I recall reading several case studies on African American genealogy that had excellent examples. Some selected court records that illustrated relationships and transfers of slaves. However, something was missing. I realized the authors had found ideal situations where the records fit, or the families and records made a nice story, or the examples illustrated how to use records in a library collection, or the records were taken from only one collection. These case studies were very informative, but they left glaring gaps in the genealogical research process. Omitted were several real problems that researchers encounter. In other words, the studies were artificial.

The dozens of examples and anecdotal stories in *Black Roots* are real. Many come from solving research problems on my family; others come from amateur and professional genealogists around the country who've been struggling with their research.

Illustrates and Analyzes Documents

Black Roots is filled with actual genealogical documents obtained from libraries, archives, courthouses, and other places where genealogists research. Examples are presented in almost every chapter. The records are not just for illustration purposes, to show readers what they look like. Each one is explained in the narrative and analyzed for its content, validity, and genealogical importance.

Illustrates Live Charts

Black Roots includes many genealogy charts to help you organize your research, keep you focused, and follow your bloodlines. These charts not only are illustrated but are filled with live information to show how they are properly filled out. But I go one step further. The charts are followed from chapter to chapter to show how new records and new information are added to them along the way. A reader doesn't have to guess at how it's done from one stage to another.

Integrates Black History with Black Genealogy

Genealogy and history are separate but related disciplines. In order to be successful, the researcher must properly merge the two. Many books on African American genealogy include African American history but do not explain when to go from one to the other. History is a broad field, and genealogical research must be placed in the proper historical context. Otherwise, the reader does not know when to study history or what history to study. For example, the history of Africa is important. However, if a beginner is researching her parents and they did not live in Africa, then studying African history will not advance her search. Conversely, if your grandparents lived through World War I, then it is important to study the history of African Americans in that war. It is directly related and in context.

Black Roots is unique in illustrating the fundamental methods of genealogy while correlating African American history that is important for the time period the genealogist is researching. When this is done properly, it is very logical and the beginner can easily and quickly grasp new concepts.

Points Out Traps

There are a number of traps beginners fall into that seriously hamper their research. Through more than twenty years of study and personal research, coupled with ten years of teaching, lecturing, consulting, and participating with genealogists on local and national levels, I have seen beginning and experienced genealogists fall into the same traps. Some genealogists don't realize these are traps until years later, and some never get out of them.

I warn you of these traps and steer you away from them so you can keep your research focused and be more successful. I have identified these traps and point them out in almost every chapter. They are also summarized at the end of the book for easy reference. There is no reason you have to fall into these same traps to learn African American genealogy. Whenever research begins to lead into a trap, you'll see the following symbol with an explanation.

 Trap: Going back too far too fast. Once genealogists find new ancestors, they immediately want to search for their parents instead of learning as much as they can about the new ancestors.

Who Can Do It?

Anyone can trace his or her family history. You don't have to be rich or famous. I attended public schools and had two working parents. When I got started, I was a schoolteacher. I spent time after school and during vacations researching.

You don't need a lot of money. When you begin, early expenses will be for telephone calls, stamps and envelopes, a few supplies, photocopies, and bus fare or gas money to visit friends and relatives in town. The only significant expenses at the beginning are for long-distance phone calls to relatives out of town and a few dollars for a few government records. I provide a list of supplies and tools in the chapter on "Organizing Before It Gets Messy." They are divided between basic, intermediate, and optional supplies.

This guide will get you started. The steps it teaches will give you a good foundation that you can build upon. Many people think there are no records of African Americans. Many people think our history is merely oral, stories passed down from one generation to the next by word of mouth. Believe me, if you are serious, diligent, patient, and investigative, your problem will not be a lack of records. Your problem will be finding the time to track down all the leads you discover!

You see, each time you go back another generation, you *double* the number of family lines you are tracing. For example, you have two parents, four grandparents, eight great-grandparents, sixteen great-great-grandparents, and so on. Just going back five generations gives you thirty-two direct ancestors! And this does not include the brothers, sisters, aunts, uncles, and cousins. Some African American families had ten, twelve, fifteen children, or more. These large families lead to huge genealogical projects. I have enough research to do to last me a lifetime. And it will, for ancestor hunting can be a lifelong hobby.

It is my belief that when starting out on a new endeavor, one should start at the beginning, square one, learning those things that are *essential* for the beginner. Therefore, things will be kept simple. Later, after progress has been made and concepts have been learned, you can progress to intermediate methods and sources. In this way your confidence and skills can grow and strengthen. You will not become confused or frustrated.

This book is a result of the classes I have taught; the genealogists I have consulted with, African Americans and others; the books I have read; and the classes, seminars, and conferences I have attended. But above all, this book comes from more than two decades of experience researching my own family's history and solving problems to progress to the next generation.

It works! This book starts from the beginning and goes step by step through procedures everyone can take. I have used these methods and have taught them to many other African Americans who have used them successfully.

Your comments and suggestions are welcome. So feel free to write and let me know if anything was easy or hard to understand and to make any suggestions. Also, please let me know what else you might expect from a beginning guide.

Follow the steps in this book and you will discover ancestors you never knew existed. So good luck, happy hunting, and enjoy the exciting journey into African American genealogy.

Part I
Preparing to Research

What Is Genealogy?

Genealogy is the study of family history. Most African Americans will not be able to go to a library and find on a shelf a published book on their family's history. They'll have to piece it together bit by bit. The process is a lot like putting together a giant jigsaw puzzle. You probably worked on jigsaw puzzles as a kid or have helped your child or niece or nephew assemble one. You dumped a box of about five hundred pieces on the table and couldn't tell one piece from another. At first you thought, "I will never be able to put this thing together." Your first step was probably to look for similar colors and group them together. Then you looked for shapes that matched. Next you put two pieces together. Then you joined two sections of two pieces together to make a section of four pieces. You connected these and made larger sections. After a long time you could see the larger picture coming together.

Well, genealogy is similar. At first you don't see how you can accomplish this enormous task. Then you collect a lot of data and perhaps think not much of it is important or related to the task at hand. Then as you proceed, you see connections between people and events. Then after a period of researching, you uncover clues that match information you heard or received during the initial stages of research that you had previously thought were unimportant. Then you see the larger picture. And hopefully, one day you are able to put all this research together to write your family history. Then you and everyone else can benefit from seeing the whole family history.

Genealogy is also a science. It involves tracing and proving one's lineage from one generation back to the previous generation. In proving our genealogy, we are bound by the same set of rules as are used in a court of law. If a person dies, leaves an estate, and does not have a will, his or her property must be divided among the heirs according to the probate law of the state. The court must determine who are the rightful heirs to the property. The heirs are relatives of the deceased, but not all the relatives—

only those that the law designates—are heirs to the property. And not just anyone can casually walk into the court and say they are related to the deceased. Once it is learned the deceased had considerable money, relatives will be crawling out of the woodwork to get part of the estate. Well, it must be *proven* that these persons are related to the deceased. The court or an attorney will often hire a professional genealogist to construct genealogy charts and submit evidence to prove these persons are related to the deceased and entitled to portions of the estate. These are the rules that govern genealogy.

Now don't become intimidated. It's not really hard. It just means you can't say anything just because you heard someone else say it. That's called hearsay. It may or may not be true. You've got to provide evidence to back it up.

Genealogy, then, first entails the collection of evidence. Evidence is any item offered to prove or disprove a fact and can be in the form of testimony, documents, or objects. However, evidence can be true or false. For example, a witness may lie or have a faulty memory. The witness's testimony is entered as evidence, but it does not have to be true and correct. Documents can also be true or false. A death certificate may contain faulty information because relatives were not around at the time of death and friends of the deceased did not know vital information about the deceased. The death certificate is evidence, but all statements recorded on it do not have to be true.

This evidence is weighted as either primary or secondary. Primary evidence is considered an original record, created at or close to the time an event occurred by someone who had direct knowledge of the event. Secondary evidence is that which is created after an event occurred, perhaps by someone who did not have direct knowledge of that event. To look at it another way, it is original records versus everything else. For example, if a doctor or midwife delivered a baby, he or she could testify as to the date of birth, the place of birth, and the mother of the child. This would be considered primary evidence if the doctor or midwife recorded the information at the time the baby was born. By contrast, a book that contains a computerized index of births from a particular locality is definitely secondary evidence. There could easily have been translation errors, data entry errors, and omissions when the book was compiled. Primary evidence is usually stronger and more reliable than secondary evidence.

Proof

Once we collect evidence, it means nothing until we prove the facts we allege. Otherwise, we could simply write anything down, which is what many people do. Just as for the rules of evidence, there are standards of proof. The standards that govern heirship and paternity in a court of law are the same standards that are used in genealogy research. Those standards are bound by a principle called "preponderance of evidence." In simple terms, this means that if there is more *credible* evidence that supports an allegation than evidence that contradicts it, proof is established. This is not as strict as the standard we often hear about in criminal court cases, called "beyond a reasonable doubt." There is often doubt when trying to prove family relationships. We know that many times it is difficult, sometimes impossible, to determine who the father of a child is today. Sometimes the only way is through DNA tests. It can be even more difficult to precisely determine the father of a child born a hundred years ago, before blood tests and DNA matching were developed. So we are not bound by the strictest standards, as in murder cases. Genealogy is not that serious. However, we do have to submit significant, credible evidence to substantiate our genealogical claims.

This evidence is judged by a jury of your peers. When a group of experienced genealogists reviews your work and passes judgment on it, you will know if you've proved your case. An example of this is when your published genealogy is accepted in a peer review genealogy journal. That means you submit it and a panel of experienced genealogists, some perhaps being certified genealogists, examines your genealogy and the evidence you submit and comes to the same conclusion. They deem it worthy, credible, and believable. Another example would be a successful application to a lineage society that evaluates lineages or a successful application to become a certified genealogist by the Board for Certification of Genealogists.

The Board for Certification of Genealogists (BCG) judges genealogists who apply for certification. They require credible evidence from different sources to prove the facts alleged in a compiled genealogy. Former BCG president Helen Leary once said, "No single document ever proved anything. It cannot prove relationship. It may prove a date, it may prove an event. But it does not prove relationship. Because, before you prove relationship you must prove identity." This is easily understood when you have several people of the same name in a small town. One document can't determine which individual it refers to.

! Trap: Many novice genealogists hear they are related to some famous person a few generations back and immediately start researching that famous person. Unfortunately, many of them find out there is no connection to that person, and they've wasted years of research. So work backward; don't try to reach back and tie the person into your family. If there is some kind of connection, you'll see how it links up along the way.

In genealogy we proceed from the known to the unknown. We research from the present to the past, one generation at a time, picking up pieces and clues of evidence like a scientist, attorney, or investigator, proving identity first and then proving lineage from one generation to the next.

For example, you start with yourself, then you proceed to your parents, then to your grandparents, and then to your great-grandparents.

When we study genealogy, we must understand that *the process is as important as the results.* Again, novice genealogists want to trace as far back as they can, as fast as they can, looking for results. But understanding records, methodology, and how you make discoveries is much more important than how far you can go back. If you understand these things, you will make progress.

Therefore you should record not only what you know and your new discoveries but also when you make new discoveries and how you made them. Then you not only can learn from your own experience but be able to apply that knowledge to other ancestors you research in the future.

Pivotal Evidence

There is a false assumption that the key to tracing ancestors lies in some pivotal document. Then either that document is missing or the researcher hasn't found it. "If only I could find this one record, it would solve all my problems." I hear it all the time. I know of cases in which genealogists had all the records at their disposal but admitted they didn't know where to start or didn't know how to put all the pieces together. Genealogy is much more than finding isolated documents. You can dump those five hundred pieces out of the jigsaw puzzle box, but if you don't know how to fit each and every piece together, you will never complete the picture.

There are other cases in which records have been burned or no longer exist in a locality or for a time period. That doesn't mean your research has stopped; it means you have to be more sophisticated in using what records do exist. A lot of genealogy is the creative use of documents. It's rarely a key document that solves a genealogical problem. Rather, it's how you interpret existing records, then assemble a series of records and compare them with each other that solves genealogical problems. The interpretation and analysis are much more important than the records themselves. Often researchers locate the records but misinterpret them.

Genealogy Versus Family History

There are many similarities but subtle differences between family history and genealogy. Genealogy tells you who the ancestors are, when and where they were born and died, who they married, and who their parents were. Genealogy links family members to succeeding generations. Family history tells you what the ancestors did between birth and death and, hopefully, why they did it and how they felt. It adds elements of history and biography and sometimes sociology to genealogy.

In family history, the entire family is researched. You try to learn as much as possible about the father, mother, and all their sisters and brothers. In genealogy you try to link that family to the preceding generation. But you can't research the family back another generation without knowing much about the history of the entire family. After teaching this, I often get the question "You mean I have to trace my cousins?" Or worse, some so-called "experienced" genealogist will say, "I'm not concerned about my grandparents' brothers and sisters. I'm only tracing my grandparents and great-grandparents."

In attempts to advance a genealogy back to another generation, many researchers neglect family history. They concentrate on only a single ancestor within that family. They do not study the brothers and sisters of their direct ancestor. They also fail to fill in the gaps between life and death. This tunnel vision restricts the majority of resources available to solve genealogical problems. Normally, siblings have the same parents, and there's nothing to say which sibling will have the important keys, records, or clues that lead to the parents. In many cases each child will leave some clue about the parents and details of the family history. Good genealogists understand the need to collect all those clues.

Unfortunately, once many genealogists discover a new ancestor, all they want to do is find out who that person's parents were. They fail to realize that *the keys to genealogy lie in family history.* Family history and genealogy work hand in hand. So study all your ancestors, try to learn as much as possible about them and their families, and you'll become very successful.

Local History

Local history is the study of counties, towns, neighborhoods, and local events. It is a microcosm of U.S. history. I mentioned earlier that history covers broad time periods; it also covers broad geographical areas. In history class in school we may have studied "Western Civilization" or "The Westward Expansion" or "The Antebellum South." An example of local history would be "Black Chicago: The Making of a Negro Ghetto, 1890–1920." It is very specific. It covers only one city and for only a thirty-year period.

Local histories study small areas during specific time periods. The good ones are very detailed. Local history must be studied to learn what events were taking place in the area and time period in which your ancestor lived. Then you can place your ancestors in the proper perspective. You can get a feel for their lifestyle and surroundings. It will also lead you to records you did not know existed. It may even tell you of friends, neighbors, relatives, and co-workers your ancestors had that you never knew.

Genealogy Versus Black Genealogy

Many genealogists state that Black genealogy is the same as traditional genealogy until you get back to slavery, prior to 1865. I cringe every time I hear those words. This statement is only partially true.

During the slavery period, enslaved African Americans were considered property and were prohibited by law from reading, writing, attending school, legally marrying, owning land, owning a business, voting, and participating in many other privileges granted to citizens of the United States. In fact, citizenship was not granted to African Americans until the Fourteenth

Amendment was ratified in 1868. These rights often determine traditional genealogical records that can be researched, such as letters, diaries, wills, census records, land deeds, voter registrations, and school records.

In order to research during the slavery period, the name of former slave owners must be positively identified to determine what they did with their property. Enslaved African Americans were generally not associated with last names to perpetuate the myth that they were sub-human and therefore didn't need surnames. Records of births and deaths of slaves were shoddy at best, and nonexistent in many cases. Letters, diaries, and other first-person recordings of slaves are also almost nonexistent. Except in rare instances, slaves were prohibited from owning property. Thus, wills and land deeds, which are traditional sources for genealogy, are unavailable for tracing enslaved African Americans.

One of the major sources for genealogical research is the United States Census records, which we'll examine in the chapter on "U.S. Census Records." They are probably used more than any other genealogical source. The census was taken every ten years, grouping persons by families. However, slaves were not listed by name, so as a genealogical source for African Americans, census records greatly diminish in value.

Many white Americans have family traditions that go back to the 1800s, or they can relatively easily trace their family history back to 1865. Many can then link to a published genealogy on one of their family lines that can vault them back to the 1600s in Europe. This is not difficult to do because there are 90,000 genealogies and family histories published on white families (see *Printed Sources*, by Kory Meyerink, in "Genealogical Reference Guides" in Bibliography). To put that into perspective, there are only a few hundred published genealogies and family histories on African American families. You'll hear many white genealogists say they've traced their family history to the 1600s or earlier. But, have they started from scratch and made every link, found every record, and solved every mystery? No. Even worse, many have piggybacked on lines that were constructed with shaky evidence that wouldn't stand up to today's rigorous standards of genealogical proof.

To say Black genealogy is the same as traditional genealogy back to the Civil War also negates 135 years of African American history, racism, segregation, and discrimination in America. These things affect genealogy just as they affect history.

Throughout the Jim Crow period (1877–1965), Blacks were discriminated against and segregated in every aspect of society. Blacks were denied housing in white neighborhoods and Black students were denied the right to attend schools with white students. Blacks were denied the right to vote or even to register to vote unless their grandfather voted, which he had not. Blacks were prevented from sitting on juries. Blacks were also denied membership in white churches and fraternal organizations.

As a result, Blacks were forced to live in segregated, all-Black neighborhoods and attend segregated elementary and secondary schools, as well as segregated colleges and universities. Blacks were forced to worship in separate churches and organize their own clubs and fraternal organizations.

There were two separate worlds, one black, one white. Segregation affected every aspect of life and was not limited to the South. Many areas of the North practiced some of these forms of segregation.

Genealogists must be aware of this segregation when researching their families because their relatives and ancestors lived through it and many of the records were also segregated. Some records of African Americans were recorded and filed by race. Some records were not recorded with the majority population but were located in the back of the book, similar to Blacks having to ride in the back of the bus. I will point out differences like these throughout this book.

There are also problems of identity. Many African Americans were very light complected. So light that they could pass for white. Since white Americans had more privileges and faced no racial discrimination, some Black Americans forsook their heritage and assimilated into the white community. They associated with whites, married whites, and moved into the white community. This makes it difficult for genealogists because many ancestors moved away, were listed as white, and will be lost forever. If you are aware that your ancestor was very light skinned, be sure to search the records listing only white people because you might find your ancestor among them instead of with the "colored" records.

Sometimes a person's race was incorrectly noted in the records. Sometimes Blacks were listed as whites and sometimes whites were listed as colored. Also, many light-skinned African Americans were assumed to be white by some clerk or recorder who didn't know their true identity.

Many of those who were not fair skinned tried to pretend they were part Puerto Rican, part Native American Indian, or some other race other than Black. Some researchers I've met are quick to research Native American ancestry without a shred of evidence other than family rumor. My grandmother told me her grandmother was part Native American Indian, but she said this without mentioning anything about the tribe or other identifying information. When I traced my great-grandmother, I learned that Native American Indians had been gone from the area long before she was born. It appeared impossible for her to be Native American Indian.

There were relations between African Americans and Native Americans. But I find it hard to believe *every* African American family has Native American ancestry. This is especially hard to believe when knowing that some Native American nations strictly prohibited the intermarrying of their people with African Americans. I also find it hard to believe when most places in the Midwest and South have not had Native American Indians in significant numbers since 1830, and places in the Northeast since long before then. As far as genealogy goes, if you have some direct evidence (documentation of an Indian name, tribe, and location), then proceed on the evidence (and not just "Grandmother was part Cherokee").

The period before Jim Crow also presents unique genealogical differences between white Americans and African Americans. Immediately following the Civil War, in 1865, the country was going through a transitional period. This was a transition from war to peacetime, a transition from slavery to freedom, and a transition from an agricultural economy to an industrial economy.

The Freedmen's Bureau (officially known as the Bureau of Refugees, Freedmen and Abandoned Lands) operated from 1865 until 1872 to assist former slaves, war refugees, and others affected by the Civil War. There is a wealth of records of the Freedmen's Bureau that African Americans need to know about. These records are difficult to research because for the most part they are not microfilmed or indexed. Traditional genealogists don't list these records as sources to research even though many of their ancestors are included in the records.

During the Civil War, African Americans fought in regiments comprising only Black soldiers with white officers. If researchers aren't aware of this, they will look for African American soldiers with the state military regiments instead of with the U.S. Colored Troops, which has a separate index to military service records. After the war African Americans continued to fight in segregated military units. Known as Buffalo Soldiers, they were organized in 1866 and remained segregated until 1952, when the army was integrated. Most whites and many Blacks were not aware of these soldiers until recently. I attended many lectures on military records, and these units and the Indian Wars they fought in were never mentioned. Nor were they mentioned in some of the major guide books.

So Black genealogy is *not* the same as traditional genealogy after 1865. It is similar in many ways, but I have pointed out just a few of the many differences. I will point out others in the pages to follow. Many of the same methods, techniques, and sources in traditional genealogy can be applied to African American genealogical research. They are very important and should be studied. They become even more important once the emancipation bridge is crossed. Then not only the Black family but the slave-owning family must be researched. Then *all* genealogical methods, techniques, and sources must be applied.

African American Genealogists

Since Alex Haley, a lot of African Americans have been researching their genealogy. They have had varying degrees of success. There are more sources opening up and more records being indexed that include African Americans.

However, there are still many problems. One of the main problems with African American genealogists is that we still don't know African American history. It was not taught in the schools and is still not taught in any depth or detail. Most of African American history in schools and Black History Month celebrations now deal with the Civil Rights Movement. This is good but not particularly relevant to the larger genealogical picture. You cannot be a good genealogist without being a good historian. So study African American history.

! Trap: Not knowing Black history. You must study it to be a successful genealogist.

Most people don't know enough about slavery and Reconstruction to research genealogy during those periods. All we know is that slaves came on slave ships to Jamestown, Virginia, starting in 1619. Blacks slaved on plantations until the end of the Civil War. Lincoln wrote the Emancipation Proclamation in 1863, freeing some slaves. There were several slave revolts and there was an abolitionist movement. Other than that, Blacks picked cotton in the field and the house slaves cooked the food and kept the house clean.

Our knowledge of Black history can be put into one paragraph. I would challenge any Black genealogist to read Herbert Gutman's *The Black Family in Slavery and Freedom,* written in 1976, or the slave narratives from the WPA Collection of the 1930s. Once an African American pedigree gets into the slavery period, it's a whole new ball game and the gears have to shift into second, third, and overdrive. Here one must be an expert on slavery, slave customs, naming patterns, and slave laws, as well as knowing how to trace white slave owners. There are many excellent studies written by historians, African American and white. What is needed is for the genealogists and the historians to know what each other has been doing.

This book will not get into that time period or those records. That's for experienced and advanced genealogists. My suggestion is, after you've mastered the methods and sources in this book and mastered intermediate research, study slavery and the antebellum period before searching for your ancestors. You'll be much more successful.

Fortunately, the future of African American genealogy is bright. There are many serious, experienced African American genealogists out there. They are developing new methods, techniques, and sources. What we need is for those genealogists to write more about what they are doing and pass along their efforts to others. Then the field of African American genealogy can progress. The onus is on us. Because these are our ancestors, we have more passion and a more vested interest in getting to the root of the matter.

What Is Not Genealogy?

Genealogy is not about collecting everyone with the same name. That's called a one-name study. I've known people who have run off and done research on the origin of their surname to see what it means and who were the first people to come to America who used that name. That may work for European Americans, but it doesn't work for people of African descent. If our enslaved ancestors were owned by a man named Smith, they were referred to as Smith's. If our ancestors were then sold to an owner named Jones, they were referred to as Jones's slaves. After slavery was over and formerly enslaved Africans could use surnames for the first time legally, some had three different surnames within the same family! And, of course, those three surnames might have had nothing to do with the first person who owned their ancestors, perhaps a hundred years earlier. So putting an undue emphasis on a surname is not doing genealogy. African Americans must concentrate on people and on tracing the lineage of a family.

Many beginners on the Internet search for names. I call it name surfing. There are thousands of people with the same name. I have ancestors who were in western Pennsylvania for over two hundred years. A relative surfs the Internet and gets many hits of people with the same surname. However, they are almost always in eastern Pennsylvania, which is like another state, and invariably white. Researchers must learn to identify a family and trace the whereabouts of that family, not everyone in the world who shares the same last name.

What Does It Take to Be a Good Genealogist?

Since there are millions of genealogists, it's hard to say what makes a good one. I have met people from all walks of life who research genealogy. However, there are a few traits successful genealogists share.

Genealogists must have a positive attitude. They have to have an open mind to think a record *might* exist and all they have to do is search for it. It's amazing how negative people are and how they immediately say there are no records on Blacks. Or they don't think there are records for a person or an area. Or they checked for records but not thoroughly.

Genealogists are junkies. They have a severe habit and can't stop researching. In order to be successful, genealogists must be open-minded, uninhibited, thorough, detailed, persistent, and patient.

A genealogist must be thorough. The more thorough you are between now and the slavery period, the more successful your research will be. The ideal goal is to locate your ancestor in a place for each and every year. You will not be able to find records for everyone in every source. But you must check every source and prove to yourself and others the ancestor is not listed in a given set of records. You cannot assume the record does not exist nor assume the ancestor is not listed in the record.

A genealogist must have focus and discipline. There are tons of records and there are many side trips and diversions to take you in different directions. You will find things you are not looking for that will be fascinating. But above all, you must possess a burning curiosity, an attention to detail, and a healthy dose of skepticism.

Why Research Genealogy?

The desire to know about one's family is older than recorded history. The Egyptian pharaohs had a record of their genealogy carved in stone thousands of years before Christ, and it still exists today. I visited the British Museum while in London in 1989. I stared in awe at a section from the Temple of Rameses II at Abydos, which showed the lineage of the kings of Egypt carved in stone in 1250 B.C.

Today genealogy is a fast-growing hobby. Some say it has become America's most popular hobby. In the nineteenth century, genealogy was done only by the descendants of royalty or those trying to find a link with royalty or famous people. Others were interested in genealogy to gain entrance into a group in which everyone could trace their lineage to a certain event or time period. Such groups are called lineage societies. The most popular is the DAR (National Society Daughters of the American Revolution). DAR members can trace their lineage to an ancestor who either served in or supported the American Revolutionary War.

Now, thanks to Alex Haley's publishing of *Roots* in 1976, ordinary people know that they, too, can trace their family history. I guess they thought if a little African American country boy can do it, anybody can. And they're right.

Genealogy enables African Americans to have a legacy of our ancestors' struggles, successes, and failures so that we can learn from our ancestors' lives—not to repeat their mistakes but to emulate their successes and use them as inspiration for the future. We did not come from a vacuum, and as former General Colin Powell said, "We stand on the shoulders of our ancestors."

To Give Our Children a Heritage

Genealogy is important for kids to know their heritage, who their ancestors are and what they accomplished. There usually are two sides to every family—good and bad. We shouldn't be ashamed of our ancestors who performed deeds we are not proud of. We need to understand them and learn from their mistakes. We should look for the good in them. We shouldn't condemn people without knowing the past. Sometimes family secrets can do more harm than good. Once these are revealed, we can glean important life lessons. This knowledge helps children develop meaningful personal role models and strive to be authors, teachers, doctors, and lawyers, not bank robbers, murderers, and drug dealers.

If African American youngsters learn genealogy early enough, it can make a big difference in their lives. Genealogy can not only help kids understand the world but can give them respect for their elders, bridge generation gaps, and heal family wounds.

Genealogy is also important for young folks to develop a sense of heritage and identity. Many African Americans are placed in environments in which they are the only one of their kind in the workplace. If they do not have a strong sense of their African American heritage and family history, they may lose their sense of identity and culture.

To Understand Family

Genealogy also helps us understand our relatives (in addition to our ancestors) and connect with those we have never met or those we haven't seen in years. Some have said genealogy has helped them identify relatives so they wouldn't accidentally marry one.

I want to understand my relatives and ancestors and why they did the things they did, good or bad. Through research I have discovered many ancestors with accomplishments that are very admirable. Genealogy gives me pride in their accomplishments. There are other ancestors who did things they were not proud of. Genealogy gives me an understanding of their circumstances.

Through genealogy research I solved a family riddle that existed in my family for almost one hundred years. The riddle created tension, controversy, and misunderstanding among family members until I solved it through researching my ancestors and the events of their lives. Unfortunately, the discovery was made so late that several of the key figures who suffered from these misunderstandings died before my research was completed. If they had not, it might have healed wounds from many ages. It did, however, give much understanding to my mother and her sister.

Some genealogists have noted the benefits of knowing family medical history, so that members can be warned of potential health risks. Many diseases are hereditary, passing down from generation to generation. If these diseases are known about in time, family members can take precautions and seek preventive cures and thereby sometimes avoid serious illness, prolonged hospitalization, and even preventable death.

To Learn About History

Genealogy teaches researchers not only about their ancestors and themselves but also about the roles their ancestors played in American history. Genealogy gives one a clearer and deeper understanding of history. Researchers must study history to understand what affected their ancestors. Their lives must be placed in context. When I think of dates and events, I immediately think of what my ancestors were doing at the time. I also look to see what role my ancestors played in historical events. My mom participated in the Civil Rights Movement in Chicago; her brother was a union organizer in Chicago; and their mom taught in a one-room schoolhouse in West Virginia. My father and his brothers served in World War II; their father litigated for public housing in the 1930s; and his dad was a Pullman porter who survived the devastating Pullman Strike of 1894. I could go on and on, but the point is, through research on my ancestors, I learned a lot about American history, as well as my ancestors' contributions to that history.

To Foster Pride and Self-Esteem

I have also found several instances of genealogy creating a tremendous sense of pride and self-esteem among African Americans. Diane said she had a nephew who always looked down and lacked self-esteem and self-confidence. She had been researching their ancestors, and when she told him about some of them and the deeds they accomplished, he started looking up and began smiling regularly. He had a newfound confidence the family had never seen before.

Betty Butler, an avid genealogist, said a young relative came up to her at a family reunion with a four-year-old in tow. This young relative said, "After you told the story of your great-grandfather named Jordan, whom you were so proud of, I thought about it long and hard. I named my son Jordan. Here he is," he said, proudly introducing the young son born after their last family reunion. Since no one in Betty's generation was named Jordan, she said it meant more to her than a million dollars. Betty said if she had ever had a son, she would have named him Jordan.

My cousin Kenten Cole is an elementary schoolteacher. He called one evening just before Halloween, asking to borrow my cavalry uniform. I had purchased it in 1992 at a dedication of the monument to Buffalo Soldiers in Fort Leavenworth, Kansas. The Buffalo Soldiers were African Americans in the U.S. Regular Army after the Civil War. It was the first time African Americans were allowed to be career military soldiers. Before then they could only volunteer for a war and return to civilian life after the war.

Our maternal great-grandfather, Preston Brooks, was a Buffalo Soldier. Kent said the teachers at his school were dressing up as famous people for the students. He wanted to dress as Preston Brooks, Buffalo Soldier.

In addition to lending my cousin the uniform, I gave him a short biography I'd written after researching Preston Brooks. I also gave him historical information on the Buffalo

Soldiers. I wanted Kenten to know about the ancestor he was portraying and something about the history of the Buffalo Soldiers so he could educate the students and to other teachers.

At the Halloween party most of the teachers were dressed as entertainers. When they asked Kenten who he was, he stuck out his chest, saluted, and said, "Preston Brooks, Buffalo Soldier!" The students and teachers looked at him curiously and asked, "Who is Preston Brooks?" Kenten relaxed into a civilian pose and replied, "My great-grandfather." He showed Brooks's biography with the picture on the cover and told the teachers and students about the Buffalo Soldiers. Kenten said he was proud to represent his great-grandfather rather than dressing like the other teachers as fictional television characters and entertainers.

Genealogy Can Be Emotional

Being a genealogist is like being a pioneer or an adventurer. The thing that we share in common is "the moment of discovery." Finally finding an ancestor's name on a record is like striking oil. It's like searching for something you've lost and finally located. It's a euphoric feeling.

Genealogy research can elicit powerful emotions. When we research our ancestors and discover their names in records, it's like we're connecting with them spiritually. It can get very eerie. I first experienced this when I had been searching for my paternal great-grandfather, Morris Burroughs, for several months and finally saw a picture of him for the first time. It was like "Wow!" I had been wondering what he looked like and suddenly I knew. Seeing his photograph was like meeting him in person.

The anticipation of receiving a document in the mail or searching a roll of microfilm can be breathtaking. I've been at the National Archives on many occasions when researchers first locate an ancestor's name on a roll of microfilm filled with old census records. Some get so excited they gasp, scream, or shout. Experienced researchers rarely even lift their heads up from their own microfilm machines when they hear the noise. They may pause briefly and say, "She found him." After all these years I still get excited and gasp and scream when I come across an ancestor I've been searching for for a long time.

There is a dramatic effect that touching original records has on researchers. George Jenkins is the great-great-grandson of Nelson Ray, a freed slave who traveled to California for the gold rush in 1849. Jenkins had researched his family for twenty-five years when he found the Missouri will that freed Nelson Ray. Jenkins made an appearance on the CBS *Sunday Morning* television show holding a copy of the will, trying to express what the piece of paper meant to him. You could feel the emotion while he said it was difficult to explain and that you have to go through it.

Sometimes when I visit the cemeteries where my ancestors are buried, the feeling comes over me again. I was in the old section of East Batavia Cemetery with Jeanne Jones, whose ancestors founded Quinn Chapel A.M.E. Church in 1847. It was Chicago's first African American church. I was interviewing a historian who was giving Jeanne and me a tour of the cemetery. He pointed out the headstone for her great-grandfather and I heard a gasp. I didn't understand why because she had visited this cemetery before. When I realized she had not located his gravesite and headstone on previous trips, I understood her excitement and emotion.

I recall when I was looking for Morris for several years in census records. Early in my research I searched the 1870 census for three hours without success. Years later I thought I might not have been thorough and searched again. It was another unsuccessful three hours. Other records indicated he was from South Carolina, but I hadn't located a single record in South Carolina with his name on it.

Finally, I was researching in Salt Lake City many years later and found his name on an 1874 school record in Spartanburg, South Carolina. When I realized it was him, I took in a deep breath and let out a big sigh of relief. I stood there motionless for a while, realizing that after all these years I had finally found him. He was right where he was supposed to be. It was a very exhilarating feeling. I probably would have screamed but I was too overcome by emotion. It wasn't because I didn't want to disturb the people in the library.

The emotionalism in genealogy is sometimes similar to that in sports when athletes win the big game or match. They jump in the air, shout, wave their arms, and move their bodies in all kinds of gyrations. Or sometimes it's like when super athletes get in "the zone." They are into the flow of the game, everything else is tuned out, and they hardly think about what they are doing. Everything just comes naturally and they perform without thinking. The body and mind are fused into one. This zone performance comes after years of perfecting a sport and teaching your body to memorize muscle reflex actions.

In genealogy this can come in two parts. The first part is when you have eaten, slept, and drunk information about your ancestors until it comes out your ears. It's as if you know them, even though you may not have lived during their lifetime. When you finally find their name or something more about them after you've been searching for years, it's a very emotional experience.

Sometimes you can't find your ancestors because you haven't done enough research. You've got some names and dates and think that's enough. It isn't. You have to know as much about them as possible in order to figure out where they came from, what they did, and where they traveled. You have to collect details of their lives so you can learn their personalities. You have to really know them, put yourself in their shoes and walk on their hallowed ground. Only after searching for every record you can and studying the history of the time and place in which they lived can you understand them.

Once you do this, you can get into "the zone," the "genealogy zone." It comes to you sometimes when you are studying your ancestors, sometimes when you are researching at a library or an archive, sometimes at night, sometimes in the shower, or sometimes when you are just daydreaming.

It's a spiritual bonding with your ancestors. You're trying to find them and they're hoping you find them, leaving you clues along the way.

Fundamentals: The Building Blocks of African American Genealogy

Beginning a new venture can be either fun or frustrating. In any sport, game, hobby, or endeavor, you do not have to read a book, take a class, or have a tutor to learn a new skill. The old method of trial and error still works. This is true in genealogy as well as other disciplines. So I would never be one to say there is only one way to do genealogy and if you don't do it that way you won't be successful. But to me, trial and error can be very frustrating.

Experience has shown that if you learn the fundamentals in a new area and follow them, you will likely become more successful and at a faster pace. You can benefit from my mistakes and those of other genealogists. Of course, if you only believed in the trial-and-error method, you probably wouldn't be reading this book.

Through solving major problems of my own, pondering the problems of others, and studying genealogy and African American history, I have developed six distinct phases of African American genealogy. If you understand and master each phase before proceeding to the next one, I believe you will be very successful.

Remember that fundamental genealogy starts from the known and proceeds to the unknown, one generation at a time. You may have the name of an old ancestor, perhaps a great-great-grandparent who was a slave. You may or may not know much about this ancestor. If you haven't completed the stages that lead back to this ancestor, you are not prepared to research that ancestor. You will not have enough information to be successful. If you thoroughly cover these phases and steps, you will pick up information along the way that will be essential in researching this ancestor. You will then be in a much better position to research that ancestor when you get your research back that far.

THE SIX PHASES OF AFRICAN AMERICAN GENEALOGY

1. Gather Oral History and Family Records
2. Research the Family to 1870
3. Identify the Last Slave Owner
4. Research the Slave Owner and Slavery
5. Go Back to Africa
6. Research Canada and the Caribbean

Phase I—Gather Oral History and Family Records

We've said genealogy starts with ourselves and proceeds backward. You are the first link in your family tree. So genealogy begins with recalling and recording things about yourself and beginning to write your autobiography. Next you'll need to interview your parents and other older relatives, pumping them for information. You'll then look at things lying around the house in trunks, attics, basements, bookcases, and shoe boxes that can add to knowledge of your family tree. Things like family papers, records, photos, and souvenirs. To sort out all this data, you'll organize it into genealogy charts that trace bloodlines and group people in family units. All these things are parts of beginning genealogy.

Phase II—Research the Family to 1870

After you exhaust sources at home, you'll venture out to locate records in the community. The objective is to research your family back to 1870. This is a key date because most African Americans were enslaved prior to the Civil War. But not all African Americans were enslaved before the Civil War. There were more than 200,000 free Blacks in the North and another 200,000 free in the South prior to the Civil War. Unfortunately, many genealogists assume their ancestors were slaves and run into a brick wall because their ancestors were actually free prior to the Emancipation Proclamation.

Additional beginning sources include records in cemeteries and funeral homes, birth and death certificates, marriage and divorce records, obituaries, published biographies and family histories, old city directories and telephone directories, Social Security records, and U.S. Census records.

Intermediate sources include records of wills, probates, estates, real estate, taxes, voter registrations, schools, churches, places of employment, military service, and civil and criminal courts. The intermediate phase also includes studying U.S. history, African American history, local history, and military history.

Phase III—Identify the Last Slave Owner

Once researchers have thoroughly completed the above records and traced their pedigree to 1870, they've arrived at the advanced stage of research. Unfortunately, many more people think they are there before they actually are. Just because you have identified an ancestor who lived in 1870 or earlier does not mean you have qualified for the advanced stage. Only after you have thoroughly exhausted the records and historical research listed above have you progressed to the advanced stage.

Once here, if your ancestors were enslaved, you have to identify the name of the last slave owner. This may sound unusual because we've all been led to believe our surnames came from the slave owner. But remember, genealogy is based on fact, not assumptions and rumor. Most African Americans are not as fortunate as Alex Haley to have the name of the slave owner passed down from generation to generation. They will have to look to specific sources to identify who was the last slave owner prior to emancipation. Even if the name of the slave owner has been passed down through the oral history of your family, you'll need to search for documentary evidence to verify it. Slave genealogy cannot be done without the name of the former slave owner.

You'll need to study the history of Reconstruction and then research Reconstruction-era sources for evidence of your ancestors and records that identify the name of the last slave owner. You'll also need to study Civil War history and records generated by the Civil War.

Phase IV—Research the Slave Owner and Slavery

Once the name of the last slave owner is identified, the next step is to research the history of slavery and understand the conditions, laws, customs, and practices that governed slavery and enslaved Africans. This subject is not taught in detail in school, so you must study it. Then you need to research the slave owner to see what he did with his property, because slaves were property—bought, sold, and traded like hogs, cattle, and tools. At this point you are doing the genealogy of the slave owner as well as the genealogy of the slave. It's double work.

Phase V—Go Back to Africa

The next phase is to look for clues and mentions of slave origins in Africa. Again, you will have to look for bits and pieces of evidence. You cannot rely on family rumors or facial features that have been altered through several generations and many years of evolution and intermixing with other races. Many people of African descent have been here for over three hundred years. You'll need to study the slave trade and the Middle Passage, which brought slaves from Africa to America.

Phase VI—Research Canada and the Caribbean

Some of you will discover your ancestors did not come to America directly from Africa; they came from the Caribbean. So you'll need to study the migrations of enslaved Africans from Africa to the Caribbean to America. You'll then search for records indicating origins in the Caribbean and then from Africa to the Caribbean.

You may discover your ancestors came to the United States from Canada. You'll have to study the Underground Railroad and trace your ancestors back and forth across the border and then to Africa or the Caribbean. But you must study the history before searching for your ancestors.

This book covers in detail only the beginning steps of genealogical research, Phase I and half of Phase II. To be most successful, these steps, or fundamentals, should be followed in sequence. I know some of you may already have done one or two of the items on this list. For example, some of you may already have talked to older relatives. You may already know three, four, or five generations of your family history from family discussions or from attending family reunions. That is good because you will need that information. You have a head start. Some of you may even have been to the National Archives to research census records but not completed earlier steps, such as obtaining birth and death certificates. Even though you have a head start on some research, you should use these fundamentals. You should read each chapter in detail because it will probably mention things you have not done, things you didn't fully understand, or things you never even thought about. You will probably need to go back to one of your earlier sources to obtain additional information.

When researchers get stuck researching an ancestor, it is often the result of skipping over fundamental steps. Others might not have been thorough in completing various steps. The process is very similar to spring training in professional baseball. Players learn the fundamentals and practice executing them perfectly, over and over again. No matter how experienced a ball player is, every spring he reports to camp and repeats the fundamentals.

Organizing Before It Gets Messy

Organization is a major key to life and to successful genealogy. If you are organized from the beginning, your chances for success are greatly increased. In tracing your family history, you will accumulate a lot of papers, documents, notes, charts, photographs, maps, brochures, and artifacts. A disorganized genealogist does not know where accumulated documents are placed, does not know where specific facts came from, cannot locate facts and documents when they are needed, and cannot find names and telephone numbers when they are needed. No matter how much research you do, if you can't put your hands on the right information when you need it, you won't be able to completely assemble and accurately analyze your research findings. My most frustrating times are when I fall behind in my filing and organization and can't find important documents. I often take several days to do nothing but file and organize papers.

Once the genealogy bug bites you, it becomes an all-encompassing monster. You become obsessed! You can't stop. You suffer from the disease called the "genealogy pox"! If you're not organized, you'll become frustrated and quit. Or, at a minimum, you will duplicate research you've already done. And no one has the time, energy, or money to needlessly duplicate research they've already done. It will also be difficult or impossible for others to help you when you run into dead ends.

Some genealogists have been researching for so long they have tons of documents. They've been very successful in collecting pieces of paper but have no system for filing and retrieving them. Therefore everything is a mess. I can't tell you how many genealogists like this I've run into. I usually come across them because they seek my help in solving a problem. When I see what they've got, the first thing I recommend is that they stop researching. They need to concentrate on organizing what they've already collected. But the genealogy bug has bitten them so hard they can't stop researching.

They get pains every time they think about organizing their papers. But an experienced genealogist not wanting to stop researching and organize his data is like a patient not wanting to take her medicine or an injured patient not wanting to attend therapy. You don't have to do it, but you're not going to get well.

! Trap: Not keeping files, notes, and papers organized.

One problem that is difficult for beginning genealogists to cope with is the enormous number of ancestors and relatives who can be included in tracing the family history. This is especially true for African Americans, who sometimes come from large families with ten, eleven, twelve children or more. The number of offspring from these large families creates huge databases. Before you know it, you have hundreds of names. I have over five hundred names in a small family database. I know another person who has over eight hundred names and another who has a database of over five thousand names! True, she has branched out to other than her own family, but when you start, you don't know where you will go. If you're organized from the beginning, you can go as far as you want. Five thousand names is an awful lot of data to manage if you are not organized.

The keys to organization are the right tools, a system, the discipline to use the system, and proper documentation.

Family History Research Tools

It doesn't cost much to begin researching your family history, and a few inexpensive tools will make the job easier. You'll probably have many of the items already. As you progress, you'll find a need for additional items to keep you organized. Here are the lists, followed by an explanation of each item.

BASIC TOOLS

- Notepaper—acid free
- Pencils—automatic (mechanical)
- Pencil lead and erasers
- Pens
- Genealogy charts and forms
- File folders—acid free
- Telephone book or list with genealogy telephone numbers
- Stationery, envelopes, and stamps

INTERMEDIATE TOOLS

- Magnifying glass or sheet
- File cabinet—legal size preferred
- File management system
- Portable cassette tape recorder
- Blank audio tapes
- Batteries for portable cassette tape recorder
- Genealogy guides and reference books
- Archival-quality polyethylene photo sleeves
- White photographer's gloves
- Briefcase
- Road atlas

OPTIONAL TOOLS

- 35mm SLR camera
- Black-and-white film
- Color film
- Videocassette camcorder
- Computer
- Word-processing and database software
- Genealogy software
- Acid-free document cases and storage boxes
- Bookcase

Basic Tools

These are the first items people need to get started. And to get really basic, all you really need is a pen and paper. Those who have started by going to family reunions and talking to older relatives probably had just a pen and paper. In fact, more genealogists would be more successful if that's all they used (except maybe a tape recorder) until they finished talking with each and every relative.

NOTEPAPER—Everyone has his or her own method for taking notes. Some people like three-ring notebooks with notebook paper, some like spiral-bound notebooks; historians like index cards, and lawyers like yellow legal pads.

Well, genealogy is different. You can use one of those systems if you want, but you may run into problems down the road. In genealogy, after you collect research data, you must be able to easily assemble every fact in one place for analysis.

Small, irregular scraps of paper can easily be misplaced and lost. If most papers and documents are a uniform size, they are easier to organize, file, retrieve, and duplicate.

Many archives and other repositories that store old, rare, and valuable documents operate very differently from your local public library. Because many of the records are original and may be the only ones in existence, archives have policies and procedures that are more restrictive than those of public libraries. Many of them do not allow notebooks, briefcases, or card files in the research room. Such items must be left in lockers outside the research room. You may be permitted to take in only single sheets of paper or a couple of file folders. Every facility is different, with its own set of rules. You shouldn't complain about these restrictions. You should actually be glad. If these policies weren't restrictive, the records on your ancestors might not exist. Therefore all notes should be taken on letter-size (8½″ × 11″) or legal size (8½″ × 14″) paper. Then if you are allowed only single sheets, you can comply with the regulations and won't become frustrated because you can't take in a spiral-bound notebook with twelve years of research in it.

In genealogy you also want to preserve your notes for as long as possible. Most papers in use today are highly acidic. Over time they will yellow and deteriorate. (More of this subject is explained in the chapter "Preserving the Past and the Present," [page 59].) So I recommend using acid-free paper for taking notes. Then your notes and records can outlive you and be around for your descendants to research, perhaps hundreds of years from now. Sticking with letter- or legal-size acid-free paper for everything minimizes the chances for loss, confusion, and deterioration.

PENCILS — Many archives, historical societies, and genealogical libraries require pencils to be used instead of pens. This is because ink can damage old documents and archivists can't take any risks with careless researchers. The two problems with using a pencil are that the lead breaks and the point always needs sharpening.

Therefore I recommend using an automatic (mechanical) pencil. An automatic pencil is made of metal and plastic. It has a thin rod of lead in the center chamber. When the lead wears down, the top is pressed and new lead is exposed at the point. One pencil can hold ten or twelve lead refills inside the center chamber. A .5mm HB lead refill is preferred. Automatic pencils are a pleasure to use. Once you start using one, you'll never want to use a wood pencil again.

PENS — Pens are used to make permanent records. After many years pencil notes can become smudged, faded, and hard to read. So if a library or research center does not require using a pencil, by all means, use a pen. However, don't use a felt-tipped pen. The ink flows through the fibers and can damage paper. Genealogy charts should be recorded in pen.

GENEALOGY CHARTS — These are needed to track research, ancestors, and relatives and to record vital information. They are explained in detail in the chapters "Family Group Sheets" (page 133) and "The Pedigree Chart" (page 146).

NOTEBOOKS—Some researchers like to use the notebook system. They place all their notes and accumulated documents in three-ring binders. This is justified by the ease of having everything in one place and being able to take it with you on a research trip. This is very misleading. A notebook is nice for displaying your research to show others, but it is very inefficient for filing and retrieving information and for conducting research.

I started with a notebook. After I gained experience and collected tons of documents, however, I had several major problems with it. The biggest problem was analysis. When using records in a notebook for analysis, you cannot assemble all the data on one ancestor in one place. You will have forms, charts, notes, documents, photographs, letters, and other miscellaneous items. All of these can easily be placed in acid-free file folders and easily filed and retrieved, but not in a notebook.

The second problem I had was that the notebook became too bulky. I had so much stuff in it the binding split! After a notebook becomes too bulky, you have to get another one and then another one. Several factors increase the bulk in notebooks, such as:

- Successful research—the more you uncover, the more documents you accumulate.
- Adding ancestors means adding more dividers to the notebook.
- If documents are placed in sleeves, the size of the notebook needed is tripled.

The third major problem with using notebooks is space. As I started accumulating loads of paper, I quickly outgrew the notebook. I realized right away I couldn't keep buying notebooks. It was bad enough finding things in one notebook, let alone a stack of notebooks. A file cabinet and file folders are designed to be flexible and grow as a project develops. Now my data is stored in four-drawer file cabinets and a few document cases. I started off with a two-drawer cabinet and progressed to four-drawer file cabinets. Currently I have five four-drawer file cabinets. But I've been researching for twenty years. That's a drawer for each year. There is no way I can put twenty drawers of data into notebooks! Notebooks cannot account for future expansion and growth the way file folders and file cabinets can.

Other problems with the notebook system are:

- If sleeves are not used, holes must be punched in documents to keep them in the binder. Researchers should never cut, tear, punch holes in, or otherwise deface documents.
- Legal-size documents must be folded, which you should not do. Folding weakens paper, which will eventually tear on the fold line.
- Notebooks cannot be taken into many archives and historical society libraries.

If notebooks were the best tool for the filing and retrieving of documents, they would be used in libraries, archives, and offices. You do find them in libraries and offices but only for limited information purposes. Libraries, archives, and offices all use file folders and file cabinets to store large quantities of documents. Therefore, use file folders instead of notebooks for the most efficient genealogical research.

FILE FOLDERS—File folders should be made of acid-free materials, just like the paper you use. Plain manila folders from office supply stores are highly acidic. The acid can migrate from a document that has a high acid concentration to one with a lesser concentration. This means acid can spread from your folder to your document. You may have seen an old book in which a receipt or newspaper article was used as a bookmark. If the book mark was there a long time, it may have left a yellow mark or stain on the page. That yellow color is the acid that migrated from the receipt to the book page.

TELEPHONE BOOK—It's a good idea to keep all telephone numbers that pertain to genealogy together. Then when you need the telephone number of someone connected with genealogy, you can easily retrieve it. This list should include relatives, genealogists, genealogy libraries, archives, courthouses, and any others you might need.

STATIONERY, ENVELOPES, AND STAMPS—Genealogy research involves mailing letters requesting information, documents, and records. Researchers should also send thank-you letters. When writing most genealogical libraries, archives, and historical societies, you should include a self-addressed, stamped envelope (SASE). Then when the recipient has a reply or a document to return, he or she can simply place the item in the SASE you provided and drop it in the mail. There is little additional time and cost to the institution. Sometimes this results in a faster reply, and sometimes it determines whether you receive a reply or not.

Intermediate Tools

MAGNIFYING GLASS OR SHEET—Some records have small print that is difficult to read. When you start to look at microfilm copies of records, you may need some help with smaller print. A magnifying glass can come in handy. Office supply stores carry 8″ × 10″ and 3″ × 5″ plastic magnifying sheets. These sheets are as thin and light as paper and can easily fit into file folders and briefcases, where they are always handy.

FILE CABINET—When first beginning, if you want to save money, you can use a box to store file folders. After you outgrow it, you should purchase a file cabinet. Again, to save money, you can buy used metal file cabinets from used office furniture stores or from want ads in the newspaper. If you are going to purchase a file cabinet, choose a legal-size one. Many court records and legal documents you will be accumulating will be legal size (8½″ × 14″). Then you can store letter-size and legal-size documents in the same file folders without having to fold the longer documents.

FILE MANAGEMENT—A file management system is designed for ease of filing and retrieving documents. If it is a good system, you can quickly and easily find information you have accumulated. The system should start simply but have room for expansion, flexibility, and complexity.

There are two types of records you'll be collecting—those that mention your ancestors' names and those that help you do genealogy. You'll want to keep them separate.

You can start a system with only a few file folders. Begin with your family genealogy files. Use one folder for the mother's side of the family (maternal) and another folder for the father's side of the family (paternal). It is a genealogical convention that women are listed by their maiden name. Their records are then filed under their maiden name, not under their husband's surname. So I'll start with a folder labeled "Burroughs" and one labeled "Brooks," since that is my mother's maiden name.

After you accumulate numerous notes and documents, subdivide your files into additional surnames or individuals. For example, my Burroughs documents go into one folder, the Brooks family documents into another folder, and the Terrell family documents into another folder. When I accumulate several documents on an individual Burroughs ancestor, I create a separate file folder for that particular ancestor. For example, my grandfather Asa Morris Burroughs has his own folder, and his brother Robert Elliott Burroughs has a separate folder. Make copies of documents that mention more than one ancestor and place in their respective folders. In this way the system can grow logically and easily as more and more documents are gathered. To make the folders easy to retrieve, file them alphabetically by surname. As simple as this seems, it will take a little getting used to at first because you'll have a tendency to think of a woman's married name and want to file her documents by family name instead of maiden name.

As for the documents within each folder, genealogist Pat Hatcher suggests filing them in chronological order as the documents were created. This builds a chronology of the person's life and is like a mini biography. I think it makes good sense.

As you collect information on cities, counties, states, and how-to-do genealogy, file it in separate folders. You want to separate your family documents from ones that have nothing to do

FILING PAPERS AND DOCUMENTS

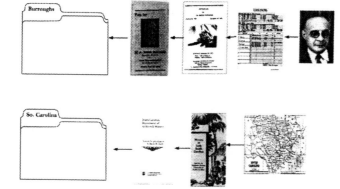

Filing Papers and Documents—A guide for filing different types of documents in a family file folder versus a state file folder.

with your family. For example, create a folder for Illinois, one for South Carolina, and a separate folder for Mississippi. Also file these alphabetically. Then if you gather a wealth of information on a particular county, start a separate folder for that county. A county folder should be filed behind its state folder. If there is more than one county folder, file them alphabetically by county behind their state folder.

A good rule of thumb to follow is, when a folder starts to get thick, sort the papers in the folder by another person if it's a family file or by another topic if it's a subject file. Then take the topic with the largest number of papers and start a separate folder for that topic. The smaller the folders are, the easier it is to find the information inside them. Pat Hatcher recommends starting another folder when they get to be a quarter of an inch thick. I have many that are a lot thinner. Keeping files thin will also help to protect the documents. If a folder is thick, the documents have a tendency to get folded, torn, and damaged. They also start to fall out and become exposed to dust and dirt. This defeats one of the main purposes of the folder, protecting the documents.

As your research gets more and more successful and you accumulate more and more records, start to group files into topics. Then place these in file drawers. For example, you might have one file drawer for the family files and another drawer with everything else. Then you can progress to a four-drawer file cabinet and have one drawer for the family; another for locality files, including states, counties, and cities; and another drawer for genealogical methods and techniques. You'll eventually divide family files between your maternal line and paternal line. Think like a library and you should have no problems retrieving your information. The Research Calendar that is explained in the chapter on "Managing Your Research" will help you keep track of research notes and documents.

GENEALOGY FILE FOLDERS

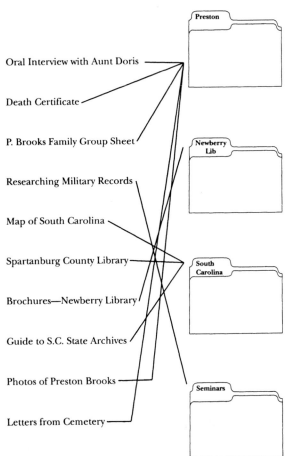

Oral Interview with Aunt Doris

Death Certificate

P. Brooks Family Group Sheet

Researching Military Records

Map of South Carolina

Spartanburg County Library

Brochures—Newberry Library

Guide to S.C. State Archives

Photos of Preston Brooks

Letters from Cemetery

Preston

Newberry Lib

South Carolina

Seminars

Genealogy File Folders—Different types of genealogical documents and how they are organized in subject folders for quick and easy retrieval.

ORGANIZING FILES
(Beginning)

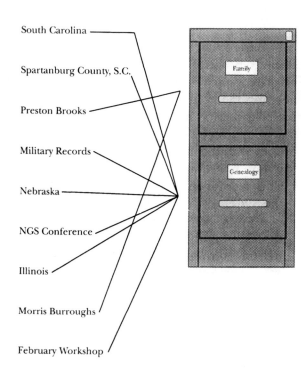

South Carolina

Spartanburg County, S.C.

Preston Brooks

Military Records

Nebraska

NGS Conference

Illinois

Morris Burroughs

February Workshop

2-Drawer File Cabinet—Beginning filing system illustrating a basic division between family documents and genealogy documents for quick and easy retrieval.

The keys to file management are:

- Use a file cabinet. If you have a lot of files, get a four-drawer file cabinet.
- Use subjects to divide the cabinet.
- Use subjects to divide the drawers.
- Alphabetize files within drawers.
- Keep filing up to date.
- Keep file folders in the cabinet, not on the desk.
- Return the used files to the cabinet at the end of the day.

TAPE RECORDER—Tape recorders are recommended to record oral interviews. They can be purchased inexpensively and come in small, handy sizes. They will definitely be put to good use. Since a portable tape recorder is so vital to research, it could be listed as a basic item instead of an intermediate item. The only reason it is listed as an intermediate tool is that it is

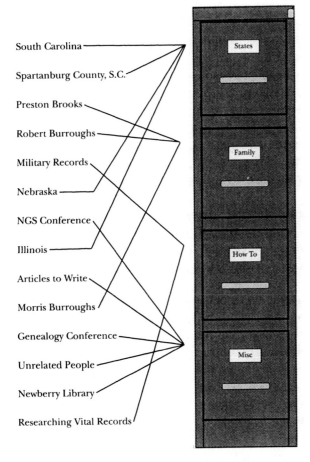

ORGANIZING FILES
(Advanced)

South Carolina
Spartanburg County, S.C.
Preston Brooks
Robert Burroughs
Military Records
Nebraska
NGS Conference
Illinois
Articles to Write
Morris Burroughs
Genealogy Conference
Unrelated People
Newberry Library
Researching Vital Records

States
Family
How To
Misc

4-Drawer File Cabinet—Advanced filing system illustrating how to organize a large, diverse collection of documents for quick and easy retrieval.

not absolutely necessary to start off. However, a whole lot is missed by not using one when interviewing relatives.

There are several things to consider when you're ready to purchase a tape recorder. The first consideration is whether to buy one with an internal or external microphone. Many inexpensive models come with a built-in microphone. That is great because the tape recorder can be placed inconspicuously next to a relative during an interview so he or she won't become intimidated by it. If a microphone is placed in front of them, your relatives may have a difficult time relaxing and thinking about the interview. They will be thinking about the microphone.

However, if a tape recorder has an external microphone, it can accommodate a lapel microphone, which you can place on the person's jacket lapel or blouse. It can also accommodate an external jack to tape-record interviews over the telephone for long-distance calls.

There are two such devices that can connect to a tape recorder. One is a suction cup that plugs into the external jack of the recorder. The suction end attaches to the telephone headset receiver.

The other device is a telephone pickup control. One end plugs into the telephone, and the other end plugs into the tape recorder. Then the voice goes directly into the tape recorder. I have used both devices successfully. There is a little better quality with the control pickup device because it has a direct connection. They both can be purchased inexpensively from a local electronics store or from a telephone or computer supply store. The control pickup costs a little more, but the better quality and ease of use are worth the minimal extra expense. Before tape-recording over the telephone, be sure to get the other person's permission.

Try to purchase a tape recorder with both an internal microphone and an external microphone jack. Then you have maximum flexibility. If you have to choose between one or the other, you're probably better off with the external jack if you have relatives out of town, and who doesn't?

The next choice to make is the size of the tapes and tape recorder. There are minicassettes and microcassettes. A minicassette recorder is small in size and takes standard-size audiocassette tapes. A microcassette recorder is the smallest you can get, usually fits into a pocket, and has the smallest tapes. These tapes are too small to fit into a standard-size tape recorder or tape deck.

The advantage of a minicassette recorder is that the tapes are usable right away in most tape players. The disadvantage occurs when the tape has to be transcribed. Some transcription machines use only microcassette tapes. If you use a standard-size tape and then need it transcribed by a service, you may have to get it transferred to the microcassette size. You'll either have to pay extra money for this transfer or do it yourself. If you do it yourself, you'll have to connect a microcassette recorder to a minicassette recorder through a cable. Other transcription services can handle either size tape. Before you buy, it's best to check with the transcription service you plan to use to see what size they prefer.

BLANK AUDIOTAPES—It almost goes without saying that you should have extra audiocassette tapes when tape-recording relatives. Since tapes have become inexpensive, they can be purchased in bulk. Drugstores, discount houses, and even electronic stores sell them in packs of five and ten to a package. It's much more convenient and cost-effective to buy them in packs of ten than to get two tapes every time you need them.

BATTERIES—Batteries for the tape recorder should be on hand for a backup source of power. However, the primary source of electric power should be an AC adapter that plugs into a wall outlet. It is more reliable than batteries, which can weaken without your knowledge. It's an awful feeling to listen to a tape recorded with weak batteries and hear a voice so slow you can't make out what is said. Also include an extension cord in your tool kit. It will come in handy in older homes with few electrical outlets.

It is also a good idea to purchase a battery recharger. A recent article in the newspaper reported a study proving that, over the long haul, recharger units save money. If you use rechargeable batteries, keep one set of regular, nonrechargeable batteries on hand for emergencies. Nonrechargeable batteries fade gradually and will last a long time on the shelf. Rechargeable batteries discharge right away, with no warning. There is no fading. They also die on the shelf if they are not used. So keep extras of both types on the shelf.

GENEALOGY GUIDES AND BOOKS—You have made the first right decision by purchasing this book. (If you got it from the library, you need to add it to your collection so you can refer to it over and over.) As you begin your genealogical journey, you will learn many new things. You will continually learn about new techniques and sources as you go along. Having a small collection of genealogy books and reference guides at home can go a long way toward advancing your knowledge and resources. When I'm up late at night studying and analyzing my ancestors, I refer to books on my genealogical bookshelf rather than waiting for the library to open the next day. Whenever I get insomnia, I get out of bed and go to my genealogy library. You'll find there are some subjects you'll refer to on a regular basis. If so, consider purchasing that book for your home library.

PHOTO SLEEVES—In the chapter "Preserving the Past and the Present," I discuss preserving old photographs and negatives. After reading that chapter, you may be inclined to purchase sleeves to store your photographs and negatives so they will last longer. These can be purchased at photography stores or from mail-order supply houses that specialize in preservation supplies.

PHOTOGRAPHER'S GLOVES—Dust, dirt, and oil naturally accumulate on our hands. If these are transferred to documents and photos, they can leave permanent marks and stains. These marks can be almost impossible to remove later on, if at all. And if they can be removed, it may be expensive if a professional has to do the work. Therefore I recommend handling photographs, negatives, and old and rare documents with white photographer's gloves. These are very inexpensive white cotton gloves that can be purchased either singly or in packs of two to five from photography stores.

BRIEFCASE—Some people already have a briefcase, but if you don't, you may want to purchase one. When you visit a library or an archive, you can copy the files you need and just pop them in your briefcase. If you're going to purchase a briefcase, buy a good leather one. The better it is, the longer it will last. The better ones also are flexible for when you *accidentally* cram more in it than was intended.

ROAD ATLAS—Maps become extremely important in doing genealogy research. You must know where your ancestors lived, where they moved, what county they lived in, where the county boundaries were, where the rivers and mountains are, and what were the closest largest cities to them. A contemporary road atlas can be purchased inexpensively and contains all the states in the United States. It is a good beginning tool to orientate you to the geography of your ancestors. If you don't have a good sense of geography, studying a map will help you get your bearings. The county boundaries may be different now than they were when your ancestors lived in the area long ago. Eventually you will have to obtain maps for the time period they lived in the area. But for now the road atlas is fine.

Optional Tools

CAMERA—We've all heard the cliché "A picture is worth a thousand words." Well, once you see the town your great-grandparents lived in or the old homestead, you'll want to take a photo to take back home and show the family. You'll also probably want to have a photograph of yourself at the site where your ancestors lived. If you don't own a camera, that may be a little difficult.

I can probably list a dozen other ways to use a camera in genealogy, but I'll mention only two. One is in copying old photographs of ancestors. Most old photographs do not have negatives. If you want a copy of the photograph, you can take it to a photo lab that specializes in copying photos. Sometimes this is feasible, practical, and inexpensive and sometimes it is not. Say you are out of town on a research trip, a thousand miles from home. A distant relative you have just met is ninety years old, and all of a sudden she produces a photograph of her grandmother. If you do not have a camera with you, you may never get a copy of that photo. This happened to me, and fortunately I had my camera with me.

Photographs can be copied with any camera, but, the results will differ depending on the quality of the camera and the skill of the photographer. I recommend purchasing the 35mm type of camera with interchangeable lenses. They let you get closer to the photograph and produce a sharp, high-quality image. Your salesperson at the photography store can recommend a good camera and a book on copying photographs. I've also recommended a couple of books in the chapter on "Preserving the Past and the Present." I suggest staying away from instant cameras. The images tend to be poor in quality and will fade faster than other images.

There is another exciting use for a camera in genealogy. Say this same relative takes you to her grandmother's gravesite. You see the gravestone of your great-great-grandmother who died in 1874. You definitely want a photograph of this headstone and the cemetery. It's even more exciting to have this ninety-year-old relative in the photo at her grandmother's grave. If you don't have a camera with you, you may lose an opportunity because you may never get to that site again. And if you do get back, your relative might not be around to pose for you.

FILM—Everyone uses color film today. That's good because it is inexpensive to process, has good tolerances, and gives true color. However, the images do not last as long as black-and-white prints. Color prints can begin to fade in as little as fifty years, whereas good black-and-white prints can last three hundred to five hundred years. I recommend sometimes using black-and-white film in your camera. When the family gathers for birthdays and holidays, it's good to shoot in black-and-white once in a while. Once you see your color photographs begin to fade and lose color, you'll be glad you shot a few rolls with black-and-white film. Black-and-white film should also be used when copying other black-and-white photographs. Your descendants will love you for it a hundred years from now. You may have to go to a camera store to purchase black-and-white film because the local drugstore and discount store may carry only color film.

CAMCORDER—A videotape of a relative is much more exciting than an audiotape. More and more family histories are being video-recorded.

When the price of camcorders started to drop, more people started purchasing them for home movies. The technology is better than that of the old 8mm movie cameras because the film doesn't have to be developed, there is instant playback, you don't need a screen, and the quality is better.

I find myself videotaping relatives as well as audiotaping them. This gives an added dimension to the person as compared to a photograph. Now when these older relatives die, our grandchildren will have more of a feeling for what they were like. What would I give now for a video of my great-grandparents?

If you don't own a camcorder or cannot afford to purchase a new one, you still have three options. If you ask around, you'll probably find you have a relative or a friend who owns one you can borrow. If not, consider purchasing a used one, or you can rent one by the day, week, or month. Again, check with your local photography store or check in the telephone directory.

COMPUTER—Computers are becoming more and more common in the home. Once they were used only by kids and hobbyists, but today even senior citizens are becoming computer literate. Because of large families and the resulting large number of names and documents to manage, using a computer for genealogy research is now very common. It has just about become a necessity. If you have a computer and are new to genealogy, I recommend starting off using only the word processor. This is a sophisticated typewriter and can be used to type letters and transcribe interviews and tape recordings, which I'll discuss later. I would hold off on buying a genealogy software program until you get some experience under your belt and you get the hang of genealogy first. Then as you gain experience, you can get an idea of what you need in a genealogy software program. There are dozens of programs on the market and even books and newsletters on using computers with genealogy. You don't need that confusion while you're trying to learn this new hobby. First finish reading this book and complete the fundamental steps. Then gain some experience doing genealogy research and filling out charts and forms. You can then read books and newsletters on genealogical computing and learn that end of the business.

For those of you who don't have a computer, this may be the thing that motivates you to purchase one. It does a tremendous job at managing and organizing data. There are some things that can be done only on a computer. Both computers and programs are getting better and are a lot easier to use than when they were first introduced.

DATABASE SOFTWARE—Databases are computer software programs that manipulate information. Some of you may be very experienced at using or programming databases. You may want to use this skill in your genealogical research. Before you attempt to create your own genealogy program, look into the market to see what genealogy software already exists. You don't want to reinvent the wheel.

The major genealogy software programs have been around for several years and have gone through several generations of upgrades. Genealogical programs of the future will be extremely sophisticated and much more complex than mere databases. They'll not only recognize the relationships of the individuals in the database but will understand how you do research and will create a paper trail of documents that leads to your genealogical conclusions.

DOCUMENT CASES AND STORAGE BOXES—I store most of my files in file cabinets. However, not everything is letter or legal size and therefore it may not fit into a file cabinet. Those items I have that are too big for the file cabinet I store in acid-free document cases. The cases fully enclose documents, protect them from dust, dirt, and moisture, and are archivally safe. They are relatively inexpensive and can be purchased through mail order.

BOOKCASE—I have several shelves in my home library devoted to genealogy. This way I can get to my books quickly and easily. My collection is steadily growing. If your books are stacked on a desk, dresser, or table, consider getting a bookcase. Books tend to last longer in a bookcase. They are usually a bit cleaner, and the bindings and paper are stronger when stored upright and fairly tight together.

Preserving the Past and the Present

One of the things that makes genealogy so much fun is the opportunity to look at old documents and records. Hearing about the past is one thing, but actually looking at old records is very exciting. It's almost like taking a step back in time. It's almost like you were there. You sit and read a document, either the actual paper or on a microfilm reader, and you imagine what life was like in another day and age.

What makes this experience possible is the *existence* of old records. Many were preserved, but many merely survived. In order for us to continue this experience and in order for our descendants to enjoy this same experience of our lives, we must preserve our records. We must preserve the ones we discover, and we must preserve the ones we create.

Most paper we use today deteriorates with age. This includes stationery, notebook paper, notepads, yellow and white legal pads, xerographic paper, and fax paper. Since we are researching records 50, 100, and 150 years old and older, we understand the importance of preserving old documents and records. With all the hard work we are doing, we don't want our research to crumble away in fifty years! We want our grandchildren and great-grandchildren, as well as future historians, to benefit from our research. More important, we don't want the documents we are creating or collecting to damage old documents. Most people don't realize that the papers and genealogy charts and forms lying in our folders can damage other valuable documents that may lie next to them in the same folder.

The preservation process begins with a little understanding of paper and how it is manufactured. Around 1850 the process of manufacturing paper changed from using cloth-based materials to using wood-based materials. The cloth fibers were nonacidic, whereas the wood-based fibers were acidic. When this change in manufacturing occurred, it was not known that it would decrease the longevity of the paper. When acidification occurs, paper fades and turns yellow. This is evidence of the deterioration process. The acid from one document can migrate to another document. Soon the paper becomes brittle and flakes. My aunt had a scrapbook that her sister created. It was fifty years old. When I picked it up from the table, there were flakes of paper left on the table and the floor. This was because the acid had weakened the paper until the slightest pressure or movement broke it into little pieces. I have even seen books in such bad shape that the pages had holes in them.

We need to slow down this process by using archival and acid-free materials. Acid-free papers are designed to last approximately three hundred years. However, the life span of documents, photographs, and artifacts is in part contingent on the temperature and humidity where they are stored. A rule of thumb is, if it is comfortable for you, it will be comfortable for your documents. If you are hot and need an air conditioner, your documents also need one. Try to avoid storing materials near heat sources (like radiators and furnaces) or in attics or basements, where there are extreme temperature fluctuations. Whereas modern research libraries and archives store materials at 55°F, the ideal temperature for documents in a home is between 68° and 72°F. The recommended relative humidity is below 50 percent, and ideal relative humidity is 35 percent.

Most acid-free paper is manufactured with watermarks. To see the watermark, hold a sheet of acid-free paper to the light. You can see an imprint that states the paper is acid free or Permabond. Although acid-free paper costs a little more, it is worth the extra cost to preserve our heritage. We would like our research to be around for at least a couple hundred years for our descendants to benefit from our efforts. Therefore, use acid-free paper whenever possible.

Acid-free paper should be used for writing notes and for creating genealogy charts and other documents during research. Some microfilm reader printers in libraries and archives print using a thermofax process. You can tell if a copy is thermofaxed if you have to let it dry for a minute. This thermofaxed copy not only will acidify but will fade after only a few years. When you acquire documents and photocopies of documents when researching, you can rephotocopy them onto acid-free paper. You can purchase acid-free paper from an archival products supplier, then take it to your favorite photocopy store. Tell the salesperson you have your own paper. Ask if he or she will insert it into the machine for you. Then you can easily photocopy any documents you have on acid-free paper and have them preserved.

Acid-free file folders should be used for storing documents. When acidic papers are placed in acid-free file folders, some of the acid in the papers migrates into the folder. This starts to neutralize the acid content of the paper, making it last a little longer. It won't completely deplete the paper of all the acid. To do that, the paper must actually be deacidified. It is a delicate process best accomplished by a trained paper conservator. Acid-free file folders are used almost exclusively in most archives in the United States.

If you follow these simple steps, the research you are doing will be around for many generations in the future. You will not reverse the acidification process, but you will preserve the documents you are currently collecting.

Preservation of Photographs

Photographs should also be preserved. Like documents, they have a limited life span. Black-and-white photographs normally last longer than color photographs, and older black-and-whites can last three hundred to five hundred years under optimal conditions. Color photos start fading after only fifty years or less. Because colors will fade from being exposed to ultraviolet rays from the sun, color photographs should be kept out of sunlight. If you see a color photograph start to turn a blue-green tint, photographers recommend copying it on black-and-white film as soon as possible. The Polaroid photos many people take will begin to fade and develop yellowish stains after only a few years. (See *The Permanence and Care of Color Photographs,* by Henry Whilhelm, "Photography" in the Bibliography, for a more detailed discussion of color photographs.) And recently some photography labs and drugstores have begun processing black-and-white photographs using a color process, which has shorter longevity. The paper and chemicals will not last as long as those of black-and-white photographs processed correctly.

Many of the ways in which we store photographs are detrimental. Older albums made with black construction paper pages are highly acidic. This acid will eventually eat into the photographs. Some photo albums have sleeves made of heavy plastic or vinyl. This vinyl also gives off harmful gases. The materials to avoid are vinyl, polyvinyl, and PVC (polyvinyl chloride).

Some inexpensive photo albums are called "magnetic" because there are no sleeves or corners attaching the photographs to the page. Plastic sheets cover the photos, which appear to float on the page. The plastic sheets actually give off harmful gases. There is adhesive that holds the prints to the page. The adhesive is often too strong, and the photos sometimes get torn when they are removed from the album.

For the best protection, photographs and negatives should be stored in archival-quality sleeves. Archival quality means the materials are good enough to be used in archives. Archives are concerned about how long they can preserve documents, photographs, and artifacts. Archival-quality sleeves are made of either Mylar, polyester, polypropylene, polyethylene, triacetate, or glassine. They can be obtained from camera stores or businesses that specialize in archival-quality products.

Photos and negatives should be kept in closed containers to be free from dust and dirt. The temperature and humidity should be comfortable to you. Remember, hot apartments and attics and damp basements are no-no's. I kept some photos in the trunk of my car once, and water seeped into the trunk. It destroyed the photos and the negatives.

Old photographs can very easily be copied. This is a lot easier than most people think. You can send them to a photographer who specializes in copying photos or contact a photo lab that does copy work. They will shoot the picture to make a photographic negative. Then you can inexpensively make as many copies as you like so all the relatives can have prints. Many drugstores now make inexpensive duplicate prints. However, they won't give you a negative, only a duplicate photograph. You'll have to ask for a copy negative in addition to the print, which is an extra charge.

If you consider yourself an amateur photographer, you can also do it yourself. You'll need a single lens reflex camera (SLR). With it, the subject you see through the viewfinder is the same as what the camera lens sees. That's because the SLR has a system of mirrors that reflect the image from the lens to the eyepiece. With a rangefinder camera, you estimate what the lens sees. You look in one area, and the lens looks in another area. That's why you get photos in which the heads are cut off. It's not the photographer's fault; it's the camera's fault. Doesn't that make you feel a little better?

It's best to copy photographs outside on a bright day. Believe it or not, sunlight is much stronger than the artificial light inside your house. The best time of day to copy photos is before or after the sun is directly overhead (a 45-degree angle is good). This prevents white spots in the middle of your photo, created when the sun's reflection bounces back into the camera lens. Then get as close as you can to focus. Once you're done, you will have not only a copy of the photograph but a negative as well. You can make reproductions for all the family members.

If you want to invest in a small amount of equipment, you can improve the quality of your copy prints. When you are photographing an object, the closer the camera is to the object, the steadier it has to be. Any small movement of the camera is magnified and the print becomes blurred and out of focus. Setting the camera on a tripod eliminates the movement of your arms while holding the camera. So the first item to purchase is a tripod.

The next item to purchase is a cable release. This is a short cable that attaches to the shutter of the camera so you don't touch the camera when shooting. You press the cable release instead of the actual shutter. This eliminates the hand vibration that occurs when you press the shutter to take a picture. The usage of these two items together will result in noticeably sharper photos.

A set of close-up filter lenses will enable you to focus closer to the photograph and also produce a larger image. These are relatively inexpensive and screw on the front of the lens just as a lens filter does. Next you might consider a copy stand to replace your tripod. This will enable you to shoot indoors and have more control over your conditions and photos. It is also easier to shoot close-ups with a copy stand than with a tripod.

If you are really serious about photography, you should buy a book on copying old photos, such as *Copying and Duplicating in Black-and-White and Color*, by Eastman Kodak (see "Photography" in the Bibliography). You can also take a photography course at the local community college. Just make sure the course covers copying photos.

This is not a book on the preservation of documents and photographs. Textbooks have been written on that subject. I suggest you spend some time learning more about preservation and conservation of documents and photographs (see "Preservation" and "Photography" in the Bibliography).

Managing Your Research

Genealogy is a fun hobby. You'll probably go to many new places, meet many new people, and examine many exciting records. Months and years later, if you are still doing genealogy, you'll think about a library or a record and ask, "Haven't I been here before?" or "Haven't I checked these records before?" or "What records did I check when I was in South Carolina last year?" or "I checked the index for Brooks and Boles—did I also check for Burroughs?" or "Now where are those documents I photocopied on Grandpa Brooks?"

If you stay with genealogy for any length of time, you will encounter a mass of data, and these questions will come up all the time. Files and a file cabinet are the first line of organization. In addition to a file cabinet, genealogical charts and forms are absolutely essential in organizing names, dates, places, events, and tasks. If all your notes were kept in narrative form, like a term paper, it would be impossible to highlight the names and vital data needed for research. It would also be difficult to efficiently track what you plan to do, whom you've written, and who's written you. Therefore, special charts and forms have been designed for genealogy research. Several of the following charts are standard—everyone expects you to have them and know how to use them. Others are designed to help you work more efficiently. The four forms that follow will help you plan your research, track the research you've conducted, and track the correspondence you've sent and received.

Research To Do

One of the first forms for organizing your research is the Research To Do form. Many people use a similar sheet in business or in their personal life but may call it a "To Do List" or a "Things To Do List." On it they list all the tasks they want to accomplish that day. With a Research To Do form used for genealogy, every time you think about a record to research, a library or an archive to visit, a relative to call or interview, a letter to write, or some other genealogical task, list the item on your Research To Do form. This way you always know what to do.

Some of my best ideas come while I'm doing daily activities. When an idea comes to me, I immediately pull out my Research To Do form and jot it down. If my form is not handy, I make a quick note and then transfer it to my Research To Do form and throw away the note. It is amazing how many items "slip our minds." Sometimes while I'm jogging around the track in the morning, I think of four or five records to check. I keep a pen and paper in my tennis bag. I jot down the ideas as soon as I can. Then when I return home I immediately transfer the notes to my Research To Do form and I throw away the note. Be careful not to accumulate little pieces of paper and notes. They will drive you crazy! Throw them away as soon as you can.

When the page gets full, continue the list on another Research To Do form and number it page 2. Then continue listing items until that form is full. At first you should merely add items to the list. Once the list becomes longer, it should be prioritized. Number each item according to its importance or according to a logical sequence. This helps you to work more efficiently. Some things should be done before others. For example, you can't interview your two

Research To Do #1—Genealogy form listing all research tasks; this will serve as a To Do List, a reminder, and a checklist.

great-aunts you've never met without making some minimal preparations. You first need to learn something about them, as well as get their addresses and telephone numbers. This will probably entail asking other relatives first. So after you make your list, prioritize each item. When an item is completed, place a checkmark next to it. After you get going, you'll probably start Research To Do forms for individual ancestors.

Things To Do

Sometimes when my list gets long, I separate genealogy research tasks from nonresearch tasks. I create a Things To Do list. My Research To Do list will include genealogical and historical sources to check, records to send for, interviews to conduct, and other research tasks. My Things To Do list will include organizational tasks such as updating charts, filing documents, typing reports, updating the computer, and buying supplies. I do the Things To Do tasks first because they keep the system in order. Then when I am ready to research or analyze my research, everything is updated and organized, and I can retrieve data when I need it. When my Research To Do form is completed and prioritized, I know what to research and what to take on my next research trip. Many experienced genealogists need to work on just their Things To Do list. They have conducted hours, months, and sometimes years of research but

Things To Do

1	Buy envelopes and stationery
2	Buy stamps
3	Buy a tape recorder with an external jack
4	Buy extra "AA" batteries
5	Order acid-free paper
6	Order acid-free file folders
7	
8	
9	
10	
11	
12	
13	
14	
15	
16	
17	
18	

Things To Do #1—Genealogy form listing organizing, office, and other non-research tasks that make research easier.

have not taken the time to update their charts and files and organize their data. If they use a Things To Do form, prioritize it, and follow it, their research will be much more productive.

Before you talk to those two great-aunts, you'll need to get some of the tools I mentioned in the chapter "Organizing Before It Gets Messy," such as stationery, envelopes, stamps, and perhaps a tape recorder. So we'll use these to start off your Things To Do List.

Research Calendar

I mentioned you will be going to many different places and checking many different records. The only way to answer the questions "Haven't I been here before?" or "Haven't I checked these records before?" or "What records did I check while in South Carolina last year?" or "I checked the index for Brooks and Boles—did I also check for Burroughs?" or "Now where are those documents I photocopied on Grandpa Brooks?" is to make an index of your research.

This index is called a Research Calendar. It records when you researched, where you researched, and what records you researched. The Research Calendar should include the date the research was conducted, the name and location of the research center, and the surnames researched. You may even want to record the first and last names of individuals and sometimes spelling variations of the surname.

When you search a book, record its title, author, and publication date. You may want to also include the publisher and city of publication. This way, if you use it at a later date or include it in a bibliography, or you decide to purchase the book, you will have all the necessary information in your Research Calendar. If you come across the book again and it is a different edition with perhaps more information or a different index, you'll know which edition you've already researched.

Next, record the book's call number or microfilm reel number. Then if you need to retrieve the book or microfilm again, you have it handy. You don't have to waste time going to the card catalogue a second time. Also, if you are in another city and you want someone else to retrieve the book, the call number will be invaluable, pinpointing the exact book and again saving time and hassle. The Research Calendar should also note if you find any information. Record a number for any documents abstracted, extracted, obtained, or photocopied.

Notes should also be made of any negative research. Negative research is when you search a source and do not find the name you're looking for. There may be valid reasons why you did not locate the name in the record. You may be looking for the wrong surname or the wrong first name, or you may be looking for a woman's married name instead of her maiden name. You may be looking for the children when you should be looking for their parents. You may be looking in the wrong time period or even in the wrong county or state. After a while you tend to forget the sources you searched and did not find anything. After the initial stages of research, there can be more negative research than positive research. It is good to track negative research so that you don't accidentally research records you've already searched and so that you can analyze why you didn't find your ancestors. With the time and expense it takes to do genealogy and to make out-of-town research trips, you don't want any duplication of effort.

Research Calendar

File Number			
Surnames Burroughs		Researcher Tony Burroughs	

Date	Repository Call No.	Description of Sources	Doc. No.
11/30/95	Chicago Public Library		
	929.1.028	"Genealogy" by Kenneth Stryker-Rodda - Boy Scouts of America Merit Badge Series No. 3383, 1973.	

Research Calendar #1—Genealogy form that tracks all research, as it is done, indicating the person researching, surnames researched, date and place of research, and all items researched including title, author, date of publication, and call number.

In some situations you may purposely want to recheck records. Perhaps when you searched a record the first time, you did not have the knowledge you now have from more current research. Or perhaps you committed one of the errors previously mentioned. As you continue to research, your base of knowledge will grow. Therefore, when you look at a record a second time, you may know ten times more than you knew the first time you searched it.

! Trap: Not creating a Research Calendar logging places you've been and sources you've checked and keeping it up to date.

If you use a computer, this index can be put into a database. Then it can be sorted by surname, research center, date, or any other useful way. A few genealogy computer programs come with built-in utilities that track research. You can also use most business database programs.

Correspondence Index

If you were wealthy, you could hop a plane and fly across the country to research every day, or you could make unlimited long-distance telephone calls. For that matter, if you were wealthy, you wouldn't need this book. You could just hire someone to do the research for you. However, if your means are more limited, you'll probably be writing a lot of letters to conduct research. It can often take several weeks to receive a reply from a genealogy request. This is due to the fact that most archives, historical societies, and genealogical libraries have small staffs and small budgets. And many of the staff in these institutions may be volunteers. When waiting several weeks for a reply to a genealogy request, you may forget whom you mailed a letter to, the date you mailed it, if you received a reply, and what the reply contained. For this reason a Correspondence Index can be very helpful in keeping track of your mailings.

A Correspondence Index is similar to a Research Calendar but is used for tracking correspondence. You'll want to record the date letters are sent and received, whom correspondence is mailed to, and if any fees are included with your letter. Also record any miscellaneous notes. Feel free to use several lines for one mailing if necessary. Be sure to include a self-addressed, stamped envelope (SASE) with your request.

Correspondence Index—Genealogy form tracking letters sent and received.

I've talked with many researchers who said they wrote a particular person or institution and never received a reply. I ask them how long it has been, and they may reply that it's been over a year. Don't let a year or two pass without receiving a reply to a request. Many people are very busy, and things happen to the mail. In the case of large governmental agencies, it helps to inquire when to expect a reply. Sometimes it's not uncommon to wait thirty to ninety days for a reply. I've waited two to four months for some government records.

If a reply is not received in thirty days, send a second request. You can copy the original letter and write or type SECOND REQUEST across the top. That usually gets the recipient's attention and adds a little bit of guilt. Or you can write a second letter and reference the first letter. Wait another thirty days and then make a phone call. There is a reason not to receive a reply in sixty days. I've been corresponding with one institution for years, trying to obtain a record they told me they have. I finally got one of the staff to admit the records were in four uncatalogued warehouses. There was no indication which of the four warehouses my ancestor's records were located in.

Some researchers keep one Correspondence Index for all their ancestors. I recommend keeping a Correspondence Index in the main genealogy file folder. Use one form for each different surname or individual. Then you can track your correspondence faster and more directly for an individual ancestor. Keep the Correspondence Index in the front of the file folder for that surname or individual and fill it out promptly when mail is sent and received.

File Folder Contents

You will gradually accumulate documents in folders for your ancestors. A handy index of the items in each folder will keep track of them, assist your organization of materials, and speed your research. This is called the Genealogy File Folder Contents form, and you keep one for each folder. It lists standard genealogy items and almost serves as a checklist of genealogical records. Among the items it might list are the forms we've just described, genealogy charts, which we'll cover in the next chapter, and the documents you collect while researching.

If a folder is used for a single ancestor, write his or her name on the line at the top of the Genealogy File Folder Contents form. If a folder is used for several ancestors with the same surname, write that surname on the line at the top of the form.

All your documents for an ancestor might not be in one folder. For example, you might have documents in another file folder, in another file cabinet, in a photograph album, in your safe deposit box, or in an oversize archival box. There is space on the form to add miscellaneous items that pertain to the ancestor but are not in the file folder. Then if you take a document out for any reason, for instance, for an exhibit or a loan, you can note what and why you're taking something out and explain the circumstances in the comments column on the right. That way you'll know where your documents are and why they might not be where they're supposed to be.

After a while you'll start to develop folders on a single topic for an ancestor. You might have a file that contains only a military pension application or a military service record. In this case the folder will be too thick for other documents. In some situations you may want to isolate a unique record. If the record is isolated, it can more easily be retrieved and the pages won't be mixed with other documents.

If the file folder contains only a single record, there is no need for a Genealogy File Folder Contents form. The descriptive label across the top of the folder will be sufficient. It should read "Ancestor's Name—Name of Document"; for example, "Preston S. Brooks—Military Pension Application File."

For your subject files, which include information on counties, states, genealogy methodology, and other topics, genealogist Pat Hatcher recommends adding a list of books and audiocassette tapes on the subject that are in your collection but not in the file.

We'll see how these charts are filled out as we go along.

	Genealogy File Folder Contents		
	Ancestor name: _Burroughs_		
		IN FOLDER Y/N	**COMMENTS**
1	Document Log		
2	Things to Do List	✓	
3	Research To Do List	✓	
4	Research Calendar	✓	
5	Correspondence Index	✓	
6	Correspondence		
7	Alphabetical list of variant surname spellings		
8	Master alphabetical list of all family surnames		
9	Soundex code		
10	Charts – Pedigree		
11	– Family Group Sheet		
12	– Descendant Chart		
13	– Soundex Charts		
14	– Census Charts		
15	– Chronology		
16	– Biography		
17	Oral history interviews		
18	Research notes, extracts, and abstracts		
19	Documents		
20	Vital statistics certificates – Birth		
21	– Death		
22	– Marriage		
23	Discrepancy charts		
24	Photographs		
25			
26			
27			
28			
29			
30			
31			
32			
33			
34			
35			

Make note in comments column of all items in separate file folders or other locations.

Genealogy File Folder Contents—Genealogy form tracking documents in each file folder.

Part II
Beginning Steps

Oral History—The Most Important Thing You Can Do

Oral history is one of the oldest customs in the African community. In West African tradition a member of the community has the responsibility to preserve, remember, and recite family and historical events in the community. These oral historians are known as griots, or *jali* in the Mandinka language. Whereas we refer to them as oral historians, Mandinka refer to them as artisans of the spoken word. *Jali* often combine their recitations with music.

Griots

Many people have heard of the old griot who kept the history of the village in his head. When anyone wanted to learn of what happened way back when, they would go to the griot and he could recite the history of the village. The griot was a living history book.

Historically, griots were employed by ruling families to recite family and community history, narrate the history of battles, and praise and entertain the rulers. Today they can be hired by others to conduct naming ceremonies, announce marriage ceremonies, and memorize family histories.

No matter how long a person's mind is trained to remember, there are limitations to how far back they can remember. The further in time a griot goes back, the less detail is recalled and the more general the information becomes. After interviewing ninety- six griots, family elders, and similar knowledgeable persons in West Africa, historian Donald R. Wright determined they could recall specific detail on individuals for about 125 years, and most of that was about famous nobility, not common everyday individuals. If one were to consult a griot today, it would be unreasonable for him to recall specific details on individuals other than famous rulers before 1875. That's well past slavery, which ended in 1865.

Oral History in Ethiopia

I was having dinner one night with Bete, a friend from Ethiopia. The discussion turned to genealogy. He got very excited and told me his uncle could remember back twelve fathers. I was amazed anyone could remember that far. Bete said his uncle used to repeat the names to his brothers and sister when they were small kids. He was upset because the uncle had died and no one had recorded the information.

Months later I talked with his sister, Yemi. I told her of my conversation with Bete and she said, "No, we do have the names. And it's not twelve generations—it's fourteen generations!" I was quite stunned. She said a cousin in Baltimore had the names. We called him on a conference call but were unsuccessful. He'd just moved and couldn't find the names.

The next time I heard from Yemi was a 5:50 A.M. wake-up call several months later. She had just returned from Ethiopia and had gotten the fourteen generations of her family line. I was very excited, and so was she.

She had gone to see an old man in Yetebon, a small village about seventy-five miles south of Addis Ababa, where her family had lived for generations. The old man's name was Aberra (she later learned he was her cousin). Yemi said he appeared to be in his nineties. She tried to date his age by relating him to her father and grandfather. She then sat down while he discussed the family lineage. After she told him who her parents were, he told Yemi the name of her grandfather, then her great-grandfather, and all the way back, fifteen generations, including hers. She recalled some of the names from talking with her cousin in Baltimore several months earlier. Yemi said she was thrilled and got the entire experience on videotape. Unfortunately, there are no dates associated with the names.

Yemi learned that Aberra's grandfather and her great-grandfather were brothers. He complained that no one is carrying on his tradition. He said people used to compete to do his job. I asked Yemi why he didn't teach someone else how to do it. She said people started migrating out of the town. Now people are only interested in their own lines, not anyone else's.

Yemi got the story of her family lineage but wishes she had taped everything the old man said. I recommended she write down what he said that she did not record, as well as the stories she told me about the experience.

As she traveled through Ethiopia, Yemi told the story to other people. The first thing everyone asked was "Who verified it?" I said wow! These people are great genealogists. They don't just take someone's word—they ask for proof. Yemi said they don't believe it until someone else, independent of them, can verify the line. That gave her a lot of confidence that the line was correct.

She then described going to Butajira, about twelve miles from Yetebon, where her parents were building a road. There was a dispute about the road and a man came by to discuss it. Someone pointed him out to Yemi and said, "He is your cousin." They then told her he knew the generations of her family. Without her telling him what she had, he recited the names going back fifteen generations, and they were the same names the old man recited, with only a slight variation of one person's name.

I told Yemi it must have been very exciting. She said it was the highlight of her trip. I told her now that she's got the story she needs to put it somewhere. She said it was funny because she and her mother had discussed the same thing. Yemi's going to make several copies for her brothers and cousins and teach the names to her son, Cole. I suggested she get the videotape transcribed and send a copy to a library or archive. She hadn't thought of that but agreed it was a good idea.

YEMI'S FAMILY TREE
(ALL MALES OTHER THAN YEMI AND HER MOTHER)

Cole Thomas Demeke Brown	(Yemi's son, born in Fort Wayne, Ind., Sept. 1995)
Yemisrach Demeke	(Yemi, who married Payne Brown)
Marta Gabre Tsadick	(married Demeke Tekle-Wold)
Gabre Tsadick Aliye	
Aliye Remsiso	
Remsiso Garro	
Garro Yazma Mendel	
Yazma Mendel Badgegrad	
Badgegrad Yarbo	
Yarbo Tayo	
Tayo Ahbo	
Ahbo Wudimo	
Wudimo Dukema	
Dukema Kenema	
Kenema Hajl Ibrahim	
Hajl Ibrahim Yahmedel Bedwi	

This patronymic naming pattern, in which the child's first name is the father's last name, helped the old man to recall fifteen generations of Yemi's lineage. However, there are no dates or events associated with the names, nor do they include brothers, sisters, aunts, uncles, or cousins.

A Lost Art

This oral tradition, which was handed down from generation to generation, preserved the names of our ancestors. But lately we've gotten away from that tradition. When the elders in our community today talk of the old days and relay stories of our ancestors, younger people don't want to listen. Now that genealogy has become popular, we are trying to recover this lost art. If young people want to learn their family history, they must begin seeking information from older relatives. By reading this book and following its principles, you are in training to become one of our modern griots. So treat your job seriously because your family and our community will depend on you.

Gathering oral history and traditions from family members is the most important first step in the genealogical process. *Before you become a genealogist, you must become a family historian.* Remember, a genealogist traces the lineage backward, whereas a family historian tries to know everything about a family unit. Without knowing the family history, you cannot trace its lineage backward.

Oral history is also the most important step in genealogy you will ever do. It is vitally important because you have limited time to get the information. Relatives grow older every day. As they age, health usually diminishes and memories tend to fade. Time is of the essence. The information stored in these human resources is not found in any library or archive. If we don't retrieve the information now and record it, family stories will be lost for eternity. Alex Haley once said, "When an old person dies, it's like a library burning."

Start with Yourself

Genealogy starts with ourselves and proceeds backward, one generation at a time, advancing from the known to the unknown. Begin by writing your autobiography, the story of your life. If we are researching the family history, *we* are a part of that family and that history. We are the first link. From here our family history extends back into time.

It doesn't make sense to do a lot of research about dead relatives and not leave your children and descendants anything about your life. This is especially true if you're a senior citizen because you don't have much time. You've lived a full life and faced difficult challenges. Many of you have made numerous sacrifices, overcome many hurdles, and accomplished worthy deeds. Many of these things you've probably taken for granted. The younger generation of today can benefit from your struggles and triumphs only if you leave the legacy for them to read.

Life is so precious, yet we take it for granted. When we are young, our life seems eternal. We often feel like we will live forever. That is, until we get older and attend a number of funerals of family and friends. Then we suddenly realize how precious and temporary our lives are. Then we see how important an autobiography becomes, not only to us but to our children and other descendants.

If you record your own story, you have a tremendous advantage over someone else researching or writing about you. You have the one opportunity to tell not only *what* you did during your lifetime but *how* and *why* you did what you did. If someone else writes a biography about you, he or she must first determine what you did during your lifetime. Major, important details and events might be overlooked. Then your biographer must determine *why* and *how* you did the things in your life. How many times have we misinterpreted someone else's life? So if you don't want that to happen to your life story, write it yourself.

Another reason to start your family history with yourself is that your brothers, sisters, and parents all have selective memories. They will remember the same events differently. You know how some people see the glass as half empty and some see it as half full. Everyone has their own opinion, their own perspective, and selective memories of the same events. They will also remember events that you either don't remember or that occurred when you were not around. Unless you are a twin, you probably did not go every place your brothers and sisters went. Your parents may have taken you some places your brothers and sisters didn't go because of differences in age, because one sibling was sick, because one went with Dad and one went with Mom, and so forth. You need to record your recollections of family events before you record how other family members remember them so your recollections aren't tainted by theirs. You'll want to differentiate what you remember from what they remember.

Starting an autobiography stimulates the brain to think about what happened when you were a child and your interaction with friends and relatives. Your brain is a miraculous machine. It stores everything you've ever done and can recall it. You just have to ask it, on a continual basis. You will amaze yourself when you start asking it for information and then record it.

A good way to start is by creating an outline of your life, listing major time periods from childhood to adulthood. Start off with things like early childhood, high school, college, adulthood, marriage. Then slowly add details to the outline by including significant factors in your life, like church, jobs, girlfriends, boyfriends, military service, moving, and retirement. The factors will vary according to your experiences. Then you can start at any point you want—with your earliest memories, or some part of your life you remember most, or something that gave you great pleasure.

After you've decided where to start, just start writing. Don't try to be perfect or fancy. This is just the first draft. You'll rewrite it later and it will read a lot better.

I suggest you keep the outline and draft notes in a file folder. Then as ideas come to you, jot them down and file them in the folder. If the folder becomes thick, you can subdivide it by the outline categories you've already created. Those of you who use a computer can create a folder for your autobiography in your word processing program. Just make regular printouts and save backups in case of computer failure.

From time to time you can spark additional memories by going through your scrapbook, photo album, and old telephone books. It's like playing games with your brain, trying to see how much information you can get out of it. Once you get going, you'll see how much fun it is and how much of your past you can re-create.

Be sure to record family activities, holidays, vacations, and trips. Make special notes of where you lived, whom you played with, and what relatives were around. Record the names of your brothers, sisters, mother, father, grandparents, aunts, uncles, cousins, and friends. List the schools you attended, the jobs you held and companies you worked for, and the churches you attended and how you participated. Record the accomplishments that made you proud, no matter how large or small.

Record how world events affected you and your community—wars like Vietnam, Korea, World War II, and the Gulf War; and sports events like the Super Bowl and the World Series. Record how you were affected by famous people like presidents, mayors, civil rights leaders, movie stars, musicians, and singers.

Do not record only the activities in which you participated; record your hopes and dreams, your successes and failures. They will be instructional and inspirational for your relatives. How many times have we heard, "If she could do it, so can I."

Don't let this autobiography intimidate you. It will not be completed in one sitting. It will take time to develop. Work on it as much as you can. Set it aside and then come back to it. Your fresh thoughts and improved memory will improve it. I write sections at a time. When I'm on the highway driving out of town, sometimes I'll take my tape recorder and record sections of my life. Other times when thoughts come to my mind, I'll go right to the computer and record my recollections of different things that happened to me.

When you finish, add a title page, table of contents, and if you're savvy, photographs, illustrations, and an index. Let people read it to make suggestions on organization, readability, and grammar. When you are satisfied it is the best you can do, make a final copy and duplicate it for family and libraries. There are books that can help you in this process (see "Writing Autobiographies" in the Bibliography). If you've had a remarkable career, you may even look for a publisher.

Keep a Diary or Journal

I also recommend starting a daily diary or journal. A diary is usually a daily entry of activities, whereas a journal is usually reflections on a unified event. I wish I'd kept a journal every time I did genealogy research and logged my theories and findings.

A journal has advantages over an autobiography because your thoughts, feelings, and activities are recorded on a daily basis. Then you're not as subject to memory lapses (although I sometimes have a little trouble remembering what I did yesterday).

When you record your daily activities, include your thoughts and reasons for making decisions. We encounter many daily dilemmas, and understanding why we make certain choices gives us insight about ourselves. We all have twenty-four hours in a day. It's how we make decisions about what to do with that time that differentiates us from everyone else and determines who we are.

Why is it so many notable historical people kept diaries and journals? I think it says something about the sense of pride, self-worth, and self-confidence of those individuals. I would almost die to find a diary or journal one of my ancestors wrote. Without such help, I have to re-create their lives, envision their daily activities, and hypothesize about how and why they made life's decisions. Without a historical perspective, those visions may be very far from reality. I wouldn't wish that burden on my descendants, and therefore I keep a journal every day.

When I started to write my autobiography, I thought about significant periods of struggle in my life. As I reflected back on specific events that transpired twenty years ago, many were just a blur. I had only the vaguest of memories, without specific details. It was a very strange feeling, almost scary.

I envisioned I would be successful one day, but I didn't want to forget where I came from. I wanted to remember the sacrifices, the bad times, the hardships and struggle it took to get there. All too often we laud our heroes but have no sense of what it took to get to the mountaintop. It's especially important for the children who look at entire lives in thirty-minute movies. If they are to get any sense of reality and learn to struggle every day to accomplish their goals, reading the diary or journal of a parent or ancestor can certainly help.

I began my journal on June 15, 1992, and wish I had started earlier. I'd give anything to have entries from my high school or college days to read. I struggled with daily entries at first. After six months I had made only eight entries. The second year I made nineteen entries. Then in the third year I made eight entries in October, sixteen in November, and thirty in December. I was getting the hang of it, and somehow I developed the discipline to keep it up each and every day. I then went more than three years without missing a day.

At first it was difficult. At times I couldn't even remember what happened the day before. I couldn't believe it. I thought to myself, "I'm keeping a journal so I can't forget my past, and I can't even remember what happened yesterday! This is not going to work." I then realized there is a difference between short-term memory and long-term memory. So I started keeping brief notes during the day on my activities. It became much better to refresh my short-term memory, and my journal entries became longer and longer. But months later when I read them they contained incredible detail, which shocked me.

During one stretch I was out of town a lot and became very busy. I fell seventeen days behind and feared I would never catch up. It was so important to me I went on a mission to catch up and made it a top priority. It took me from September 18 to November 4, 1997, to catch up. It was a big relief when I did.

I've found this journal has additional benefits I hadn't planned on. I gave a lecture in Salt Lake City one day, and part of my talk was based on genealogical discoveries I had recorded in my journal. On other occasions I've used my journal to pinpoint when key events occurred when I needed the exact date. It has proved invaluable.

Leave a Legacy

In addition to keeping a daily diary or journal and writing an autobiography, there are several things you can do to preserve your life for your descendants. The first is to publish that autobiography once you've written it. This can be as simple as typing it and getting the local photocopy store to make copies and put a binder on them. You can spend as much or as little as you want. Then send it to family members and libraries. That way it will be around to benefit descendants.

You know how much it would mean to you to hear a tape of your great-grandparents. It will mean the same for your great-grandchildren to hear a tape of you. Take a tape recorder and from time to time record your thoughts and activities.

Similarly, set your video recorder on remote and record your thoughts and activities. I tried doing a daily video diary but failed after the first day. But I've heard it works for others.

Keep a scrapbook of brochures, programs, and tickets to events you attend, along with other mementos. It's like giving souvenirs to yourself. Do you save your cards and correspondence? This is a record of family, friends, and business dealings. It paints another picture of you from others' point of view.

You also might want to save items in your wallet when they expire rather than throw them out. I found one of my old wallets from college days and the jobs I had right after college. I was fascinated by the old identification cards and how I looked with different hairstyles and out-of-date clothes. The expired credit cards brought back memories of clothes I'd purchased and cars I'd owned. Now I make a habit of saving cards when they expire and have an enormous collection. I go through it from time to time, and the items bring back good memories.

Then go through your photo album and label your photographs. You know who the people are, but will your children and grandchildren know when you are gone and you become an ancestor?

When you save these things, be sure to use the acid-free file folders and other preservation supplies discussed earlier.

Living Relatives

Before you start interviewing relatives, pull out a sheet of paper and make a list of *all* your living relatives. Start with your parents if they are alive. Then list the oldest living member of the family. List any of your great-grandparents if they are alive and any of their brothers and sisters if they are alive. Then list your grandparents and any of their brothers and sisters if they are still living. Next list your aunts and uncles who are living.

I've heard people say, "All my parents and grandparents are deceased. I have no one to interview." If your parents, grandparents, and great-grandparents are deceased, list their friends, neighbors, classmates, co-workers, business associates, and church members. Close your eyes and think about it for a while. Somebody who knew them could still be alive. Our best friends and associates often know more about us than our relatives.

We should seek out these associates even if they did not know our ancestors. Professional genealogist Sharon DeBartolo Carmark, author of *Italian-American Family History*, says, "Friends and neighbors share similar experiences. We should interview them to get stories of the neighborhood and find out what it was like growing up during that time period."

! Trap: Not seeking out relatives we haven't met before or those we haven't seen in a long time.

Don't neglect in-laws (people who married into the family) and divorced relatives. They often lived with relatives and can know as much about the family as blood relatives. I knew about my aunt Irene's first of three husbands but had never met him. That part of the family moved to California when I was very young. His son Claude is my first cousin. I had not talked to Claude in twenty-five years. When we got back in touch with each other, he told me his father and mother had lived with a cousin of our grandfather in Tuskegee, Alabama, during World War II.

I quickly realized he was referring to Cousin Pearl. I discovered Cousin Pearl's name when researching and traveled to Tuskegee to meet her. Unfortunately, she died before I got that chance. I then researched Cousin Pearl's life for several years. I struggled to find out how she was related to our family. It never dawned on me that Claude's father (who was a divorced in-law) had known Cousin Pearl and actually lived in her house while training as a Tuskegee airman.

So be sure to include on your list of people to interview not only relatives who are close (and you know well) but also distant relatives (whom you may not know too well or haven't seen in a long time). You never know who has the missing piece to the puzzle you're trying to put together.

Finally, list the names of your living brothers, sisters, and cousins. Yes, you need to interview your brothers and sisters. We all lead different lives, go through different experiences, and have different memories. I recall sitting around with my brothers and cousins once, reminiscing about when we were young, and they talked about things I didn't remember. It was funny. It was like I hadn't even been around, but I had. I also recall my brother Asa saying once, "Well, you know Mom didn't cook. Dad did all the cooking." I was stunned. When I thought about it, I knew he was right. But it was something I'd never thought about. When you're young, you don't consciously analyze your family. (Often you don't analyze anything. You just enjoy life.) Well, my father's mother loved to cook. Grandma Burroughs didn't work, and it seemed as if all she did was cook. My dad must have picked it up from her. I recall my mother getting upset the first time she ate at my grandmother's house. At the table were Grandma and Granddad, my dad and her, and Dad's two brothers and sister. Grandma took orders like she was a chef in a restaurant and cooked whatever anyone wanted. My mom said whenever she was the cook, she cooked one thing and everyone had to eat it.

When a person dies and can no longer be interviewed, their children become much more important. The children sometimes know things about their parents that no one else knows. In addition to interviewing your brothers and sisters, don't hesitate to interview the children of your older deceased relatives.

This list of living relatives you've written is now prioritized so you can begin with the most important persons and then proceed to everyone else by age. Try to interview the oldest relatives as soon as possible. Make it an objective to interview each and every one on this list. It doesn't matter how much they know about the family history; it only matters that they know something. If they don't know a lot about their older relatives, they should still recall a lot about their own lives.

! Trap: Asking only for the names of parents and grandparents.

Genealogists fall into the trap of asking only for the names of parents and grandparents. Then when relatives don't know about distant relatives, they are dismissed as not knowing anything. I often hear genealogists say, "They don't know anything about our family history. I know more than they do," or "They don't remember anything." Don't focus on what a person doesn't know. You and your relative will only become frustrated, and your interview session will be unproductive. Older memories will sometimes improve as people start to think about time in the past. Genealogists neglect to get the things relatives *do* remember, the story of *their* lives. You want your relatives to talk about themselves and their experiences. As their stories unfold, they will mention relatives, friends, events, and places. They will indirectly tell you about their older relatives. You have to analyze what they say, draw inferences from what they tell you, and assemble the pieces, envisioning the larger story. So focus on what your relatives do remember, and your interview will be a lot more productive.

On Which Side to Start—Mom's or Dad's?

A frequent question arises as to which side of the family you should start tracing first. The answer to this question lies in front of you on your list. You should trace the side with the older living relatives on it. You want to get to these relatives while they are alive. Then when you begin researching in libraries and archives, you should share your results with these relatives. This can often refresh their memories and add more stories to the family history.

At the time I started tracing my family history, November 1975, all of my great-grandparents were deceased and three of four grandparents were deceased. My paternal grandmother was eighty years old and had a decent memory. Within a year and a half, I'd lose my father, an aunt, and an uncle.

Like most people, I was interested in my surname and therefore began researching on my father's side of the family. However, not only was my grandfather deceased, but my father's only aunt and uncle were also deceased. There were few relatives living on his side of the family. I did not let this deter me and interviewed my father and grandmother a few times.

When I went to interview my mother and her sister, I realized Mom's aunt and uncle were still living. Aunt Roxie was eighty-two years old, and Uncle Dan was eighty-six. Also still living was Aunt Hannah, my *great*-grandmother's sister, who was ninety-four years old. Neither Roxie nor Hannah were my aunts, nor was Dan my uncle. However, as in many African American families, all older relatives were referred to by the titles of "aunt" and "uncle" as terms of respect. When your relatives refer to another relative as aunt or uncle, try to determine whose aunt and uncle they really are and how they are related to you.

Since these were the oldest living relatives on either side of my family, I stopped researching on my dad's side of the family and quickly switched to my mom's side. I decided to concentrate my efforts on these older relatives who were still living. Once they passed, all of their stories and memories would go with them.

Descendants of Preston S. Brooks and Anna Griffin

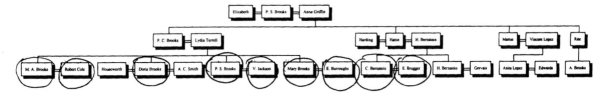

Descendant Chart—A three-generation genealogy chart illustrating an early ancestor and his children and grandchildren. Circled are living descendants who should be interviewed.

After I made significant progress, I eventually returned to researching my father's side of the family. Sometimes researchers are not able to make this decision when they first begin. When you talk to a few relatives, they may tell you of older relatives still living whom you may not know. Once you learn of older relatives, don't hesitate to change direction, seek them out, and interview them. If they are very elderly, you may not have much time.

TIP—It's good to draw a genealogy chart from the oldest known member of the family down to the youngest. This is called a Descendant Chart because it illustrates all the descendants of the oldest known ancestor for that line of the family. This Descendant Chart includes in-laws because it shows marriages. Then circle everyone on the chart who is living and interview each one. These in-laws and children of deceased ancestors could all have information on the family, as well as family papers and photos. A photograph album of nineteenth-century and early twentieth-century tintypes was handed down to me from my aunt. It had been passed down to her from her mother, who got it from the in-law who raised my grandmother.

Homework Before the Interview

Before you interview a relative, there's some homework you need to do. When you interview someone you've never met before, not only is he or she a stranger to you, but you are a stranger as well. You may be excited by your new interest in genealogy and be all pumped up to meet your relative, but she may not feel the same way. As far as she's concerned, she doesn't know you and may be "ticked off" that you took so long to find out she existed and waited until the end of her life to learn who she is and "what she did." Some senior citizens have been taken advantage of and won't know if "you are just another one to take advantage of them" until you prove your sincerity to them. So anything you can do to put them at ease will help your task.

If this is a relative you've never met before, find out something about him before you knock on his door. What is his physical condition and what are his likes, dislikes, turn-ons and turn-offs? Does he have a good memory? Is he hard of hearing? Does he live alone? Is he confined to a wheelchair? These types of health questions give a feel for the person.

If you can, find out if the person is sensitive to anything you should be aware of, because you do not want to unknowingly offend her. Everyone has skeletons in the closet (things we are embarrassed about and don't want others to know). If you can safely talk around these areas or discuss them tactfully, you can get through your interview successfully on a positive note. Sometimes if you hit the wrong button, a person will clam up and you'll never get any more information out of her. If you sense this happening, quickly divert to another topic and perhaps return to this topic at the end of the interview.

You also want to find out what the relative is fond of so you might be able to develop some common bonds. A good technique that Dorothy Spruill Redford, author of *Somerset Homecoming*, uses is to find out what kind of food the person likes. Then when you arrive at the house for an interview, carrying the favorite food, you develop an instant rapport. My Grandmother Burroughs had a bad case of rheumatoid arthritis. Her fingers would swell and ache, and she'd be very uncomfortable. As she aged, it got worse, and she was eventually confined to a wheelchair. So she rarely got out of the house. She loved root beer, and whenever I went by, I almost always had a can of root beer with me. When she saw that can of root beer, her face would light up in a great big smile. No matter how depressed she may have been before I came by, when her lips touched that cold root beer, her worries were totally forgotten. She was straight for the rest of the day. Sometimes I thought she appreciated that root beer more than seeing me!

It's usually best to call ahead and make an appointment before you show up on a relative's doorstep. You want to be sure he's not out of town, at the doctor's office, or watching his favorite afternoon program. When you do phone, have your pen, paper, and tape recorder ready. You're not calling to conduct the interview, only to set the appointment. But many a time I have called to ask when I could come by and a relative has given a half hour's worth of information before I could get off the telephone. So be prepared.

Before you go to the interview, make sure you have extra supplies of pens, pencils, and acid-free paper. You'll be taking plenty of notes. You should also have an extension cord, extra film, batteries, and tapes. If you have more supplies than you need, you won't run out.

The other important item to take to the interview is your Research Calendar. This will be our first research activity, other than reading to prepare to research, and it will be the first item on your calendar. Remember, you are to record every time you conduct research.

	Research Calendar		

File Number   *1*   **Researcher** *Tony Burroughs*

Surnames *Burroughs*

Date	Repository Call No.	Description of Sources	Doc. No.
11/30/75	*Chicago Public Library*		
	929.1.028	*"Genealogy" by Kenneth Stryker-Rodda - Boy Scouts of America Merit Badge Series No. 3383, 1973.*	
12/4/75	*Home of Alma Burroughs - 505 E. 60th St, Chicago, Ill.*		
		Interview Grandma Burroughs	*1*

Research Calendar #2—Research Calendar that includes second day of research, which resulted in producing a document.

Note Taking

Have your pen and acid-free paper handy so you can take notes during the interview. I recommend taking notes on acid-free paper so they will be around for a long time. I still refer to original notes I took twenty-three years ago. Those that I made on yellow legal pads browned and deteriorated years ago. I have since photocopied them on acid-free paper.

I record the date of the interview and the name, address, and telephone number of the person interviewed. Then when I'm ready to write a thank-you letter or call for a follow-up interview, the phone and address are handy. I also indicate the relationship of the person to me or to another of my relatives (e.g., my father's uncle). Then it's not just a name. I immediately know how the person is related in the family.

Next, record your name. At different times during your research, you may have other family members, friends, or professionals conduct interviews for you. It is important to know who conducted each particular interview. The person may tell you one thing and tell someone else a different story. For example, sometimes older people won't tell the same stories to younger people that they'll tell their peers. They figure you're too young to know certain things. And when a person gets up in age, young is a relative concept. A person who is eighty years old may consider a person who's fifty young. So after you interview a person, you may also want your mother or aunt to also interview them. She may get completely different information than you did. If you find that you came out of an interview without any information, it may be because you weren't the right age or gender.

Elizabeth Clark-Lewis, Howard University professor and author of *Living In, Living Out: African American Domestics in Washington, D.C., 1910–1940,* has a technique she finds successful. If a female interviews a female and a male interviews a male, sometimes you will get more information. For example, an old man will tell some stories to what he considers a young boy about "learning the ropes" and what he did as a growing young man. He might not tell these same stories to someone he looks upon as a young lady. Similarly, an older woman may confide thoughts and experiences about men to a woman that she'd never tell to a man. So you might think about conducting multiple interviews, one by yourself and one by your brother or sister or mother or aunt.

During the interview you'll want to write down the exact spelling of unusual names and places. Many times the sound of a name is completely different from the spelling. Also write down notes for follow-up questions. When a person is talking, you don't want to interrupt her, especially if she's telling an interesting story. You may forget a follow-up question unless you immediately jot it down.

Questioning

First ask if anyone else has traced the family history. You want to benefit from the work of other family members, and you don't want to duplicate any research that has already been done. If someone has researched the family, you want to get copies of any information that was compiled. Then you should evaluate and verify the research. If the researcher made errors and mistakes, you don't want to duplicate them. You verify someone else's research by first checking to see if he or she recorded the sources of information written in the family history. Then check those sources to see if the data in the family history was recorded fully and accurately. I'll explain verifying oral history later in this chapter. If the relative is an experienced genealogist, there may be reams of information. In this case the relative may not be willing to make copies of years of research for you. You will have to develop another level of trust and credibility to share significant amounts of information. I've found fellow genealogists very willing to share information, but if they have several file cabinets of data, it can be difficult to share everything. You'll want to have good discussions with your relative and not duplicate research. You may decide to research different lines and share each other's results.

Also find out if there are any family reunions that you are unaware of. Reunions can be a good opportunity to talk to several distant family members at one time. Relatives are also in a good mood for talking about the family history. If you've already talked to family members through family reunions, be sure you've asked all the questions listed here. If you do a thorough job, you will interview a relative two, three, four times or more. Elizabeth Clark-Lewis interviewed one aunt twelve times! I thought that was pretty amazing until I talked with my aunt about twenty times.

You will probably know something about your family history and about the person you are interviewing. You have to be careful this knowledge does not tip off your relative to answers for your questions. Leading questions usually influence answers. For example, if you know a fact, don't ask the relative to verify the fact. Ask an open-ended question to see if the relative knows the fact. For instance, if you know Davie moved from Uniontown to Brownsville, don't ask when Davie moved from Uniontown to Brownsville. Ask, "Do you know where Davie lived?" Then ask, "When did he move?" Next ask, "Where did he move when he left?"

Another technique is to ask several different relatives the same questions about an event or ancestor. This way you'll get several different perspectives on the same event.

I sometimes ask relatives to recall their earliest memory, their childhood, and the people in their lives. This is oral autobiography. You can use the same outline you used earlier in your own autobiography. I often have my genealogy class close their eyes and think of their earliest memories. After a while I have them open their eyes and discuss what they were thinking. I've heard some of the most incredible stories come out of people's mouths. I asked this of a distant cousin, Jim Truman, who was seventy-four years old. He could remember back when he was four years old, playing in the country on a Pennsylvania farm. He grew up with his grandparents, who were my great-great-grandparents! He described how he rode horses around a ring, which helped harvest the food.

Other genealogists suggest that the interview start with more recent times and proceed backward. Many times I start by talking about something I know about that relative and then proceed with logical questions from there. For example, I told my Uncle Leonard I had a photo of him and his wife cutting their wedding cake. They were married for only a few years, but I knew her and remembered her. I asked him when they got married. That started a whole conversation about her, him, how they met, where he worked, where she worked, and what else was going on in the 1950s in Chicago.

In all families many marriages do not work out and the couple gets divorced. Always find out if the couple you inquire about stayed married or got divorced. Sometimes we miss information because we naively assume a couple stayed married and don't even inquire if they got divorced. Unfortunately, sometimes divorces are very bitter and ex-spouses will not give you a lot of information about their "ex" in an interview. Or the information they give you might be very biased. But you're not making a judgment; you're just collecting one version of a story.

Next, ask vital questions about dates and places of birth, death, and marriage. When it comes to dates, most persons' memories are vague. Many won't remember exact dates but may remember how old they were when an event happened, or how old a child was when an event happened, or what major event a date was associated with. For example, they'll remember their grandmother died the year of the big flood, or Mom died when John was two years old, or you were in high school when Aunt Mary was in the hospital. Later you can analyze the information and determine the approximate date. Ask relatives how old they were or what grade they were in school or how old their kids were when an event occurred. Most people don't remember dates; they remember events.

Ask in what cemetery an ancestor was buried. What funeral home handled the burial? Did they attend the funeral? What church did they attend? You'll need to know where each event occurred, including the city, county, and state.

Did any of your ancestors own property? If they owned property, where was it located and who were the neighbors? When was the land purchased? Whom did they buy it from? How much did it cost? Where did they get the money to buy the property? When was it sold? Whom did they sell it to? Why did they sell it?

Other questions to ask are, Did anyone serve in the military? Where did they work? Where did they go to school? Did anyone leave a will? Was anyone a slave? There are hundreds of questions to ask.

Oral History Questions

1. EARLIEST MEMORIES
   What is your earliest memory?
   What games did you play as a child?
   What was your favorite toy?
   Do you remember getting into trouble as a child?
   Who were your playmates?

2. PERSONAL
   What do you enjoy doing?
   What is important to you?
   Did you like to party?
   Do you smoke or drink?
   What was your favorite book?
   What was your favorite movie?
   What is your favorite color?
   What kind of clothes do you like?

What makes you mad or upset?
What injuries and illnesses have you had?

3. RELATIVES
   What relatives do you remember?
   Who was the oldest relative in the family?
   What do you remember about him or her?
   What relatives did you admire?
   What relatives did you dislike or despise?
   Do you have family reunions?
   When did they start? Why?
   Who comes?
   What do you do at family reunions?
   What do you like about them?
   What do you dislike about them?

4. FAMILY ACTIVITIES
   What do you remember about celebrating your birthdays?
   What do you remember about celebrating Christmas?
   How did you celebrate Thanksgiving?
   What do you remember about other holidays?
   Did the family go on picnics or to amusement parks?
   Did the family go on vacations together?
   Have you traveled much?
   Where have you been?

5. EDUCATION
   What elementary school did you go to?
   How far was the school and how did you get there?
   What do you remember about it?
   Did your brothers and sisters attend the same schools?
   What high school did you go to?
   What college did you go to?

What were your favorite subjects?

What subjects did you hate?

Who were your favorite teachers and what do
your remember about them?

What teachers influenced you the most and why?

What classmates do you remember?

Do you keep up with any of your classmates?

Do you attend class reunions?

6. WORK AND OCCUPATION

What was your first job?

Did you like it?

How much were you paid?

What other jobs have you had?

What companies did you work for?

How did you get each job?

Did you like them?

Did you ever own a business?

7. CHURCH

What religion are you?

What church did you attend?

Where was the church located?

What time did you attend church?

How often did you attend?

Were you active in the church?

Did you attend any other churches?

Why did you change?

8. REAL ESTATE

Where did you live?

Were you raised on a farm or in a city?

Do you live in a house or an apartment?

Describe your house.

Tell me about your room.

Who else lived in the house?

Was the house in the family a long time?

Who was the original owner?

How much did it cost?

Who were the neighbors?

When did you buy your first house?

Describe the experience.

Did you ever invest in real estate?

9. MILITARY EXPERIENCES

Were you in the military service?

Did you enlist or were you drafted?

What branch of the service?

What do you remember about the service?

Was your husband in the service?

Were your brothers or sons in the service?

Do you remember any other relatives or ancestors in the service?

10. FRATERNITIES AND ASSOCIATIONS

Were you in a fraternity or sorority?

Did you hold any offices?

Did you belong to any clubs or organizations?

Were you ever in politics?

11. SPORTS AND RECREATIONAL ACTIVITIES

Were you on any athletic teams?

Did you play tennis, golf, bowling, or cards?

What is your primary form of exercise?

Did you have any pets?

Did you have any plants?

12. HOBBIES

What are your hobbies?

Did you have any hobbies as a kid?

Do you or did you ever collect anything?

What are your favorite things to cook or eat?

Do you sew?

13. LIFE

Who was the biggest influence in your life?

Who were your other mentors and heroes?

What was your greatest success?

What was your biggest failure or disappointment?

Did you have any goals in life?

Was life easy or a struggle? How so?

What is your biggest accomplishment in life?

Where did you get your values?

14. RACE RELATIONS

Were you ever discriminated against?

How did the Civil Rights movement affect you?

Did you hear of any ancestor being a slave?

Do you recall any stories of slavery?

Bob Greene and D. G. Fulford's book, *To Our Children's Children: Preserving Family Histories for Generations to Come*, is devoted entirely to questions for family history (see "Oral History" in Bibliography).

Try to have a flexible outline of questions. If you see your relative pursuing a certain subject that he enjoys discussing, by all means follow it. Don't interrupt him. If it's important to him, it will be important to the family history. Most of the time it is impossible to know in advance what details a person may remember from before you were born. That's why we have interviews. After your relative finishes talking, ask follow-up questions on the subject to get more in-depth information. Your natural curiosity will lead you to logical questions. You can always come back to your prepared list of questions. And write down everything, no matter how seemingly unimportant.

When interviewing, you'll need to develop the skill of reading between the lines. Oral historians remind us that African Americans and women are not always open and forthright with painful memories of the past. We need to listen for implications, suggestions, hesitations, incomplete sentences, and stumbling blocks. These clues should not be dismissed or overlooked. Make note of them for later interpretation.

Interviewing Tips

Interviews come in two types, easy and difficult. The easy ones are taken from people who are talkative and outgoing. In fact, sometimes they talk so much you can't shut them up. Often they know a lot about the family history or will lead you to believe they know a lot about the family history.

The difficult interviews are with people who are quiet, shy, introverted, or have poor memories. Sometimes they can't remember anything, or they just give one-word answers. Sometimes people have something to hide and are afraid to say much of anything. These interviews are like pulling teeth.

Sometimes you won't know which type an interview is going to be until you get into it. If you are prepared, you will have different techniques and questions at your disposal. It's up to the interviewee whether you have to use them. In some of my best interviews I rarely asked any questions at all. The interviewee just sat and talked about everything. In other interviews I asked dozens of questions and got only a little bit of information. Hopefully, yours won't be difficult.

One technique you can use to open people up is to ask about mementos and souvenirs in their house or apartment. People usually have objects displayed in their home that have meaning to them. It could be something on the dresser or a shelf, on a coffee table or the fireplace mantel, in a bookcase or china cabinet, or a painting hanging on the wall. If you are observant when you walk into someone's house, you will immediately notice personal items the owner has on display. If you ask, "Where did that object come from?" there is usually a story behind it that illuminates the relative's personality and perhaps the family history.

You can also use the "close your eyes technique" mentioned earlier. Ask the relative to close her eyes and describe walking to school and being in school—the route she took, the school building, her friends and teachers, and what the day was like. Once she opens up and starts talking, you can follow up with logical questions that can eventually lead to more family history. Similarly, you can ask her to close her eyes and describe the house she grew up in or the experience of going to church.

Professional genealogist Sharon DeBartolo Carmack adds some creative ways of stimulating memories and getting relatives to talk. She suggests taking them to their old neighborhood and interviewing them while walking down the block. Here the relative can reminisce about the people, houses, stores, and playgrounds. She also recommends having the person give you a tour of his house and discuss the objects and the rooms.

How Much Should You Interview?

You have to interview relatives more than once. After the initial interview, review what was discussed. Think about it and analyze the things mentioned. There will be natural follow-up questions. Your Aunt Mary may have mentioned the elementary school she attended, but she may not have mentioned many other things, like where the school was located, how she got to school, if all her brothers and sisters attended the same school, who were her classmates and what she remembered about them, who were her favorite teachers and worst teachers, what were her favorite subjects and worst subjects, and what other schools she attended. All of these could be follow-up questions, just about the school she attended. There are other follow-up questions to be asked about each and every area discussed.

You may interview Aunt Mary many times over the years. After you return with research you've done and ask her additional questions, her mind may become stimulated. She may remember things she didn't recall during a previous interview. Or you may open up an area that you did not touch upon the first time you talked with her. The brain stores all our experiences. Most of them are lying dormant in the back of our mind, the subconscious. Once we begin stimulating the memory, things begin to come to the forefront, the conscious part of the brain. We have the ability to recall things we have not thought about for seventy years or more. This cyclical process helps us retrieve more and more information.

Ask yourself, "If a relative is fifty, sixty, seventy, or older, how long do you think it will take to tell his or her life's story?" That's what you have to consider in interviewing someone for genealogy. Some researchers think they can talk to a relative for an hour or two on one occasion, and they will have what they need. No way.

I have talked to my Aunt Doris maybe twenty times in the last fifteen years about the family history. My latest line of questioning was about her Uncle Ed. He was a half-brother to her father. She had a pension paper that had belonged to him and was passed to her from her father. Her father had cared for Uncle Ed when he got old and sick. Aunt Doris couldn't find the paper but kept telling me tidbits about Uncle Ed. Finally one day she mentioned that Uncle Ed was a porter and worked for the Pullman Company. She had never before mentioned he was a Pullman porter. I said wow! Those records are right here in Chicago at the Newberry Library.

The Pullman Company was the largest employer of African American men at the turn of the century. In 1925 Pullman porters started one of the first African American trade unions, the Brotherhood of Sleeping Car Porters, headed by labor leader A. Philip Randolph. (A union of African American dockworkers in Cairo, Illinois, may have started prior to 1925.) Randolph later became a Civil Rights leader and helped African Americans win the right to work in defense plants in 1941. Employee records of Pullman porters are very important for African American genealogists.

I went to the Newberry Library and located the Pullman Company records. They take up half a floor of space. I found a record for Uncle Ed, which indicated when he started working for the Pullman Company, when he left, why he left, when and where he was born, and his date of death, none of which I had known before. His date and place of birth told me where my great-grandmother was living at the time! That was the person I was ultimately seeking, but you see how the oral history and an aunt and uncle got me there.

> **!** Trap: Not getting biographies from Mom and Dad, thinking that we already "know" them.

One of my biggest mistakes was not taking enough time to talk to my father. I didn't ask him enough questions about his life or his parents. He never knew his grandparents and only aunt. They died before he was born. He met his uncle only one time. The times I did talk with my dad, I did not tape-record him or take adequate notes. He's deceased now, and I don't have material sufficient enough to review his thoughts, remembrances, or words. I have only brief, sketchy notes, written too long ago to accurately analyze or place in context. Some of the things that I recall I have not found in my notes. Knowing the tricks memory plays on you, I wonder now did he say them or are they things in my mind that I attribute to him?

Record the Interview

When interviewing, it is best to use a tape recorder. There are two advantages to tape-recording your relatives. The first is to get an accurate record of everything they say. The second is to capture their voice on tape. Once the relative passes away, this becomes an invaluable memento. It gives you a different dimension of that person, more than just a memory, some documents, and a photograph or two.

Speaking of photographs, you should also consider purchasing a camcorder to videotape your relatives. A videotape of your relatives is even *more* valuable than an audiotape. Hearing and seeing your relatives after they have gone is almost like bringing them back to life.

> **!** Trap: Not tape-recording Mom and Dad, thinking they will be around for years.

Another big mistake I made (you can see I made many) was never taking the opportunity to tape-record my mother when I first started tracing my genealogy. I was more interested in talking to her older sisters, aunt, and great-aunt. It was the biggest mistake of my genealogical career. She died suddenly after a short hospital stay when she was only sixty-one years old. Ironically, my nephew (her grandson) had his first birthday party at Mom's house. Nate, a friend of the family, came by and videotaped the party. Mom is the most prominent person on the videotape. She is vibrant, laughing, joking, and in rare form—nothing like her last days in the hospital. Looking at that videotape is much more realistic than looking at two-dimensional photographs of her. It is one of my most prized possessions. So don't let that happen to you. Do not take your parents for granted, as if they will live to the age of Methuselah (in the Bible, Methuselah was said to have lived 969 years). And if you can get access to a camcorder, video-tape them whenever you can.

Uncle Dan died in the summer of 1990, just before his one hundredth birthday. I drove back to western Pennsylvania to attend his funeral. At the funeral I met Charlie, another elderly cousin I'd never known. Cousin Charlie was excited and enthusiastic when I asked him for an interview and drove over to my hotel room. I got a great interview filled with incredible stories and rich details about Charlie working in a steel mill and the racism African Americans faced. He told me Uncle Dan held the highest-ranking job of any African American at the mill and explained his job as a roller. Cousin Charlie talked for two hours, and I thought he was through. I decided to pop another tape in the camcorder and Cousin Charlie talked for another hour! He tired me out. I think reflecting on his life and having someone interested in it helped him as much as it helped me.

! Trap: Waiting to travel to see distant older relatives instead of interviewing them over the telephone.

For relatives who live out of town, you don't have to travel just to tape-record them. You can tape-record an interview over the telephone. Refer to the chapter on "Organizing Before It Gets Messy," where I describe the kinds of tape recorders and telephone connection devices that can be attached to your telephone. Another method of recording a long-distance tele-phone call is with a telephone answering machine. Some machines allow you to press a but-ton while talking to record the call. If you don't have a tape recorder handy, it may be your only option. Check the instruction manual to see if your answering machine has this feature and learn how to activate it. If you record a long-distance interview over the telephone, you can initially save a lot of money—like airfare, hotel, and food to travel to see the relative in person. You still need to visit that relative in person, but it could mean the difference in a six-month delay before you can travel. It could even mean the difference in that relative still being around or not. If the relative is elderly, don't wait until the family reunion or your vaca-tion to interview him or her.

After you tape-record the interview, check to see if the tape is OK. (I have recorded sessions and pressed the play button instead of the record button. Fortunately, I was also simultane-ously videotaping and still had the critical thirty minutes of the interview. But I still felt kind of dumb.) If everything came out OK, break the tabs on the rear of the cassette. This will prevent you from accidentally erasing the tape. Then store the tape in a safe place. It will become extremely valuable as time marches on. If you made a long-distance trip to interview a distant relative, you may not get another opportunity to record the same information again. Debra is an avid genealogist whose husband's passion is jazz music. He needed a tape one evening and recorded beautiful music over all her interviews with relatives who are now deceased! You can imagine how she felt. But it wasn't his fault. She should have clearly labeled the tapes, broken the tabs to prevent re-recording, and stored them in a special place—away from his jazz music.

Contrary to popular belief, audiotapes will not last forever. They are very fragile and their longevity is in part contingent on how well you care for them. Keep the tapes in their cases. If they are left exposed, dust and dirt can get inside and damage the recording. Dust and dirt can also damage the tape recorder. It is also a good idea to store tapes in a cassette storage cabinet for better protection. Then store the cabinet away from electronic devices and heat sources, such as radiators and sunlight. They are very sensitive to heat and humidity, which can vastly shorten their life span. The tape is composed of magnetic fields, which will deteriorate and can be suddenly erased when the tape is placed too close to a magnetic field generated by some electronic devices.

I also recommend making backup copies of tapes. If you damage the only one you own, you'll be sick. If you have a dual cassette tape deck, you can make duplicates very easily. If you make a copy right away, label the original as the master and the duplicate as a copy or backup. When transcribing or listening to the recording, use the backup copy. Keep the original stored away. Then if you damage the copy, you still have the original. Some people recommend periodically copying the tape, thinking the copy will outlast the original.

I have written my ancestors' birth dates, death dates, and wedding anniversaries on my calendar. On those special days I listen to tape recordings I recorded years ago. It's like Grandma is still alive. It's an incredible feeling. If I don't have a tape recording of particular ancestors, I pull out their files and look at their photographs and read their biography I've written. Or I work on research in their folder on their birthday. I do things like write or update their biography, put their photos in archival sleeves to preserve them, put their documents in acid-free folders and sleeves, develop genealogy research plans, or write to courthouses or archives for their records. In addition to ensuring I do a little genealogy all the time, it's a way of remembering them, celebrating their birthday, and paying homage to them.

If you video-record relatives, don't think that the videotape is a family history, a final product, or will be interesting for someone else to view. It is merely a raw product, not a finished product. In order for a videotape to become interesting for others to view, it must be edited. If you do not have editing skills and you want a professional job, go to a professional company. If you want to attempt it yourself, refer to Duane and Pat Strum's book, *Video Family History* (see "Oral History" in Bibliography), or look to computer editing software. Whichever route you take, keep your original footage intact. It will be valuable for your research.

Don't Forget to Send a Thank-You

After the interview, write a nice thank-you note to your relative. Let her know how appreciative you are and that you'll stay in touch and may have follow-up questions. If you've promised anything, like names and addresses, copies of photographs, or genealogy charts, include them in your correspondence. Try not to let more than a week or two pass before you send this thank-you.

Transcribe the Interview

Immediately after the interview, write or type your notes and recollections of the interview. If you do this right away, you will retain a higher percentage of what transpired during the discussion. If I don't have the opportunity to use a tape recorder during an interview, I write notes immediately afterward. If it's a telephone interview, I write my notes as soon as I hang up the telephone, before I do anything else. If the interview is at a relative's house, after I leave I'll drive around the corner, park the car, and write my notes in the car. I'll also rewrite any scribblings I made on my notepad. My handwriting is very bad, and I have a tendency to write very fast. Afterward I have difficulty reading my own handwriting. If I go over the interview right away, I have a better chance of deciphering what I wrote. I can also add in little details I didn't have time to record during the interview. The longer you wait, the more details you'll lose, and it's the details that you need.

! Trap: Not transcribing tape recordings.

If you tape-record a relative, you should transcribe the tape. It is exciting to listen to an audiotape of an older relative reminiscing about many details of family history you've never heard before. However, when you are analyzing the family tree and trying to figure out where the family came from, you need to look at the data. It is quicker and easier to examine a few sheets of paper than to listen to an hour-long tape that may have what you need in the middle or at the end. At other times you'll want to concentrate on certain segments of the interview, perhaps as little as a sentence or two. This is better done from a transcript. Another critical reason to transcribe the tape is the transcription will last longer than the fragile tape. If you lose the audio quality, you still have the information from the transcription.

I'll record my name unless another relative conducted the interview, in which case I'll record his or her name. I'll also record if the interview was in person or on the telephone. Then I'll type everything that was discussed.

PERSONAL INTERVIEW
(Reconstructed interview from note fragments)

With: Alma (Rice) Burroughs
Who: Paternal Grandmother
By: Tony Burroughs
Date: December 4, 1975

My husband was born in Chicago in 1893. He died in 1971. We were married in 1915 in Chicago. We had a small private wedding.

His dad worked on the railroad. I think he was from North Carolina.

His mother went to Spelman (African American female college in Atlanta, Georgia). Her maiden name was Williams and she was born in Memphis, Tennessee.

He went to Crane High School and had no military service. He went to Kent Law School and passed the bar in 1920. He became president of the bar association. He got the first home for the bar association on Michigan Avenue.

Once you transcribe the tape, do not destroy it. It is a different document than the transcription. It will reveal emphasis, voice inflection, excitement, laughter, hesitation, and other emotions not revealed in a transcript. You will probably listen to it at a later date. After you conduct other research, the tape will have new meaning. Some things might take on new meanings that previously did not seem important.

Some oral historians advocate a formal transcription in which the questions are clearly delineated and separated from the answers, similar to what you see in a magazine article. For example:

QUESTION: *When and where were you born, Grandma?*
ANSWER: *I was born in Memphis, Tennessee, in 1895.*

That clears up any ambiguity in the transcript but takes more time and paper. If you have the money to have the transcription done professionally, I'd advise having it done. Professional transcribers are trained in preparing transcripts in this format. Some of my interviews were so brief the questions are obvious.

Disseminate the Information

Another advantage of transcribing tapes is to disseminate the information. You need to copy certain segments of your interviews and place the information in the folders of other ancestors and relatives. For example, if Grandma Burroughs mentioned something about her husband, I want to make sure I have that information recorded in her folder *as well as* his folder, with a footnote stating the information came from an interview with Grandma Burroughs on December 4, 1975. This should be done with every name mentioned. Otherwise, when I am analyzing my grandfather, I may miss some of the facts of his life. So if she mentioned three different people, I'll record those items with the respective ancestors, in three different folders. If you are using a computer word processor, this is easy to do. Just copy the section and paste it into a new document. Otherwise, you might want to photocopy the transcript and then cut and paste segments for their respective folders. Just make sure when you transfer information, you also transfer the notations on where that information came from.

When you do this for each and every person in every interview, you begin to build a wealth of information on several different relatives without doing any other research than interviewing.

ORAL HISTORY

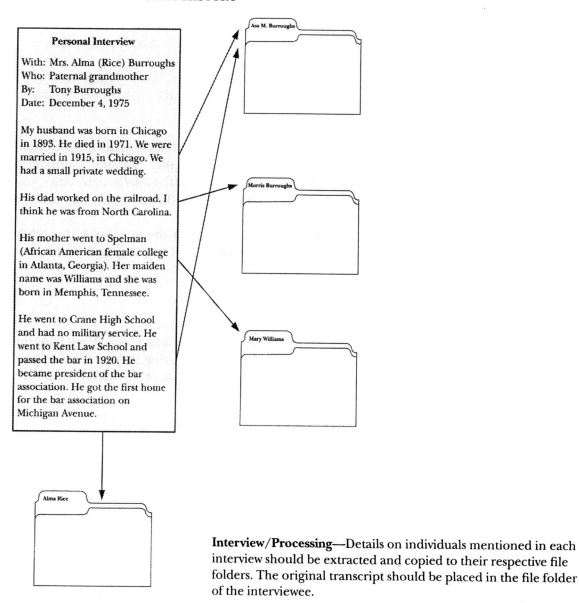

Personal Interview

With: Mrs. Alma (Rice) Burroughs
Who: Paternal grandmother
By: Tony Burroughs
Date: December 4, 1975

My husband was born in Chicago in 1893. He died in 1971. We were married in 1915, in Chicago. We had a small private wedding.

His dad worked on the railroad. I think he was from North Carolina.

His mother went to Spelman (African American female college in Atlanta, Georgia). Her maiden name was Williams and she was born in Memphis, Tennessee.

He went to Crane High School and had no military service. He went to Kent Law School and passed the bar in 1920. He became president of the bar association. He got the first home for the bar association on Michigan Avenue.

Asa M. Burroughs

Morris Burroughs

Mary Williams

Alma Rice

Interview/Processing—Details on individuals mentioned in each interview should be extracted and copied to their respective file folders. The original transcript should be placed in the file folder of the interviewee.

When you conduct research in libraries, archives, and courthouses, you may obtain documents that have several names on them. You will use the same process to record the information in several different folders. That way you are always operating with all the information you have accumulated for each relative and ancestor. Otherwise, you are operating with half a deck and you'll miss some things. Those of you who have genealogical experience and have not done this, you need to return to all your interviews and research notes because you'll have information buried in other ancestors' files. Disseminate the information and you might solve some problems.

After you transcribe an interview tape and convert it to paper, read it and analyze it. Think about the information in the document. Why did these events occur? Why didn't other things happen? Who else was involved? What details were omitted? This is where your inquisitive nature and your investigative skills come in handy.

As you're reading, thinking, and analyzing, have a sheet of paper handy. As questions come to your mind, write them down. You should have tons of questions. Also refer to your questionnaire. Did the person answer every question? If not, add these to your list. Now you're ready to call your relative for a follow-up interview. Add this task to your Things To Do sheet. After you conduct the next interview, repeat the process: type the interview, disseminate the information, read and analyze the information, develop follow-up questions, and conduct another interview. Date the new interview and type it up as a completely separate interview. If a relative gives you additional information on the telephone, also record that as a separate interview. Do this until all your questions get answered or until your relative has no more answers.

The importance of oral history cannot be overstated. Records that you will be searching have been around for a long time. They will continue to be around for a long time. Your relatives will not.

When I attended Uncle Dan's funeral in Pennsylvania in 1990, I recalled interviewing him and Aunt Roxie thirteen years earlier, in 1977. He was eighty-six years old at the time and she was eighty-two. I soon discovered that eight of the nine relatives I interviewed that year had died since I last visited Pennsylvania. In the same time period I lost my mother, father, two uncles, two aunts, and a grandmother. It was a sobering feeling. However, I was elated that I had the opportunity to meet them and glad I took the time to record most of them on audiotapes. Now those audiotapes are some of my most valued possessions. I have information on them that is priceless. There is no way I could have found some of the information in a library or an archive.

Our relatives hold very valuable clues, some of which may be obvious, others not realized for years to come. You should attempt to locate each and every relative who is even remotely related to you. Go back to your list of living relatives developed earlier. This is your guide. Interview all of them. After you begin your genealogical journey, you will discover relatives you never knew existed. Move fast to interview them.

Verify Oral History

As exciting as oral history is, you'll soon learn that the words spoken are not gospel. Oral history is fraught with many potential hazards. You must be aware of these hazards, for they can stifle your progress and lead you astray. They can also impair the credibility of your research and reflect on your reputation as a genealogist. These hazards include the following:

- Relatives' memories will fade and facts will become cloudy and distorted.
- Senility or Alzheimer's disease can develop, which can distort or block key facts.
- Some events can become confused with others.
- Unfavorable events might be hidden, disguised, or omitted.
- Some relatives or ancestors can be confused with others.
- Rumors can be repeated from one generation to another, the story changing as it filters down.
- Some stories grow into myths.
- Gossip can become mixed with fact.
- Stories can be exaggerated.
- Some stories are actually lies.

As a family historian, you may not know which of these aspects are coming into play. Therefore, your only recourse is to verify as many stories as possible. No longer can we use the excuses "African Americans have only an oral tradition" or "There aren't any records for African Americans." We must verify as many people, places, and events as possible. All oral history cannot be taken as fact. Much of it can be used only as a guide, a clue, or a direction showing where to look. Some stories will be verified and some will not. In the verification process you will clarify some stories and learn a lot more about your family. It will be very exciting once you start seeking answers to questions like mine: "Did Grandma Brooks actually teach in a one-room schoolhouse?" "Was Great-Grandpa Brooks really a Buffalo Soldier?" "Did Grandpa Terrell actually kill a guy?" Now you are on a mission!

! Trap: Getting stuck on myths of oral history.

Verification is done by searching through records and obtaining documents to substantiate the stories. We'll look for records in the next chapter and see if our oral history is correct.

Genealogist and travel agent Collette DeVerge has been researching her family for more than fifteen years. Her mother died when she was seventeen years old, so when Collette began genealogy, she turned to her grandmother for the oral history of her family. When Collette reached the ten-year mark, she compiled a book of her research and gave it to her grandmother on Mother's Day. That's when Collette learned the real family history. The grandmother she'd given the book to realized how serious Collette was about the family history and confessed she was not Collette's grandmother! Collette was stunned. She realized the family history this "grandmother" had told Collette about during their interviews was not true. Collette's real grandmother never married, and Collette's mother was born out of wedlock. This "grandmother" Collette knew was really her step-grandmother. She raised Collette's mother from the age of five, when her real mother had died. So ten years of genealogy research was done on the wrong family, not Collette's blood relatives. Fortunately, Collette was eventually told the truth and was able to locate information on her blood relatives.

Talking to your relatives and collecting oral history is the most important thing you can do in genealogy. Records in libraries, archives, and courthouses have been there for years and will be there long after we're gone. However, our relatives will not. They have a limited lifetime, so get to them while they are alive.

> **!** Trap: Neglecting living relatives by researching in libraries, archives, and county courthouses before all of the relatives have been thoroughly interviewed.

Now we'll check our Things To Do, Research To Do, and Research Calendar to see that they are up to date.

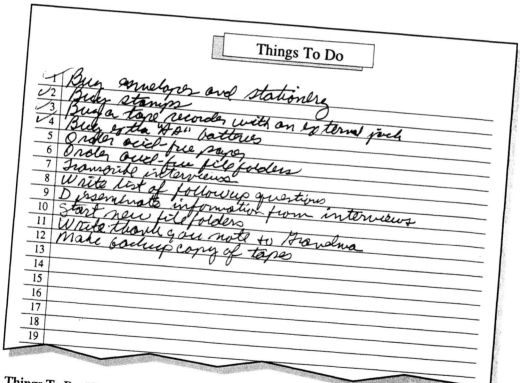

Things To Do #2—The second Things To Do form, which has completed items checked off and additional items listed.

Research To Do

Name *Burroughs*

✓ 1	Finish reading genealogy book
✓ 2	Make list of relatives to interview
3	Get current telephone numbers and addresses
4	Start my autobiography
5	Type first draft of my autobiography
6	Prioritize list of living relatives by age
7	Call grandma to set date for interview
8	Call mom to set date for interview
9	Call Dad to set date for interview
10	Call Aunt Doris to set date for interview
11	
12	
13	
14	
15	
16	
17	
18	
19	

Research To Do #2—The second Research To Do form, which has completed items checked off and additional items listed.

Research Calendar			

File Number   /

Surnames   Burroughs

Researcher   Tony Burroughs

Date	Repository Call No.	Description of Sources	Doc. No.
1/30/75		Chicago Public Library	
	929.1.028	"Genealogy" by Kenneth Stryker-Rodda - Boy Scouts of America Merit Badge Series No. 3383, 1973.	
12/4/75		Home of Alma Burroughs - 505 E. 60th St, Chicago, Ill.	
		Interview Grandma Burroughs	1
12/10/75		Home of Elmer & Mary Burroughs 10215 So. LaFayette - Chicago, Ill.	
		Interview Mom	2
		Interview Dad	3
12/12/75		Telephone interview with Aunt Doris Smith	4
12/12/75		Follow up interview with Grandma (telephone)	5

Research Calendar #3—The Research Calendar after four days of research, illustrating trips to the library, relatives' homes, and telephone interviews.

The Family Archives—Researching Family Records

After family members are interviewed, the next step in the genealogical process is to begin researching records to verify the oral history you have just obtained. Unfortunately, everything a person says may not be true. We outlined some of those reasons in the previous chapter. Obtaining records and documents will help you either substantiate or refute the oral history. Records will also begin to add pieces to the family puzzle. Finally, these family records may also reveal additional ancestors to add to your family tree.

The first place to search for records is in the family archives. Everyone has family archives but might not realize it. An archive is a place that stores old records. Most people have old records lying somewhere around the house. Some of us have older records than others, and some of us have better-organized records than others.

What are family records? They are things like the family Bible, an old baby book, a high school yearbook, old scrapbooks, or the family photo album. Other items would include:

- newspaper articles
- obituaries clipped out of newspapers
- funeral programs
- letters
- deeds and mortgages
- apartment leases
- contracts
- stocks and bonds
- insurance records
- bills and receipts
- payroll stubs
- military discharge papers
- fraternal records
- pension records
- wills
- death certificates, birth certificates, and marriage licenses
- baptismal certificates
- confirmation records
- artifacts

They would include anything and everything that could list a family member's name. Most of the time they are things we have taken for granted for years. Sometimes they are things we haven't seen for years, and sometimes they are things we have never seen. They could be items that Grandmother left in a box that no one ever opened.

Where do you find the family archives? Right under your nose. They can be found anywhere in the house: in the basement, in the attic, in a closet, in a suitcase, in an old trunk, in a bookcase, in a file cabinet, in shoe boxes, in between book pages, and in dresser drawers. Family papers have no boundaries as to where they can be located. You must look anywhere and everywhere.

Everyone has some of these family documents and records. But you must look for them. Most people do not know these things are useful for tracing the family history and do not see them as records and documents. Often we think about them as old papers and garbage. Most people throw them away without knowing their value.

Think about what happens when a person dies. The family takes care of the funeral arrangements and greets friends and relatives who come to the house and the funeral. They then proceed to attend to the personal affairs of the deceased. This means checking for insurance policies and disposing of personal possessions and assets. The first things to go are the car, furniture, television, stereo, and VCR. Clothing, if fashionable, jewelry, and other items of obvious value may be distributed to relatives and friends. The other items of no apparent value—the personal papers, bills, photos, and such—are either kept by the spouse, handed down to the children, or thrown in the garbage.

These are treasures to the genealogist: the personal papers, bills, books, and photos. This is why it is so important to interview *all* of your living relatives. In many cases important family papers are in the homes of the children of your grandparents, great-grandparents, or aunts and uncles. So even though these children may be younger than you, they have access to the family records of their deceased parents and grandparents that will be extremely valuable to you.

Family Bible

In conducting your search, the first family record to look for is the family Bible. Many families kept a large Bible. If you do not know of a Bible in the family, ask all the relatives you interview to see if anyone has one. Often births, deaths, and marriages were recorded in the front or center pages. Some Bibles even had ancestor charts in them. During the eighteenth and nineteenth centuries, most states did not require the registration of births and deaths. Although some New England localities have vital records that date from the seventeenth century, most states did not require vital registration until the twentieth century. We'll look at these in detail in the "Vital Records" chapter. In many cases the family Bible has the only written record of a birth or a death. So treat family Bibles as the valuable and rare records they are when you come across them.

If you find a family Bible with the names and dates of ancestors in it, don't accept them as fact. Just because names and dates are written in the Holy Book does not make them true and

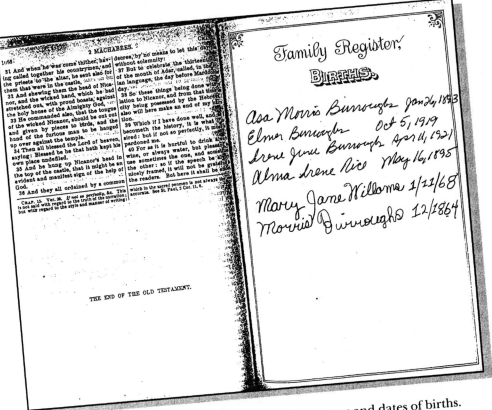

Bible Birth List—Page from the family Bible listing names and dates of births.

correct. As genealogists, we cannot just accept information as fact. We must validate and verify it. There are several ways to substantiate the information recorded in a family Bible.

TEST 1 —First look at the list of births. Are they listed in chronological order, are they in clusters, or do the dates jump around? If the dates are in chronological order, it increases the likelihood they might have been recorded when the babies were born. This is very important, because if they were *not* recorded when the babies were born, they were recorded from some other source or from someone's memory—both of which are subject to error.

TEST 2 —Check the handwriting in the Bible. Does it appear the inscriptions were all written with the same pen and in the same handwriting, even though the dates occurred over a one-hundred-year period? Or are there different handwriting styles and different colored inks? Does it appear that someone picked up a pen or pencil at the time a baby was born and recorded the birth in the Bible? If so, that further increases the validity of the information in the Bible.

Test 3—Examine the copyright page. What is the copyright date of the Bible? Is it before or after the dates of birth in the Bible? Any event recorded with a date *preceding* the copyright date of the Bible was recorded *after* the event occurred, not *at* the time of occurrence. For example, suppose a Bible was published in 1950. If it lists a birth occurring in 1935, the birth was recorded based on notes written somewhere else or based on someone's memory fifteen or more years after the fact. However, if a birth was recorded for 1955, it might have been recorded when the baby was born. Examine the Bible the same way for deaths and marriages.

If your family Bible can hold up to these three tests, it is considered a primary source. It strengthens the possibility that the names and dates are true. However, if the Bible doesn't meet these tests, that does not mean the information is not true, so don't disregard it. You just

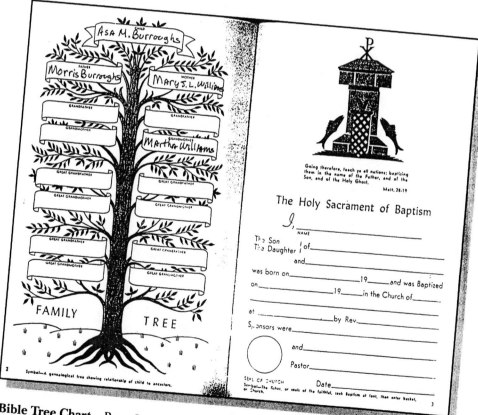

Bible Tree Chart—Page from the family Bible illustrating a baby and his ancestors.

have to check further. See if you can locate the original source of the information that was recorded in the Bible.

Once you locate a family Bible, don't carry it around every time you want to research or discuss the family history. Photocopy the pages with family names and vital statistics. Also photocopy the title page and copyright page and record the name and address of the owner of the Bible. If the Bible is at a relative's home out of town, ask him or her to photocopy those pages and mail them to you. Include these new documents in your genealogy file folders. Then you can show people the photocopied pages, and the Bible will be kept safe and secure.

Notebooks

My grandfather had a small Bible given to him by his mother, but only one of the cover pages survived and it did not contain any family data. However, he kept a little red notebook in which he recorded the names of his parents, Morris Burroughs and Mary Jane Lillie Williams, along with their birth and death dates and the cities where the events occurred. His father (my great-grandfather) was listed as being born in 1864 in Spartanburg, South Carolina.

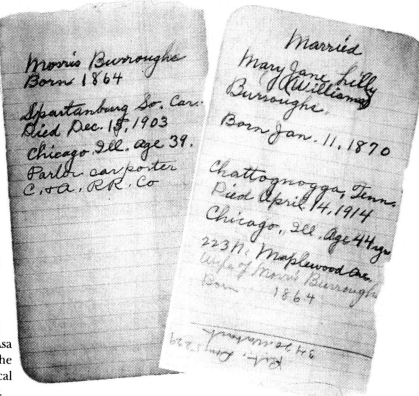

Red Notebook: Morris (left)—Page from small red notebook owned by Asa Morris Burroughs where he recorded brief biographical information on his family.

Red Notebook: Mary (right)—Page from small red notebook owned by Asa Morris Burroughs where he recorded brief biographical information on his family.

Robert Burroughs's Insurance Policy—Nickel life-insurance policy from 1901 on Robert Burroughs, found among family papers. It illustrates Robert's age and his mother and brother's names.

When I interviewed my grandmother, she said Morris was from North Carolina. Her memory is contradicted by this little red notebook. It saved me a lot of work and headaches because there's a big difference between North Carolina and South Carolina. Whereas the information on Granddad's parents was probably not recorded in the red notebook at the time of their deaths, it was important information. It provided the first concrete written information on my great-grandparents and refuted Grandma's recollections. But I still had to corroborate the information with other sources because the notebook appears to be a secondary source. Most of the dates seem to have been written at the same time.

My grandfather also recorded vital information for his brother, Robert Burroughs. He recorded the births of all his children, along with the names of the doctors who delivered them, and meticulously recorded every time he moved, along with the address of each house and apartment the family lived in. It is a fascinating book and I've spent hours going through it.

Genealogist Charles Brewer went through his mother's closet after she died in 1970. He discovered two small shirt-pocket notebooks, very similar to my grandfather's little red notebook. The books had been kept by Charles's maternal great-great-grandfather, Matthias T. Teackle. Handwritten notes in one notebook provided the information that the Teackle family had left Baltimore in 1853 and relocated in Toronto, Canada.

Charles then found Canadian and United States naturalization documents for his maternal great-grandfather, William Dyer. Charles said had he not retrieved the notebooks that had been handed down through the family for over 120 years, he never would have known of these migrations.

Old Trunks

In 1976 I had been tracing my family history for several months. One day my grandmother mentioned that her husband's brother, Robert Burroughs, who died in 1958, had an old trunk. Granddad had gathered up his belongings, placed them in the trunk, put the trunk in the basement, and never opened it. It sat there for eighteen years. Grandma asked me if I wanted to look in it. I said, "Of course!" We spent the entire day going through the trunk.

It was a mind-boggling experience. We found antique pens, cigarette lighters, a flute, chess pieces, books, old clothes, photographs, a marriage license, and employee badges from the Chicago Park District, Arlington Park Jockey Club, and Hawthorne Stables. There were also payroll stubs from Lincoln Fields Jockey Club in 1937, when he made $24.50 a week! There were welfare applications that showed addresses, occupations, employers, and wages. There were letters—one from a "Cousin Hazel" living in Joliet, Illinois, whom I hadn't known about.

Robert Burroughs's Business Card— Business card belonging to Robert Burroughs; found in his trunk. It illustrates his occupation and address.

Earl Gaither's Business Card—Business card for Earl P. Gaither, a cousin to Asa Morris Burroughs, indicating his address, occupation, and telephone number.

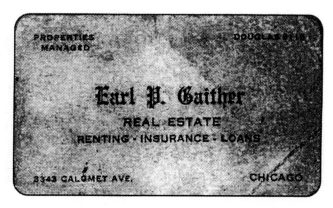

There were nickel insurance policies that listed his mother and brother as beneficiaries. These were very valuable because they were additional documents validating the relationship between my grandfather, his mother (my great-grandmother), and his brother.

There were business cards, including one on which Robert advertised himself as an auto mechanic and a radio specialist. Another business card was from an Earl P. Gaither. My grandfather had only the one brother, Robert, and no sisters. I once said to my grandmother, "Granddad had to have *some* relatives. Wasn't there a cousin somewhere?" She said yes. He had cousins named Gaither. She recalled a heavyset, dark-skinned lady whose first name she couldn't remember. Grandma said she hadn't seen them since they got married. That was in 1915, sixty years earlier. Now with this business card I had a first name, address, telephone number, and occupation. I used that information to locate Earl Gaither in telephone directories and city directories. (See the chapter "Going to the Library" to learn how I traced his family.)

Also in the trunk were six driver's licenses, twelve state vehicle registrations, and thirteen city vehicle registrations going back to 1917. I found cars I had never heard of—a Kissel, a

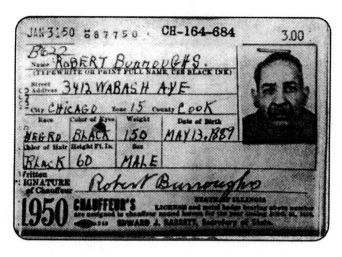

Robert Burroughs's License—Robert Burroughs's driver's license, found in his trunk, providing his birth date, height, weight, color of eyes and hair, address, occupation, signature, and photograph.

CARS OWNED BY ROBERT ELLIOTT BURROUGHS
(owned nine cars and one motorcycle in twenty-seven years)

Model Year	Car	Model	Year Owned	Age of Car	Age of Owner	City License Fee	Address
	?		1917*		28	$2.00	225 N. Hoyne
1921	Liberty		1925	4	36	$10.00	2951 S. Vernon
1921	Liberty	Tour	1926	5	37	$10.00	320 E. 41st Street
	Stearns	K	1928		39	$10.00	4711 S. Prairie
	Stearns	K	1929		40	$10.00	3420 S. Wabash
1928	Kissel	Roadster	1930	2	41	$10.00	4957 S. Calumet
1928	Kissel	Roadster	1931	3	42	$10.00	710 E. 47th
1928	Kissel	Roadster	1932	4	43		Chicago Heights
1928	Kissel	Roadster	1935	5	46	$5.00	2625 S. Dearborn
1929	Cadillac	Sedan	1937	8	48		3435 S. Wabash
1929	Graham Page	Coupe	1938	9	49		3116 S. Michigan
1930	Ford	Coupe	1939	9	50		3305 S. Michigan
	International	Panel	1949		60		3412 S. Wabash
1938	Mercury	Sedan	1949	11	60	$10.00	3412 S. Wabash
1938	Mercury	Sedan	1950	12	61		3412 S. Wabash
1938	Mercury	Sedan	1951	13	62	$10.00	3412 S. Wabash
1938	Mercury	Sedan	1952	14	63	$15.00	3412 S. Wabash
1942	Harley	Davidson	1952	10	63	$4.50	3410 S. Wabash
1941	Dodge	Panel	1952	11	63	$30.00	3410 S. Wabash
1941	Dodge	Panel	1953	12	64	$30.00	3410 S. Wabash
1940	Buick	Sedan	1953	13	64	$15.00	3410 S. Wabash

*1917 registration is torn and the name of the vehicle is missing.

Kissell License—A 1932 Ilinois vehicle license for a 1928 Kissell roadster owned by Robert Burroughs; found in his trunk.

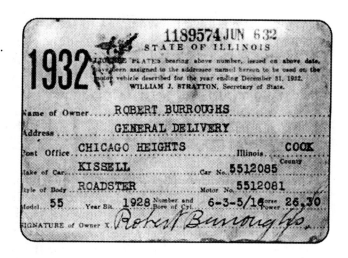

Liberty License—A 1926 state of Illinois vehicle license for a 1921 Liberty touring car owned by Robert Burroughs; found in his trunk.

Stearns License—A 1929 city of Chicago vehicle license for a 1921 Stearns K owned by Robert Burroughs; found in his trunk.

Liberty, and a Stearns. Then I wanted to see what the cars looked like and learn what had happened to the companies. In the early days of automobiles, there were hundreds of manufacturers. I made a chronological list of the cars he owned and how old they were. This gave me a picture of Robert's economic status. Family oral history said he drove fast cars and had lots of women. Reality showed he owned newer cars when he was young but drove old beaters as he got older.

There were newspaper clippings. One of the clippings was for my grandfather when he was elected to head the Cook County Bar Association in 1928. The other newspaper clipping was for Robert when he and his boys robbed the Illinois Tool Works of $5,700 in 1917. Robert served five years in Joliet State Penitentiary. It's ironic he robbed a bank and kept the evidence to tell about it. We also found poems in the trunk. Robert started writing poetry in the penitentiary. I guess he had a lot of time on his hands.

Some researchers don't like to find this kind of thing. When you research genealogy, you find good and bad. Here we have a case in which one brother was president of the bar association and the other was a bank robber. There is good and bad in all families. Sometimes you'll find more information on those who got into trouble than on those who were "goodie two-shoes" and never did anything wrong.

I think they are interesting and try not to pass judgment on people's lives. I have found that even undesirable information has helped me solve family riddles. It also has provided more information to help me fully understand why people develop certain attitudes, make certain decisions, and lead different lives. One of the reasons we research family history is for a deeper understanding of people, family, and history.

I learned more about my grandfather's brother through this trunk than I could ever have learned anywhere else. Before I started tracing the family history, I never even knew

Bar Association Article—1928 *Chicago Defender* newspaper clipping announcing Asa Morris Burroughs's election as president of the Cook County Bar Association.

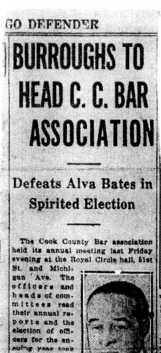

GO DEFENDER

BURROUGHS TO HEAD C. C. BAR ASSOCIATION

Defeats Alva Bates in Spirited Election

The Cook County Bar association held its annual meeting last Friday evening at the Royal Circle hall, 51st St. and Michigan Ave. The officers and heads of committees read their annual reports and the election of officers for the ensuing year took place.

Attorney C. Francis Stradford, president of the body for the past year, presided. The reports showed that the year just ended was the most progressive in the history of the association.

Attorneys A. Morris Burroughs and Alva L. Bates were the two candidates for the office of president. Both men are popular with their fellow lawyers and each had campaigned vigorously. As a result, their friends came out to vote. Of the 110 members of the association, 108 voted. Attorney Burroughs was elected by a large majority.

Other officers elected for the year were: Thomas R. Johnson, first vice president; Harold M. Tyler, second vice president; Samuel A. Beadle, third vice president, James Morehead, general secretary; Arthur H. Bellamy, financial secretary; William K. Hooks, treasurer, and Benjamin G. Pollard, attorney for the body. Members elected to the board of directors were: Judge Albert B. George. Attorneys Nathan K. McGill, Violette N. Anderson, George C. Adams, Milton Oldham, C. Francis Stradford and Richard Hill, Jr.

The newly elected president is well qualified for the office and has been engaged actively in the practice of his profession for eight years. Mr. Burroughs was secretary of the association for three years. The new president is anxious that the association shall have its own home and law library and will endeavor to have a site purchased while he is in office.

$5,700 Pay Roll Robbers Confess; Two Sentenced

Five pay roll robbers, implicated in the robbing of the Illinois Tool works, 154 East Erie street, of about $5,700 on May 9, pleaded guilty before Judge Barrett in Criminal court yesterday. Robert Burroughs and Harry Williams, Negroes, were sent to Joliet and Pontiac, respectively, for terms of a year to life. Sentence was deferred on William Webb, a Negro, and Alex Clifton, 21 years old, 3720 Cottage Grove avenue, and Vincent Sheehan, 28 years old, 4422 Vincennes avenue, cashier and bookkeeper of the company. Sheehan and Clifton admitted planning the robbery. Clifton said he was in debt from trips along the primrose path.

Bank Robbery Article—Newspaper clipping found in trunk belonging to Robert Burroughs. He and two others robbed the Illinois Tool Works in 1917.

my grandfather had a brother. You can see how the items painted a picture of him, as well as providing the names of ancestors. All these things are important. Just an envelope with a name and address can be very important. On the surface it may appear worthless, but if there are several people in the same location with the same name, this could differentiate your ancestor from the others.

I am so lucky that Robert's things weren't thrown out when he died. I wonder how many other things were thrown out by other ancestors? Robert's brother, my grandfather, was a meticulous record keeper. However, his things were stored in the garage and were soiled and destroyed before I began researching the family. I am still going through items from Robert's trunk, preserving and organizing the documents. I placed the documents in acid-free file folders and then made a list of the records. There were fifty-six folders. I originally placed them in an acid-free document case and later in the file cabinet.

This source lay dormant for eighteen years and no one touched it. There are probably similar sources in your family's basements and attics. I talked with a genealogist named Betty whose uncle's basement was so cluttered with family memorabilia she could hardly get down the steps.

When my grandmother Burroughs died twelve years later, I discovered another gold mine. I thought I had seen everything she owned when I first started researching. We had talked many times and she had brought many things out for me to see. What I didn't realize was there were things in that old house that *she* probably didn't know were there. She had lived in the house for forty years, and a lot of things were buried and forgotten.

There was a black tin box that probably belonged to my great-grandfather Morris Burroughs before he died in 1903. One of the items in the box was the organization papers for an association of "colored railway workers" in 1901! I am currently researching this association. My great-grandfather was the president and appears to have written the document. The association was organized twenty-four years before A. Philip Randolph organized the Brotherhood of Sleeping Car Porters, the first African American union.

Also in my grandmother's house was a shoe box full of letters. These were letters her sons wrote to her during World War II. About one hundred letters were in the box, most from my father. I've been preserving, organizing, and cataloging the letters since they were discovered. They chronicle an important period in the history of this country and the role that African Americans played in it. Grandma never mentioned the letters in any of my interviews. She might have forgotten about them since they were almost fifty years old.

Funeral Programs

After you look for the old Bible and any trunks and shoe boxes, next check for funeral programs and newspaper obituaries. Funeral programs often include a short biography of the deceased, usually prepared by the next of kin. However, since a funeral program has to be written and printed right away, in a time of mourning and stress, the accuracy of the information can vary. My grandfather died in 1971 when I was out of town. My grandmother gave me a copy of his funeral program, which told a lot about him. Most of it I did not know because he was just "Granddad." It told of his parents, his date of marriage, and highlights of his law career.

When genealogist Belzora Cheatham went through her family's archives, she found a chest of drawers full of funeral programs. She then began asking relatives for additional funeral programs they'd saved. One relative gave her a funeral program for a cousin of her father. It listed many relatives Bell did not have in her genealogy computer database. Eventually she collected more than 560 funeral programs from relatives. The oldest is for an ancestor who died in 1945. These funeral programs not only provide biographical information on the deceased, but usually give the name of the funeral home and a list of surviving relatives.

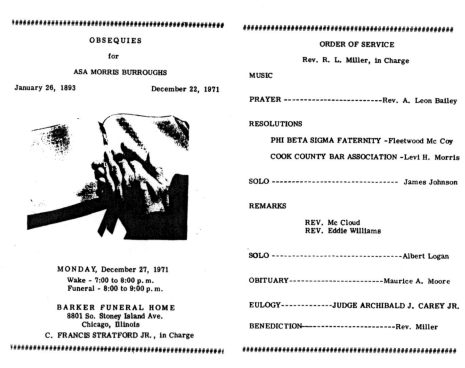

Asa Burroughs's Funeral Program—1971 funeral program for Asa Morris Burroughs; saved by his widow, Alma Burroughs.

Obituaries

After researching individual ancestors for weeks, months, or even years, it is a lot of fun and very exciting to locate an obituary for an ancestor. Obituaries are short biographies of recently deceased individuals, usually published in newspapers. They notify the public that a person died and contain basic facts about the person's life and sometimes a wealth of information. When all we know about an ancestor's life is a date and place of birth, death, and marriage, locating an obituary can be very rewarding. An obituary can paint a picture of the ancestor's life and provide the names of other relatives.

Usually written by the next of kin, newspaper obituaries almost always list other relatives and sometimes the parents and descendants of the deceased. Sometimes they give limited biographical information. At a minimum, they usually list the funeral home and may list the cemetery.

Fortunately, many obituaries are clipped and saved by family members. So the first place to look for obituaries is from family members. When doing oral history, always ask if family members kept any newspaper obituaries. Sometimes the clippings were saved and placed in scrapbooks, photograph albums, purses, dresser drawers, and shoe boxes.

###

OBITUARY

ASA MORRIS BURROUGHS, was born January 26, 1893. Parents Morris and Mary Burroughs a native of Chicago raised on the West Side. Attended Grammer School, High School and Kent College of Law.

United in marriage to Alma Rice on January 7, 1915 to this union 4 children were born.

His father died in 1903 therefore, he became sole support of his invalid mother. At the age of 16, he went to work as an office boy in the firm of Hallam, Laramie, Levy, O'Donnell, Stephens, Korn and Borrelli from 1909 - 1923, during which time he studied law. He was admitted to the Bar in February 1921.

Specialized in Real Estate Property and Probate Law. Also Workman Compensation cases and Chancery cases.

When the Ida B. Wells Housing Project was ordered abandoned by Attorney General Cummings in 1937 Attorney Burroughs was the one Attorney to object to the motion and the Project became a success.

One of his greatest legal achievements was the Conversion of the area between 115th & 119th Streets, Ashland Avenue & Morgan from a manufacturing District to a residential district, now known as Maple Park.

The swimming pools in Washington Park stands as a monument to his activity in civic matters. In 1942, Attorney Burroughs appealed to the newly elected Governor and the Mayor to have the streets in the 31st and 33rd streets section to be improved with public funds that also, was a success.   (Continued on back..)

###

OBITUARY-Cont'd.

Secretary of the Cook County Association in 1925, 26, and 27. President of the Cook County Bar Association in 1928 and 1929. Organizer and President of the Chicago Democratic Lawyers - 1932. Attorney and Director of Mid South Side Property Owners League and Mid South Side Business League. Member of the Executive Committee of the Boy Scouts. Chairman and Director of the Color Big Brothers 1937 - 1943.

Founder of the Cook County Bar Association Law Library in 1928. Candidate for Judge in Primary in 1936. Member of PHI BETA SIGMA FRATERNITY. Candidate for Judge in Primary in 1936.

He remained in his law practice until his health began to fail in the early 60's.

ASA MORRIS BURROUGHS leaves to mourn his passing:

A Devoted Wife, Alma.

Three Sons: Morris, Leonard and Elmer Burroughs of Chicago, Illinois.

One Daughter, Miss Irene J. Spencer of Santa Clara, California.

Seven Grandchildren and Five Great-grandchildren; and MANY friends.

(INTERMENT - OAKRIDGE CEMETARY
Tuesday, December 28, 1971)

###

When I started tracing my family history, my Aunt Doris shared an obituary that had been passed down through the family, of an ancestor who died in 1927, Ella Batch Simmons. The obituary reveals Ella's date of death, birth date, place of birth, residence, parents' names, mother's maiden name, surviving brothers and sisters, and their residences, children, minister, and the name of the A.M.E. church she attended in Elizabeth, Pennsylvania. It also indicates the name of the funeral home and the name of the cemetery where she is buried. This obituary contains a lot of valuable family information.

Newspaper clippings about family members are often saved by older relatives, sometimes in scrapbooks. Newsprint is the cheapest paper made. It deteriorates extremely rapidly. It will often crumble in your hands, so handle it very carefully. If you locate any obituaries, be sure to photocopy them on your acid-free paper. If the newspaper publisher has gone out of business, it may take a lot of work to locate a library that has a copy of the newspaper and the issue that ran the obituary. Treat these obituaries as valuable documents. I know of one researcher who has copies of newspapers that no longer exist and have not been microfilmed. These items we take for granted are much more valuable than we realize. But even if

THE DEATH RECORD

Simmons

Mrs. Ella Batch Simmons, one of the best known colored residents of Elizabeth, died at her home on Seveth avenue Wednesday afternoon, March 30th, aged 67 years, 4 months and 12 days. She was born in Perryopolis, the daughter of the late Stephen and Margaret Goe-Batch. She was a faithful member of the Allen Chapel A. M. E. church.

Mrs. Simmons is survived by the following: One daughter, Mae Simmons, one son, Lloyd G. Simmons; and a foster daughter, Lydia Brooks, all of Elizabeth; two sisters, Mrs. Elizabeth Catlin of Monongahela and Mrs. Rebecca Catlin of West Newton; two brothers, James W. Batch of Homestead and Stephen Batch of Monongahela.

Funeral services were held from her late home on Friday afternoon in charge of her pastor, Rev. F. W. Collins. Interment was in Elizabeth cemetery.

Ella Batch Simmons's Obituary—Pennsylvania newspaper obituary from 1927 for Ella Batch Simmons; saved by author's aunt, Doris Smith.

the family did not save obituaries, sometimes they can still be obtained from the library. I'll discuss those in the chapter on "Going to the Library."

Autograph Books

Also look for baby books, school yearbooks, and autograph books. Everyone remembers autograph books from when they graduated from elementary school. Well, who signs autograph books? Your classmates, teachers, best friends, and relatives. I received an autograph book that belonged to my grandmother's favorite aunt, Lovie. It was given to her by her sister in 1889. One night I had insomnia, and you know what genealogists do when we have insomnia? We do genealogy.

I started going through the autograph book, as I had done many times before. I had meant to photocopy the pages but never did. I decided to enter the names into my computer. Then I entered the dates people signed their names. Then I noticed that some were from Chicago and others were from other cities. So I also entered the names of the cities. Well, when you sign an autograph book, where do you sign? On your favorite page, of course. Some people like the first page, some like the last page, some like the green pages and some like the pink pages. The signatures are all in random order. After I entered the information in the computer, I decided to sort the names.

I sorted the names by date and got an interesting pattern. There were dates from Chicago and then dates from Cairo, Illinois, and then dates from Chicago again. I recalled Cairo from an interview I did with Grandma. I went back to that interview, which I had typed and filed away. Grandma said her Aunt Lovie had a godmother who lived in Cairo. She would go down to visit her, but Grandma didn't like it because the godmother lived by the Ohio River and it was very smelly. Knowing my grandmother, the wife of a prominent attorney, I figured she didn't want to be around any smelly river. I could envision her turning up her nose whenever she heard the word Cairo.

Well, I drove to Cairo and found a record of that godmother. In addition, I also found Aunt Lovie living there with her mother, Fannie Barker, my great-great-grandmother. Little did I know they had lived in Cairo before moving to Chicago from Tennessee. After studying the old Cairo city directories, I concluded they came up the Mississippi River on a steamer from Memphis, Tennessee, to Cairo, Illinois. It's a natural migration pattern. This placed my ancestors in Illinois seven years before I thought they were there. It also qualified me to obtain an Illinois Pioneer Certificate, reserved for those who can identify ancestors who lived in Illinois prior to 1881.

If you're lucky, you might find a diary or an autobiography written by one of your ancestors. One genealogist I know found an autobiography that listed the name of the plantation and the former slave owner of her ancestors. This document was extremely valuable because this information is rarely passed down through oral history. Ask your relatives for each one of these items. They will probably not have all of them, but anything they have will add to your store of knowledge.

Keep Family Records Organized

When researching family records, be careful to keep documents in the order they are found. It may help later in interpreting the records. For example, my Cousin Kent had an old photograph album. He could identify some of the ancestors in some of the photographs but not all of them. One day he purchased a beautiful new album and gave the old photos a new home.

What Kent failed to do was transfer the captions below the photographs, which identified the people in the photos. Now the photos are separated from the captions, and he can no longer identify the people in them.

Charles had a nice collection of nineteenth-century letters written by one of his ancestors. Some of the letters had newspaper clippings and photographs enclosed in the envelopes with the letters. Charles nicely separated these items from the letters, not realizing they would be important years later. Now when analyzing the letters with newfound information, he cannot identify which newspaper articles and photographs the writer is referring to in the letters.

Make copies of each item you find on acid-free paper. Then place the copies (and originals if you are the current owner) into acid-free file folders. Be sure to use a separate folder for each person's records. These old pieces of paper and scraps have now become genealogy documents. Treat them with care.

Family Photos

Now pull out the old family photo albums and pictures. Sometimes the names of the persons in the photographs will be written on them or listed on the back of the photograph. I received one photograph of my great-grandmother Terrell seated next to her sister and cousin. Fortunately, the names of all three girls are written on the back of the photograph, as well as where they were living at the time. The photograph was taken (probably in Perryopolis) to give to Grandma Terrell's other sister, Hannah, who was living in Fayette City.

I received another photograph of Grandma Terrell's parents, David and Anna Truman, my great-great-grandparents. It was a picture postcard that was very popular at the turn of the century. The postcard had their names inscribed on the front border in pencil and the words "Grandpa and Grandma Truman" inscribed on the mailing side. Postcard photographs were very popular between 1905 and 1930, which helps to date the people in the photo. They were often given as photographs instead of mailed to family and friends.

Unfortunately, you'll find many photographs without names on the front or back. It's very sad to see photographs of your ancestors and have no idea who they are. I found a photograph in which I could recognize my Aunt Irene as a young girl. I wondered if she recalled the photograph and the occasion. However, she was living in California, while I was in Chicago. I made a copy of the photograph and put labels under each photograph. I mailed it to her with a cover letter, asking her to identify the other four girls in the photograph and tell me when it was taken. It took her a while, but she returned it with all the girls' names on the labels. She also remembered where it was taken and the name of the photographer. It so happened her girlfriend's father was the photographer.

Perhaps the most important find I made in Robert's trunk was an old photograph. It had no names, dates, or places written on it. However, I was able to identify several people in the photo from earlier photos of my great-grandparents, Morris and Mary Burroughs, which my grandmother had identified and given to me. From these I was able to identify Morris and Mary in the photo found in Robert's trunk. I identified Morris as the man standing on the left and his

Truman Girls/Front (above)—Photograph of
three Truman sisters; found among family papers.

Truman Girls/Back (right)—Rear of photograph
reveals names of girls and also indicates town where each is living
and that the photograph is a gift to their other sister, Hannah Truman, who lives in
Fayette City, Pennsylvania.

wife, Mary, sitting on the bench. Sitting next to Mary is an older woman who looks just like her
and is dressed like her. It is probably Mary's mother, Martha, my great-great-grandmother. I
later found out Martha died in 1900, so identifying her on a photograph was exhilarating!

Also pictured in the photo is a baby, who I'm sure was my grandfather's brother, Robert,
the owner of the trunk. He's less than a year old, so the photo would have been taken in 1889,
soon after he was born.

Mary had a sister and two brothers. I believe the man next to Morris is one of her brothers.
Oral history says Mary's father was white. I'm not saying the white-looking man in the photograph is her father, but I wonder why he's in the photo. I haven't been able to identify the older
man on the far right because no man was listed in the household on early census records.

Anna and David Truman— Photograph of David and Anna Truman, author's great-great-grandparents.

Mary was born in Chattanooga, where her family was still living at the time of the photo. They did not move to Chicago until the 1890s. I can tell the photograph was probably taken in Chattanooga rather than Chicago because of the wood-frame house and the foliage in the background. Their Chicago residence in 1889 was a brick two-story apartment building I was able to identify from addresses in the Chicago city directory. The Chattanooga city directory indicated that the block where they lived on Grove Street consisted of single-family homes.

Since Robert was born in Chicago, I imagine Morris and Mary were eager to return to Chattanooga for her family to see their firstborn child. While there, they decided to have a family photograph taken. Robert was so proud of it he kept it all his life. This would have been his baby picture.

> **!** Trap: Not encouraging Mom, Dad, and other relatives to label their photographs. This can lead to unidentified ancestors in the future.

So there are ways of identifying photographs even though they are not labeled. The photographs in your family may not be labeled either. However, a distant relative may have duplicate photos that are labeled. Most of the time family photos are not labeled or appropriately identified. Once you locate photographs, if your relative knows the people in the photo-

Mary Jane Burroughs (left)—Photograph of author's great-grandmother, Mary Jane Lillie Burroughs; found in the basement.

Morris Burroughs (right)—Photograph of author's great-grandfather, Morris Burroughs; found in the basement.

graph, have him or her immediately write the names on the back of the photo. Photos should be labeled in pencil. If you write in pen, over time the ink can seep through to the front and damage the photo. An alternative is to place a label on the back of the photo and write in pen on the label. Special foil-backed labels with archivally safe adhesive can be ordered from archival supply companies. To properly label the photograph, identify the people in the photo, the ages if possible, and the approximate date and location of the photo. If older relatives die without identifying the people in photos, many of your ancestors' names will be lost forever. So take the time to label your photos.

Trying to get to family photographs is not always easy. Relatives know they may have the only copy of a photograph. They want to keep that photograph and may not be willing to risk losing it. Relatives may therefore tell you they can't find it or may not allow you to look at it. Assure them you do not want to take the photograph; you merely want to look at it.

You should try to get copies made of the photos. Refer to the section on preservation of photographs in the chapter "Preserving the Past and the Present" to see how to make copies. Once you have negatives and copies made, family members can have one and relatives won't feel so protective and hoard their photos.

Family in Country—Photograph of Burroughs family found in trunk belonging to Robert Burroughs. Sitting, left to right, Mary Burroughs, Robert Burroughs (baby), and Martha Williams. Standing, left to right, Morris Burroughs, Malachias or Lee Williams, and two unidentified men. Analysis of the photograph reveals it was probably taken in 1889, in front of Martha Williams's home in Chattanooga, Tennessee.

Looking at photographs is also a good way to stimulate memories and get additional family history. Use them as a tool after conducting oral interviews. Your initial questionnaire will answer a lot of questions, and the later showing of photographs will stimulate additional memories. If you use the questionnaire first, then go through the photograph album, you will get more information.

As you look at each photograph, ask, "Who is this in the picture?" You will often get a long, detailed answer about who the person is, how the person is related, where the photo was taken, why the photo was taken, and how the photograph was acquired. Have your tape recorder handy so you can capture the entire story with all the emotion. Afterward you probably won't remember the whole story. If you try to tape the story later, you will probably never get it again as you will when your relative first starts reminiscing.

I had a photograph of my aunt when she was about thirteen years old. She stood with a group of girls in front of a church. A priest was in the photograph, and the girls wore white-and-black church vestments as if they were in the choir. Because my aunt's children, my first cousins, went to a Catholic elementary school, I assumed this was probably a Catholic church. My aunt was living in California when I started to research this photograph, so I couldn't contact her immediately. I also recalled that when I first interviewed her she had a poor memory.

I planned to ask several older members of the community to identify the photograph. Before I could do this, I happened to include it with a group of photographs I took over to my Uncle Leonard's apartment for identification. When Uncle Leonard looked at the photo, he immediately identified the church as the *Episcopal* church the family attended, not a Catholic one. The church garments of Episcopalians and Catholics are very similar and hence the misinterpretation on my part.

This led me to St. Thomas Episcopal Church, which has records dating back to 1917. In these records I found listings for my aunt, my uncle, and my father. In addition to identifying the church in the photograph, Uncle Leonard also revealed that his brother had been married three or four times, which I had not known. Uncle Leonard also told me *he* had been married three times and gave me the names of his former wives. He talked of his fondness for women and attending Club DeLisa, a legendary Chicago nightclub showcasing African American entertainers from around the country, like Duke Ellington, Cab Calloway, and Nat King Cole. It was very popular on the south side of Chicago in the 1930s, '40s, and '50s and was visited by white entertainers like Bob Hope and Bing Crosby. Uncle Leonard also gave me a long account of his experiences in Burma during World War II. I ended up with a lot of information, and we had a

Girls in Front of Church—Photograph found among Burroughs family papers of Father William Suthern and girls in front of St. Thomas Episcopal Church in Chicago. Author's Aunt Irene Burroughs is standing in front row at far left.

lot of fun. I had my video recorder on the whole time. These later stories had nothing to do with the photographs but had everything to do with the family history.

This leads me to another important point to stress. Try not to let your biases and prejudices affect your interviews or other aspects of your research. The more objective you are, the more information you'll get, and the richer your story will be. For example, Uncle Leonard was very shy and private. He was sensitive about his bald head and always wore a hat, outside and inside the house. He refrained from being photographed. He did not like to go to public or family gatherings and did not attend funerals, weddings, or picnics. He lived in the same building as his mother until she died when he was sixty-nine years old. Uncle Leonard had a great sense of humor, and we loved him dearly. Because of his shyness, we always looked at him a little differently, but he was family. I had talked with him briefly about the family history, but he could never remember anything. So I was reluctant to conduct a formal interview with him. When I called Uncle Leonard to set a time to review the photographs, he was so shy he broke about ten appointments. Considering the wealth of information I got when he looked at the photographs, I shudder to think that I did not want to interview him again and thought he had no information about the family history. So try to interview everyone, regardless of his or her personality and your personal biases.

Make a list of all the documents and photographs you obtain for each individual ancestor. Make notations as to when and where the documents were obtained. Then place this list in their respective file folders. You will need this list in the next step. For an example, below is a list of the documents found in Robert's trunk. Some of these will be used later to document the family history.

ITEMS FROM TRUNK BELONGING TO ROBERT ELLIOTT BURROUGHS
(Discovered in basement of 505 East 60th Street in 1976)

1. Metropolitan Life Insurance Company $100 policy no. 20336808 for Robert Burroughs, issued 14 October 1901, and payable 5 cents weekly. Mother, Mary Burroughs, beneficiary; later changed to Asa M. Burroughs, brother.
2. Metropolitan Life Insurance Company $25 policy no. 8808889 for Robert Burroughs, issued 6 March 1916. Mother, Mary Burroughs, beneficiary; later changed to Asa M. Burroughs, brother.
3. Crown Point, Indiana, Marriage Certificate for Robert E. Burroughs and Malvina V. Holman—18 October 1929.
4. Robert Burroughs, 2625 Dearborn, application to Employment Relief Service, Vocational Record—1930.
5. Arlington Park Jockey Club Stable badge number 1072 to Robert Burroughs—1932.
6. Claim of Robert Burroughs, 3420 Wabash, against Reliable Auto Parts and Charlie Consontine, owner—1932.

7. Robert Burroughs, 2625 Dearborn, application to Cook County Bureau of Public Welfare—1933.
8. Letter to Robert Burroughs, 2625 Dearborn, from the Secretary of State regarding assigning engine number to Kissel roadster—20 October 1934.
9. Hawthorne Stable badge number 645 to R. Burroughs—1936.
10. Groom License no. 895 issued to Robert Burroughs from the Illinois Racing Commission—29 May 1936.
11. Payroll stubs from Lincoln Fields Jockey Club—1937.
12. Robert Burroughs, 3305 S. Michigan Ave., application to Chicago Relief Administration—12 August 1941.
13. Blank Federal Income Tax Return form for 1943.
14. City of Chicago, Delayed Birth Certificate for Robert Elliott Burroughs, born 13 May 1889; filed 2 November 1943.
15. Federal Income Tax Return for Robert Burroughs, 3305 S. Michigan Ave.—1944.
16. Receipt from Dr. Harry S. McCray, optometrist, for Robert Burroughs, c/o The Pullman Company—20 October 1944.
17. Certificate of Junking issued to Robert Burroughs, 3412 Wabash, from Edward J. Barrett, Secretary of State, for an International panel vehicle—1949.
18. Bankers Life and Casualty Company, application for Robert Burroughs, 3410 S. Wabash, receipts, business card—1954.
19. Robert Burroughs, 1135 W. 59th St., application for general assistance, City of Chicago Department of Welfare—20 January 1955.
20. Letter to Robert Burroughs, 1139 W. 59th St., from Morris Ellman, Cook County Department of Welfare—16 May 1955.
21. Letter to Robert from cousin Hazel, Joliet, Ill.—1985 (letter currently misplaced).
22. Chicago Relief Administration cover letter and blank forms.

Where's That Town?

Before any meaningful outside research can begin, you'll need to determine where the towns and cities are located that your ancestors lived in. If you've interviewed all your living relatives and checked all the family records, you've probably come up with some places you've never heard of. You'll also need to place these towns in a county and near another town or river or some other geographical landmark. Many records you need to search were created by county governments and are located in county courthouses. The county seat was the town where all official business took place. Today we think of a courthouse as a building. When a county was originally formed, however, the location where the county commissioners transacted business was called the courthouse. It might have been in the back of Mr. Jones's store. Later, if a town developed on that location, it might adopt a name like Jonesboro Courthouse. Later many cities dropped "Courthouse" from the end of their names. So if you see a name like Jonesboro Courthouse on records or maps, you'll know what it means. The county was often broken

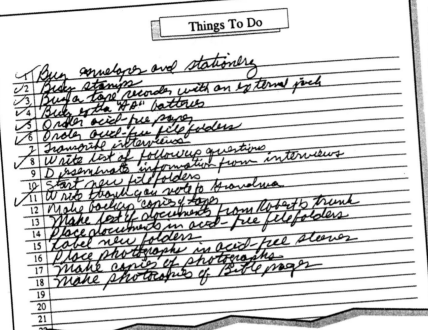

Things To Do #3—Third Things To Do sheet checking off items completed and adding tasks to preserve family records.

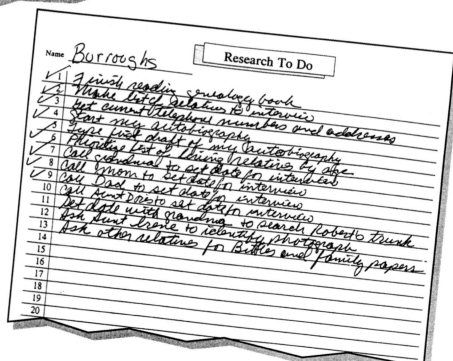

Research To Do #3—Third Research To Do sheet, checking off items completed and adding tasks to research family records.

```
                        ┌─────────────────────┐
                        │  Research Calendar  │
                        └─────────────────────┘

File Number      1              Researcher  Tony Burroughs
Surnames  Burroughs

  Date      Repository          Description of Sources           Doc. No.
            Call No.

1/30/75  Chicago Public Library

         929.1.028  "Genealogy" by Kenneth Stryker-
                     Rodda - Boy Scouts of America
                     Merit Badge Series No. 3383,
                     1973.

12/4/75  Home of Alma Burroughs - 505 E, 60th St.
                                   Chicago, Ill.
         Interview Grandma Burroughs                     1

12/10/75 Home of Elmer & Mary Ellen Burroughs
          10215 So. Lafayette - Chgo, Ill
          Interview Mom                                  2
          Interview Dad                                  3

12/21/75 Telephone interview with Aunt Doris Smith      4

12/21/75 Followup interview with Grandma (telephone)    5

1/15/76  Search Robert's trunk with Grandma          many
          505 E, 60th Street - basement              documents
```

Research Calendar #4—Fourth Research Calendar, adding research in family records at Grandma Burroughs's house.

down into smaller subdivisions called townships. When you interview older family members, they may mention a name or an area where they lived, and it might not be a city or the county but a rural area, which may be a township.

There are a few towns that are not situated in a county. They are referred to as independent cities, and almost all of their records are with the city government, not in a county office. Sometimes people lived in places we've never heard of. That's why you need to ask relatives where those places were located.

Pull out your highway map or atlas and see if you can find the town. If you don't have a highway map, get one from the drugstore, a map store, the highway department, or the chamber of commerce in the area you're researching. From your map you should be able to locate the town and determine what county it is located in. If you can't find the town right away, be sure to look at the index of cities and towns on the map or atlas; it's usually in the back. If you

		IN FOLDER Y/N	COMMENTS

Genealogy File Folder Contents

Ancestor name: *Robert Burroughs*

		IN FOLDER Y/N	COMMENTS
1	Document Log		
2	Things to Do List	✓	
3	Research To Do List	✓	
4	Research Calendar	✓	
5	Correspondence Index	✓	
6	Correspondence		
7	Alphabetical list of variant surname spellings		
8	Master alphabetical list of all family surnames		
9	Soundex code		
10	Charts – Pedigree		
11	– Family Group Sheet		
12	– Descendant Chart		
13	– Soundex Charts		
14	– Census Charts		
15	– Chronology		
16	– Biography		
17	Oral history interviews		
18	Research notes, extracts, and abstracts		
19	Documents	N	See List of documents & Folder
20	Vital statistics certificates – Birth		
21	– Death		
22	– Marriage		
23	Discrepancy charts		
24	Photographs	Y	
25			
26			
27			
28			
29			
30			
31			
32			
33			
34			
35			

Make note in comments column of all items in separate file folders or other locations.

File Folder: Robert Burroughs—Genealogy File Folder
Contents form indicating items in Robert Burroughs's folder.

still can't find the town and it's not listed in the index, you'll have to do some further research. The chapter "Going to the Library" describes sophisticated sources for locating hard-to-find towns.

In conclusion, scrapbooks, papers, photographs, and things around the house that we take for granted are extremely valuable for genealogical research. They can also be very exciting. Most genealogists overlook these things, not knowing their value. They hold valuable details not found in libraries and archives. They are the second important step in your journey to reconstruct the family history. Don't neglect them. Try to go through every relative's basement and attic. And once you get clues to where ancestors lived, try to pinpoint the locations on a map. I'll show you what to do with all this newfound data in the next chapter.

Family Group Sheets

By now you have amassed tons of information about the family. You have written your autobiography, which includes remembrances of relatives and family events. You have interviewed many different relatives several times. The tape recordings from these interviews are now transcribed onto paper, either typed, computerized, or neatly handwritten. You now have file folders labeled with the names of relatives and ancestors. You have placed your transcripts, as well as numerous family documents found in the basement, attic, or other places around the house, in these folders.

Now that all this information is gathered, you must sort it out. You have identified relatives and ancestors and heard juicy stories about their lives. They may include brothers, sisters, aunts, uncles, cousins, grandparents, in-laws, outlaws, (remember Robert?), and even friends of the family. Eventually you may have hundreds or even thousands of names. Researchers sometimes get confused and distracted dealing with so many names. It is often difficult to separate relatives from friends of the family.

Genealogy charts were developed to sort out these relationships and keep research focused. The mind works in pictures. You've heard the phrase "A picture is worth a thousand words." Well, that's one of the purposes in using a genealogy chart. It draws a picture of the family tree.

Some of the information you've collected will be extracted and placed on genealogy charts and forms. But much of it will remain to be compiled later into biographies and the family history.

The first information you will extract will be placed on a Family Group Sheet. A Family Group Sheet is the first major genealogy chart used to organize and sort data. It organizes the vital statistics for a family unit. It also includes notes on where you found the information. It ensures that no vital information is overlooked. Most researchers have notes on legal pads, scraps of paper, backs of envelopes, in file folders, and in notebooks. As a result, when an important date or place is needed, it can't be located. The Family Group Sheet helps to solve this problem.

The Family Group Sheet includes the names of parents and their children and the dates and places of birth, marriage, and death for each of them. If you have children, start with yourself and your spouse as parents, then list your children. Record your given name, then your middle name if you have one, and then your surname (last name). Record only the maiden name for women. It is also useful to include nicknames, which should be enclosed in quotation marks (e.g., "Butch"). In your interview notes or on your biography sheets (not on the Family Group Sheet), you should state where this nickname came from. When you begin to search for your ancestors' names in records, you'll find they might be listed by their first name, middle name, nickname, and sometimes merely their initials. If you have all their names handy, you will not miss them if they show up in a record. You can also search for your ancestors under their nicknames if you do not locate them under their given names. Genealogist Carolyn Grant has an eighty-year-old relative named Blossom. She never found her in the household or census records. However, she found a girl named Charlotte who was eight years old, which was the right age for Blossom. When Carolyn asked Blossom about this, she verified that Charlotte was her given name. She said she never liked the name Charlotte and therefore never used it.

Sometimes men used their initials instead of their first names. For example, my grandfather's name was Asa Morris Burroughs. However, most records list him as A. M. Burroughs, which is how he usually signed his name. I even found him listed in the 1920 census under only his middle name, Morris Burroughs. His mother's name was Mary Burroughs. Her full name was Mary Jane Lillie (Williams) Burroughs. I have located records for her under Mary Williams, Mary Burroughs, Mary J. L. Burroughs, Mary J. L. Williams, Mamie Burroughs, and Lillie Williams. I haven't found her under Jane Williams yet, and I hope I don't! A handy little book to add to your collection is *Nicknames: Past and Present* by Christine Rose (see "Genealogical Reference Guides" in Bibliography). It lists many names and the nicknames that are associated with each name. You'd be surprised to know some of the common nicknames that were used in the nineteenth and early twentieth centuries. For example, how many people realize Polly was a nickname for Mary, or that Bess, Liz, and Liza were nicknames for Elizabeth? Genealogists often miss their ancestors in records because they don't know their nicknames or they only know their ancestors' nicknames and not their real names.

The Family Group Sheet includes a space for the names of the parents of the father and mother. After you record the parents, record the names of the children. They should be listed in order of birth, from the eldest to the youngest. Do not record the surname of the children if it's the same as the surname of the parents. Record it only if the surname is different from that of the parents or other siblings. If there were previous marriages, they should be noted on the line that says "Other husbands" or "Other wives." Then another Family Group Sheet should be used to record that relationship. It should note the first marriage and any children of that relationship.

Family Group Sheet

FATHER *Asa Morris Burroughs*

Born	City	County	State
Married	City	County	State
Died	City	County	State
Buried	City	County	State
Father *Morris Burroughs*		Born	Died
Mother *Mary Jane Lillie Williams*		Born	Died
Other wives			

MOTHER *Alma Irene Rice*

Born	City	County	State
Died	City	County	State
Buried	City	County	State
Father *William Henry Rice*		Born	Died
Mother *Minnie Ophelia Barker*		Born	Died
Other husbands *None*			

SEX M/F	CHILDREN List each child in order of birth (whether living or dead).	Date	City	County	State	SPOUSE
1 *M*	*Morris*	Born				1st *Marie Hines*
		Married				2nd *Jean Simmons*
		Died				
2 *M*	*Leonard*	Born				1st *Gladys Hamilton*
		Married				2nd
		Died				
3 *M*	*Elmer*	Born				1st *Mary Ella Brooks*
		Married				2nd
		Died				
4 *F*	*Irene June*	Born				1st *Claude Davis*
		Married				2nd
		Died				
5		Born				1st
		Married				2nd
		Died				
6		Born				1st
		Married				2nd
		Died				
7		Born				1st
		Married				2nd
		Died				
8		Born				1st
		Married				2nd
		Died				

Date prepared: *10 Feb 1976*
Prepared by: *Tony Burroughs*

Family Group Sheet—Family Group Sheet for the family of Asa Morris and Alma Burroughs, recording vital statistics data for their family.

The question always comes up, "My parents weren't married" or "What should I do about single parents, divorced and separated couples, half brothers and sisters, or 'illegitimate children'?" We all have them in our family tree somewhere. I recommend several things.

First, I recommend recording "half" brothers and sisters (those of a previous marriage) in two ways. (Some people are offended by the term *half brother*. If you have a better term, by all

Family Group Sheet

FATHER Asa Morris Burroughs

	City	County	State
Born	Chicago	Cook	Illinois
Married	Chicago	Cook	Illinois
Died	Chicago	Cook	Illinois
Buried	Hillside	Cook	Illinois
Father	Morris Burroughs	Born	Died
Mother	Mary Jane Lillie Williams	Born	Died
Other wives			

MOTHER Alma Irene Rice

	City	County	State
Born	Chicago	Cook	Illinois
Died	Chicago	Cook	Illinois
Buried	Hillside	Cook	Illinois
Father	William Henry Rice	Born	Died
Mother	Minnie Ophelia Barker	Born	Died
Other husbands			

SEX M/F	CHILDREN (List each child in order of birth (whether living or dead)).	Date	City	County	State	SPOUSE
1 M	Morris	Born	Chicago	Cook	IL	1st Marie Hines
		Married				2nd Jean Simmons
		Died				
2 M	Leonard	Born	Chicago	Cook	IL	1st Gladys Hamilton
		Married				2nd
		Died				
3 M	Elmer	Born	Chicago	Cook	IL	1st Mary Ellen Banks
		Married				2nd
		Died				
4 F	Irene June	Born	Chicago	Cook	IL	1st Claude Davis
		Married				2nd
		Died	Woodland Hills	Los Angeles	CA	
5		Born				1st
		Married				2nd
		Died				
6		Born				1st
		Married				2nd
		Died				
7		Born				1st
		Married				2nd
		Died				
8		Born				1st
		Married				2nd
		Died				

Date prepared: 10 Feb 1976
Prepared by: Tony Burroughs

Family Group Sheet with Places—Family Group Sheet for the family of Asa Morris and Alma Burroughs, with places of birth, death, and marriage added.

means use it.) They belong on a separate Family Group Sheet with their birth mother and father and any other brothers and sisters. Then if they live in the household with their half parent, list them in the order of their birth with their half brothers and sisters. Include a footnote to explain that they are from a previous marriage. Some genealogists list them only on the Family Group Sheet with their birth parents. I like to do both. This gives me a biological picture and a realistic picture of the household. I want to know who lived in the house.

If a father did not marry the mother of his children, his name should also be footnoted to explain they never married. Then you won't needlessly search for marriage records that don't exist. Likewise, children out of wedlock should be footnoted and explained. Sometimes these are very sensitive subjects, especially with older relatives. You'll have to make a decision if these situations can easily be discussed and listed correctly on your Family Group Sheets. If not, then you must determine if these circumstances will embarrass anyone. If they will, you might want to keep two sets of records, one for public view and the real one under lock and key for research purposes until it will not embarrass any family member.

If a parent was divorced, place a footnote stating the couple was divorced. If you know the date of the divorce or approximate date, also indicate it in the footnote. I'll tell you later on about researching divorce records.

Once you have the names listed, then record the places of birth, death, and marriage. Be sure to include the city, county, and state where the events occurred. The county is very important. Most official vital records were originally recorded at the county courthouse. That is one of the places you'll have to research for further information.

Next, record the dates of birth, death, and marriage. If an event occurred on May 21, 1870, recording it as 5/21/70 could be misleading. In genealogy the event may have occurred in 1970, 1870, or 1770. Therefore dates are recorded in military style (21 May 1870): two digits for the day come first, the month is spelled out, and four digits for the year come last.

If you do not know an exact date, there are several abbreviations you can use to indicate approximate dates. The letters *ca.* in front of a date are an abbreviation for *circa,* meaning "about" or an approximate date (ca. 1910). *Abt.* can be used for "about" (abt. 1910), *bef.* for "before" (bef. 1910), and *aft.* for "after" (aft. 1910). You may wish to include a date range (for example, Born: 1900–1910) to indicate the earliest and latest possible dates. You don't want to search for records in 1920 or 1930 if the ancestor died before 1910. You should always try to put dates in a ballpark range and then constantly narrow that range.

If you do not have all the dates and places for an ancestor, fill in what you know. For example, suppose your grandmother told you her grandmother's name was Fannie. All she could remember about Fannie was that she was sweet, baked cookies, and was from Virginia. You would record her first name on the Family Group Sheet but not her last name. Since maiden names are recorded, not married names, this space would remain blank. The blank space helps to remind you that there is some missing vital information. Once the maiden name is found, it is then recorded next to her first name. A footnote would go next to the maiden name with an explanation of where the information was found. You would record Virginia as a place of birth. As of yet, you do not know the city or county where she was born, and so these spaces are left blank. If your grandmother told you where her grandmother died but not *when* she died, record the place but not a date.

Once you go through all your records, you may realize you do not have some of the information needed to complete the Family Group Sheet. Write down follow-up questions to ask

Family Group Sheet

FATHER ASA Morris Burroughs

Born	26 Jan 1893	City	Chicago	County	Cook	State	Illinois
Married	7 Jan 1915	City	Chicago	County	Cook	State	Illinois
Died	22 Dec 1971	City	Chicago	County	Cook	State	Illinois
Buried	28 Dec 1971	City	Hillside	County	Cook	State	Illinois
Father	Morris Burroughs			Born	CA 1864	Died	15 Dec 1903
Mother	Mary Jane Little Williams			Born	11 Jan 1870	Died	14 Apr 1914
Other wives							

MOTHER Alma Irene Rice

Born	16 May 1895	City	Chicago	County	Cook	State	Illinois
Died		City	Chicago	County	Cook	State	Illinois
Buried		City	Hillside	County	Cook	State	Illinois
Father	William Henry Rice			Born		Died	
Mother	Minnie Ophelia Barker			Born		Died	
Other husbands							

SEX M/F	CHILDREN (List each child in order of birth (whether living or dead).)	Date	City	County	State	SPOUSE
M	Morris	Born 10 Feb 1916	Chicago	Cook	IL	1st Marie Hines
		Married				2nd Jean Simmons
		Died				
M	Leonard	Born 27 July 1918	Chicago	Cook	IL	1st Gladys Hamilton
		Married				2nd
		Died				
M	Elmer	Born 5 Oct 1919	Chicago	Cook	IL	1st Maryellen Banks
		Married 2 Jul 1947				2nd
		Died				
F	Irene June	Born 11 Apr 1921	Chicago	Cook	IL	1st Claude Davis
		Married				2nd
		Died	Woodland Hills	Los Angeles	CA	
5		Born				1st
		Married				2nd
		Died				
6		Born				1st
		Married				2nd
		Died				
7		Born				1st
		Married				2nd
		Died				
8		Born				1st
		Married				2nd
		Died				

Date prepared: 10 Feb 1976
Prepared by: Tony Burroughs

Family Group Sheet with Dates—Family Group Sheet for the family of Asa Morris and Alma Burroughs, with dates of birth, death, and marriage added.

your relatives for the missing areas. When you contact them, have your tape recorder handy. Asking a simple question like "Where was Uncle Bob born?" may lead to a half-hour discussion. If your tape is not rolling, you may miss a valuable story. I have learned that if you don't record an interview the first time and are lucky enough to get the story the second time around, it will not be the same. It will not have the same enthusiasm, excitement, or interest as the original interview. After you finish, type the interview and date it. This is treated as a follow-up interview. It should be viewed as a separate interview from your other ones even though it may be only a one- or two-sentence statement and even though it may come the day after your first interview.

You should fill out two Family Group Sheets for most of your relatives and ancestors, one as a child and another as a parent. For example, your mother would appear on one Family Group Sheet listing her and your father as parents of the household. Their children would be listed on the same Family Group Sheet in chronological order. Your mother would also appear on a second Family Group Sheet as a child, listed with her brothers and sisters and your grandparents as her mother and father. If you don't know an ancestor's parents, you should still list him or her on a Family Group Sheet as a child. The space for the parents' names should be left blank. Then when you locate one of the parents, enter it on the appropriate line.

So check all the ancestors who had children and make sure they are recorded on two Family Group Sheets. After these are filled out, you will have blank spaces on some of the lines. This is where your future genealogical research will focus. Your mission is to locate the data to fill in all of these lines on each of your Family Group Sheets. As you search for this information, it will give you additional details about the family and their surroundings.

Documentation

Now comes the most important part of being a good genealogist, documenting where you found the information you've gathered. It's really a simple task. When you gather information, write down where you got it. The information might come from a book, from a newspaper, from a microfilm, or from the "horse's mouth." Well, maybe not literally. But if the information came from an interview, state whom you interviewed, when you interviewed her, where you interviewed her (or if the interview was on the telephone), if you have a transcript, and where the transcript is located. If the information came from your personal knowledge, it should be included in your autobiography, which would be listed as a source.

After you record the vital information on your Family Group Sheet, record the sources of that information. If the information is gathered from an interview with Alma Burroughs on 4 December 1975, that source and date should be footnoted in the same manner as in a term paper. Place a small superscript number at the top of the line and record the explanation at the bottom of the page, on the back of the Family Group Sheet, or on a separate sheet attached to the Family Group Sheet. If you have formalized your interviews and transcribed and dated your tapes, this information will be at your fingertips. Those of you who have already started and have not named and dated your interviews, go back and do it. Check your old calendars, datebooks, and notes and come up with a date. If you can't remember an exact date, estimate one. It might be December 1988 or the Summer of 1995.

The goals of proper source citation are to use the best possible sources and to direct others to your sources. For example, stating "An interview with Grandma" is not enough for another genealogist to locate the information. However, if the citation reads "Personal interview with

Family Group Sheet

FATHER *Asa Morris Burroughs*

	Date	City	County		State
Born	26 Jan 1893	Chicago	Cook		Illinois
Married	7 Jan 1915	Chicago	Cook		Illinois
Died	22 Dec 1971	Chicago	Cook		Illinois
Buried	28 Dec 1971	Hillside	Cook		Illinois

			Born		Died
Father	Morris Burroughs		CA 1864		15 Dec 1903
Mother	Mary Jane Little Williams		11 Jan 1870		14 Apr 1914

Other wives

MOTHER *Alma Irene Rice*

	Date	City	County		State
Born	16 May 1895	Chicago	Cook		Illinois
Died		Chicago	Cook		Illinois
Buried		Hillside	Cook		Illinois

			Born		Died
Father	William Henry Rice				
Mother	Minnie Ophelia Barker				

Other husbands

SEX M/F	CHILDREN List each child in order of birth (whether living or dead)		Date	City	County	State	SPOUSE
M	Morris	Born	10 Feb 1916	Chicago	Cook	IL	1st Marie Hines
		Married					2nd Jean Simmons
		Died					
M	Leonard	Born	27 July 1918	Chicago	Cook	IL	1st Gladys Hamilton
		Married					2nd
		Died					
M	Elmer	Born	5 Oct 1919	Chicago	Cook	IL	1st Mary Lou Banks
		Married	2 Jul 1947				2nd
		Died					
F	Irene June	Born	11 Apr 1921	Chicago	Cook	IL	1st Claude Davis
		Married					2nd
		Died		Woodland Hills Los Angeles		CA	
5		Born					1st
		Married					2nd
		Died					
6		Born					1st
		Married					2nd
		Died					
7		Born					1st
		Married					2nd
		Died					
8		Born					1st
		Married					2nd
		Died					

See documentation sheet.

Date prepared: *10 Feb 1976*
Prepared by: *Tony Burroughs*

Family Group Sheet with Footnotes—Family Group Sheet for the family of Asa Morris and Alma Burroughs, with footnotes tracking sources of the names, dates, and places.

Mrs. Alma Burroughs by Tony Burroughs on 4 December 1975 at home of Mrs. Burroughs (505 E. 60th St., Chicago, IL). Transcript in possession of Tony Burroughs (P.O. Box 53091, Chicago, IL). Mrs. Burroughs is now deceased," another genealogist will know who was inter-

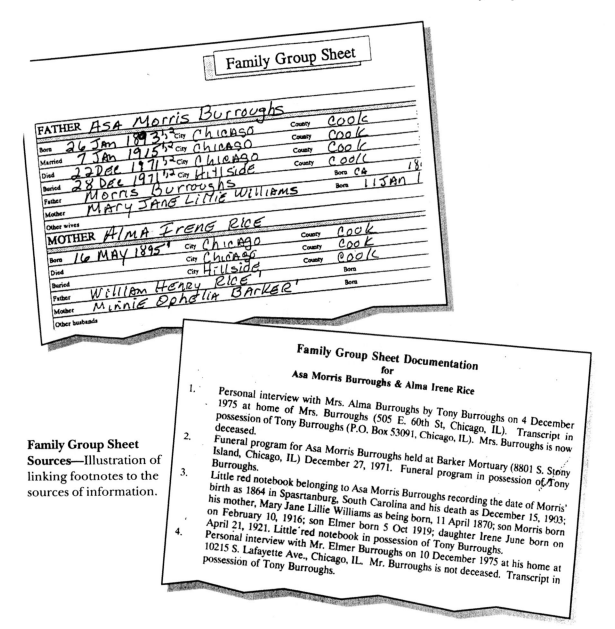

Family Group Sheet Sources—Illustration of linking footnotes to the sources of information.

The handwritten Family Group Sheet reads:

FATHER ASA Morris Burroughs — County Cook
Born 26 Jan 1893 City Chicago County Cook
Married 7 Jan 1915 City Chicago County Cook
Died 22 Dec 1971 City Chicago County Cook
Buried 28 Dec 1971 City Hillside Born CA
Father Morris Burroughs Born 11 Jan
Mother Mary Jane Lillie Williams
Other wives

MOTHER Alma Irene Rice County Cook
Born 16 May 1895 City Chicago County Cook
Died City Chicago County Cook
Buried City Hillside Born
Father William Henry Rice Born
Mother Minnie Ophelia Barker
Other husbands

Family Group Sheet Documentation
for
Asa Morris Burroughs & Alma Irene Rice

1. Personal interview with Mrs. Alma Burroughs by Tony Burroughs on 4 December 1975 at home of Mrs. Burroughs (505 E. 60th St, Chicago, IL). Transcript in possession of Tony Burroughs (P.O. Box 53091, Chicago, IL). Mrs. Burroughs is now deceased.

2. Funeral program for Asa Morris Burroughs held at Barker Mortuary (8801 S. Stony Island, Chicago, IL) December 27, 1971. Funeral program in possession of Tony Burroughs.

3. Little red notebook belonging to Asa Morris Burroughs recording the date of Morris' birth as 1864 in Spasrtanburg, South Carolina and his death as December 15, 1903; his mother, Mary Jane Lillie Williams as being born, 11 April 1870; son Morris born on February 10, 1916; son Elmer born 5 Oct 1919; daughter Irene June born on April 21, 1921. Little red notebook in possession of Tony Burroughs.

4. Personal interview with Mr. Elmer Burroughs on 10 December 1975 at his home at 10215 S. Lafayette Ave., Chicago, IL. Mr. Burroughs is not deceased. Transcript in possession of Tony Burroughs.

viewed, when and where the subject was interviewed, the location of the transcript, and a contact person who has a copy of the transcript. Always think in terms of others who do not know the information—do you provide enough information for them to duplicate your research to prove your findings, or come up with different conclusions?

The best possible evidence means as close to the original as possible. We talked earlier about primary and secondary records, primary being original records and secondary being derivative works, essentially everything else. If records are indexed, don't cite the index; cite the original source. Of course, that means after you search an index, you have to examine the original source. If original records have been microfilmed and the original is not accessible, cite the microfilm copy. If records are transcribed and published in a book, search for copies of the originals. A transcript could contain a transcription error or misreading of the records. If you locate a record on the Internet, search for the originals and cite the originals, not the Internet.

The description of your sources will be too lengthy to be placed at the bottom of the Family Group Sheet. Therefore I recommend placing them either on the reverse side of the sheet or on a separate note sheet that remains with that Family Group Sheet. If you choose to record footnotes on a separate sheet, title the documentation page with the names of the parents it belongs to at the top, as a heading. Then write a note in the note section on the Family Group Sheet to refer to the separate documentation sheet.

These footnotes and sources are called your *documentation.* Documentation serves several purposes. If a discrepancy occurs in the future, and it will, you will know the sources of the conflicting data. After you get conflicting data, you will have to determine the correct facts. As in a court of law, you will have to look at the evidence and determine if one record is more valid than another record. At times you will have several different records either all saying something different or some supporting one date and others supporting opposing dates. The point to stress here is that your goal at this point is not to determine which pieces of evidence are valid but to be sure that the sources of each bit of information are recorded. Validity will be judged at a later date, which will be covered in a later chapter.

At some time in the future, you may want to consult a source again. If the information is properly documented, you should have no trouble rechecking it. If you're discussing your genealogy with a fellow researcher, you can easily refer him or her to the same source if needed. This documentation will also be needed if you want to publish your research in the future or if you want to apply to a lineage, hereditary, or patriotic society. These organizations consist of genealogists who can trace their lineage to a particular ancestor and members of an event, such as the American Revolution.

If someone wants to evaluate or critique your research or if someone wants to start researching where you stopped, this documentation will prove invaluable. At some point in the future, you may want to hire a consultant or a professional genealogist to conduct research or to help you solve a major problem. The genealogist will ask where you got the information listed on your Family Group Sheets, as well as what sources you consulted.

The last reason for documenting your sources is a personal one. Are the names, dates, and places on your Family Group Sheets assumptions and opinions, or are they the results of hard, honest research that someone else can duplicate? If you never cite any sources, it appears that your words are either merely your opinion, information you fabricated, or a display of unprofessionalism. When you put something on paper, your words should be believed, trusted, respected, and relied upon. If citations are done properly, they will be—if not, you will be the laughing-stock of the genealogy community. Citing sources enhances your credibility and reliability.

There are several guides to citing genealogical sources and evaluating evidence. *Evidence: Citation and Analysis for the Family Historian* was written by Elizabeth Shown Mills, a certified genealogist and past president of the Board of Certification of Genealogists. Another useful book is *Cite Your Sources: A Manual for Documenting Family Histories and Genealogical Records,* by Richard S. Lackey. These and other useful books, articles, and pamphlets are listed in the Bibliography.

You may want to keep both a permanent and a working Family Group Sheet. When information is updated and verified, the old information should be crossed out on the working copy. The new facts should be written above the old. After the information is updated, analysis can be performed years later on the original Family Group Sheet. Then prepare a permanent Family Group Sheet. This sheet can be kept neat and clean or printed from a computer program.

Collateral Ancestors

When you're having trouble locating records for your direct ancestors, you can often find records on their brothers and sisters. Since these are not your direct ancestors, we refer to them as "collateral ancestors." They are the key to overcoming stumbling blocks. Usually some siblings leave more records than others. You don't know which sibling is going to leave the most records or have the best clues to their parents until you search them all. Out of three brothers, one may have been a writer, extroverted, and a very public person. His brother may have been very shy, introverted, and private. Another one may have gotten in trouble all the time and been in and out of jail. Each one of these siblings will have left different kinds of records, though each one had the same parents.

Since siblings were also born at different times, the family may have moved or their economic or employment situation may have changed between the births of the children. Therefore, the data contained in the records of each sibling may yield different information about the family in general and about the parents in particular. *In many cases, the records of a parent ancestor are found* only *among the records of a brother or sister of your direct ancestor.*

Cousins

Thinking about collateral ancestors brings up the subject of cousins. When researching family history, we often hear phrases like "She is your cousin" or "He was your grandfather's cousin." Ordinarily we might assume the person referred to is a first cousin, but that might not be the case. If you assume that the person is a first cousin, you may have difficulty locating a common grandfather. It may never occur to you that this person might be a second cousin, a third cousin, a first cousin once removed, or not related at all, merely a friend of the family.

Out of respect for older people, African American families often refer to them as aunt, uncle, and sometimes cousin, whether they are or not. Relatives usually know who their first cousins are—the children of their aunts and uncles, which means they have the same grand-parents. However, all other cousins are usually referred to as second cousins, even though relatives might not know how they're related.

The term *second cousin* refers to a distinct relationship between members of the family, as do *first cousin once removed, first cousin twice removed,* and *second cousin once removed.* Second cousins are the children of first cousins. Similarly, third cousins are the children of second cousins, which means they are the grandchildren of first cousins. First cousin once removed is the relationship between a first cousin and the child of a first cousin.

Perhaps the best way to understand these relationships is to see them on a chart. Substitute your name in the appropriate space to determine who your cousins are. To figure out relationships of other relatives, substitute their names in spaces and then add children, brothers, sisters, aunts, uncles, or grandparents to see how others are related.

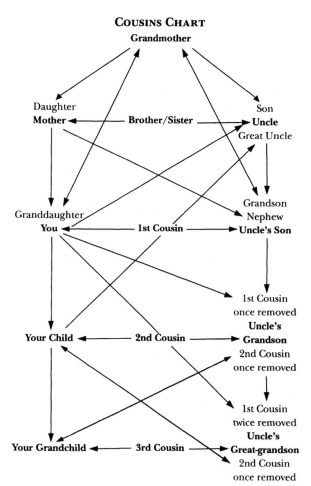

COUSINS CHART

Cousins Chart—A diagram showing family relationships, particularly the differences between first, second, and third cousins and cousins removed. To determine relationships in your family, substitute known parents, siblings, and children in the respective spaces.

It's good to understand these technical relationships, but I'm not sure I'd go into detail explaining it to nongenealogists. It gets complicated, and most relatives probably do not want to be bothered. At a family reunion genealogist Saundra Brown told one relative she was a first cousin once removed. The relative got insulted and smarted back, "Don't remove me from the family."

! Trap: Not keeping genealogy charts up to date.

So extract the vital information from your oral interviews and family papers. Enter them onto your Family Group Sheets. Fill out a separate Family Group Sheet for each family unit. Footnote the source of each item of information. From here your objective is to try to fill in all the blanks on your Family Group Sheets and keep them up to date!

Things To Do #4—Things To do sheet, adding items to complete genealogy charts.

The Pedigree Chart

The only dog I ever owned was a playful little mutt. He chewed up everything in the house before I could train him, and he didn't last very long. I've always admired pedigreed dogs for their beauty, distinctiveness, and personality. A pedigreed dog is one that has a family tree and whose ancestors have supposedly not mated with dogs of other breeds. I don't know why they don't call them thoroughbreds.

The second major chart in genealogy is the Pedigree Chart. Some genealogists despise the term "Pedigree Chart" because of the dog implications. I think they also despise it because in the early days genealogists were very snobbish and thought that genealogy was worthwhile only for those who came from nobility and hence could claim a royal or pure pedigree. I've never thought of the dog connotation and also realize that the world is made up of common folks as well as descendants of kings and queens. So I don't let the term bother me and I don't think you should let it bother you.

The Pedigree Chart in genealogy traces your direct bloodline backward. The word *pedigree* means a list of ancestors or a record of ancestors. *Pedigreed* means having a known or recorded pedigree or list of ancestors. The Pedigree Chart in genealogy is sometimes referred to as an ancestor chart or a family tree chart. The latter is a generic term, and I've seen dozens of different formats for family tree charts, so genealogists don't use the term.

Pedigree Charts keep your genealogy research focused. You can sometimes become distracted by dozens and often hundreds of names. There will be brothers, sisters, aunts, uncles, cousins, in-laws, and friends of the family. The Pedigree Chart organizes all these relatives and ancestors and shows direct blood lineages to distant ancestors. Many genealogists begin with a Pedigree Chart instead of a Family Group Sheet, think it is more important, and hence place more emphasis on it. I think that is a critical error. Once researchers place more emphasis on the Pedigree Chart, they focus on how far they can go back on the chart. They also focus on how quickly they can go back. That's when they lose sight of the brothers and sisters of their ancestors, who are just as important as their direct ancestors. That's why I emphasize the Family Group Sheet. Remember, you don't know which of the brothers or sisters will leave important clues about their parents, and they all have the same parents.

The Pedigree Chart looks like a reversed tennis or basketball tournament seeding chart. It includes spaces for your name, your parents' names, and all of their parents' parents' names

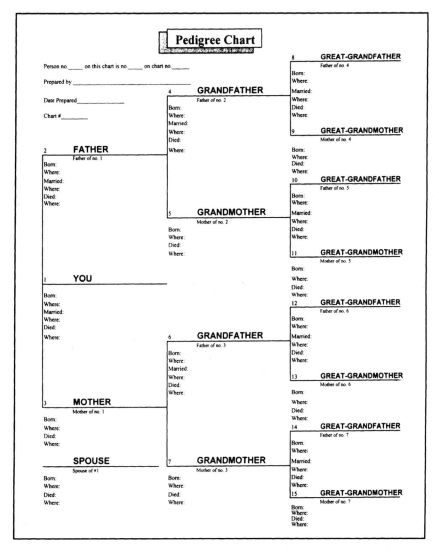

Pedigree Chart—Sample Pedigree Chart indicating which ancestors go in which position. Pedigree charts trace a person's bloodline backward.

(i.e., grandparents, great-grandparents, great-great-grandparents, and so on). The Pedigree Chart does not include any of your brothers, sisters, aunts, uncles, or cousins. They are recorded on Family Group Sheets.

Begin by filling out the identifying information in the upper left corner of the page. Since this is your first Pedigree Chart, fill in the blanks so that the first line reads, "Person no. 1 on this chart is no. 1 on chart no. 1." On the next lines, write in your name, the day's date, and Chart #1.

You will use names, dates, and places from your Family Group Sheets to fill out the Pedigree Chart. Since you are the first link in your family history, the Pedigree Chart begins with you. Record your first, middle, and last names in position number 1 on the left side of the chart. Record your father's name in position number 2 above your name. His father's name goes above and to the right. This is continued in the same order until all the fathers' names are recorded above and to the right of their children.

In a similar fashion, record your mother's name in position number 3, below your name. Record her mother's name in position number 7, below and to the right of her daughter's name. This continues in the same order until all the mothers are recorded below and to the right of their children and below their husbands' names. If you are married, your spouse's name goes in the bottom left corner for identification purposes. Your spouse is not in the bloodline of your ancestors.

Once you get names recorded you can often see naming patterns in the family. It is interesting to observe middle names in addition to first names. My middle name, Preston, came from my grandfather, Preston Brooks. Some patterns you will not be able to see because everyone on your chart will not be the firstborn child. Firstborn sons are sometimes named for their fathers or grandfathers.

Now record dates and places of birth, marriage, and death. Remember to use military style dates and to include the name of the county, in parenthesis, after the city. As in the Family Group Sheets, leave spaces blank for whatever information you don't know.

I don't recommend footnoting the Pedigree Chart because the Family Group Sheets are documented with sources. However, in her book *Evidence: Citation and Analysis for the Family Historian*, Elizabeth Shown Mills recommends footnoting Pedigree Charts. I think it's double work, but she brings up a good point. If you ever give out a copy of your Pedigree Chart without documented Family Group Sheets, the receiver will not know where the information came from. My solution is to include Family Group Sheets with any Pedigree Chart you send out.

After you complete the four generations, the fifth and subsequent generations are recorded on other Pedigree Charts. These are linked by numbering the charts. The first Pedigree Chart is number 1 and the second is number 2. The first chart is referenced on the second chart. In the example, my paternal grandmother told me about her grandmother, Fannie Barker, who is my great-great-grandmother. I continued the first Pedigree Chart onto the second one by starting over with my great-grandmother, Minnie Ophelia Barker. She's number 11 on the first Pedigree Chart but became number 1 on the second Pedigree Chart. I referenced the original Pedigree Chart at the top of the second by filling in the blanks, "Person no. 1 on this chart is no. 11 on chart no. 1." Then I wrote her mother's name, Fannie Barker, in position number 3.

This way all charts are on 8½″ × 11″ paper. They all can be neatly filed and retrieved for analysis and research. If you try to place all generations on one sheet of paper, it will become large and unwieldy or you will not be able to record all the vital data needed for analysis and research. You can purchase a large chart to place on your wall for display purposes.

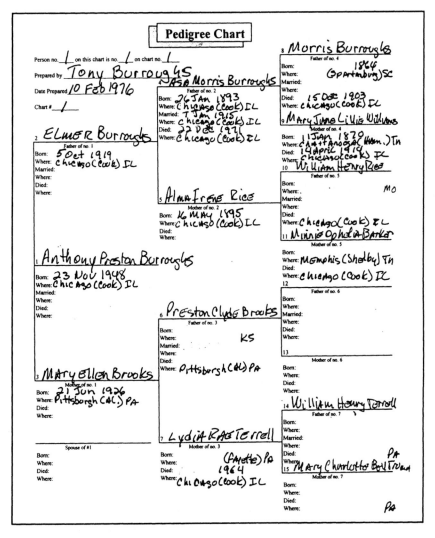

Completed Pedigree Chart—Pedigree Chart #1, filled in with names, dates, and places of birth, death, and marriage—the same information on the Family Group Sheet.

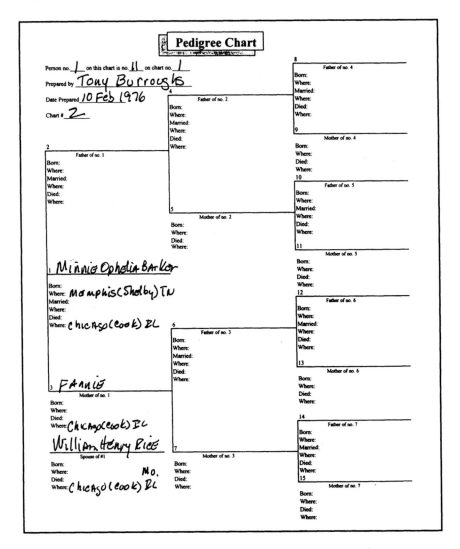

Pedigree Chart

Person no. _1_ on this chart is no. _11_ on chart no. _1_

Prepared by _Tony Burroughs_

Date Prepared _10 Feb 1976_

Chart # _2_

Father of no. 1
Born:
Where:
Married:
Where:
Died:
Where:

1 _Minnie Ophelia Barker_
Born:
Where: _Memphis (Shelby) TN_
Married:
Where:
Died:
Where: _Chicago (Cook) IL_

3 _Fannie_
Mother of no. 1
Born:
Where:
Died:
Where: _Chicago (Cook) IL_

William Henry Rice
Spouse of #1
Born:
Where: _Mo._
Died:
Where: _Chicago (Cook) IL_

4   Father of no. 2
Born:
Where:
Married:
Where:
Died:
Where:

5   Mother of no. 2
Born:
Where:
Died:
Where:

6   Father of no. 3
Born:
Where:
Married:
Where:
Died:
Where:

7   Mother of no. 3
Born:
Where:
Died:
Where:

8   Father of no. 4
Born:
Where:
Married:
Where:
Died:
Where:

9   Mother of no. 4
Born:
Where:
Died:
Where:

10   Father of no. 5
Born:
Where:
Married:
Where:
Died:
Where:

11   Mother of no. 5
Born:
Where:
Died:
Where:

12   Father of no. 6
Born:
Where:
Married:
Where:
Died:
Where:

13   Mother of no. 6
Born:
Where:
Died:
Where:

14   Father of no. 7
Born:
Where:
Married:
Where:
Died:
Where:

15   Mother of no. 7
Born:
Where:
Died:
Where:

Pedigree Continuation—Pedigree Chart #2, which continues from person #11 on Pedigree Chart #1.

Blank spaces and gaps immediately tell you what information is lacking. That's where your research should focus. Update your chart as soon as you get new information to fill in the blanks and keep it up to date. As I stated in the previous chapter, one of the big traps genealogists fall into is not keeping their charts up to date—that includes both Family Group Sheets and Pedigree Charts.

You should fill in all the gaps for the children before pursuing their parents. It's difficult to do because there is a natural tendency to research the next generation as soon as you get a name. But with only a name, you do not have enough information to research the ancestor. Pursuing as much information as you can about the children will give you a stronger foundation for pursuing the parents. Clues to the parents lie in their children. For example, once you know where a child was born, you immediately know where the parents were living at the time.

This Pedigree Chart is very important. It should remain with your research all of your genealogical career. If someone else is going to assist you with your research, the first question he or she may ask is "Can I look at your Pedigree Chart?" When you are researching, you will refer to it on a regular basis.

Genealogy charts can be purchased from genealogy supply companies and from some libraries and archives. I recommend using acid-free charts to preserve your research as you create it.

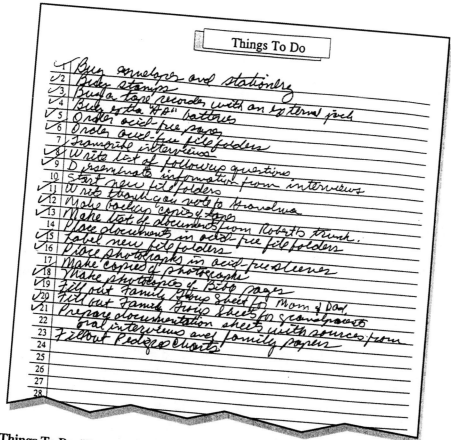

Things To Do #5—Things To Do sheet indicating completed items checked off and adding item to complete the Pedigree Chart.

Records in Cemeteries

Cemeteries as sources for genealogical information are often overlooked by beginning genealogists. The cemetery is the final resting place for our ancestors. It is the next venue we should visit after interviewing relatives and researching family papers. Many people have not been to the cemetery since their relatives passed away. Some people visit the cemetery on Memorial Day, Veterans Day, or on the birthdays of their deceased spouses or parents. Some people are even afraid to go into cemeteries. However, once you start visiting cemeteries for genealogical research, you'll find that many of them are very beautiful and serene places. And they can be an excellent place to learn of ancestors you never knew about. That's what happened to me.

After talking with my parents and grandmother about the family's history and seeing all the photographs and family documents, I was fired up! I was eager to visit Oakridge Cemetery, where my grandfather is buried. I was not living in Chicago in 1971 when he died, so I had no idea what the cemetery was like.

It was a long drive to Hillside, Illinois, a suburb west of Chicago. I arrived at the office and gave the clerk the names of my grandfather and his parents, who were buried there. She pulled out a large ledger and showed me the list of names entered for two different lots my family owned. Each had a diagram of the graves and indicated which ones had gravestones. She then gave me a map to show where the grave site was located and how I'd recognize the section when I got there. I then drove along the winding road inside the cemetery and located it near the rear of the cemetery, close to the fence.

I saw the flat two-toned gray headstone for my grandfather, which merely stated "Asa M. Burroughs 1894–1971." I thought about his life and what I remembered about him when I was a kid, in addition to the things I had learned about his legal

Oakridge Ledger—Sexton record from Oakridge Cemetery for the Burroughs family lot.

career from his funeral program. Close to his stone was one for my grandmother's mother, "Minnie Rice 1875–1949." I was only a baby when she died, and Grandma mentioned her only briefly.

Having learned we had two family lots from cemetery deeds and correspondence saved by my grandfather, I sought out the second lot, which was closer to the road, only a few steps away. I was quite surprised to see a large granite stone, pinkish in color, about three feet high, for my great-grandfather and another great-grandmother, Morris and Mary Jane Lillie Burroughs. It read "Burroughs" at the top, and on the face "Father: Morris 1864–1903" and "Mother: Mary J. L. 1870–1914." I realized the words "father" and "mother" had come from my grandfather, who bought the stone.

These were two ancestors I had never known and had learned about only through genealogical research. After researching their lives and seeing photographs of them, I was emotional being at their grave site, knowing their remains were a few feet underground. It was as if I had made another connection and we were communicating. I thought about the challenges they'd overcome and thought they were probably thanking me for uncovering their past and telling their descendants (and the public) about them.

After paying homage to my ancestors, I drove back to the office and asked the clerk for a copy of the record in the large ledger. At first she balked at photocopying the pages because

Asa Morris Stone—Gravestone for author's grandfather Asa Morris Burroughs.

Burroughs Stone—Gravestone straddling graves of author's great-grandparents, Morris and Mary Jane Lillie Burroughs, in Oakridge Cemetery.

of the unwieldy size. I looked at it and showed her how the book could be turned and the posts taken out in order to make it easier to photocopy. She realized it would take only a couple of minutes. She smiled and said it was no problem. When she returned, I examined the record more closely. This time I saw the listing for my grandfather's brother, Robert Burroughs. I realized he did not have a headstone. But I noticed there were other names, also without markers, I did not recognize—Malchias Williams, age twenty-two, interred June 15, 1905; Georgia Martin, age thirty-four, interred June 15, 1905; Martha Williams, age forty-seven, interred June 15, 1905; and Bertha Lewis, age fifteen months, interred January 26, 1911.

I asked the clerk about them, and she said there was no relationship listed or other information. So there was no way of telling who they were.

I drove home wondering who these people were. I showed the list to my father; he said he didn't have a clue as to who they were. He told me to ask my grandmother. I then showed the list to her and she said she had no idea who they were. Naturally, I was perplexed. I wanted to know who all these individuals were who were buried in our family cemetery lot, and I was determined to find out. I went on a mission. It wasn't until I did more genealogical research that I began to unravel the mystery and identify the individuals.

I began getting death certificates and census records, which I'll cover later. Slowly I began to identify the names on the list. I found out Martha Williams was Mary Jane Lillie (Williams) Burroughs's mother. She was my grandfather's grandmother and my great-great-grandmother! I was stunned. Malchias Williams was Mary's brother, my grandfather's uncle. Georgia Martin was Mrs. Georgia (Williams) Martin, Mary's sister and my grandfather's aunt. These were Mary's relatives—my ancestors. They all died before my father was born, even before my grandmother met my grandfather. And my grandfather did not leave a record of them in his little red book. His grandmother died when he was only seven years old, and his aunt and uncle died when he was six years old. He had very little memory of them, if any, and there was no oral history to bring their names down to other family members. Here they were, buried in the family cemetery lot, right where they were supposed to be, and none of their descendants knew who they were. It was a very sad feeling. (Incidentally, I still don't know who Bertha Lewis is, but I'm on her trail.)

So you need to visit each cemetery where your ancestors are buried. Request copies of all the cemetery's records. I also suggest taking older relatives to the family cemetery and doing another interview in the cemetery. Reminiscing about the people buried in the cemetery and looking over the area will stimulate old memories. Have your tape recorder with you so you can record these spontaneous stories.

I also thought about the three people who were interred on the same day, June 15, 1905. I had figured they had died in an accident or from an epidemic. Several ancestors died of tuberculosis, which is highly contagious. It was the leading cause of death at the turn of the century. However, after I began receiving death certificates, I realized they did not all die on the same day. That's why you have to be very careful with cemetery records. They record the date of interment, not the date of death.

The date of interment versus the date of death cannot be taken lightly. They can be far apart. In northern cities that get severe winter weather, grave diggers could not penetrate the frozen ground. Bodies were stored in receiving vaults until the spring thaw. So the severity of the weather sometimes determined when the remains were put into the ground. With modern technology that problem no longer exists, and most receiving vaults have been destroyed.

Coffin plates were placed on the front of caskets so grave diggers could identify them. Once the remains were interred, the coffin plate was given to the family. I had one of these for years before my friend Helen Sclair explained what it was. Everyone calls Helen "The

Cemetery Lady" because she researches only cemeteries. She's not a genealogist. The coffin plate was silver metal with a ribbed border and had the following inscription:

Morris Burroughs
Died Dec. 15, 1903
Aged 39 years

I found out my ancestors had been reinterred in Oakridge Cemetery on June 15, 1905, from Forest Home Cemetery in Forest Park, closer to Chicago. After analyzing the dates of death and interment and Mary's cemetery deeds, I figured out what had happened. After Mary's husband, Morris, died in 1903, she bought a cemetery lot in the newer Oakridge Cemetery, farther out from the city. After burying her husband, she had her other relatives disinterred from Forest Home Cemetery and reinterred in the newer Oakridge Cemetery so the family would all be together. Forest Home Cemetery opened in 1873, and it may have been difficult to get a cemetery lot for all the family members. Even though Oakridge was a little farther from the city, it was only four years old in 1905 and undoubtedly had more space. Price and competition between the two cemeteries may also have played a role in the change.

I then went to Forest Home Cemetery and checked for records of the original interments. When I got copies of their records, I realized Georgia Martin was actually *Mrs.* Georgia Martin, Mary's sister. So be very careful in analyzing records in the cemetery.

Determining the Cemetery

Use your filled-out Family Group Sheets as your guide. Try to determine the cemetery where every deceased person on each of your Family Group Sheets is buried. Then contact each cemetery, even if you know when the ancestor died and even if you have already visited the cemetery for the ancestor's burial. You were probably not there for genealogical research.

If you do not know the cemetery, you'll have to conduct research to determine it. First ask your relatives. If they don't know, seek out friends of the deceased. Also ask the minister of the church if he or she is still around. If you know what funeral home handled the burial, check with them. If the funeral home has a record of the funeral, they can tell you which cemetery your ancestor is buried in. (I'll discuss funeral homes in the next chapter.) While you were uncovering family records, if you located an obituary, funeral program, or death certificate, the name of the cemetery should be listed on one or all of those.

If you still don't know the name of the cemetery where your ancestor is buried, there are several other steps you can take to ascertain it. Determine the ancestor's religion. Many churches had cemeteries, and many people were buried according to religious custom. For example, Catholics were rarely buried in non-Catholic cemeteries. Military veterans were sometimes buried in veterans' cemeteries, not with their families.

If the death was in a small town, you can often guess the name of the cemetery. There may be only one or two cemeteries in town anyway. Even in large cities, during segregation there were usually a limited number of cemeteries that buried African Americans. You can often contact the African American churches in the town where your ancestor lived. The ministers at the churches conduct last rites at burials and know the cemeteries in town. If the ancestor died in the North but was born in the South, his or her remains may have been shipped back South. For this reason many African Americans are not buried in the city where they died.

Segregation

During segregation, most African Americans were buried in all-Black cemeteries. When I go to a city where an ancestor died, I ask other African Americans the names of the Black cemeteries in town. Once you contact one Black cemetery, the employees there can tell you the names of the other ones in town. My own search took me to an African American cemetery in Spartanburg, South Carolina. The name of the cemetery was the Colored Cemetery. I soon discovered there were two African American cemeteries in Spartanburg, both named the Colored Cemetery.

However, this is not an ironclad rule. Blacks were buried not only in cemeteries owned by African Americans. During some time periods they were buried in "colored" sections of white-owned cemeteries. If there is not a "colored" cemetery in town, researchers should look to white cemeteries and inquire about the "colored" section or "colored" burials. Sometimes employees won't admit there is a "colored" section, but the records will often reveal this fact.

Abandoned Cemeteries

RIP. I had seen these initials associated with gravestones and cemeteries for a long time and wondered what they meant. One day a light went off and I realized they meant "Rest in Peace." If that's what you think happens when you're buried, think again.

When I first encountered an abandoned cemetery, I was quite shocked. I was relatively new to genealogy, and my knowledge of cemeteries consisted of tall and short monuments of stone, beautiful green lawns, winding roads, tall trees, beautiful flowers, and sometimes lakes and ducks, even swans. That a place of dignity and reverence could become abandoned and not recognizable as a cemetery never entered my mind. But my sense of history was also somewhat naive, and I hadn't thought in real terms about what happens when populations expand, people migrate, and buildings take over what used to be vacant land. I soon learned our oldest cemeteries are being forgotten, abandoned, and reused to build highways, homes, shopping malls, and country clubs.

Greenlane Cemetery—Brownsville, Pennsylvania

On one of my early genealogy trips east, I visited an old cemetery in Brownsville, Pennsylvania. It's a small town on the east bank of the Monongahela River, about twenty-five miles south of Pittsburgh. Brownsville was settled in the late 1700s and was incorporated in 1817. I don't think the cemetery is nearly that old, but when I came to it I wouldn't have known it was a cemetery unless someone had told me. Called Greenlane Cemetery, it resembled a forest more than a cemetery. The weeds had grown so tall they were mistaken for trees by most folks. You needed a pitchfork to see any broken gravestones that had long since fallen down. It had long been abandoned.

I had a difficult time navigating through the weeds and sticker bugs, but I managed to find a few old stones that belonged to some of my ancestors. One was a Civil War veteran in the Massachusetts 55th Volunteer Infantry, Thomas Sorrell. The Massachusetts 55th was created when the Massachusetts 54th was filled. You may recall that the Massachusetts 54th was the all-Black army regiment that was depicted in the film *Glory*, starring Denzel Washington. It wasn't the first regiment of African Americans to serve in the Civil War, but it was the first one authorized by Congress. The 54th gets so much publicity that few people have heard of the 55th, which fought in some of the same engagements.

A colleague of mine, former Ambassador Ronald Palmer, published a list of the African Americans buried in the cemetery who had served in the Civil War (see the chapter "Going to the Library" for details on his list and others). The list had previously been published in the *Uniontown Herald-Standard* newspaper by Paul Sunyak. There were twenty-four African Americans from the cemetery on the list. I'm not sure if they all had gravestones because the list came from the Local Veterans Administration. However, they were all eligible for free military markers from the VA because of their military service. That day was a real eye opener for me about what can happen when descendants move away, and neglect and poverty move in.

Mount Forest—South Holland, Illinois

The South Suburban Genealogical and Historical Society in South Holland, Illinois, transcribes interments in small cemeteries in the suburbs south of Chicago. One of the cemeteries they transcribed was an abandoned African American cemetery named Mount Forest. They were nice enough to give me a list of names from the interments. Abandoned cemeteries are maintained by the Cook County Forest Preserve, and that's what it looks like. I went by there one fall, and the only way you could tell it was a cemetery was the indentations for each grave. Leaves fell from the trees and seemed to settle only on the sunken graves.

The cemetery opened in 1909 on two and a half acres of land. There were only twenty-three stones with legible names on them, the earliest dated 1910. However, county records indicate there were fifty lot owners, and undoubtedly many people were buried in single graves without markers. The last lot was purchased in 1947, but the bulk of the burials were done by 1930.

Freedmen's Park—Dallas, Texas

In 1990 construction crews were excavating to expand the Central Expressway in Dallas, Texas, when they struck bones. Archaeologists were brought in, and they uncovered more than 1,100 graves in a five-acre cemetery of former slaves—the largest such find in the United States at the time. Half of the graves were for children.

The cemetery was dedicated in 1869, but burials appear to date from 1861. At that time the place was called Freementown, a village of former slaves on their road to independence. The cemetery was closed in 1925. As in many African American burial grounds, many of the graves do not have traditional markers. The cemetery fell into disrepair and was neglected for decades, until no one remembered it was a cemetery anymore. A highway was built through part of the land in the 1940s, and the city of Dallas turned the remaining area into a park in 1965.

Even though traditional gravestones were not found, archaeologists did uncover the outlines of sheared-off wooden markers and artifacts for traditional Black burials, such as seashells, bottles, and personal effects. Many of these have been placed in the African American Museum in Fair Park in Dallas. The excavated remains of 1,513 African Americans were reinterred in another cemetery. The remaining land was designated a historic site by the city of Dallas and the Texas Historical Commission, and a memorial sculpture was designed by an African American, David Newton, and built on the site in 1998.

Washington Park Cemetery—St. Louis, Missouri

Established in the 1920s, Washington Park Cemetery was the largest cemetery for African Americans in St. Louis, Missouri. Families were able to use homemade gravestones until the 1980s, when only granite was permitted.

When the St. Louis Lambert Field Airport underwent renovation and expansion in 1993, the MetroLink light-rail transportation system wanted to connect the airport to downtown St. Louis. Washington Park Cemetery was in the way. A court order approved moving the remains of 2,200 people to two white-owned, previously segregated cemeteries instead of the African American–owned cemetery in town. This raised a lot of controversy, and the owner of the African American cemetery filed suit for violation of his civil rights. However, he abandoned his own cemetery and lost it when the St. Louis County Circuit Court appointed a receiver for it in 1999.

South Carolina

Among the worst cases I've heard about concern some of the oldest African American cemeteries. I'd always heard and read that Blacks first came to America in 1619, to Jamestown, Virginia. Quite naturally I was intrigued when I read of the first Negro slave revolt occurring in America in 1526 at the mouth of the Pee Dee River, near present-day Georgetown, South Carolina. Historian Herbert Aptheker's *American Negro Slave Revolts* documented the instance of Spanish slave owners who left the Caribbean in 1526 for the mainland and took enslaved Africans with them. The slaves revolted and the whites who survived returned to the Caribbean. The Africans stayed and lived among the Native American Indians. In the years that followed, the islands off the coast of South Carolina, Georgia, and northern Florida became heavily populated with slaves.

This area is known as the Sea Islands. The population has been predominantly people of African descent since that time. When Hilton Head Island, South Carolina, was captured by

Union forces during the Civil War, whites abandoned their plantations. Some of the white slave owners were absentee owners, living elsewhere; others left to fight for the Confederacy; still others fled the area before the Union troops arrived in 1861. African American slaves flocked to the Sea Islands. In 1865 General William Tecumseh Sherman issued Special Field Order 15, reserving the land from Charleston to Jacksonville and thirty miles inland for former slaves. Guess what size the lots were? No more than forty acres. Sound familiar? That's when the rallying cry became "Forty acres and a mule!" (Blacks in other areas of the county also got access to abandoned lands.)

Many former slaves worked this land; some leased land and others purchased land. However, after Abraham Lincoln was assassinated, Andrew Johnson became president and pardoned many former landowners for abandoning their land to support the Confederacy, which allowed them to regain ownership of their land. That's how we lost the forty acres. However, the land was still populated by a majority of African Americans, some as owners but many more as laborers and sharecroppers.

The islands were isolated from the mainland, and the residents had "culturally closed communities." Because of this, they were able to retain much of the language and customs they'd brought from Africa. This rich heritage has caused the area to be widely studied by historians, folklorists, archaeologists, anthropologists, and linguists.

Most middle-class people today know of Hilton Head as a luxury-resort island but probably have not equated it with former slaves, plantations, and the Civil War. Land was purchased by developers beginning in the 1950s and turned into golf courses, tennis resorts, and condominiums. Taxes rose so high that many of the few native people who owned land could not afford to pay them. Many sold out and moved, and the native population dwindled while the white population soared. However, their cemeteries remained, at least theoretically.

Now some of those cemeteries are in the middle of golf courses and resort condominium complexes, some fully enclosed by private property. In order to visit their ancestors' graves, people must get permission from security guards at the entrance to the resort plantations. Braddock Cemetery, also known as Harbor Point Cemetery, is close to the fairway of the eighteenth hole at Sea Pines Plantation, where the MCI Heritage Golf Classic is held and viewed on national television. Native islanders say that part of the cemetery without grave markers was plowed over to make room for condominiums and the golf course.

Dafuskie Island, just south of Hilton Head, is also threatened by developers who want to turn it into a resort island. When thinking of the future of her family cemetery, an eighty-six-year-old resident was so angered she said, "I could shoot alligators between the eyes. I buried two husbands on Fuskie, and now those folks are talking about removing the cemetery. If the construction companies bother my husbands' graves, that is the day I'll put them in one."[1]

[1]Charles Blockson, "Sea Change in the Sea Islands," *National Geographic* 172, no. 6 (Dec. 1987), p. 756.

Braddock Cemetery—Braddock Cemetery in Sea Pines Plantation on
Hilton Head Island, South Carolina.

City Cemetery—Newark, New Jersey

One of the saddest stories I've heard is about a genealogist who searched for years to find the
cemetery where her grandfather was buried. It was the old City Cemetery in Newark, New Jersey, where poor people who could not afford funerals were buried. No one knew where it was,
despite the fact that 18,000 bodies were buried there. She finally located it on a tax map. But
when she arrived at the location, she couldn't believe her eyes. It was now a garbage dump!
She cried and almost fainted. She then sued the city, which agreed to remove the garbage and
restore the land to a cemetery.

African Burial Ground—New York City

Probably the most famous abandoned African American cemetery is beneath the heart of
New York City. In June 1991 construction crews were digging at Broadway and Reade Street in
lower Manhattan, on the site for a $276 million thirty-four-story federal office building. They
were working on a section to build a pavilion and suddenly hit bones and stopped digging.
They discovered a five-acre cemetery two blocks from City Hall. Maps in the historical society
said it was a Negro burial ground that was closed two hundred years ago. What was strange was
that it was uncovered sixteen to twenty-eight feet below street level! Skeletal remains had

never been located this far below ground before, and the discovery changed the thoughts and techniques of urban archaeology.

Research revealed the cemetery opened around 1712, or more likely earlier (enslaved Africans were brought to New York as early as 1625 with the Dutch). The burial ground closed in 1795, and later landfills wiped out remaining surface evidence of it. Historians, archaeologists, and anthropologists now say it's the oldest municipal and only pre–Revolutionary War African burial ground known to exist in the United States. The Landmarks Preservation Commission in New York described it as "the most important archaeological discovery of this century."

Archaeologists uncovered 390 burials before they stopped excavating. They theorize there may have been up to 20,000 burials. Ninety-two percent of the discovered remains had African ancestry. It appears that a few white paupers and Native American Indians were also buried at the site. Forty percent of the unearthed skeletons were children, which is similar to the ratio in Freedmen's Park Cemetery in Dallas. Childhood diseases that can be treated medically today (measles, chicken pox, whooping cough, diphtheria, and scarlet fever) were often fatal in the seventeenth and eighteenth centuries.

Despite the excitement the discovery of this historic burial ground created, all did not go well. Newspapers reported a number of problems with the construction and excavation of the remains.

- Construction workers accidentally poured concrete over twenty graves.
- Grave robbers stole teeth and damaged a skull.
- Archaeologists did not have space in their labs to preserve all the remains.
- Drawers were overpacked with remains.
- Rooms weren't properly air-conditioned.
- Not having a research plan violated historic preservation guidelines.
- Bones were wrapped in acidic newspaper.
- One year after the first skeleton was removed, the cleaning, conservation, and study had not been done.

African Burial Ground—Burial 369 is an adult male. He was evidently wearing a shroud. At least one shroud pin was found associated with his remains. Photograph furnished by the U.S. General Services Administration.

To add insult to injury, the archaeological team was almost all white and was accused by the African American community of being insensitive to their interests. They said the team had no experience in African American history or New York City history. They primarily identified skeletal remains for police investigation. Leading African American anthropologists in the country had not been consulted on the project.

The community protested, and things got so bad that on July 21, New York Mayor David N. Dinkins wrote a letter to the General Services Administration (GSA) regional administrator, William Diamond, asking him to suspend construction of the pavilion section of the federal building. Dinkins thought they needed to evaluate what had transpired and plan a new course of action. He also thought there should be a memorial and a museum and interpretive center built. After all, this was one of the most significant finds of the twentieth century, and it was about the role Africans and African Americans played in building New York, a story that had never been told. However, his pleas fell on deaf ears. Diamond thought the delay would cause needless cost overruns and rejected Dinkins's request on July 24.

Mayor Dinkins then appealed to the Congressional Black Caucus, and Gus Savage from Chicago, chairman of the Subcommittee on Public Buildings and Grounds in the House of Representatives, came to New York and held a congressional hearing on July 27. Savage listened to testimony about why the federal building construction should be halted. Testimony was presented by Mayor Dinkins, anthropologist Michael Blakey from Howard University, Laurie Beckelman, chairperson of the Landmarks Preservation Commission, GSA representatives, and others.

Transcripts from the congressional hearing reveal that Diamond still did not see a need to suspend construction and refused to recommend it to his superior. Savage stated that the GSA was in violation of Section 106 of the Historic Preservation Act of 1966 and had also failed in an agreement with the city of New York and the Landmarks Preservation Commission. He therefore demanded the GSA submit an amended prospectus for the construction of the new federal building. He said until he received it, he would not approve any further funding for GSA construction projects, which included a new Justice Department building, nor would he sign off on or renew any GSA leases. Savage then terminated the hearing before all remaining witnesses testified.

Considering that the GSA constructs all government buildings (except for the Department of Defense) and leases most government offices, he effectively shut down government buildings. That's powerful. It was so powerful that two days later the GSA acquiesced. They caved in to all the community's requests. Richard Austin, the commissioner of GSA, met with Mayor Dinkins and agreed that the future of the African Burial Ground would be decided by a national advisory panel established by the mayor. They further agreed that the pavilion area would probably become a museum under management of the Smithsonian.

Helen Sclair points out that burial grounds get bulldozed all the time. The only reason this one was saved was because people from the African American community became incensed and brought public attention and pressure to the mess. Mayor Dinkins was African American, and Gus Savage was African American. If these key people had not coordinated and fought for this issue, the fight could easily have been lost. In fact, there have been other African burial grounds in New York that weren't saved.

We used to fight to save our lives; now we have to fight to save our ancestors. Hopefully, the fight to save your ancestor's family cemetery will not be so monumental. The first step is to be aware of your family burial ground and then properly care for it.

Howard Dodson, head of the Schomburg Research Center of Black Culture in New York City, was appointed by Mayor Dinkins to chair the advisory council. In December 1992 the council decided the remains should go to Howard University. They were transferred the following November, in 1993.

Further examination of the remains revealed links to practices in West Africa. Beads on the top of one skeleton were in the shape of a heart, which was identified as the Ghanaian symbol *sankofa*. It means "Look to the past to inform the future. One can correct one's mistakes."[2] In 1995 Ghanaian chiefs from Africa visited Howard University to see the remains and to pay homage. They also apologized for African ancestors who participated in the slave trade.

Plans are under way to build the memorial and interpretive center museum. The interpretive center is scheduled to open in 2001, and the exterior memorial will open in 2002. Six works of art were commissioned for the interior of the federal building. Research on the remains at Howard University is also planned to be completed in 2002. The remains will then be placed in wooden coffins and then porous vaults for reinterment with a proper ceremony. The cycle will then be completed, eleven years after the discovery.

The Sexton's Office

In many cases the cemetery you want to research will be located in the same town where you now live. Visit each one that is within driving distance of your home. If the cemetery is located out of town, write a letter requesting copies of the records of your ancestors. If you live in a major city, the local library may have a telephone directory for the city where the cemetery is located, so you can look up the address and telephone number. Then when you get the opportunity to travel, include the cemetery in your list of places to visit and research.

Some cemeteries have a Sexton's Office with records of the cemetery. Always check with the office to see what they have. When you give the clerk the name of the ancestor you are researching, he or she will look up the record and tell you the section of the cemetery where your ancestor is buried. Larger cemeteries are usually divided by sections. These are identified by names, letters of the alphabet, or numbers. The sections are then usually subdivided by blocks, rows, or lots. A lot is made up of several graves. Many offices use preprinted forms they fill out with your ancestor's name and the section, lot, and grave number. However, as a genealogist, you'll want more information.

[2]Patrice Gaines, "Bones of Forebears: Howard U. Study Stirs Ghanaian Chiefs to Honor Ages-Old Link to U.S. Blacks," *Washington Post*, August 3, 1995, p. B1.

The records of interments may be recorded on 3″ × 5″ cards, large ledger cards, or in bound book volumes. You'll want to see the lot card or other record, which will have a map of the lot illustrating each interment, the size of each grave, placement of graves within the lot, and where each marker is installed, if any. Also ask if there are any legal papers associated with the grave. There could be a separate file in addition to the bound records. It might include names (and relationships) of those eligible to be buried on the lot.

Clerks in the office are usually nice and will do what they can to assist you. Some of them are intrigued by genealogy and are more than happy to talk with you. Sometimes they have brochures on the cemetery, which you'll want to collect. They may even have a list of names and burial locations of notable people interred in the cemetery.

You'll want photocopies of any records they have listing your ancestors' names. Don't settle for their preprinted form. Remember, you always want a copy of the original record. Sometimes it will reveal information you may overlook for years or that won't become important until you discover new information years from now. Sometimes you'll get clerks who don't want to be bothered with genealogists and don't want to do any extra work. Don't lose your temper. Be patient and nice, and usually they will come around. Offer to pay for the photocopies. What can they cost, a quarter or even a dollar? Whatever the cost, it's worth it, and usually you won't be charged.

However, despite what I've just said, things are changing, at least in major cities. Some cemeteries are now charging fees for records I got for free years ago. Two large cemeteries in Chicago both charge five dollars a name to search their records. That can become prohibitive and inhibit research. One cemetery refuses to make photocopies of any records, citing privacy, which actually doesn't pertain to dead people. They also told me someone could bring in a photocopy of a cemetery deed and say that's all they had for property they owned. I pointed out they could easily stamp a photocopy, illustrating it is a copy, to prevent any fraudulent use, but they haven't changed their policy.

As in my experience, information from cemeteries can often reveal additional ancestors. I've seen records that listed all the surviving relatives so the cemetery would know who else could be buried in the family lot in future years. I've even seen family tree charts in cemetery records, and military records for those who qualify for military markers. One genealogist named Sylvia found a burial permit from 1934 with the names and addresses of all the surviving relatives.

Be sure to ask the clerk if the burial is in a single-grave or multi-grave lot. Sometimes families purchased cemetery lots that contained several graves. As family members died, they were buried in the family lot. This lot would have older ancestors buried with more recent family members. In one cemetery where my ancestors are buried, they are all in single-grave lots. None of them have markers, and none are buried close to each other. When a family member died, relatives went to the cemetery, purchased a single grave, and buried their loved one.

No Sexton's Office

Often older and smaller cemeteries do not have an office on cemetery grounds. You'll have to find out who has possession of the records. There are several ways of determining this.

Usually you can ask the funeral home in the area. They make burials in the cemetery and will know who owns it. Also, the nearest churches usually know the owner. Parishioners often have funerals in the church and then take the body from the church to the cemetery for burial. As I mentioned earlier, the minister may have presided over the burial and administered last rites to the deceased. In many cases churches owned cemeteries. Then the records are either at the church or in the house of the minister or some officer of the church.

A cemetery is a business and usually needs a license to operate. Burial permits are usually required before a body is committed to the ground. Therefore, the local chamber of commerce

Mt. Washington Letter—Letter from Donald R. Martin, secretary and treasurer of the Mt. Washington Endowment Association, to the author, indicating Truman burials in the cemetery.

or the city or county office issuing business licenses and burial permits will know the owner of the cemetery. The county recorder's office may also have information on the cemetery. In Cook County, Illinois, purchasers of cemetery lots often recorded their cemetery deeds, just as they did their home deeds. Fortunately, they were recorded in separate deed books called cemetery books. They are arranged alphabetically by name of cemetery. These are not records of burials, only the names of persons who owned cemetery lots.

You may also find the name of the monument dealer in town. They know who owns the cemetery, as well as any previous owners, and they may have old records of the purchasers of grave markers. Check to see if they have records for the surnames you are searching. This can be a valuable source of information.

Ask residents living near the cemetery. They usually know who their neighbors are and can often give you the whole history of the cemetery and its previous owners. In small African American rural areas, usually everyone knows one another, and they tend to be more friendly and talkative. Finding out information like this isn't usually difficult.

You can also check with the local newspaper. It may have carried a story on the cemetery, and editors usually know what's going on in a town similar to Brownsville, Pennsylvania, where Greenlane Cemetery is located. If the cemetery you're researching is very old, the local historical society may have obtained records for it. And finally, a local genealogical society may have transcribed the names from the gravestones. Remember the South Suburban Genealogical and Historical Society, which published the names from the abandoned African American cemetery Mount Forest? Genealogical societies do this all over the country. So there are various ways to obtain information on cemeteries, even on abandoned ones. We'll explore cemetery records that are published and microfilmed in the chapter on "Going to the Library."

In 1976 my brother Mike and I visited a rural cemetery called Mt. Washington Cemetery, in Perryopolis, Pennsylvania. There was no sexton's office, but a caretaker was mowing the lawn. As we walked down the hill to his shed, I told him my Truman ancestors were buried in the cemetery. He gave me the name and address of the owner, who had the records. A month later a letter arrived in the mail with a list of seven Trumans buried in the cemetery.

Institutions

Helen Sclair enlightened me again, as she had with the African Burial Ground, and said one of the places genealogists miss when looking for cemeteries is institutions. These include prisons, mental health hospitals, and poorhouses. Many of these institutions have cemeteries on the grounds. You cannot always tell from a map because it will show just the institution, not all the buildings and grounds associated with it.

In many cases these will affect Black and poor people. If you know your ancestor was in an institution and you cannot locate his records among your ancestors' in their family cemetery, remember that he may have died in the institution and been buried on the grounds. Helen suggests looking for the records of the institution to see if there are burial records. The record could also be in the state archives. However, some records may be unobtainable without a court order.

Grave Markers

Be sure to ask the sexton if any of the graves of your ancestors have markers on them.[3] Cemetery records usually indicate if there is a marker on a grave. If your ancestor did not have a

marker, the clerk can indicate the closest marker to your ancestor's grave. Then you can count the graves over to where your ancestor is buried. Many poor Blacks did not have the money to purchase gravestones, so the lack of one may be an indicator of the financial condition of the family. Other graves do not have stones but have funeral home markers. Genealogist E. Renee Ingram reported several funeral home markers in her family cemetery. She believes they were meant to be temporary, until the family could afford a gravestone. They are metal signs driven into the ground on a stake with the deceased's name, age, death date, and funeral home name. Some have survived for more than sixty years. In some country cemeteries markers were wooden and no longer exist, and some were only large rocks (field stones) that marked the spot of the grave.

Some graves of African Americans in rural communities are marked with homemade markers. In an article on gravestones, researcher M. Ruth Little described an African American grave digger in North Carolina who earned extra income by making inexpensive tombstones from concrete. He pressed commercial letters into the soft, wet concrete to make the inscriptions. About the only decoration on some were marbles that kids play

Othello Gravestone—Gravestone for Othello, an African slave buried in Harvard, Massachusetts, in 1818.

with. There are a few rare stones in New England that mention Africa and sometimes locations in Africa where enslaved Africans were born (see illustration above).

If there is a marker on your ancestor's grave, try to find out when it was purchased. If the family did not have a lot of money, the marker may have been purchased several years after the bur-

---

[3]We used to call markers "tombstones" or "headstones." Now we know there are headstones, footstones, and markers not even made of stone, but metal, wood, and every other known material. The proper term is now "grave marker."

ial. In that lapse of time, information might not have been recorded correctly on the headstone. My maternal grandmother died in 1964. Her marker was a triple headstone for a three-grave lot. She was buried with the family who raised her. The stone was purchased sometime after the first burial in 1952. At the time of her death in 1964, the family had moved from Pennsylvania to Illinois. After she was buried, no one contacted a monument company in Pennsylvania to have the stone engraved for her burial. Thirty-six years later it is still not engraved! When and if it does get engraved (I'll probably have to do it), will the right death date be recorded? I once erroneously recorded her death as 1965 instead of 1964 on a chart I made. When my cousin pointed it out, I checked my records, realized he was right, and corrected that chart. This is why it is important to document your sources and to keep your records up to date.

One of my paternal great-grandmothers is named Fannie Barker. She's one of the relatives buried in Oak Woods Cemetery. She is listed in the cemetery records as Fannie Barker. Her name is also recorded as Fannie on several other records, including her death certificate, the U.S. Census schedule, the Chicago city directory, and a cup that has been passed down through the family since 1910. When I finally located her headstone, it did not say Fannie Barker. It said *Frances* Barker! This is the only record I have located that lists her name as Frances. Now when I research, I look for Fannie Barker and Frances Barker. So when doing your oral interviewing, remember what I said earlier about asking for nicknames as well as given names and middle names.

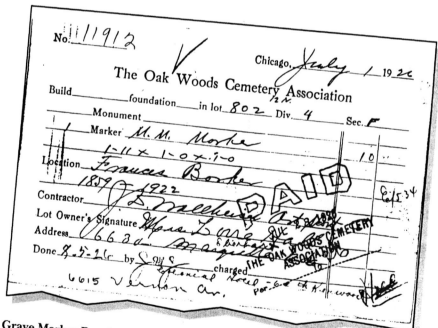

Grave Marker Receipt—Receipt for Frances Barker's grave marker, paid for by her daughter, Lovie Hall, in 1926.

Ask the cemetery for a photocopy of the grave marker record if they have one. When I received a photocopy of the headstone receipt for Frances, it contained some additional information. Her daughter Lovie paid for the headstone. So Lovie's name was listed, along with several addresses where she lived. Apparently she did not pay for the headstone all at once but in installments. This gave me a record of the places where Lovie had moved in the years it took to pay off the bill. This small record and the new addresses I received added a few more pieces to the family picture being developed. Incidentally, Lovie sacrificed for a grave marker for her mother but doesn't have one for her own grave.

When you visit the cemetery, try to go on a good day. A good day is when it is not raining or snowing and the ground is dry. Fall or early spring are the best seasons because of thin foliage and fewer bugs. You'll have to walk through the grass and may have to get down on your hands and knees to locate a grave marker. So wearing thick shoes or boots, long pants (jeans), and perhaps a pair of gloves will be best.

The headstone I found for the ancestor who served in the Massachusetts 55th in the Civil War proved very important. His regiment number was engraved on the front of the stone. I used this information to obtain his Civil War pension application file and military service records from the National Archives in Washington, D.C. In addition to details about the engagements of his regiment, the files gave me his dates of military service, the name of his widow, the names and ages of their children, and the name of the cemetery where I located his headstone. As you see, military records can hold a wealth of information. So keep an eye out for military gravestones, markers, and stones recording military regiment numbers. If you discover an ancestor with prior military service, contact the National Archives. They will send you a form to fill out to receive copies of his military service record and pension application file if he applied for a pension. You can also obtain a copy of his grave marker application. If he's buried in a national cemetery, that's proof he was in the military.

Calculating Tombstone Dates

Sometimes the cemetery record or the tombstone inscription shows the person's date of death but not the date of birth. For example, the record or the tombstone might show that a person died on May 6, 1889, and was 71 years, 7 months, and 9 days old. In this case the date of birth can be determined. You can use a calculation called the 8870 formula to quickly calculate the exact date of birth.

8870 FORMULA

	18890506	person died 1889 May 6
subtract	710709	71 years 7 months 9 days
	18179797	
subtract	8870	constant
	18170927	birth date is 1817 Sept. 27

This can be a tremendous help to genealogists when checking tombstone or death record dates. But let me give you a word of warning: just because a date is engraved in stone, that does not mean it is correct. Gravestone inscriptions were made many years after a person was born and are subject to many errors. They are secondary records and should be used as an estimate of the year of birth. We'll see as we go along how you can verify the accuracy of these dates.

Photographing Grave Markers

We've stated that many African Americans did not have gravestones. However, if you locate one, be sure you take a photograph of it. There are a few techniques that will help you get better-quality photographs. I met a lady in western New York named Laurel Gabel. She's a cemetery researcher like Helen and a member of the Association for Gravestone Studies. She was nice enough to share her photography secrets with me, and I'm going to share them with you.

There are four main keys to photography: composition, exposure, sharpness, and lighting. Composition for us is easy. We have a stationary subject and the same background for every shot. Make sure you get close enough to the grave marker to fill the frame so you'll get the detail you need. Also look around all sides of the stone to see if there are engravings on different sides, because you'll also want to take photographs of them. Look on the rear of the stone near the bottom to see if the engraver left his signature. If he did, take a shot of it too. If there are other family members' or friends' markers close by, you'll want to pull back and get a wider angle to include them in a shot. I also take shots of the entrance to the cemetery and the sexton's office if there is one.

Most of the keys to exposure can be solved by having a good camera. If you have difficulty manually adjusting exposure, make sure your camera has an auto-exposure mode. Most cameras do. If your camera has an adjustable lens opening, set it on a smaller opening for a sharper photo, something like f11 or f16. You can widen it a bit to blur the background for shots when you want to get a little of the cemetery background, but eliminating that will get the most detail on the stone. If you have a steady hand, you can get a decent photograph. But to get the sharpest image, you'll want to invest in an inexpensive tripod and cable release. They compensate for shaky hands and the slightest of movements. You'll also tend to get sharper images from slower film (100 to 200 ASA for color).

The last item is the one most amateur photographers fall down on, and this is where Laurel helps us out. After you master the first three items, great shots are all in the lighting. If you've ever looked at photographs of people's faces and couldn't see the whites of the eyes, the wrinkles in the face, or where the nose stops and the mouth begins, it was because of the lighting. Shadows covered the subject's face.

When you're in the cemetery, if the sun shines in your face, that means nothing is lighting the gravestone in front of you and therefore the photograph will come out like the face, with no features, very dark. If the sun shines directly on the face of the gravestone, the light will drown out the indentations of the engravings and they'll be too light to read. This is why flash photographs also result in washed-out images.

The trick is to shoot in bright sunlight and get the sun to hit the engravings at just the right angle to create tiny shadows in the carvings. A thirty-degree angle is good. This way the carvings on the stone are accentuated. Laurel does this by using a mirror to reflect the sunlight to hit the stone the way she wants it. Then she is in control instead of the sun. She recommends buying an inexpensive large mirror like the kind you get in a discount store to put on the back of your bedroom door. It can easily ride in the backseat or in the trunk of your car. For out-of-town trips, you can purchase a folding reflector from a camera store.

Most people use color film, but as mentioned earlier, black-and-white will last ten times as long. Of course, if you want to make slides, color will be best. Be sure to record the section and location of every marker you shoot. And above all else, practice shooting in a cemetery at home before going on the road to record your ancestors in a faraway country cemetery. Then you can evaluate your results and make adjustments until you get great shots. The last thing in the world you want is to go to the ancestral homeland for a rare visit, shoot a roll or two of film in the cemetery, and have nothing come out.

When your prints come back from the lab, be sure to label each one with the city, the name of the cemetery, the section of the cemetery where the stone is located, and the date photographed. If the name of the deceased is not obvious on the photo, also record that.

Photographing grave markers is very important. Markers for African Americans are often rare, and older ones wear with the weather. Unfortunately, some stones have been or will be vandalized, broken, stolen, or abandoned. So your photographs become valuable documents as years progress. Treat them as the valuable documents they are. Follow these techniques and hear your friends and relatives go "Wow!" when they see photos of your ancestors' grave markers.

Rubbing

Older gravestones are sometimes difficult to read. Engraved letters on soft limestone may have withered away. If this has happened, the inscription may be easier to read if you place a piece of paper over it and take a rubbing of the stone. This used to be a common practice until all the damage it caused was revealed. You need to know what you are doing before attempting this. Many stones have been damaged because of careless rubbing and careless applications of ink and wax. Some state laws require a permit to rub a cemetery stone, and for many stones rubbing is forbidden.

A stone should not be rubbed if a grain falls when you test with a finger, if cracks are in the stone, or if a hollow sound is heard when you thump it. Some stones have been found to contain asbestos-causing cancer and therefore should not even be touched. If you don't know what kind of material you're dealing with, you should not touch a stone anyway. Any rubbings should be done under supervision with an experienced rubber who follows preservation guidelines.

You may have read that some genealogists recommend using shaving cream to bring out highlights on gravestones. Don't buy that. Research has shown that shaving cream and other chemicals will harm some gravestones. You should never use anything other than water and mild detergent to clean a marker. The Association for Gravestone Studies strongly recommends against shaving cream, chemicals, cleaners, flour, cornstarch, or anything other than water. The best and least destructive way to get a good reading on a marker is to use the photographic techniques described earlier.

Preservation

If you stumble into a neglected or an old abandoned cemetery, you'll probably want to restore and preserve it. But don't jump in with both feet and bring the neighborhood rehab crew down the first Saturday you have a free moment. You'll need to do some planning to do a proper job. Not only are cemeteries sacred places, but they are also delicate places. You want to be careful not to do more harm than good. It's best to seek professional help before trying to do anything pervasive. You should contact the Association for Gravestone Studies, the local or state historic preservation office, or the National Trust for Historic Preservation (for addresses, see Appendix). If there needs to be any conservation work done on stones, permission might be required by the governing authority of the cemetery. Some areas have state laws that govern work in cemeteries.

The first thing preservationists recommend in preserving cemeteries is to record information about the cemetery and the markers. They recommend carefully and fully documenting the markers in the cemetery, as well as their locations. Surprisingly, written words sometimes outlast words engraved in stone. Amazing!

You'll want to record the information on each marker exactly as it appears on the original, using abbreviations only if they are used on the original, using upper and lower case letters as they are on the original, and using a separate line for each line on the original. If you can't make out any individual letters, use a question mark in the space. It's also recommended you record the marker's age, condition, type of stone, and any damage.

It's also a good idea to take photographs of the markers. The tips earlier in this chapter will help, but even if you do take photos, you still need to record the information on paper. You'll also need to make a diagram of the cemetery, noting the dimensions, directions of the graves and markers, and distinguishing geographic features. And if you have a camcorder, it would also be a good idea to shoot a video of the cemetery.

Use extreme care if attempting to clean any stones. Only water and mild soap are recommended. Don't apply any foreign matter such as epoxies, cleaners, or sealers to stones. Don't do anything abrasive on stones. Careless brushing and rubbing can damage some stones. Never paint stones and do not discard any fragments. To avoid further damage to stones, do not use a power mower close to them. Use hand clippers.

Other useful information is contained in *A Graveyard Preservation Primer* by Laynette Strangstad, available from the Association for Gravestone Studies. It explains for nonprofessionals step by step how to preserve and restore a small to medium graveyard. You should follow its guidelines. That way you'll avoid many of the costly mistakes others have made.

Strangstad's *Preservation of Historic Burying Grounds* is another helpful booklet that emphasizes planning the preservation and includes ancillary areas such as the entrance, walkways, roadways, retaining walls, and buildings.

There are computer software programs for indexing cemeteries, including one developed by the Association for Gravestone Studies. They can save you a lot of time and make your project more professional.

If yours is a large cemetery, you'll need to enlist help from the local genealogy society, the Boy Scouts or Girl Scouts, church members, or local school students. But do your homework first so you can instruct them and have a successful project.

Cemeteries of the Future

I don't think cemeteries will ever be a "thing of the past," but the future is looking very different from the past. As busy baby boomers age and migrate around the country, and as time and space become more rare, more and more people are opting for cremation instead of direct burial. The Cremation Association of North America reported the number of cremations rose by 75 percent from 1984 to 1994. In 1963 only 4 percent of Americans chose cremation. Current figures are at 21 percent, and estimates are that cremations will make up 42 percent of all dispositions by 2010.

However, these figures vary by region of the country, religion, and ethnic group. Some people will never choose cremation (Orthodox Christians, Jews, and Muslims), and many view it as anathema. African Americans do not request cremations as much as the rest of the population, but many do. If you or some of your family members decide on cremation, you can still have the remains interred in your family cemetery lot. And this kind of interment is much cheaper than the cost of opening and closing a grave for a regular burial.

There is also evidence of cemeteries becoming "high tech." Have you ever tried to read an old tombstone and barely been able to make out the name and date? If that was all you knew of an ancestor, didn't you drive yourself crazy trying to figure out what that person was like? Mark Howells, a genealogist and computer professional, describes new stone markers that have not only an inscription of the deceased's name but embedded computer chips and a screen on which viewers can see photographs of the deceased and read an entire family history! Of course, they'd better have some good batteries. And there are growing sites on the Internet listing memorials for loved ones.

Unfortunately, there's also a darker side to the future of cemeteries. With more baby boomers aging, death has become a growth business. Some people are capitalizing on this in unscrupulous ways. More and more mom-and-pop funeral homes and cemeteries are being bought out by large conglomerates and international corporations. This has led to much higher prices and questionable practices. The price of dying has risen three times faster than the cost of living.

Because African Americans tend to be less educated, have a higher rate of funerals versus cremations, and opt for more expensive funerals, they have been targeted by the large corporations.

So be very careful when looking toward the future. Don't be afraid to compare prices when shopping for funeral and cemetery services. You'd do it with most other expensive purchases.

Update Your Charts

If you receive any new information from cemetery sources, update your Family Group Sheets and Pedigree Chart. Be sure to footnote the sources, which should be done in the following manner:

5. Asa M. Burroughs's gravestone, Lot 38, Section 11, Oakridge Cemetery, in Hillside (Cook County), Illinois. Photographed by Tony Burroughs, 1 March 1977.
6. Sexton's ledger for Lot 38, Section 11, at Oakridge Cemetery, in Hillside (Cook County), Illinois, indicates Asa M. Burroughs interred on 28 December 1971 at 77 years of age. Tony Burroughs has photocopy.
7. Sexton's ledger for Lot 487, Section 11, Oakridge Cemetery, in Hillside (Cook County), Illinois, indicates Morris Burroughs interred on 17 December 1903 at 40 years of age. Tony Burroughs has photocopy.
8. Sexton's ledger for Lot 487, Section 11, Oakridge Cemetery, in Hillside (Cook County), Illinois, indicates Mary Burroughs interred on 17 April 1914 at 44 years 3 months and 3 days of age. Tony Burroughs has photocopy.

Family Group Sheet #2—Updated Family Group Sheet after adding footnotes and sources from cemetery research.

In the chapters that follow, we'll look at ways to follow up on new information we've found at the cemetery.

Remember, when doing research, the cemetery where your ancestors are buried may not have an office with records. There may not be a grave marker for your ancestor. If there is not one, it's a good project for your family to invest in one. You may want to start a project for your family to purchase grave markers and install one at each family reunion, holding a ceremony memorializing the ancestor.

In spite of these potential obstacles, you must always check to see if cemetery records exist. This is a basic source that is often overlooked. But as you can see, cemeteries can reveal vital information and save time, money, and effort.

Research To Do #4—Fourth Research To Do sheet indicating completed items checked off and adding cemetery research to do.

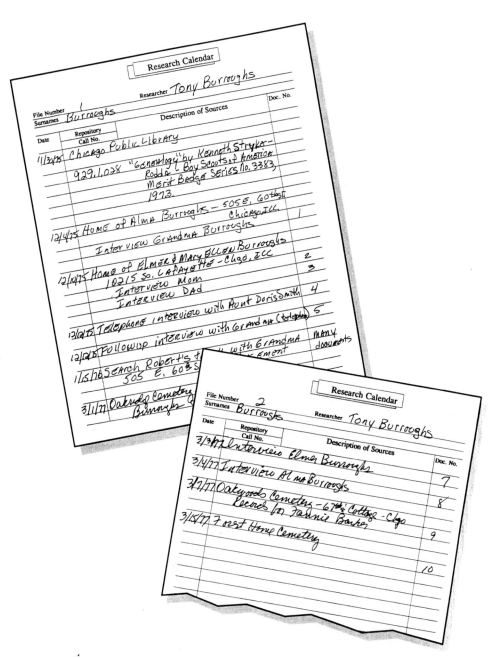

Research Calendar #5—Research Calendar after adding more interviews and cemetery research.

Things To Do

Things To Do
✓1 Buy envelopes and stationery
✓2 Buy stamps
✓3 Buy a tape recorder with an external jack
✓4 Buy extra "D" batteries
✓5 Order acid-free paper
✓6 Order acid-free file folders
✓7 Transcribe interviews
✓8 Write list of followup questions
✓9 Disseminate information from interviews
✓10 Start new file folders
✓11 Write thank you note to Grandma
✓12 Make backup copies of tapes
✓13 Make list of documents from Robert's trunk.
✓14 Place documents in acid-free file folders
✓15 Label new file folders
✓16 Place photographs in acid-free sleeves
✓17 Make copies of photographs
✓18 Make photocopies of Bible pages
✓19 Fill out Family Group Sheet for Mom & Dad.
✓20 Fill out Family Group Sheets for grandparents
✓21 Prepare documentation sheets with sources from oral interviews and family papers
22
✓23 Fill out Pedigree Charts
24 Update Family Group Sheets with cemetery findings
25 Update Pedigree charts with cemetery findings
26
27

Things To Do #6—Updated Things To Do sheet after checking off completed items and adding notes to update charts after cemetery research.

Genealogy File Folder Contents

Ancestor name: Robert Burroughs

		IN FOLDER Y/N	COMMENTS
1	Document Log		
2	Things to Do List		
3	Research To Do List	✓	
4	Research Calendar	✓	
5	Correspondence Index	✓	
6	Correspondence	✓	
7	Alphabetical list of variant surname spellings		
8	Master alphabetical list of all family surnames		
9	Soundex code		
10	Charts – Pedigree		
11	– Family Group Sheet		
12	– Descendant Chart		
13	– Soundex Charts		
14	– Census Charts		
15	– Chronology		
16	– Biography		
17	Oral history interviews		
18	Research notes, extracts, and abstracts		
19	Documents		
20	Vital statistics certificates – Birth	N	See list of documents & folders
21	– Death		
22	– Marriage		
23	Discrepancy charts		
24	Photographs		
25	Oakdale cemetery records	Y	
26	Oakridge Cemetery Map	Y	
27			
28			

File Folder Contents #6—Genealogy File Folder Contents sheet after adding cemetery records in file.

Records in Funeral Homes

Funeral homes can be excellent sources for genealogical data but are often overlooked by beginning genealogists. Before your ancestors were buried, their remains were normally handled by the local undertaker.

The information found in funeral home records is similar to that found in cemetery records. However, it's from a different source, and you need to look for confirmation of information you already have, as well as those small pieces of bonus information. As you'll see in a minute, there are sometimes small bits of different information in funeral home records that are not in cemetery records.

Funeral home records are also important because you won't always find cemetery records. Small, old county cemeteries get filled up and no longer make burials. Others become abandoned and the records are lost. In this situation, the records in funeral homes are very important.

Another value in locating funeral home records is in obtaining the exact date of death, which will save you time and money in obtaining copies of death certificates. In other instances, you'll discover some ancestors do not have death certificates, and the funeral home record may be the only written record of the ancestor's death.

My paternal grandfather's funeral home record listed his first, middle, and last names, race, date and place of birth, date of death, address, occupation, Social Security number, address, and names of parents. His widow was the informant and didn't know his mother's maiden name.

Also listed were the fees for the funeral, cemetery burial, and two certified copies of his death certificate. The record also indicated how these charges were paid—from his insurance. Grandfather had a Met Life nickel policy! At five cents a week, he must have been paying on it all his life. Even then, it amounted only to $166.67. The funeral cost over $1,300! So much for life insurance. But it did list the beneficiary of the policy, his widow. Beneficiaries are usually relatives but are not always the spouse.

One distant ancestor I was tracking lived in Detroit. He had a fairly common name, Roscoe Lewis. I didn't have a lot of information on him and found several Roscoe Lewises in old Detroit telephone directories. So many, in fact, I couldn't tell which one was the one related to me.

I collected other information and found a Roscoe Lewis who died in 1984, about the time I estimated. I obtained a death certificate and thought this was the Roscoe Lewis I was tracking. The name of the funeral home was listed on the bottom of the death certificate, and I called to see if they were still in business. They were and I drove by to get copies of their records.

Much to my surprise, on the back of their data sheet, they'd written the names of the people to be picked up for the funeral procession. One of the ladies, Barbara Sanders, was staying in a motel and had obviously come in from out of town. Below her name was her address in California. Next to her name was written "sis" for sister. Those were the two pieces of evidence I needed. They were the smoking guns. Not only did I know the name Barbara Sanders and her address, but I'd talked with her years before and collected stories about Roscoe Lewis. Barbara Sanders is since deceased, but she's the one who told me about her brother Roscoe and put me on his trail. I then went to the cemetery and got additional information.

Funeral Home Records

Unfortunately, the records from African American funeral homes are a mixed bag. Some funeral homes have good records and some don't. I talked with one funeral home in South Carolina whose records went back to their beginning, close to the turn of the century. However, they were organized chronologically and then by the name of the person who paid for the funeral. It would have been very time-consuming and next to impossible to locate any of my early ancestors in the records.

Some funeral homes don't realize the value of their records. Many know there are death certificates created by the county and feel their records are important only to the owners as a business record. They don't have a feel for history, genealogy, or many of the problems and obstacles genealogists encounter.

Unfortunately, many times records are destroyed. I talked to a mortician in Chicago who said they had so many records they couldn't house them all, and so they destroyed all records that were over seven years old.

Funeral Programs

I've briefly mentioned funeral programs in the preceding chapters on oral history, family records, and cemetery records. Many of you are probably familiar with them and perhaps take them for granted. I certainly did until I started doing genealogy.

At most African American funerals, a written program is passed out to everyone attending the funeral. It is usually an 8½″ × 11″ sheet of paper folded lengthwise, with the name of the deceased, birth and death dates, often a photograph, an obituary, the order of service, the name of the officiating minister, the name of the cemetery, and the name of the funeral home. Recently these programs have gotten quite elaborate. I just saw one from South Carolina that ran eight to ten pages and was filled with photographs. They're taking on a life of their own.

Helen Sclair made me realize these funeral programs are unique to the African American community. Funerals in the white community normally have prayer cards, which merely list a prayer, the date of death, and the time and place of the wake, funeral, and burial.

This was confirmed by Alice Houston, of Houston's Secretarial and Printing Company in Chicago. She printed the funeral program for my grandfather in 1971. When Mrs. Houston started her business, she almost exclusively designed and printed funeral programs for African American families. Just recently she started getting business from three white-owned funeral homes that were handling a few burials of African Americans. When the relatives asked for funeral programs for the funeral service, the white funeral directors didn't know what they were talking about. Somehow the owners got in touch with Houston's Secretarial and Printing, and now when they get African American funerals, they send the families to Mrs. Houston to print the programs.

Family members usually save these programs after the funeral. Genealogist Bell Cheatham not only saves funeral programs but collects ones she doesn't have from other family members. In discussions with her we tried to determine why funeral programs are a phenomenon in the African American community. Her theory is that, because of racism and segregation, African Americans were not permitted to have obituaries published in local white newspapers and therefore African American funeral programs were born out of necessity.

In contacting several African American–owned funeral homes, I learned that many save funeral programs for the clients they bury. They are part of the funeral records. When I contacted Barker Mortuary, which buried my grandfather in 1971, they still had the copy of the program designed and printed by Mrs. Houston. If I hadn't already found it through family records, I would have been elated by all this new information. When you contact funeral homes for information, be sure to ask if they save funeral programs. Most will be willing to copy the one you want. However, be very careful about the information. It can be very inaccurate, depending on who supplied it and what state his or her mind was in while writing the obituary. Remember, the biographical information was collected and written in haste.

Determining the Funeral Home

There are several sources for determining the name of the funeral home that buried your ancestors. The first step is to ask family members. Many family members may have attended the funeral and have a detailed recollection of the funeral services. Others may recall that there was only one funeral home in town that everyone used. I have a relative who knew one of the funeral directors and still keeps in touch with him.

⌐ ACCIDENT .— (Specify) SUICIDE ~~~~ HOMICIDE	21b. PLACE OF INJURY (e.g., in or about home, farm, factory, street, office bldg., etc.)	21c. (CITY, TOV
⌐ TIME (Month) (Day) (Year) (Hour) OF ~~~ ~~~ m. E.S.T. NJURY	21e. INJURY OCCURRED While at Not While Work □ at Work □	21f. HOW DID I
⌐ I hereby certify that I attended the deceased from JULY.9.. 1949.. to D alive on .Dec. 4..... 1953, and that death occurred at.10:00P.m, E.		
⌐a. SIGNATURE	M.D. or other M.D.	23b. ADDRESS S. Pitt
⌐BURIAL CREMA- N, REMOVAL (Specify) Removal	24b. DATE 12-6-53	24c. NAME OF CEMETERY OR CREMATORY Anatomical Board
⌐E REC'D BY LOCAL REGISTRAR'S SIGNATURE FQ.. 12-5-53 Nola C Castlick		25. SIGNATURE Yahuc

Anatomical Board—Bottom section of death certificate indicating deceased was not buried in a cemetery but that the body was donated to science to use for studying anatomy.

If you already have a death certificate for an ancestor, it will indicate the name of the funeral home on the bottom. Even if the person was cremated and not buried in a cemetery, the name of the funeral home should still be listed. If there was no burial or cremation and the body was donated to science, there will be something like "Anatomical Board" listed in place of the funeral home or cemetery.

If you know where the ancestor is buried, check the cemetery records, which sometimes indicate the name of the funeral home. If not, ask to see a copy of the burial permit. It is normally delivered from the funeral home, whose name is recorded somewhere on the form.

Sometimes the local newspaper or the African American newspaper will publish an obituary or death notice, often listing the name of the funeral home. Newspaper obituaries are often saved by family members as souvenirs and mementos and may be in a scrapbook, photo album, or a file cabinet. You may have run across them when researching family records earlier. If not, contact your relatives and ask if they have any. Old newspapers can be researched in libraries, which I discuss in a later chapter.

When going through Robert's trunk, I located several business cards I discussed in the chapter on family records. One I didn't mention was from J. L. Marr Funeral Parlor. Handwritten across the top in Robert's handwriting is "Buried my wife." The rear of the business card served as his receipt. Dated July 25, 1937, it reads, "Rec. from Mr. R. Burroughs $215.00 for funeral. Bill paid in full. J. L. Marr."

Robert E. Burroughs's first wife divorced him while he was in prison. His second wife, Malvina, died in 1937 and was buried by J. L. Marr Funeral Home. J. L. Marr is no longer in business. It was bought out by another African American funeral home and remained in the same location. The new owner, Samuel B. Rawl Mortuary, took it over when Mr. Marr died. Samuel B. Rawl is an uncle of Lou Rawls, the famous singer. (It's not uncommon in genealogy for

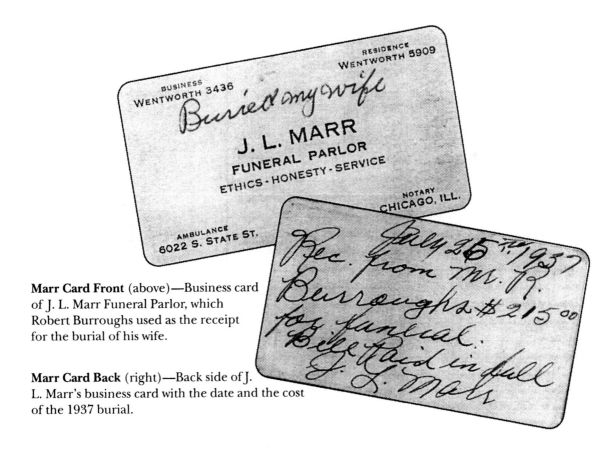

Marr Card Front (above)—Business card of J. L. Marr Funeral Parlor, which Robert Burroughs used as the receipt for the burial of his wife.

Marr Card Back (right)—Back side of J. L. Marr's business card with the date and the cost of the 1937 burial.

some family members to keep the "s" on the end of a last name and others to drop it.) I plan to contact Rawl Mortuary to see if they have records from J. L. Marr.

Contacting Funeral Homes

A local business telephone directory will include a list of all the funeral homes in a town. There are also directories of funeral directors, which is covered in the library chapter, as well as associations of funeral home directors. You should contact funeral homes in the areas where your ancestors lived to see if they handled any of your ancestors.

When you locate one, find out when it started business. Then find out when the other African American funeral homes began in the area. I was researching the death of Ellen Burroughs, who died in Spartanburg, South Carolina, in 1910. I located the name of the African American funeral home and paid them a visit. There was no death certificate for Ellen Burroughs, and I asked if they had a record of her death. Surprisingly, they told me they weren't even in business in 1910, and they were the first Black funeral home in town. I asked who buried the African Americans before them. She told me the white funeral home across town.

RECORD OF FUNERAL

Name of deceased _Ellen Burroughs_ P.O. _Taly_ Date _Aug 3_ 1910

To whom charged _Daughter of Wesley_ P.O. "

Order given by _Geo Chew & John Oedus_ P.O. '

Date of death _Aug 2nd_ Place of death _# 363 Convent_

Cause of death _____ Duration of disease _____

Date of funeral _Aug 4th_ Date of burial _Aug 4th_

Funeral services at _Church_ Place of burial _Cal Cem_

Time of funeral services _10 oclock_ Race _Col_

Age _74 years_ Casket _3/6_

Clergyman _Cooper_ Coffin _____

Physician _Hardy_ Embalming _____

Occupation of deceased _____ Hearse _____

Name of father _____ Wagon _____

Name of mother _____ Bricking grave _____

Name of husband _____ Opening grave _____

Name of wife _____ Burial robe _____

Body to be shipped to _____ Burial slippers _____

Arthur Rutherford Lot Hose _____

Gloves _____

2 Landau Washing and dressing _____

1 Crest Shaving _____

3 St Hack Disinfecting room _____

Carriages _____

Funeral Record for Ellen Burroughs—1910 funeral record for Ellen Burroughs from J. F. Floyd's Mortuary in Spartanburg, South Carolina.

I'd never even thought of that. And being from the North, I was a little leery about going to a white funeral home in a small town in South Carolina. However, the clerk was very friendly and said they had the record. It would be no problem making me a copy, and she didn't even charge me.

The record listed the name of the deceased, the date of death, the place of death, and who paid for the funeral. When I saw "Daughter of Wesley," I got very excited. I have circumstantial evidence Ellen is my great-great grandmother, and now I'd gone back another generation. However, I did research on the church she attended, and my elation quickly diminished. I found out Ellen was a member of the Daughters of Wesley, a church organization. They paid for her funeral. So Wesley was not her father, after all.

I then reexamined the funeral record and realized George Clements and John Revis ordered the funeral. George was Ellen's son-in-law. The record also listed her age, seventy-four years, which meant she was born in 1836! That was exciting. It listed the minister's name and the physician's name. It also listed the fees for the funeral: a casket, a hearse, a charge for opening the grave, and others I didn't understand.

The funeral was held in the church, and Ellen was buried in Arthur Rutherford's lot in the Colored Cemetery. Rutherford was her granddaughter's husband. I asked where the Colored Cemetery was located, and the response was "Which one?" There happened to be two cemeteries in town where African Americans were buried, and both were called the Colored Cemetery.

One of the things I neglected to do was contact the church for their record of the funeral. Many funerals were held in the church, which created records. The question is, do the records still exist? Sometimes these records are held by the minister who performed last rites.

So when searching your ancestor's community, be sure to find out when the Black funeral homes started and what churches existed at the time. If you're looking for records before the African American funeral home began, definitely consider the white undertakers.

Discovering Other Ancestors

The information from funeral homes can often reveal additional ancestors. If families used the same funeral home, which they usually did, it would have information on other ancestors that you might not previously have known. You should make a list of the ancestors who lived in that area. You may find that the same funeral home buried your ancestors' parents and brothers and sisters. The record might also list a relative who paid for the funeral or who owned the cemetery lot where the burial took place.

Sometimes family members moved to a new community, and a funeral home shipped the body back to where the family originated. This happened for my maternal grandmother, Lydia Brooks. She died in Chicago in 1964 and her funeral was in Chicago. But afterward the African American funeral home shipped her body back to Pennsylvania for another funeral and eventual burial. In a case like this, a funeral home might have received the body of a long-lost ancestor who died in some far-off place. You may have lost track of an ancestor in your research, only to find out where he or she migrated through funeral home records. If the funeral home locates any records for your ancestors, ask for photocopies and offer to pay any fees.

Out of Business

Remember, older funeral homes may have gone out of business. When this happened, the business was often passed down to another family member and thus stayed in the family. If there was no one around or no one was interested in maintaining the business, sometimes i was taken over by another undertaker. One or several of the other African American under takers in town will know the history of their competitors and predecessors. Sometimes there was no other option and the business closed. This often happened when the owner died and the family did not want to take over the business. In this situation the records may still be in the hands of the family. Or there is a slight chance the records were deposited at a local historical society or a library or an archive. You don't know until you check. I mention one case in the chapter "Going to the Library."

You will need to write to or visit each funeral home that buried your ancestors. Be sure to ask who the undertaker was when conducting your oral interviews. Again, use your Family Group Sheets as a guide. Contact the funeral home for every deceased person listed.

Research To Do #5—Updated Research To Do sheet after checking off cemetery research done and adding funeral home research to be done.

If you receive any new information from the funeral home, remember to update your Family Group Sheets and Pedigree Chart. Be sure to create a footnote that says the source was the funeral home (e.g., Funeral home record from Barker's Mortuary in Chicago for Asa Morris Burroughs, 27 December 1971).

Now having visited the cemetery and the funeral home that buried your ancestors, you have the dates and places of death. We'll now use that information to locate vital records, discussed in the next chapter. Later, in the library chapter, we'll cover information on researching funeral home records in libraries, locating published funeral home records, and locating original records for funeral homes that are no longer in business.

Research Calendar #6— Updated Research Calendar after adding visit to the funeral home.

Vital Records

When I discuss genealogy, I often run into people who say, "I can't trace my family tree. Everybody's dead." What these people don't realize is that all our ancestors are dead! That's what this game is about—finding dead folks. Often the easiest way to find out who a person's parents are is to obtain a vital record.

Vital records are birth certificates, death certificates, marriage licenses, and divorce records. If interviewing your living relatives is the most important task in genealogy, obtaining vital records is probably the second most important in unlocking genealogical mysteries. The exciting thing about birth certificates and death certificates is that they often provide the names of parents and immediately extend your pedigree back another generation. The names of these parents are often previously unknown ancestors.

If you already know the dates and places of these vital events, you may not think a vital statistics record is necessary. Well, in genealogy research *every* record is important. Remember the rule "Let no stone go unturned." This means you look at every record. You don't know what it will say until you see it. There are often surprises and bonuses.

Each vital record will sometimes give small bits of information, in addition to the date and place of the event—what I call "bonus information." It's a bonus because you didn't ask for it. You're searching for the date of birth of the baby, but often the birth certificate will go a lot further. Many times the names of parents will be listed. This is invaluable because if you didn't know the parents' names, it takes you back another generation. Sometimes the maiden name of the mother is listed, sometimes the places of birth of the parents are listed, and sometimes the occupations of the parents, their employers, their addresses, and how long they lived in the city or state are listed.

Death Certificates

In genealogy research, always look for death records before birth records. This is in keeping with the principles of proceeding from the known to the unknown, starting from the present and working toward the past, and tracing backward one generation at a time. You may have heard that an ancestor was born in a certain city or state, but when you get the death certificate, you may find something different on it.

! Trap: Trying to obtain a birth certificate before a death certificate. The death certificate will lead you to the birth certificate.

For which ancestors do you request death certificates? Again, use your Family Group Sheets as a guide. By now you should be getting the picture that Family Group Sheets are used as guides in every stage of genealogical research. You need to get a death certificate for every person who is listed as deceased during the period that vital records existed in each county and state. This is the official record of their death.

To obtain a death certificate, you need to know the approximate date of death. Having this date will also expedite your order. If you do not know the exact date of death, the clerks in vital records offices will search only a few years before and a few years after the date of death you provide. This is usually five years before and five years after. If the record is not located, you are still charged the same fee, which is a search fee. Some states charge additional fees for each year they search, so you need to be as accurate as possible before you apply for the certificate. This is why you should research records in cemeteries and funeral homes before applying for death certificates. These records will provide the exact dates. Often our relatives' memories are very hazy about exact dates of death. They can be off by ten or twenty years. If they are that far off, you have only a slim chance of obtaining a death certificate. So be sure to check with the cemetery and funeral home first.

Other records that indicate death dates:

- Cemetery gravestones
- Cemetery sexton's records
- Burial permits
- Funeral programs
- Newspaper obituaries
- Newspaper death notices
- Newspaper articles
- Hospital records
- Police reports
- Insurance records
- Military pensions
- Social Security records

If you did not know the name of the cemetery before you received the death certificate, you should find it on the death certificate. Now you can contact the cemetery and obtain their records. Refer back to the chapter on "Records in Cemeteries" and do all the things necessary to get additional information from the cemetery. Remember, there may be other ancestors buried there. The same goes for the funeral home. If you did not know it previously but the name and address are listed on the death certificate, contact them. You may want to go back and review the chapter on "Records in Funeral Homes."

Information on Death Certificates

The information contained on death certificates varies from state to state, from county to county within the state, and even for different time periods within the same county. You usually don't know what you're going to get until it arrives in the mail. That's what makes anticipating the mail so exciting.

The death certificate for my paternal grandfather, Asa Morris Burroughs, listed his father's name but not his mother's. Fortunately, I knew the name from family records and cemetery records. But the death certificate did list his Social Security number, which I used to obtain information I'll discuss in a later chapter.

The death certificate for Asa's brother, Robert, listed his father's name and his mother's maiden name. It also listed Robert as widowed, so I needed to look for a marriage record. And it listed his address at the time of death, so I had a location from which to trace him backward, which I'll cover in the chapter on "Going to the Library." Robert died in a hospital, and the informant was listed as "county hospital records." That means he supplied the information himself and the information tends to be reliable. However, he must have been very sick, because neither his date of birth, Social Security number, nor occupation was listed. He had been in the county hospital for four days with pneumonia and died from it.

The death certificate for my maternal grandmother Lydia Brooks listed both her parents' names, William and Mary Terrell, which took me back another generation on both sides of the family. It also listed the length of time she'd been in Chicago, which was important because I didn't want to waste time searching for records in Chicago if she was living in Pennsylvania. It also indicated the cemetery where she was buried. She died in Chicago but was buried in Elizabeth, Pennsylvania. Many people died in one city and their bodies were shipped back home to be buried. This can sometimes cause difficulty in obtaining death certificates. Once we see ancestors buried in the cemetery, we don't think they may have died in another city or state, and that's where the death certificate is located.

The death certificate listed her place of birth as Fayette County, Pennsylvania. Great—can you imagine how big that county is? She could have been born anywhere in the county. I asked her daughters where she was born, and none of them knew. It took quite a bit of searching, but I finally figured it out.

I got the death certificate for my grandmother's mother, who was my great-grandmother, Mary Terrell. It listed her parents and her mother's maiden name. Naturally, I was excited to

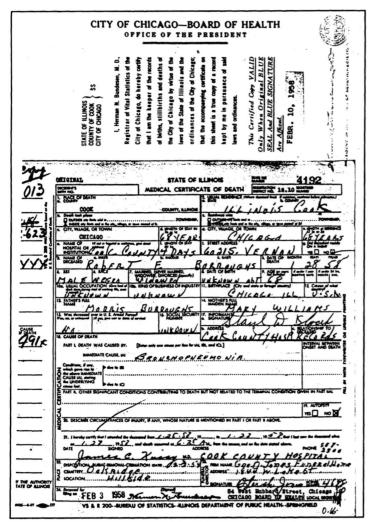

Robert Burroughs's Death Certificate—1958 Death Certificate for Robert E. Burroughs.

receive it because that gave me the names of my great-great-grandparents, David Truman and Anna Smothers. David Truman died in 1916, and I got his death certificate. It listed his parents' names, Samuel Truman and Mary Goe, who were my great-great-great-grandparents. Then I got the death certificate for Anna Smothers, who died a few months after her husband, and it listed her parents, O. P. Smothers and Charlotte Simpson. I was on a roll. That's the beauty of death certificates— they take you back another generation if they list the parents.

Both David and Anna Truman were listed as being buried in the Quaker Cemetery near Brownsville. I bought a book on Quaker genealogy, *Our Quaker Ancestors,* which was very interesting and educated me on how the records were divided in different locations for the different branches of Quakers. They have excellent records, and I ended up traveling to Swarthmore, Pennsylvania, not far from Philly, to search Quaker records. I didn't locate any of my ancestors in the records (never finished researching), but I learned a lot of interesting history, saw some beautiful rolling hills, and met a lot of nice people. I also learned that the Quaker Cemetery near Brownsville was the only cemetery around, which was perhaps why my ancestors were buried there.

Unfortunately, death certificates don't always list the names of parents of the deceased, which can be disappointing. My paternal great-grandmother, Mary Jane Lillie (Williams) Burroughs, had her father's name listed on her death certificate. It was Mr. Williams! Thanks. That doesn't tell me a lot. I think my grandfather, the informant, just made that up.

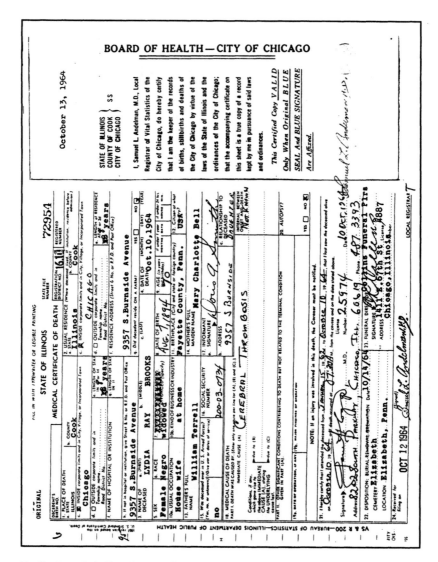

Lydia Brooks's Death Certificate—1964 death certificate for author's maternal grandmother, Lydia Brooks.

My paternal grandfather's father, Mary's husband, Morris, died in Chicago in 1903 when he was only forty years old. There's not even a space on the death certificate to list his parents. That caused me untold grief for years as I tried to determine his parents. But it did indicate the length of time he'd been in the state of Illinois, twelve years, which meant he migrated around 1891.

One day I looked at his death certificate again and noticed something I had not noticed before. I looked at the very top and saw the word "Corrected." Now, why hadn't I noticed it before? Probably because all I was interested in was his parents' names, and I was extremely disappointed when they weren't listed.

I returned to the county vital records office to locate the original death certificate. After a week's worth of waiting, a supervisor finally brought a copy of the original. I also received three affidavits, each saying there was an error on the original as to the place of birth, which should have been South Carolina. One was signed by the widow, one by the physician, and one by the funeral director. I seriously doubt if the physician and funeral director knew where my great-grandfather was born.

The original certificate listed his place of birth as Tennessee. I knew right away that Tennessee is where his wife, Mary, was born. I figured in the stress of his death, she inadvertently said he was born in Tennessee. However, after pondering this for a long time and trying to analyze why this error occurred, I thought of something else. I knew Morris and Mary had to have met somewhere. I wondered if he lived in Tennessee for a time and met Mary there. If that was the case, he did live in Tennessee; he wasn't only born there. As a genealogist, I knew that when I searched for Mary in Chattanooga, I should also search for Morris, even though I know he was born in Spartanburg, South Carolina.

I also compared both certificates and discovered other interesting things. First, his race changed, from Colored to Black. Both certificates indicated Morris died of tuberculous, but the original indicated the length of his illness was eight months! That means he suffered with the disease and could have been hospitalized. There are records for Cook County Hospital during that period, and I'll also search for records of the tuberculous sanitarium in Chicago.

Other things on Morris's death certificate proved interesting. It listed his address as 619 Park Avenue, but Park Avenue doesn't even exist anymore. I had to go to the city library to obtain a list of street name changes to figure out where he lived. In the process I discovered his address number was also different. The city changed the east-west axis in 1908 and therefore all the numbers changed. The library had a conversion book that helped me figure out what the equivalent new number was. I drove by the address, only to see a vacant lot! However, some of the houses on the block were very old, so I could tell what his house probably looked like. Those of you trying to locate the house where an ancestor lived, be sure to check with the city to see if there have been any name and number changes in the past.

As we have seen, the name of the informant is always important. However, death certificates don't always indicate the relationship of informants to the deceased. Too often genealogists assume they were relatives. If you don't know the relationship, you can go crazy trying to figure it out. I had one such case for the death of a distant collateral ancestor in Detroit. I hadn't done a lot of research on him, and the name of the informant on the death certificate was not familiar. I wondered if she was related. After getting the death certificate, I proceeded to the cemetery. I located the grave and took photos of the marker. I then went to the sexton's office and got copies of the burial record. It indicated the cemetery charges and who made the arrangements. It was the same lady who was the informant. However, this time her relationship to the deceased was listed—friend.

Reliability

We cannot accept all the information on a death certificate just because it's a government document with an official seal. As with all documents, we must analyze and validate the information. My maternal grandmother died in 1964. Her death certificate listed her father's name and her mother's maiden name. That took me back another generation, to my great-grandparents. However, when I followed up on my great-grandmother's name, it didn't pan out. The name on the death certificate was Mary Charlotte Bell. If I had looked for that name, I never would have found it. Her real name was Mary Charlotte Bell *Truman*. Bell was part of her middle name.

I looked at the informant's name on the death certificate, and it was her daughter's. She knew her grandmother and probably knew her maiden name. However, deaths are very stressful, and family members have to make numerous decisions, often about things that are not important to them. When a loved one dies, who cares about the death certificate? People are concerned with making funeral and cemetery arrangements, notifying family and friends, taking time off from work, negotiating with the insurance company, searching for money to pay for everything, and a million and one other things, let alone grieving.

So the information on a death certificate can be notoriously inaccurate. It can only be as accurate as the knowledge of the person who supplied it. Sometimes no family members are around, and sometimes family members are not very knowledgeable about their genealogy. The only thing reliable on a death certificate is the date of death. Even the person's name is contingent on who was around and knew the deceased at the time of death. The person's age is often incorrect. It is normally supplied by someone else, who may not have been around when the person was born. Therefore, take everything with a grain of salt and search for supporting evidence.

If an ancestor died while in a hospital, the hospital should have a record. You can usually tell if the ancestor died in a hospital because the death certificate will list the hospital's as your ancestor's address or it will give the name of the hospital as the residence. It will probably also list the informant or the source of information as "medical records." This can be verified by researching the medical records department of the hospital. If the death occurred long ago, the records may be in the hospital's archives. They should contain additional information. When the person was admitted, the doctor or nurse probably took a medical history and recorded personal information.

Creation of Death Certificates

Death certificates are normally initiated by funeral homes. They interview the family to get information on the deceased. They next fill out their name, license number, and signature.

Then they obtain the signature of the physician, who fills in the immediate cause of death and any contributing causes, although I have some old death certificates that do not indicate a cause of death. The funeral home then delivers it to the board of health, which is a county or city department, and submits an application for a burial permit, or they directly exchange it for a burial permit. The board of health then creates a certified copy of the death certificate, and the funeral home submits the burial permit to the cemetery, which needs it to inter the remains.

When an individual dies in a hospital, the staff often initiates the death certificate, filling out information on the deceased from medical records. They then forward the death certificate form to the funeral home, which finishes the process.

Coroner's Records

If an ancestor was killed, committed suicide, died from an injury, accident, or other unnatural cause, or the cause of death could not be immediately determined, the coroner or medical examiner was probably involved. A coroner is a political official who investigates a death, whereas a medical examiner is a physician who conducts the investigation. Most coroners have been replaced by medical examiners to ensure that investigations are more scientific than political.

Whenever a death is due to unnatural causes, there is usually an inquest. An inquest is an investigation to help determine the cause of death and the circumstances surrounding the death. Normally, people are interviewed who knew the deceased, including relatives if they were around at the time. This would have created other records you want to explore. In Illinois, early Cook County coroner's records include the name of the deceased, date and location of the inquest, verdict of the coroner's jury, names of jurors, and the names, residences, and occupations of witnesses. They also contain the names of alleged assailants in murder cases and persons assigned blame in negligence.

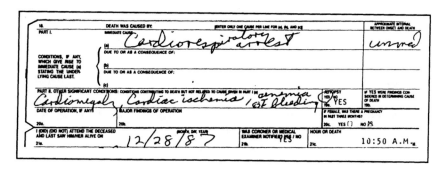

Coroner's Death Certificate—Bottom portion of death certificate indicating an autopsy was performed (19a) and the coroner was notified of this death (21b).

There is a line on some death certificates that asks if the coroner or medical examiner investigated. You may never have noticed it because you were looking only for the names of the parents. If the answer is yes, contact the medical examiner's office in the county where the death occurred. You should follow up by researching for newspaper articles, court records, and police reports, all of which may give additional information.

One African American genealogist told me her ancestor was lynched in the South. She wanted to know if there are records of lynchings. Fortunately or unfortunately, there are records of lynchings. They happen to be unique death records that many African Americans have to deal with. Although they are very painful for me to think about, I've described how to access records of lynchings in the library chapter.

Birth Certificates

If you do not have a copy of your own birth certificate, start by ordering one. Remember, you're the first link in your own family tree. Some people are surprised when they receive their own birth certificates. One of my students had her dad order a copy of his birth certificate. He was sixty-five years old and had never seen his birth certificate. The vital records office had a hard time locating it, and he was shocked when they found it. The last name recorded on his birth certificate was different from the one he was using. His family theorized his mother was between marriages and had a child by a man she didn't marry. The father was not her first marriage nor her second, and no one had ever told the student's father. Unfortunately, he did not find this out until he was sixty-five years old!

You also want to get copies of birth certificates for your children. One of my other students had eight children. He was also shocked when the birth certificates arrived. There were errors on several of them he'd not known about.

Determining Dates

Pinpointing dates of birth in order to obtain birth certificates is usually more difficult than pinpointing dates of death to obtain death certificates. Whereas the cemetery and funeral home can provide the exact date of death needed to obtain a death certificate, there is no equivalent for exact birth dates. However, there are ways of determining approximate dates of birth. If you were lucky enough to turn up a family Bible when searching for family records, it may give you a reliable date of birth. Remember, though, to compare the date of birth in the Bible with the copyright date in the front of the Bible and the other tests of validity (see the chapter "The Family Archives"). If the date of birth occurred before the copyright date, it was not entered in the Bible at the time of the birth. It was entered from someone's memory or from another record. It is therefore subject to error.

You can also determine approximate dates of birth from other family records like driver's licenses, identification cards, school records, and church records. Try to locate items on which the deceased person had to supply his or her birth date. They are usually more reliable than a record on which another person had to supply the date, such as in an obituary or a death certificate. And try to find records created closer to the date of birth.

Reliability of Age at Death

The age or date of birth on a death certificate can be unreliable. The informant on the death certificate usually would not have had access to the deceased person's birth certificate. How well the informant knew the deceased will in part determine how reliable the date is. And we all know people often lie about their age. They do it for various reasons: to get a job, to obtain a pension or Social Security, to get married, to join the military service, or just because they don't want other people to know their right age.

The same goes for information on gravestones. The date of birth on them is unreliable. Many times the stones were purchased years after the person was dead and buried. You'll recall from the previous chapter my grandfather's gravestone, which read, "Asa M. Burroughs 1894–1971." Asa was born before his parents had decided on his name. So his name does not appear on his birth certificate, but his date and place of birth do, as well as his parents' names and other identifying information. From this certificate we see Asa was born in 1893, not

Asa Burroughs's Birth Certificate—1893 birth certificate for author's grandfather Asa Morris Burroughs.

1894. This kind of error is not uncommon. So use dates on gravestones as a guide—do not accept them as fact until they are corroborated with other records.

Despite the fact that my grandfather's birth certificate did not show his name, it proved very valuable. It verified that Asa was the second born, gave his mother's maiden name (Williams), and verified his parents' states of birth (South Carolina and Tennessee). It also contained bonus information about his parents, listing their address and their ages. This is great information. I obtained a birth certificate to verify someone's date of birth, and the certificate also verified the *parents'* years of birth. That would assist me in getting birth records for them.

Asa's birth certificate also listed his father's occupation, which I already knew to be railroad porter. But now I knew that he was a Pullman porter. I had been tracking down records from the Chicago and Alton Railroad, which I found to be in Alabama. The Pullman Company records were in Chicago, at the Newberry Library. I had direct and quick access to them. I searched through the payroll records and discovered he was working for Pullman in Chicago in 1887, two years before any other evidence I'd uncovered.

This is why we leave no stone unturned and check all records. I'd already known Asa's date and place of birth before obtaining his birth certificate. What I didn't realize until I obtained it was that it included his father's employer and would lead to new discoveries that I'll cover later.

Short Form Versus Long Form

Sometimes birth certificates are produced in both long and short forms. If you have a choice, always obtain the long form. It may cost a little extra money, but in the long run it is worth it. The short form will usually have just the name of the person and the date and place of birth. This form exists because the person requesting it may merely need to get an official verification of his or her age, usually to satisfy requirements to obtain Social Security benefits, apply for a pension, apply for a job, obtain a passport, or enter school. The applicant is not concerned with the other miscellaneous information on the birth certificate.

My father was born in 1919 in Chicago and had a short-form birth certificate issued in 1942, three months before he was drafted into the army for World War II. The certificate recorded very little information, only his name, sex, date of birth, and place of birth. I found it among family papers after he died. After analyzing it, I realized it was merely a form filled out by a clerk, not a photocopy of the original record. I checked with the vital records office, and they did have a long form for him, which was a photocopy of the original record of birth. In addition to the information listed above, the long form included the time of birth; his parents' full names and mother's maiden name; his parents' race, age, place of birth, and occupation; the number of children they had; the number of children still living; and the physician's name and address. However, the birth certificate was not filed until three months after my father was born. It appears the physician was late in filing it.

In analyzing this birth certificate, I saw that the place of birth was listed as the address of the mother and father. This was undoubtedly a home delivery, which is verified by a footnote

Elmer Burroughs's Birth Certificate—1919 birth certificate (long form) for author's father, Elmer Burroughs.

at the bottom of the form that reads, "If birth occurred in hospital or institution, give its name instead of street and number."

I called my cousin in California, Jackie Jarrett. I asked if she remembered the family doctor. She said she remembered the doctor coming to the house and said she never went to a hospital or doctor's office until she moved to California. I asked if she remembered the doctor's name. She said, "No. When he came to the house, we ran under the table. We hated to see him come. We knew we were going to get a shot, and we hated shots."

For genealogy research the additional information on the long form is just as important as the date of birth. It gives you additional pieces to fit into your puzzle.

Remember, my maternal grandmother's (Lydia Brooks's) death certificate listed her place of birth as Fayette County, Pennsylvania. In trying to determine where in the county she was born, I applied to Pennsylvania for a birth certificate for her first daughter, Margaret Ann Brooks, in hopes it would list the birthplace of the baby's mother. It did—Pennsylvania! No city, no county, just the name of the state.

No Birth Certificates—Registration of Birth Certificates

In some instances you may order a birth certificate and find one does not exist for your ancestor. To understand why, we need to look at how and when registration began. In the Virginia Colony in 1639, ministers were required to report burials, christenings, and marriages. But the first modern vital registrations began in 1841 in Massachusetts, where standardized forms were used throughout the state and collected on a statewide basis. Some states followed suit before the Civil War, but the content of the forms varied, responsibilities for filing records varied, and the legal status was weak.

After the Civil War the federal government and the American Medical Association, concerned about the health of the country and seeking to lower the high infant and maternal mortality rate, set out to generate complete, accurate, and uniform vital statistics for births and deaths. Mortality schedules were introduced with the 1850 and 1860 census population schedules. Census takers were instructed to list every person who had died within the twelve months preceding the census enumeration. However, the government discovered a high percentage of deaths were being missed on the mortality schedules, almost 40 percent. States were then encouraged to pass legislation mandating registration of births and deaths on a statewide basis. When a state hit 90 percent registration, the government would purchase vital records from it to compile reliable statistics.

The Census Bureau tested the degree of completeness of birth registration throughout the United States in 1930, 1940, and 1950. As you would expect, the rates of incompleteness in birth registration were higher in Black communities than anywhere else. In 1940 rural communities of African Americans in southern states had the highest rates, averaging 24 percent of babies without birth certificates. The rural areas of the five states of South Carolina, Oklahoma, Tennessee, Arkansas, and Texas ranged from 30 percent to 39 percent. Most of these areas were served by midwives.

Midwives

Many African American babies were delivered in the home by midwives, especially in the rural south. As late as 1940 almost half of all African American babies were birthed by midwives and only 26 percent were born in hospitals. By 1945 the rate had dropped, but only to 38 percent. In addition to births by midwives, another 22 percent of births were home deliveries by physicians. Just over 40 percent of African American babies were born in hospitals.

AFRICAN AMERICAN BIRTHS

Year	Midwife Delivery	Physician Home Delivery	Total
1936	55.0%	25.5%	80.5%
1937	53.5%	25.5%	79.0%
1938	52.3%	25.0%	78.3%
1939	50.9%	24.8%	75.7%
1940	49.2%	24.1%	73.3%
1945	38.1%	21.7%	59.8%

Note: Remaining births were in hospitals. However, the figures are undoubtedly higher because statistics were compiled from birth registrations and a much lower rate of registration occurred in the African American community.

Source: Historical Statistics of Black America; Negro Handbook; U.S. Office of Vital Statistics.

Midwifery in the Black community dates back to slavery. Plantation midwives delivered the babies of other slaves, as well as the white babies of the owner's family. They referred to their skill as "catching babies."

These women were often elderly, most having passed the childbearing age, and were referred to as grannie midwives and sometimes just grannies. They learned the job through trial and error and passed the skill on to their daughters, nieces, or granddaughters, who often lent a helping hand. Some were also herbalists and spiritual healers.

After the Civil War there continued to be a need for grannie midwives. Most who began midwifery after slavery said they received messages from the Lord to deliver babies. The cycle of life has always been a spiritual event in the African and African American communities. Because they were called upon for this work, midwives were always held in high esteem in the African American community.

Because of racism, segregation, and poverty, large parts of the Black community did not have access to doctors, hospitals, and adequate medical care. This was particularly true in the rural South, where most Blacks lived. Even in areas that had adequate medical care, many poor Blacks could not afford hospital deliveries. Using a midwife was usually the only option. Plus, midwives were a tradition in the Black community. Many families had several generations delivered by the same midwife.

This tradition continued well into the twentieth century. Even as late as the 1930s, estimates are that African American midwives in rural Louisiana delivered ten times as many babies as African American doctors. In 1936 over half of all Black babies born in the United States were delivered by midwives. The Children's Bureau of the Census estimated that in 1940 midwives delivered 66 percent of all Black babies born in Mississippi, Alabama, Arkansas, Louisiana, Georgia, South Carolina, and Florida and from 33 to 66 percent in Virginia, North Carolina, Texas, Oklahoma, and Delaware.

Registering Births

There's a perception that births attended by midwives were not recorded in vital records offices and that birth certificates do not exist for these babies. There are no hard and fast rules. Sometimes births were recorded and sometimes they weren't.

During the public health movement, grannie midwives were phased out in favor of nurse midwives who received training in preventing infection, sterilizing equipment, and filling out birth certificate registration forms. New state laws for vital registration required midwives to register their deliveries, but this was difficult for many midwives because they could not read and write (nor could many of their patients). Near the bottom of most birth certificates is a space to sign that says, "Physician or midwife."

Genealogist Rosetta (Tines) Thomas's great-grandmother Commie Tines Wilson was a grannie midwife in Cahoma County, Mississippi. Commie's husband's family was sold to different slave owners in Alabama, and he was determined to have a strong family after slavery. He and Commie had fourteen children. Commie lived to be 104 years old and was a midwife for seventy-five of those years. One of Rosetta's prize possessions is her own birth certificate signed by the midwife, her own great-grandmother.

Many midwives recorded births in the mother's family Bible. Genealogist Dee Woodtor had an ancestor who was a midwife. Her ancestor kept a book of all her deliveries, but no one in the family can find it. If you know of any records created by midwives, try to get them into an archive. They will be invaluable to genealogists and historians.

If a birth certificate is not recorded for your ancestor during the period when birth certificates were recorded in the county or state, the delivery may have been done by a midwife and not recorded with the county. This is when family Bible records are invaluable. So check doubly hard to see if any family member has a family Bible with recordings of births. Later, when you travel to libraries and archives, be sure to search for the records of midwives (as well as Bible records). They are rare, but you might get lucky. When you progress to advanced research, you'll see that some slave births were recorded in the slave owner's Bible.

Delayed Birth Certificates

Before you get discouraged and think there is no birth certificate for your ancestor because he or she was born in the South and delivered by a midwife, there is one more possibility to explore.

We now know that when some people were born, they did not have a birth certificate recorded in the vital records office. This was sometimes because the person was not born in a hospital, was delivered by a midwife, or even because the physician was negligent in filing a record of the birth. Sometimes people did not find this out until years later, when they needed to apply for a pension, Social Security, a passport, or military service. They needed a birth certificate and learned that one had never been filed. They were given the option to file a delayed birth certificate. These were official birth certificates but were recorded sometime after the birth, in many cases *years* after the birth.

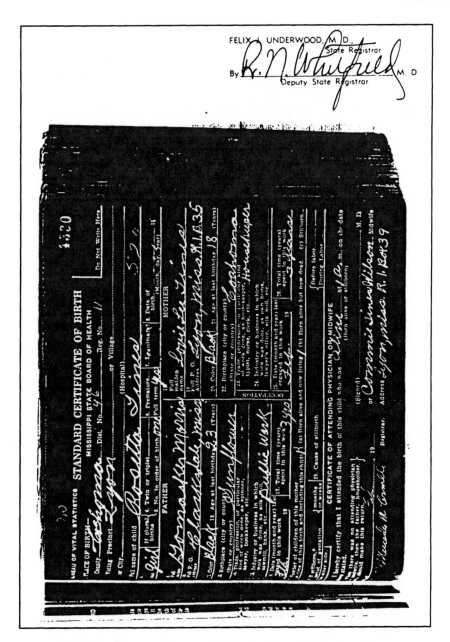

Rosetta Tines's Birth Certificate—Birth certificate for Rosetta Tines, signed by her great-grandmother Commie Tines Wilson, the midwife.

Delayed Birth Certificate (front)—Blank form for application of a delayed birth certificate, found among Robert Burroughs's papers.

There was a rapid increase in registrations of birth certificates beginning in 1940 because of World War II. Citizenship was required to obtain food ration books and to work in defense industries. Birth certificates were proof of citizenship and had been heavily promoted by public health organizations. Birth certificates were also required for dependent children of servicemen to qualify for family allowances.

But because of discrimination, African Americans were not allowed to work in defense industries or the federal government, except in janitorial positions. A. Philip Randolph, leader of the Brotherhood of Sleeping Car Porters (Pullman porters), and the Black community exerted pressure on the federal government and threatened a march on Washington. Bowing to pressure, President Franklin D. Roosevelt signed Executive Order 8802 on June 25, 1941, declaring racial discrimination in the defense industry and federal government illegal. Thousands of jobs opened up for African Americans in defense industries, but they needed proof of citizenship to get them. Many were without birth certificates, having been delivered by midwives, and applied for delayed birth certificates.

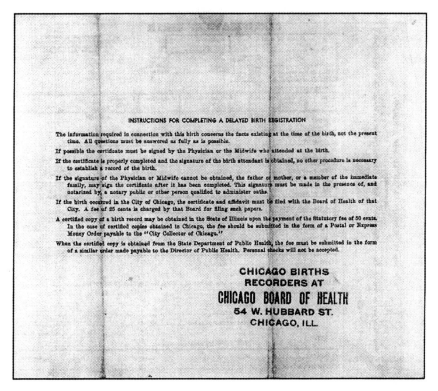

Delayed Birth Certificate (back)—Instructions for filling out application for delayed birth certificate.

My grandfather's brother, Robert Elliott Burroughs, was not issued a birth certificate when he was born in Chicago in 1889. It appears he needed one in 1942 to apply for a job as an electrician with the Pullman Company, which manufactured troop train cars for World War II. A blank application form for a delayed birth certificate with instructions on the back was found in his trunk after his death.

The procedure for processing a delayed birth certificate varied from state to state and even by time period. The board of health regulations at the time Robert applied specified several options. The first proof of birth was the signature of the physician or midwife who delivered the baby. If they were not around, the signature of one of the parents or immediate family was required. Both of Robert's parents were deceased in 1943 so he brought in his only brother, Asa. They accepted his testimony, but I'm not sure I would as a genealogist. Yes, his brother was an upstanding lawyer in 1943, but he was Robert's *younger* brother. Asa wasn't even born in 1889. Incidentally, Robert got the job at Pullman, but it lasted only three months.

My mom was born in Pittsburgh in 1926 and did not have a birth certificate. Her sister said she was delivered by a midwife who lived down the street. Mom needed a birth certificate in

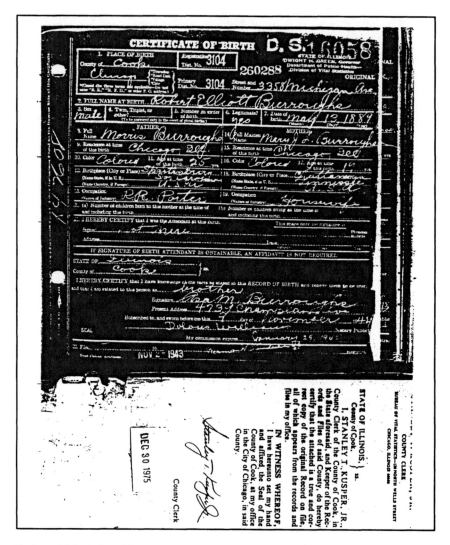

Delayed Birth Certificate for Robert Burroughs—1943 delayed birth
certificate for Robert Burroughs, born in 1889.

1943 to obtain war rations and apparently was not aware she did not have one. The Pittsburgh
office of vital records returned the fifty cents she sent in with a letter stating they had no
record and she could order a delayed birth certificate.

So all of you who decided there were no birth certificates for your ancestors who were born
before the state began registering births need to think again. There's a good possibility they
applied for a delayed birth certificate. Make sure the vital records office searches the delayed

birth certificates. Sometimes they are in the files with regular certificates, and sometimes they are appended to the end of original certificates and clerks have to do additional work to find them.

When you obtain a birth certificate for genealogical research, always check to see if it is a delayed birth certificate. This is not always evident. Sometimes the initials D.B. (for delayed birth) on some part of the form will indicate it is delayed. The key is to look for the date of filing and compare it with the date of birth. If the certificate is delayed, it is not as reliable as a

Pittsburgh Vital Statistics Letter—Letter to Mary Ellen Brooks from the Pittsburgh, Pennsylvania, Bureau of Vital Statistics notifying her that they were unable to locate a record of her birth.

copy of an original that was recorded at the time of the birth. A delayed birth certificate is a secondary source, whereas a certificate created at the time of birth is a primary source.

If you do encounter a delayed birth certificate, ask the clerk (or usually the supervisor) if the office maintained copies of the evidence your ancestor brought in to prove his or her birth. If they did, this evidence could prove interesting. Some offices request Bible records or other documentary evidence. Had I no other documents on my grandfather, his name and signature on the bottom of his brother's delayed birth certificate would have proved very valuable.

If neither a birth certificate nor a delayed birth certificate was filed, there may be a record of the birth in the hospital or clinic. So if you know what hospital or clinic the baby was born in, check the hospital records department or the hospital archives for evidence of birth.

No Father

Unfortunately, sometimes genealogists receive birth certificates, only to learn there is no father listed. This can be very frustrating. In some states, if the mother and father were not married, the law prohibited the father's name from being recorded on the baby's birth certificate. I've heard of a case in which the mother and father stayed together for quite a while and the father had to go to court to get his name recorded on his daughter's birth certificate. In some places the term *bastard* was recorded on the birth record. There are even places where bastardy bonds had to be taken out when the couple was not married.

Divorce Records

Unfortunately, divorce records are often neglected by genealogists. They are good sources for genealogy information, are easy to use, and are normally typed and well indexed. They should be researched before marriage records because you have to prove marriage before getting a divorce. The transcript of the court proceedings usually mentions the date and place of the marriage, in addition to revealing dirt and gossip about the relationship. If you don't know the exact date of the marriage when you're researching marriage records, you will usually be charged a search fee whether or not the record is located. But the charges for copies of divorce records are usually just photocopying charges. Researching divorce records before marriage records is also consistent with the fundamental of researching backward, one step at a time. The divorce occurred *after* the marriage and therefore is closer to you in time.

New Information

The new information I obtained from the divorce record of my uncle's first marriage included his wife's maiden name, the date and place of their marriage, the address where they lived while married, and the name of his brother. This uncle's second marriage also ended in divorce, and I gleaned additional information from the record of that divorce. It gave the address of the house they purchased as well as a legal description and information on when it was purchased, where it was located, and what were the price, down payment, and mortgage holder. There was also the name and address of the beauty shop his wife owned. I recall going to the beauty shop when I was a child.

From the divorce records of Aunt Irene's first marriage, I gleaned even more information than from my other uncle's divorces. I learned of her husband's military service, his occupation, his employer, his salary, his address five years after the divorce, and how long they had known each other before they were married. I also learned the name and date of birth of their child, my oldest cousin. There were also names of neighbors and school classmates who were witnesses at the divorce proceedings.

Some divorce records span many years because of child support. With this information you can track migrations well after the divorce decree. These little bits and pieces can help give a fuller picture of the ancestor and also lead to other genealogical records. However, I wouldn't place too much credibility on the reasons for the divorce in the court testimony. It was often difficult to obtain a divorce, and therefore some of the testimony may have been fabricated or stretched in order to obtain it.

Open to the Public

Divorce records are open to the public, and you can usually search the indexes yourself. The tricky part is you have to know the state and county where the divorce was filed. With people moving all the time, this is not always easy. If the divorce occurred in the county you are living in, you can probably go to the county building and obtain the record. If it occurred in another county or state, you'll have to write for the record. Divorce records are housed in different places in different states. A divorce is a court proceeding, so the record is usually found with the records of the court, which could be the chancery court, circuit court, district court, or superior court. In Louisiana the records are located in the parish clerk's office. To find out which court in your county and state has the records, consult guides like *The Handy Book for Genealogists* and *Ancestry's Red Book,* both listed under "Genealogy Reference Guides" in the Bibliography, or contact the county courthouse where you think the divorce occurred.

Once you locate the proper court, look for an index of the records. They will probably be organized by year, so if you don't know the date, you may have to search several years. There should also be an index by plaintiff and defendant. If you don't know who filed for the divorce, you'll have to search for both the husband's and the wife's name.

Under the divorce listing, there will probably be a case number or docket number associated with the divorce. You can either use this number to locate the case yourself or give it to a clerk who will pull the record for you. In larger cities records are sometimes stored in warehouses, and it can take a few days for a file to be transferred to an office where you can examine it. When you get the file, you can usually make photocopies. Hopefully, the record will mention when and where the couple got married. With that information you will be able to obtain the marriage record.

Marriage Records

Obtaining marriage records at first sounds pretty routine, just like obtaining birth and death certificates. However, obtaining marriage records can be very tricky. One reason is that you often don't know if the couple got married in the state the bride was from or the state the groom was from.

More tricky than that, though, is the fact that even if a couple lived in the same state and county all their lives, they may not have gotten married there. If they were in a hurry to get married or if the bride was underage, the couple may have traveled across the county or state line to get married. I know one Chicago genealogist whose parents lived in Chicago but were married in Valparaiso, Indiana.

Determining the Bride and Groom

The first step in locating marriage records is determining the bride and groom. Sometimes this is obvious, but other times you may know one spouse but not the other. Then you'll have to determine the date and place of marriage before ordering a record.

The divorce records discussed above will indicate marriage dates and places. A review of your Family Group Sheets, oral interview notes, and files should also reveal this information for some of your ancestors. If not, be sure you asked questions about marriage dates and places when you talked with your relatives during the oral history phase. Your search of family papers such as letters, receipts, and the photo album may also have turned up evidence of marriages. One of the items I acquired was a replica of a marriage certificate. This was obtained by my grandmother's sister Roxie and her husband, Daniel Phillips, for their wedding anniversary.

Speaking of anniversaries, records of these events may reveal marriage dates. Couples often had parties on their tenth, twenty-fifth, fiftieth, and other wedding anniversaries. They may have sent out to friends and relatives announcements that were then saved in scrapbooks and photo albums. These probably won't give the place of the marriage, but it only takes simple subtraction to calculate the marriage date.

If you still don't know details of the marriage, there are several additional sources to research:

- Family Bible
- Newspaper obituaries
- Funeral programs
- Newspaper notices of marriages and anniversaries
- Newspaper commemorative souvenirs

Those of you who have had some experience in genealogy but are having difficulty locating marriage records may want to check the 1900 U.S. Census. Column number 9 asks whether the person is single, married, widowed, or divorced. Column 10 asks for the number of years married. Then you can calculate the date of marriage. The next two columns are not about

Replica Marriage Certificate—A 1971 commemorative marriage certificate for Daniel Phillips and Roxie B. Terrell indicating that a record of their 1914 marriage is on file in New Castle, Pennsylvania.

marriage but are helpful because they help analyze the family and could indicate if the mother was previously married. Column 11 asks, "Mother of how many children," and column 12 asks for the number of those children who are still living. For those of you who are real beginners, we'll cover census records a little later.

Different Types of Marriage Records

The term *marriage record* is generic. It could mean anything. There are different types of marriage records, and you need to be familiar with all of them. They were probably not all issued in the county where your ancestor lived, but you need to check for each and every one, just in case. Plus, you may have ancestors who had marriage records in one county and other ancestors who lived in other states and counties that had a different kind of marriage record.

When a couple got married, more than one record was created, which produced multiple documents. Most people are familiar with the *marriage license* and *marriage certificate*. When a couple decided to get married, they applied to the county for a marriage license. If they met the requirements, this license was issued by the county and the couple had to take it to someone authorized to perform a marriage. This was usually a minister or justice of the peace. After the wedding, the officiating person often gave the couple a marriage certificate saying he married them. The couple was then required to return the signed marriage license to the county clerk, proving they actually got married.

For those of you who are married, this is old hat. However, we need to review the process from a genealogical point of view to understand what records and documents are created and what we should look for.

If you've found a marriage record among family papers, it is most likely a marriage certificate. You can usually tell because it says "Certificate" in bold letters on the front. It will also usually have flower designs and a fancy border around the edge. I found the marriage certificate for my mom and dad among the family papers after they died.

When you apply at the county courthouse for a marriage record for your ancestor, you'll probably receive a copy of the marriage license, which was recorded in the official record. Examine it to see exactly what you have. I purchased a marriage license from the Cook

Pittsburgh Newspaper—Page from the 1950 *Pittsburgh Courier* showing photographs of couples married in Tennessee, North Carolina, and Georgia.

County clerk in Illinois that had more information than the marriage certificate. It included the bride and groom's ages, which meant I could calculate their years of birth.

Sometimes the records in county courthouses are called *marriage returns,* meaning the marriage license was returned after the marriage was performed. Just because a marriage license was issued does not mean the marriage took place. Many a bride or groom has gotten cold feet at the last minute and walked out. Sometimes you'll receive a *marriage register,* which will show not only your ancestor's name but that of everyone else who got married that day.

What researchers often don't realize is this whole process began with the couple applying for the license. That means a *marriage application* was filled out. It existed at the time of the marriage; the question is, does it still exist? Researchers need to inquire for marriage applications and obtain them when they exist. They will provide additional information and can solve genealogical problems.

My aunt remembered the date her parents were married, November 6, 1918, because it was exactly one year before their first child was born. That was my aunt's older sister, and she couldn't forget her birthday and therefore couldn't forget her parents' date of marriage.

Since I knew this date from my aunt, I was never in a hurry to order a marriage record for my grandparents Preston Brooks and Lydia Terrell. But leaving no stone unturned, I finally

Burroughs Marriage Certificate—Marriage certificate for author's parents, Elmer Burroughs and Mary Ellen Brooks, found among family papers.

Burroughs Marriage License—Marriage license for author's parents, Elmer Burroughs and Mary Ellen Brooks, obtained from the Cook County (Illinois) clerk's office.

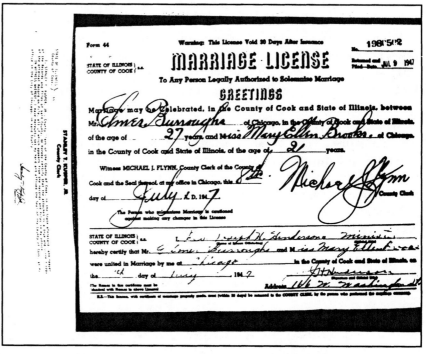

applied for the marriage license. I knew I could also get the marriage application for more money, and I figured it would give me more information. Boy, was I right! I was amazed at some of the new information I obtained.

One of the questions the application asked was "Have you been previously married?" My grandfather indicated yes! I was shocked. I never knew he was married before and my grandmother was his second wife. I asked two aunts, who both said it was true. They even said they knew his daughter by his first marriage, but neither remembered her name or the name of the first wife. The marriage application indicated she died in 1910, which gave me a little to go on.

The other information the application provided was my grandfather's age, the names of his parents, the maiden name of his mother, the residence of his father and mother, the occupation of his father and mother, and the birthplace of his father and mother (unfortunately, only the state). Most of this other information I knew, but it was a verification of my other sources.

The next shocker came from my grandmother. No, she wasn't previously married, but she had to provide her place of birth. She listed Fayette City, Pennsylvania. I was ecstatic! Remember all the trouble I'd been going through trying to identify her place of birth? I had looked at her death certificate, on which her place of birth was listed as Fayette County, Pennsylvania.

This was frustrating because she could have been born anywhere in the county. Fayette City is a small town on the Monongahela River, south of Pittsburgh and at the northern edge of the county. This is the only record I've found that indicated her city of birth. This is proof of why we search every record, even if we think we know what it will say. It's the bonus information we don't ask for that solves our genealogical problems.

The information on marriage records tends to be reliable because it comes from the individuals themselves. However, we all know people don't always tell the truth. I was shocked for the third time when I looked at who my grandmother listed as her parents, Lemuel (Simmons) and Ella Batch. They were not her parents but the people who raised her. I shudder to think what would have happened to some unsuspecting genealogist who obtained this record before others, then searched for records confirming this couple as her parents.

Genealogist Ron Smith located a marriage record for his mother's grandparents (his great-grandparents), who were married in 1872. Attached to the marriage certificate was the marriage application. The application indicated the parents of both the bride and groom. This gave Ron his great-great-grandparents! He said he was so excited he couldn't contain himself. His great-great-grandfather was born in the 1840s.

Sometimes marriage applications did not remain with other marriage records at the county courthouse. Sometimes you'll find them at the state archives, a historical society, or a university library. But it will be advantageous for you to search for them if they are not still with the marriage licenses and other records.

In some states at different times in history, a *marriage bond* was required to be posted before the marriage. (This proved the sincerity and the ability of the groom to marry the bride.) Often the witnesses signing these marriage records were relatives. Treat their names very carefully.

Brooks/Terrell Marriage Application—1918 marriage application for author's maternal grandparents, which indicates Lydia's birthplace and that Preston was previously married.

Louisiana Marriage Bond—1905 marriage bond for Augustin and Sylvestre Baptiste, required in Thibodaux Parish, Louisiana.

If you've already collected marriage records, check to see which ones you have. Then see if the others are available. If you are about to search, obtain all the records that exist in your county. If they don't have the marriage applications, ask the clerk what happened to them.

Different Types of Marriages

There are also different types of marriages. We all know many couples did not have big church weddings. Many had small ceremonies at home, and many went to city hall or to a justice of the peace. Different types of marriages create different types of records.

When a couple is married by a justice of the peace, this is a legal civil proceeding. There are legal records created that I've already described. When a couple is married in a church, it is a

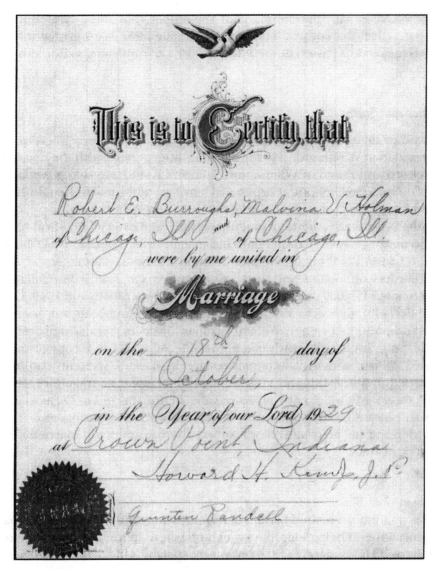

Crown Point Certificate—1929 Crown Point marriage certificate for Robert E. Burroughs and Malvina V. Holman; found among Robert's papers.

religious ceremony. Normally the same legal records are created, but religious records are also created. The church and minister create their own records, which may be overlooked by genealogists. If you know what church the couple attended, by all means ask if they retained records. Sometimes when marriage records are not found in the county courthouse, the only record of a marriage is with the church. But remember that some churches have better recordkeeping practices than others. They are not as systematic as government agencies. I've even seen marriage records passed down to the children of ministers, so don't overlook them as sources.

Border Counties and States

I mentioned earlier that many people did not get married in the area where they lived. My older brother settled in Wilmington, North Carolina, after serving with the marines and married a woman born and raised in Wilmington. It wasn't until I was doing genealogy that he told me they were married in South Carolina. When I asked him why, he said his wife had a friend there and it was quicker to get married there than in Wilmington.

My grandfather's brother, Robert Burroughs, was born and lived all his life in Chicago. However, his second marriage was in Crown Point, Indiana, in 1929. Thousands of Chicago couples were married in Crown Point because neither a blood test nor a waiting period was required. Crown Point borders on Illinois and was a short trolley car ride from Chicago. The city attracted an estimated 175,000 couples getting married between 1915 and 1940. Leading up to World War II (1937–40), they were so busy the office stayed open twenty-four hours a day.

My great-grandmother's brother, William Truman, lived in Pennsylvania all his life. His wife, Anna Able, also lived in Pennsylvania all her life. When I got a copy of their marriage license, it stated William and Anna were married in Maryland. I asked my cousin Chuck why they were married in Maryland, and he said his mother was underage and they ran off to Maryland to get married. And many couples traveled all the way to Las Vegas to get married.

So if you can't locate marriage records, check the bordering county and the bordering state. Ask the clerks in the marriage records office where couples got married if they wanted to get married right away.

Chronologies

Because people migrated, it is often hard to determine when and where they got married. One of the techniques I use to help determine when and where to look for marriage records is to create a chronology. This is merely a list of events in a person's life, in chronological order.

One of my paternal great-grandfathers, William Rice, was born in Missouri, moved to Illinois, and died in Chicago in 1900. I've found evidence of him living in St. Louis and Cape Girardeau, Missouri, and in Cairo and Chicago, Illinois. It was difficult determining where I should write for his marriage license, so I created a chronology of his life.

I figured he probably married before his first daughter was born in 1893, when he was about twenty-five years old. I decided to check marriage records in Chicago from shortly after he arrived in 1888 through 1893, when Frances was born. The county clerk located a marriage license for July 20, 1891. He was twenty-three and his wife, Minnie Barker (my great-grandmother), was nineteen years old.

CHRONOLOGY FOR WILLIAM RICE

1867   Born in Cape Girardeau or St. Louis, Missouri
        (oral history and death certificate)
1880   Lived in Cape Girardeau, Missouri (U.S. Census)
1885   Lived in Cairo, Illinois (city directory)
1887   Moved to Chicago (death certificate)
1889   Lived at 1329 State St. (Chicago city directory)
1891   Lived at 2913 Armour Ave. (Chicago city directory)
1892   Lived at 2712 Cottage Grove (Chicago voter registration)
1893   First daughter, Frances Mae Rice, born in Chicago
        (birth certificate)
1894   Lived at 24th & Dearborn (Chicago city directory)
1899   Lived at 386 33rd St. (Chicago city directory)
1900   Lived at 477 38th St. (death certificate)

So if you're having trouble determining when and where your ancestors were married, try a simple chronology and you should be able to make good guesses.

Dates of Records

Many counties began registering vital records around the turn of the twentieth century, but by 1920 all states required registration of vital records. However, some states, towns, and counties began registering births and deaths before 1900. For example, Virginia has birth and death records from 1853 (including slaves); Chicago has births from 1871 and deaths from 1878; Charleston, South Carolina, has births from 1877 and deaths from 1821; and New Orleans has birth records from 1790 and deaths from 1803. Many people assume early vital records were not kept on African Americans. Sometimes this is true, but more often than not, records were kept. In genealogy we can't assume records were not kept. We have to look and let the clerks prove to us that they do not exist.

Where to Obtain Records

Before you go running off to obtain vital records, check with your family members first. They may have copies of their own birth certificates and marriage licenses (be sure to ask if they do during the oral interview process). Or you may have discovered one of these certificates while researching family papers. In either case, make a photocopy of the record and indicate on the back that you got it from a family member and who it was. This way you won't confuse yourself later, thinking you got it from the vital records office. Then return the original to the family member.

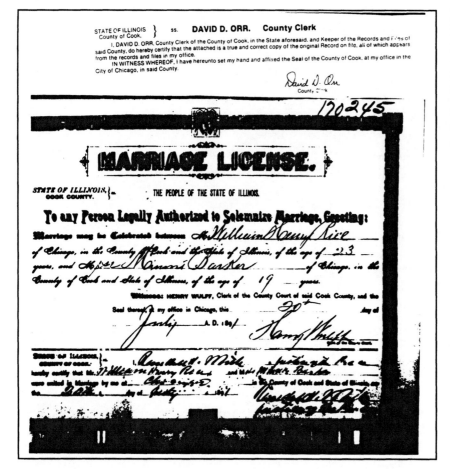

Rice Marriage License—1891 marriage license for author's paternal great-grandparents, William Henry Rice and Minnie Barker, obtained from the Cook County (Illinois) clerk's office.

Refer back to your Family Group Sheets. You should try to obtain a birth, death, and marriage record (and divorce if applicable) for *every* individual who lived during the period that vital records were kept.

Vital records can be obtained from several sources. State laws were enacted mandating birth and death certificates in every state by 1920. So for any of your ancestors who died between then and now, the state vital records office, usually in the state capitol, has a copy of the record. However, you can't always rely on records only being available at the state level since the state law. Desmond Walls Allen, a professional genealogist from Arkansas, said there were 550,000 birth certificates filed for people born prior to the Arkansas state law in 1914. They are called "priors." Marriage and divorce records are almost exclusively maintained at the county level. So you'd apply to the county clerk in the county courthouse.

Before the recording of birth and death records became law in many states, it was done in many counties and cities. Therefore, if an event occurred before the state law, you'll need to check with the county vital records office (or the county department of health) to see if they have records prior to the date of the state law. In some cases records were recorded in major cities before they were recorded in the county. So you'd contact the city vital records office.

However, some records that were created in the counties were transferred to the state, and in some cases the state and county have duplicate records. Early vital records in some states were transferred to the state archives, some to historical societies, and some to universities. It varies by locality.

Guides to Records

There are several guides to assist your research. The following are listed in the Bibliography under "Vital Records" or "Genealogy Reference Guides."

Where to Write for Vital Records lists every state in the union (plus Puerto Rico, the Virgin Islands, and other U.S. territories), the dates for which the state office has records on file, the cost of a record (at the time of publication), the address of the state office where you can obtain a copy, and where to write for earlier records in major cities. It is available for a nominal fee from the U.S. Printing Office (Superintendent of Documents, U.S. Government Printing Office, Washington, DC 20402), from a government bookstore, or from the library.

The *International Vital Records Handbook* is similar to *Where to Write,* listing the dates for which each state office has records, the cost of a record (at the time of publication), and the address of the state office where you can obtain a copy. The difference is the scope is international and it includes sample forms for obtaining records. Some states will not process requests unless they are on the official state form.

Neither *Where to Write* nor *International Vital Records Handbook* provides a county-by-county listing. There are approximately 5,000 counties in the United States. The *Handy Book for Genealogists* and *Ancestry's Red Book* both give a listing for every county in the United States. They also list the types of vital records available in each county and the dates records started in each county.

The *United States County Courthouse Address Book* gives the names, addresses, and telephone numbers for every county in the United States. It is smaller, cheaper, and updated more often than *The Handy Book* and *Ancestry's Red Book.* Telephone numbers at county offices do change. Also, old buildings get demolished and replaced by new facilities, so addresses change.

Fees and Waiting Time

You don't have to travel to the location to obtain copies of records. You can order them by mail. But before ordering, contact the city office or county courthouse for the vital records office where the event occurred. Double-check to see what years they have for birth, death, marriage, and divorce records. Also ask about fees and if there are different charges for certified copies and noncertified copies. You don't need certified copies except for a court case, as in probate. Sometimes county offices sell the same vital statistic record that the state office sells, but for a cheaper price. For example, in 1994 the city of Detroit charged seventeen dollars for a death certificate, whereas the state of Michigan charged thirteen dollars for the same record. At the same time the city of Chicago charged five dollars for a death certificate, whereas the state of Illinois charged ten dollars.

Also ask about the time it takes to receive records. The time will often vary between the city, county, and state. It takes four to six weeks to receive a record from the city of Detroit, whereas the state of Michigan takes up to four months. However, if you walk into the state office, you could pick up the record in forty-five minutes. Detroit will mail the certificate in a week if the request is received by priority mail. Butler County, Ohio, mails a certificate the same day they receive a request, whereas the state of Ohio can take from four to six weeks.

Some county courthouses will let you search older records yourself. This is a lot of fun. Sometimes you can locate records that the clerk may have missed. If you search the records yourself, you can also browse for other ancestors whose names you know or for surnames you suspect are related.

The Internet

Incidentally, don't think you can get vital records on the Internet. Remember, as a genealogist, you want the best available evidence. That's a photocopy of the original record. An index, transcription, or other representation from a book or the Internet will not do. At best, it may give you the date and location where you can obtain a photocopy of the original record.

Segregation

Since most African Americans have roots in the South, segregation can never be forgotten. Some birth, death, and marriage records are segregated by race—white and colored. This is very tricky because there is no consistency. Records were segregated in some southern states and not others. They were segregated in some counties and not in others within the same state. And they were segregated in some time periods and not in others. If you order a record and it is not found, it may be because the person was African American. In this case you may want to write again and be sure the clerk checked both records. In "Going to the Library" I'll cover strategies to help you determine if records were segregated.

No Records

There are many reasons you may be unable to locate vital records. You may be using a nickname and the record is filed under the person's given name. For a woman you may be searching under a married name and the record is under her maiden name.

Sometimes a person lived in a city but died in a suburban hospital. Cook County, Illinois, is so large that the county has regional vital records offices. So a record normally found at the county building in downtown Chicago may actually be located at a regional office in a suburb.

If you have trouble getting death certificates but have found ancestors in cemeteries, be sure you've checked with funeral homes in the area. Also remember that some white-owned funeral homes handled African American burials. And some Blacks in rural areas may have had their own funeral and burial and never reported the death to the county for a death certificate to be recorded.

Many marriage records for African Americans were segregated. Make sure the "colored" records were checked. Sometimes records are not found because the couple never got married. The child was born out of wedlock, and sometimes the parents stayed together and sometimes they did not.

Also be aware of state and county boundary lines. Some people living near a border crossed over for certain events. In addition, these lines are not permanent. They do change from time to time, mostly for political reasons. Your ancestor could have lived in the same house all her life, but the county boundary could have changed several times, placing her in two or three different counties during her lifetime. Check to see where the boundary lines were for the time you're looking for a record. Maps and geographical references are covered in the library chapter.

When no birth record is located, you may want to ask the county to check again for delayed records. Sometimes delayed records are filed separately and clerks may not have checked them. When all else fails, check the church for baptismal records, which were often used in place of birth records. Also look for family Bible records. When death certificates are not recorded, cemetery and funeral home records become more important.

Even if you suspect that there are no birth or death records, you should still make an attempt to search for vital records. You will need a letter from the county or state vital records office that states no record is on file. This is part of your documentation. That still does not mean a record does not exist. It only means you checked and they checked. We'll see later how clerks can be proved wrong.

Restrictions on Records

Unfortunately, vital records are becoming harder to access in some areas of the country. Some states have deemed them private records and restrict access to persons named in the record. This is OK for living individuals, but genealogists are concerned primarily with deceased individuals. Restrictions were instituted because people were obtaining vital records to create illegal identification cards. Lack of access makes it tough not only on criminals but also on genealogists.

This happened in Illinois, but a genealogist came to the rescue. Loretto Szucs, a professional genealogist, author, and editor, had a genealogy client who was in the state legislature. She discussed the problem with him, and he sponsored a new vital records law in Illinois. It opened up the records and made a provision for genealogists to obtain records but with a stamp on them that states, "FOR GENEALOGY PURPOSES ONLY."

In 1994 a bill was circulating in the California legislature to close access to vital records. Genealogists banded together to lobby the state and were very instrumental in blocking the bill's passage. Now they monitor potential bills and work with the state legislature. Local and state genealogical societies in Arizona were successful in getting a new vital records law passed in 1997 that is favorable to genealogists.

Some states have worked with the genealogical community, and others have not. A first step is to contact the state genealogical society, which probably has encountered the problem before you and may know of a work-around. If that doesn't work, contact the Federation of Genealogical Societies and the National Genealogical Society, which have combined efforts and formed a Records Preservation Committee. They push to keep open access to records and monitor situations around the country. The *FGS Forum* publishes a column called "Records Access," which monitors access to all kinds of genealogical records by state. (To contact the FGS or NGS, see "National Genealogical Organizations" in the appendix.)

Computerized Records

The other problem of access to records is computerization. As we all know, computers are both a blessing and a curse. More and more vital records are being computerized because it is faster, cheaper, and requires fewer clerks to punch a name in a computer and print a record than to search a cabinet for a roll of microfilm, then search for a name at a microfilm machine and print out the record. Unfortunately, for this speed we lose accuracy and information. We also lose the pleasure of seeing old handwriting and ornate certificates from different time periods.

The birth certificate for my Aunt Margaret Brooks from Pennsylvania is a computer printout. Her sister Doris Brooks's birth certificate is also a computer printout. Aunt Doris's middle name is Althea, but her computerized birth certificate has her middle name spelled "Alpha." She gets upset every time she looks at it or even thinks about it.

The marriage record I received for my aunt Irene Burroughs was a computer printout from the Cook County clerk. It spelled her name wrong. The data input operator mistook a *u* for an *n* and it came out Burronghs. Also missing were the place of marriage and the address of the minister, both important facts for analyzing the place and type of marriage. I wanted to know if they married in a church or at city hall. I know vital record forms varied tremendously over the years, and I doubted the computer database was flexible enough to include everything from the original certificates, which changed over the years. These programs were designed for efficiency, not for genealogy. So I made another visit to the county clerk's office.

I applied for a copy of the original marriage license and showed the approving clerk my computer printout. He said there would be no problem, which was surprising. However, when I got to the cashier to pay my seven dollars, she said I could not get a photocopy of the original marriage license, only a computer printout. I told her I could get a copy and I already had the computer printout. The cashier said she would ask her supervisor, who had worked in the office for thirty years.

Over walked a tall lady with a badge on her blouse that read "Kathy S." I explained I had a computer printout and wanted a copy of the original marriage license. Kathy said they didn't issue copies of originals anymore. I told her they still had them and a lady upstairs had told me I could get a copy. Kathy said I could talk to *her* supervisor.

A few minutes later another lady came to the counter with a badge that read "Louisa." She also told me I could not get a copy of the original marriage license. She said the computer printout had the same information as the original. I said I'd like to have a copy of the original because there could be some little item on it I might need. She said it had only the names of the bride and groom and that the parents' names weren't added until 1968. I told her a lady upstairs had told me I could get a copy of the original but I couldn't remember her name.

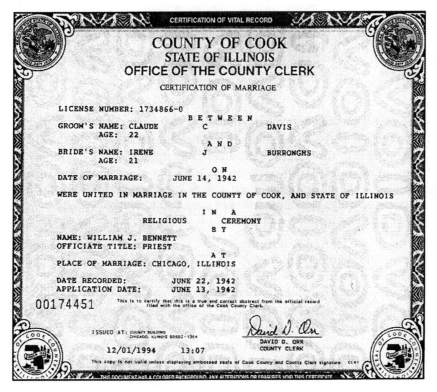

Computer Marriage License—1942 computerized marriage certification for Claude C. Davis and Irene J. Burroughs, obtained from the Cook County (Illinois) clerk's office; Burroughs is misspelled, the name of the priest is incorrect (William J. Bennett), and the name of the church is omitted.

Original Marriage License—
Photocopy of original 1942 marriage license of Claude C. Davis and Irene J. Burroughs, obtained from the Cook County (Illinois) Clerk's office, with proper spelling of Burroughs, correct name of priest (Wm. B. Southern Jr.), and name of church (St. Thomas).

Louisa asked to see what was on my printout, and I showed it to her. I told her the name Burroughs should be spelled with a *u* instead of an *n*. She said it was probably a typo and explained how I could return the printout and they would change it. I told her I wanted to keep the printout *and* get a copy of the original. She said she'd check the marriage application.

Within ten minutes my name was called for the photocopy of the original, which was marked "FOR GENEALOGY PURPOSES ONLY." As I suspected, the computer printout did omit a lot of key information. The original included the birthplace of both bride and groom and the name and address of the church where the wedding was held, St. Thomas Episcopal Church at 3801 Wabash. I immediately recognized it as the family church, and it dawned on me they probably had a big wedding that might have been mentioned in the African American newspaper, the *Chicago Defender.* The date the license was returned was also omitted, June 16, 1942.

I kept reading and found another error. The name of the officiating minister on the printout was obviously different from the one on the original. It appears the data input clerk couldn't read the writing and made up a name. The name of the priest on the computer printout was Wm. J. Bennett and on the original license was Wm. Southern Jr. I was incensed. If I'd tried to look for records for a Reverend William J. Bennett, I would have been on a wild goose chase.

We as genealogists need to question what is happening to the original records and determine what it takes to get copies of the originals. Hopefully, they are not being destroyed. But if we don't take a proactive role, they will be destroyed and can never be recovered.

After Obtaining Records

So order some vital records and then wait for your mailbox to fill. I always get excited when these things arrive in the mail. In addition to obtaining birth and death certificates for your parents, grandparents, and great-grandparents, get them for their brothers and sisters. Because they all were born and died at different times, the information about their parents may have changed, including address, occupation, employer, or spouse. In addition, information missing on one certificate may have been filled out on a sibling's certificate. Obtaining certificates for a large family may help to fill in gaps in migration patterns when a family moved from one location to another.

When records arrive, make photocopies on your acid-free paper and file them in their respective folders. Then you can work with the photocopy and leave your original neat and clean. If these certificates give you new information, update your Family Group Sheets and Pedigree Chart. A footnote should be created next to the date and place of the event. These footnotes should be numbered consecutively. Then the description of the source should follow in the notes section at the bottom or on another page. The description should be detailed enough so that someone else could pull the record. For example, if it is for a death certificate, the note should list the name and date of death of the deceased and the death certificate number (for example, [1]City of Chicago Board of Health Death Certificate No. 4192 for Robert E. Burroughs, January 28, 1958).

Analyze each certificate thoroughly by studying each and every item on the certificate. Check to see if it is a short form or a long form, a photocopy of the original, a form filled out by a clerk, or a computer printout. Realize the record is only as accurate as the informant's memory. For example, the date of death recorded on a death certificate is normally very reliable. However, the age, place of birth, and parentage of the deceased can be unreliable because it was not supplied by the deceased. Record what new information you learn, what information is confirmed, what is contradicted, and what new questions are raised, and make a list of follow-up things to do. When these certificates mention other people, remember to add that additional information to their respective folders.

Birth, death, and marriage are, unfortunately, the vital necessities for genealogists. I say unfortunately because many genealogists are concerned only with the dates and places of birth, death, and marriage. They neglect the other aspects of a person's life. These three events account for only three days in a person's whole life. It's the other days that make up 99.9 percent of their lives and will tell you about their personality, lifestyle, habits, education, travels, and other things that will give you clues for tracing their parents. So read on to see how to fill in other aspects of your ancestors' lives. In the chapter that follows, we'll also examine sources of published vital records.

Going to the Library

Haven't been to the library lately? Don't be intimidated—it's fun. To some people a library sounds like school or work or something hard. Using the library for genealogy is different from using it when you were in school. Back then you had to go to the library whether you liked it or not. With genealogy a library is a major source for finding your ancestors, so you want to go. Once you find an ancestor, you'll really get excited and you'll love going to the library. This chapter will guide you through the library so your trip will be fun and successful.

How to Find a Genealogy Library

Rather than a regular public library, you'll want to find a library with a lot of genealogy books. Many major cities have large public libraries with a genealogy department on one floor. Cities such as New York, Los Angeles, Dallas, and Cincinnati have some of the largest genealogy collections of public libraries in the country. Okay, you say you don't live in one of those cities. The local public library in your community will probably have a small genealogy or local history section. It may not be the biggest or the best in the area, but it should be a place to start.

There are libraries that specialize in genealogy or have special genealogy collections that are larger than the one in the local public library. This is important not only for where you live but for where your ancestors lived (eventually you'll want to visit the library in that city). Genealogy libraries are not difficult to find. A quick and easy way is to ask the reference librarian at your local public library for the best and largest genealogy collections in your area. You can also consult reference directories that list libraries. The *Directory of American Libraries with Genealogy or Local History Collections*, edited by P. William Filby, lists major genealogy collections within libraries, as well as libraries that specialize in genealogy. It lists 1,500 libraries in the United States alphabetically by state and city and 128 in Canada. Each listing includes the library's name, address, telephone number, hours, policies, size of collection, and major reference works owned. If there are printed guides to the collection, they are noted. This and other reference books that list libraries with genealogy collections can be found under "Libraries" in the Bibliography. The following are a few of the most useful volumes.

The *American Library Directory,* published by R. R. Bowker, attempts to list every public, private, and academic library in the United States. Published annually, it is a multivolume set arranged alphabetically by state and then city. Listings include the library's street address, e-mail address, telephone number, branches, staff names, size of holdings, subject interests, special collections, publications, date founded, and automated information.

The *Genealogist's Address Book,* by Elizabeth Bentley (see "Genealogy Reference Guides" in the Bibliography), is in three parts: national addresses, state addresses, and ethnic and religious organizations and research centers. It gives names, addresses, and telephone numbers. Part 2 lists addresses and telephone numbers of libraries and archives that specialize in genealogy in each state. It also lists historical societies and genealogical societies, some of which have genealogy collections. The national section lists large institutions like the National Archives and the Library of Congress. The ethnic and religious organizations and research centers listed in Part 3 are not all genealogically related, nor do they all have research facilities. *The Genealogist's Address Book* is also available on CD-ROM.

The *Ancestry Family Historian's Address Book,* by Juliana Szucs Smith, is organized alphabetically by state but then alphabetically by name of library rather than name of city. This makes it a little difficult to locate libraries in the same city. Listings include names, addresses, some telephone numbers, and some Web sites.

By using these guides' listings of addresses and telephone numbers, you can contact libraries before visiting, which, as you'll see, might be a wise decision. You can also find some of this information on the Internet, which I'll discuss in the chapter on "Electronic Genealogy."

Mormon Family History Library—Salt Lake City, Utah

The largest genealogy library in the world, the Family History Library, is operated by the Mormons, the Church of Jesus Christ of Latter-day Saints (LDS). Tracing their ancestors for purposes of church ceremonies is important to them. So the church sends teams around the world to microfilm original records in churches, courthouses, and other repositories, including birth and death certificates, baptismal records, wills, land deeds, and other genealogical records. The Family History Library has more than 2 million reels of microfilm. These records include everyone in the original records, not just Mormons.

One copy of the microfilm stays with the original records. Another copy goes to Salt Lake City and is available for researchers at the Family History Library. The library is free to use and open to the public. The records are the exact same records you'd see if you traveled to Mississippi, Alabama, or other places where your ancestors lived. The Family History Library also lends microfilm to their branch libraries around the country, called Family History Centers. The LDS church operates more than 1,600 Family History Centers around the country, which are also free and open to the public. They can be located in the telephone directory under "Church of Jesus Christ of Latter-day Saints." Researchers can rent microfilm to view at the centers for a small fee, about the cost of postage.

There are several resources that describe how the Family History Library operates. The LDS church publishes three small pamphlets that are very useful: *Family History Library, Library Services and Resources,* and *In a Granite Mountain.* Two excellent books are *The Library: A Guide to the LDS Family History Library,* by Johni Cerny and Wendy Elliott, and *Going to Salt Lake City to Do Family History,* by J. Carlyle Parker (for both, see "Libraries" in the Bibliography). Elizabeth L. Nichols wrote a book on using the Family History Library's computer systems, *Understanding Genealogy in the Computer Age: Family Search* (see "Electronic Genealogy" in the Bibliography).

Specifically for African American genealogy, see the Family History Library's *African American Records Quick Guide* and *Family History Library Bibliography of African-American Sources,* both compiled by Marie Taylor; and Margo Williams's article, "Using the LDS Family History Library in Building Your Genealogy," published in the *Journal of the Afro-American Historical and Genealogical Society.* I gave a lecture on using the Family History Library for African American genealogy at the 2000 Federation of Genealogical Societies conference in Salt Lake City, Utah ("Using the Resources of the Family History Library for African American Research"). A tape of the lecture can be obtained from Repeat Performance (see "Libraries" in the Bibliography for all resources).

Learning About the Library

By this stage in the game, you may have identified many new ancestors who lived in many different locations. Plus, genealogy can be a never-ending hobby as you try to track down all these ancestors. Therefore, you know you cannot finish this job in a day. You'll have to return to the library many times. So it's best to have limited objectives on your first trip to the library. Then you won't be overwhelmed or disappointed if you don't reach Adam and Eve on your first try.

There are several things you need to determine first: Where is the library? What days and times is it open? What are parking facilities? And how is it accessed by public transportation?

Some genealogy libraries have limited staff and are closed on Mondays. Some are closed on weekends, and others are closed in the evening. That can make it tough for people who work from nine to five. I received a call from an out-of-town genealogy group that scheduled a two-week research trip to Mississippi. They had a twenty-four-hour layover in Chicago and wanted to visit the Newberry Library, a major genealogical library. Fortunately, they contacted me first, and I told them the library was closed the day they'd be in Chicago. They then wanted to visit a branch of the National Archives, but the location made it difficult for public transportation from the train station and back. So it pays to check ahead.

Be sure to check for admission fees. Some libraries charge admission, and you don't want to be surprised at the door. While you're at it, check on costs for making photocopies and procedures for making photocopies. Some libraries have self-service photocopying, whereas others allow only staff to photocopy so that materials won't be mishandled. In these facilities you have to fill out a form and submit a request to photocopy a book or document and retrieve it sometime later. This can make a big difference if you have limited time to research.

There might be other rules and regulations you must follow, and you need to find out what they are before visiting. Is the library for members only, or do members get special privileges? Do you need to register or need a special library card to use the library? Can you bring your portable computer? Are there limited electrical outlets for computers?

What are the security procedures? Since genealogy books are normally the oldest in the library, special procedures are sometimes implemented to ensure the books remain in the collection and in good condition. You'll want to know if you can bring in notebooks and purses. Some facilities prohibit purses, notebooks, and even file folders to be brought into the research room. Some libraries have lockers outside the research room, and personal belongings must be placed in them. Anything you bring in and out of the research room must be searched. Many facilities with genealogy collections have old, rare, and valuable books and documents. Some of these items are the only ones in existence, and libraries don't want to lose them. I never complain about strict security procedures. I want to be sure what I want to see is there when I need it. These procedures could dramatically affect how you research if you are used to constantly referring to your notes and documents. So it is wise to find out what they are beforehand.

If you plan on spending the day at the library, you'll also want to inquire about eating facilities in the building or nearby. Some have lunchrooms where you can bring a sandwich, and others have cafeterias. For those that don't, you'll want to know how far you'll have to go for lunch. I've heard of people trying to work through the day without eating and getting sick.

Once you get to the library, you'll want a tour. In fact, before you visit, ask about tours. Sometimes they are given only on certain days at certain times. Sometimes they are given by available staff only when they have time. But you need to know the layout of the room(s) and where everything is located. You don't want to find out at the end of a day of fruitless searches that what you needed was just on the other side of the room.

You'll also want to know who the reference librarian is and if there is a curator or archivist. They will usually be the most knowledgeable people in the library or in the genealogy department. I can usually find the easy stuff myself, but when I get to the hard questions, I need the person who knows the most about the collection. It's very important to know who that person is and get to know him or her. Reference librarians and archivists can solve many problems and save you valuable time. But use their time wisely, or you'll be avoided like the plague. That means learn the basics and the easy stuff. The more you do on your own, the more reference librarians will be happy to help you.

I always like to get the name and business card of the genealogy reference librarian or the person who helped me the most. You will have to visit the library again, and if you develop a personal contact, your life will be easier the second time around. The name will also come in handy if you have to call the facility in the future. "Hey, Mr. Jones. Remember me? I was there on Friday and you helped me locate the book on Spartanburg County. I neglected to copy the copyright page and wondered if you could assist me with it." Or "Do you also have books on Edgefield County?"

So your initial objectives are to get to know where the library is and how it operates. As a beginner, when you get down to actual researching, your research objectives should center on twentieth-century research. You'll need to search records from the present back to 1920. This will prepare you for the census records we'll discuss later. Some of these twentieth-century records you've gathered already from the sources we've already covered. But there are others you'll need to explore.

How Materials in Libraries Are Organized

Some genealogy libraries or genealogy collections are just like the libraries when you were in school. You know, books are on the shelves and you just go browsing down an aisle to find what you want. However, many libraries with genealogy collections are very different. To preserve valuable books and documents, they store them in climate-controlled rooms too cold for most researchers to work in comfortably. The books are in one room, and the researchers are in another. In order to get the books and materials you need, you have to find them in the card catalogue (or computer catalogue) and then submit a request for a book to be retrieved by a staff member. This is called a "closed stack" collection. Closed because the collection is behind closed doors and retrieved by the staff. One of the questions you should ask when you call is if the library has an open or closed stack collection.

In addition to books, genealogy libraries may have records that have been microfilmed, and you'll have to load them on a machine to read. There might also be a collection of photographs, which is always exciting. When I visited a genealogy collection in Pennsylvania for the first time, my colleague suggested I first look at the photographic collection, which was very renowned. I ended up spending so much time there that I only had time to see the book collection for a couple of minutes. But it was worth it because I found a photograph of a distant ancestor who fought in the Civil War!

Almost all of today's libraries have some kind of integration with electronic technology. Many are converting old card catalogues to computer. Some use both types of catalogue during conversion periods, and you may need to search both. It is very different to search for books and records in a card catalogue than on a computer. There are advantages and disadvantages to both methods. In addition to the card catalogues on computer, many libraries have actual genealogy records and indexes on the computer. Some have drawers of CD-ROM disks you can use on a computer, while others have direct access to the Internet.

Books and records are catalogued according to one of three systems, in some cases more than one. The one we're familiar with from high school is the Dewey Decimal System. It has three-digit numbers, like 900 to 999, which is for History, followed by the first initial of the author's last name. The numbers are further subdivided within the series; for instance, 929 is for Genealogy. Many larger public and academic libraries are catalogued by the Library of

Congress Classification System, which uses letters and numbers. For example, C, D, E, and F are for History. The numbers are further subdivided by double letters and numbers; for example, CS1-3090 is for Genealogy, and CS42-2209 is Genealogy by region of the country, and CS2300-3090 is Genealogy with Personal and Family Names.

There are some libraries that use both, the Dewey Decimal System for older works and the Library of Congress System for newer works. Once you know the system, you can walk in any library and go to the section for the books you need. Finally, some libraries use a proprietary cataloguing system unique to their library. Believe it or not, there are other libraries, or collections within libraries, that don't even have card catalogues. They use printed guides to their collections, called "finding aids." These are booklets or other reference publications that describe collections, sometimes giving numbers or codes for the librarians to locate the materials and for you to order the materials.

This may sound like an academic discussion that you'd rather not be bothered with, but it will affect your ability to locate items in a library. This is especially true if the cataloguing is by computer and uses the Library of Congress system. Knowing the Library of Congress subject headings will greatly improve your ability to find materials. All books are classified by subject, and the Library of Congress publishes lists of these subjects. For example, should you search under the subject term Blacks, Black Americans, African Americans, Afro-Americans, or Negroes? It's a good question, and the multivolume set *Library of Congress Subject Headings* (1997) answers it and other questions about which terms computer catalogues recognize. These will also be the terms used in many library card catalogues under subject categories. This set of subject headings can be found in larger libraries. (To answer your question, the old Library of Congress term was "Negroes," and the current term is "Afro-Americans." "Blacks" would include people from other countries.) Below are some genealogical subjects and the terms used by the Library of Congress.

SUBJECT	LIBRARY OF CONGRESS SUBJECT HEADINGS
Autobiography	Douglass, Frederick
	Autobiography
	Autobiographies—Bibliography—Union lists
	Afro-Americans—Biography
	Afro-Americans—Biography—Bibliography—Union lists
	Slaves—United States—Biography—Bibliography—Union lists
Biography	Douglass, Frederick, 1817?–1895
	Afro-Americans—Biography
	Blacks—Biography
	Afro-Americans—Mississippi—Biography
	Afro-Americans—Mississippi—History
	Mississippi—biography
	Mississippi—History

Subject	Library of Congress Subject Headings
Biographical dictionaries	Blacks—United States—Biography
	Afro-Americans—Biography—Indexes
	Afro-American families—Biography
	Afro-American soldiers—Biography
	Afro-American women—Biography
	Afro-American musicians—Biography
	Afro-American lawyers—Directories
	Afro-American Baptists—Biography
	Afro-American Episcopalians
	Women, Black—United States—Biography
	Afro-Americans—Biography—Bibliography—Microform catalogues
	Blacks—Biography—Bibliography—Microform catalogues
	Afro-Americans—Mississippi
Blacks	Afro-Americans—Genealogy
	Afro-Americans—History
Birth records	Birth certificates
	Registers of births, etc.
Cemetery records	Cemeteries—Mississippi
Churches	Churches—Mississippi
	Hinds County (Miss.)—churches
	Methodist
	St. Marks Church
City	Jackson (Miss.)
City directories	Jackson (Miss.)—Directories
County	Hinds County or Hinds County (Miss.)
Court records	Court records—Mississippi
Death records	Cemeteries—Mississippi
	Death notices—Mississippi
	Epitaphs—Mississippi
	Tombstones
	Sepulchral monuments
	Obituaries—Mississippi
Divorce records	Divorce records
Family	Burroughs family
Family history	Genealogy
	Haley, Alex
	Haley family
	Kinte family
Funeral records	Funeral homes
	Undertakers
	Undertaking
Gazetteers	Mississippi—Gazetteers
	Mississippi—Description and travel

SUBJECT	LIBRARY OF CONGRESS SUBJECT HEADINGS
	Names, geographical—Mississippi
	Postal service—Mississippi
Genealogies	Genealogy
	Genealogy—Research
	Burroughs family
	Washington, Harold, 1922–1987—Family
	Afro-Americans—Genealogy
	Afro-American families
	Mississippi—Genealogy
	Family reunions—Mississippi
Genealogical dictionary	Afro-Americans—Genealogy—Bibliography
Genealogy journals	Mississippi—Genealogy—Periodicals
History	Mississippi—History
	Southern states—History
Land records	Deeds—Mississippi
	Land grants—Mississippi
	Land titles—Mississippi
	Settlement
	Land tenure—Mississippi
Maps	Hinds County (Miss.)—Maps
	Mississippi—Maps
	Mississippi—Description and travel—Maps
	Mississippi—Atlases
Marriage records	Marriage licenses—Mississippi
	Marriage records
	Marriage customs
Military records	Afro-Americans—Soldiers
	Pensions, military—Mississippi
	United States—History—[insert name of war]—Regimental histories
	United States—History—[insert name of war]— Cemeteries
	United States—History—[insert name of war]— Rosters
	United States—History—[insert name of war]— Registers
	United States—History—[insert name of war]— Biography
	Mississippi—History—[insert name of war]
State	Mississippi—Genealogy
	Mississippi—History
	Afro-Americans—Mississippi
State census	Mississippi—Census
Taxation	Taxation—Mississippi
Vital Records	Registers of births, etc.
Wills	Wills—Mississippi
	Probate records—Mississippi
	Estates

The best guide I've read that covers library research is *A Guide to Library Research Methods,* by Thomas Mann (see "Libraries" in the Bibliography). A librarian at the Library of Congress, Mann teaches classes on how to research and is also a former private investigator. His guide is used in many schools to teach students the techniques of researching. He informs readers of specialized encyclopedias and indexes and explains how to master the Library of Congress subject headings and everything else in a library.

Getting to Know the Library

Once you've identified a genealogy library and you generally know how it operates, you need to get to know it personally. The better you know it, the easier it will be to use and the more things you'll be able to find in it.

The first questions you want to ask are, What is its specialty, and how does it differ from other genealogy libraries? Every institution has its own specialty, or uniqueness. That's the reason it's in existence. If it is not unique, researchers can go somewhere else.

One library may have the largest collection of genealogy materials in the area; one may have the most maps; one may have the most papers created in the nineteenth century. One may have the largest collection of newsletters and journals, and one may have the most family histories. You never know until you ask. For example, the Chicago Public Library has a small collection of genealogy materials on Chicago and Illinois, and the Chicago Historical Society collects published and original manuscripts on Chicago history. The Illinois Historical Society collects private papers and documents concerning the history of Illinois. The Newberry Library, also located in Chicago, collects genealogical materials from throughout the United States, including Chicago and Illinois, but concentrates on the Midwest, New England, and pre-twentieth-century materials. The National Archives collects only records created by the Federal Government and has a branch in Chicago, and the Illinois State Archives collects records regarding Illinois state, county, and municipal governments. There is often a little overlap, but each collection has some primary reason for existence.

It's a good idea to request booklets, pamphlets, and flyers the library publishes on its collection. These can be obtained on your first visit or often by mail or the Web. Depending on the size and the age of the collection, someone may have written a guide to the library or genealogy collection. If so, you'll want to examine it before arriving. It will detail the uniqueness of the collection and list many items in the collection. It will not list everything because libraries purchase materials on a continuing basis. By the time such a book is published, it is out of date. However, that does not mean you should not read it. It only means the card catalogue or finding aids are the ultimate answer to what is in the collection. The guide is a good starting point.

Next you need to understand the floor layout. Where is the catalogue? Where are the books, if any are on open shelves, and what subjects are where? Is the collection on more than one floor, and if so, what is on each floor? Many of these questions will be answered on a tour if you take one. There may also be a map and floor layout to illustrate where items are stored.

You also want to know if there is a bookstore or gift shop. This may be the place to buy a guide to the collection or other genealogy books or forms you may need.

After you've gone this far, it's time to check the card catalogue. Is it the old kind with cards in drawers or the new kind with a computer terminal? If the latter, are all the materials in the system or only ones after a certain date? In the latter case you'll have to consult both for most research projects. Some systems will have Internet connections and perhaps locate materials on their Web site, which we'll discuss in the "Electronic Genealogy" chapter.

Are there any "finding aids" or bibliographies for special collections that you need to be aware of? Where are these located? Several genealogy libraries have developed African American bibliographies listing a sampling of genealogy materials in their collections to assist those doing African American genealogy. Florida, Maryland, Pennsylvania, and South Carolina have guides to researching African American families using records in their state archives. The Newberry Library, Detroit Public Library (Burton Historical Collection), and Allen County Public Library (Fort Wayne, Indiana) have similar guides for using their collections. These guides won't contain everything of use to you in the collections, but you wouldn't want to research for very long without using one.

Using the Collection

Now that you're getting down to serious business, you need to be sure you have the right tools with you to research successfully. What are those things needed to get the job done? Two forms you've been using are a must for any research trip, the Research To Do list and the Research Calendar. The first reminds you of research you plan on doing; the other is for research you have completed. They should be with you at all times. If this is not your first trip to the library, the Research Calendar should include all your previous trips. You do not want to duplicate research, and you may need to review previous research to put the current trip into perspective.

The first thing to do after sitting down in a library is to take out your Research Calendar and record the day's date and name and location of the library. Then record the author, title, date of publication, version or edition, and card catalogue number or microfilm reel number for every book or record you examine. Record the name or names you're searching for in each particular record. Then note if you find something or not and if you make a photocopy from the item. If you do not find anything, be sure to record "none" or "nil" to indicate it was a negative search. Negative research can be as important as positive research. There are reasons you don't find what you're looking for, and this is something you need to analyze. If you have to leave the library before you are finished with a book or record, note where you stopped reading so you can return where you left off. This procedure will keep a running tally of all your research.

! Trap: Not using a Research Calendar and keeping it up to date.

If ideas come to you that you want to research later, immediately record them on your Research To Do sheet. Some of my best ideas come while I'm concentrating on my research.

The next items of importance to bring to the library are your Family Group Sheets and Pedigree Charts. They should be up to date with all the information you've collected thus far. If your genealogy charts are not up to date, you'll be researching without all the data you've collected and therefore might miss some things. And while you're at it, it's a good idea to bring blank genealogy charts and forms. You never know when you'll find a new bunch of names you need to sort out.

! Trap: Going to the library and not having your charts up to date.

I suggest making an alphabetical list of all your ancestors' surnames, and another of spelling variations of those surnames (see examples that follow). We've stated that names were sometimes spelled differently in the past. The further you go back, the less consistently names will be spelled.

! Trap: Ignoring spelling variations in names.

LIST OF ANCESTORS' SURNAMES

Barker	Hansberry	Simpson
Brooks	Hunt	Smothers
Burroughs	Hutton	Swygert
Clemons	Kinner	Terrell
Dyer	McGruder	Thayer
Gaither	Moultrie	Truman
Goe	Norton	Twitty
Griffin	Rice	Williams
Hall	Rutherford	

If you do not take the list of spelling variations with you, you might miss your ancestors in some records because you're looking under the spelling you're used to, not other variations they could be listed under.

SPELLING VARIATIONS FOR SURNAME BURROUGHS

Barrow	Brows	Burrills
Barrows	Burow	Burris
Barrus	Burows	Burriss
Borah	Burrall	Burrough
Borahs	Burralls	Burroughs
Boris	Burras	Burrow
Borough	Burrell	Burrowes
Boroughs	Burrells	Burrows
Borroughs	Burrill	Burrus
Bouroughs		

I also advocate making a list of the cities, states, and counties where your ancestors lived. These will be the areas you will be researching for records. After you create the list, alphabetize it (see the following example). Then it will be easy to check a card catalogue using your organized list of localities.

LOCATIONS RESEARCHING—TONY BURROUGHS

States (or Countries)	Cities	Counties
Arizona	Tempe	Maricopa
	Nogales	Santa Cruz
Arkansas	Hot Springs	Garland
California	Berkeley	Alameda
	Los Angeles	Los Angeles
	Palo Alto	Santa Clara
	San Jose	Santa Clara
Colorado	Denver	Denver
Florida	Jacksonville	Duval
Georgia	Atlanta	Fulton
Illinois	Cairo	Alexander
	Chicago	Cook
	Joliet	Will
Indiana	Indianapolis	Marion
Kansas	Fort Riley	Riley
	Junction City	Geary
Kentucky		
Maryland		Prince George's

States (or Countries)	Cities	Counties
Michigan	Detroit	Wayne
Missouri	Cape Girardeau	Cape Girardeau
	St. Louis	St. Louis
Nebraska	Crawford	Dawes
	Fort Robinson	Dawes
	Valentine	Cherry
New Jersey	Orange	Essex
Ohio	Cincinnati	Hamilton
	Cleveland	Cuyahoga
	Oxford	Butler
Pennsylvania	Belle Vernon	Fayette
	Bridgeport	Fayette
	Brownsville	Fayette
	California	Washington
	Charleroi	Washington
	Coal Center	Washington
	Coolspring Township	Mercer
	Donora	Washington
	Elco	Washington
	Elizabeth	Allegheny
	Farrell	Mercer
	Fayette City	Fayette
	Jefferson Township	Fayette
	Monessen	Westmoreland
	Monongahela	Washington
	Newell	Fayette
	Perry Township	Fayette
	Perryopolis	Fayette
	Pittsburgh	Allegheny
	Red Lion	Fayette
	Redstone Township	Fayette
	Roscoe	Washington
	Sharon	Mercer
	Twilight	Washington
	Washington	Washington
	Washington Township	Washington
	West Middlesex	Mercer
South Carolina	Columbia	Richland
	Spartanburg	Spartanburg
	Blockers Township	Edgefield
	Saluda Township	Edgefield

States (or Countries)	Cities	Counties
Tennessee	Chattanooga	Hamilton
	Jackson	Madison
	Memphis	Shelby
		Giles
Virginia		Clark
West Virginia	Kingwood	Preston
	Monongah	Marlon
	Morgantown	Monongalia
	Newberry	Preston
	Wheeling	Ohio
Wyoming	Buffalo City	Johnson
	Cheyenne	Laramie
	Fort McKinney	Johnson
Japan	Nagasaki	
	Yokohama	
Philippines		
Hawaii	Scofield Barracks	
England		

I also carry a list of subjects I like to search for, things like African Americans, Blacks, Negroes, coloreds, slaves, freedmen, free persons of color, and A.M.E. (African Methodist Episcopal) Church. These are key words that pertain to African Americans and might lead me to books in the collection.

You'll also need some office supplies, things like pens, pencils, and paper. But for a really efficient toolkit, pack the list of items below so you'll have a portable office on the road with you. It makes life very comfortable.

pens	stapler and extra staples	rubber bands
pencils	file folders	correction fluid or tape
eraser	sticky notes	magnifying glass or sheet
acid-free paper	tape	stamps (if out of town)
scrap paper	scissors	envelopes (if out of town)
paper clips		

These small items can be stored in small "pocket secretaries" (sometimes called portable desks) that fit easily in a briefcase or purse. I keep one loaded and handy to drop into my briefcase whenever I leave for the library.

Believe it or not, there are some things you should *not* take to the library, especially to out-of-town libraries. Those are old, original, and rare documents. You don't want to risk losing them or handling them too much. If they are unprotected, they will pick up dirt and oil every time you touch them. If they are folded, each folding and unfolding weakens the paper, and it will eventually tear. Old documents are very expensive to clean and repair professionally and impossible to replace if lost. They are best left at home or in a safe deposit box. If you need the information, make a photocopy and work from the copy.

Also don't take the family Bible or old photographs to the library. Pages of births, deaths, and marriages from the Bible can be photocopied, as well as photographs. You want to preserve these items as much as possible for your descendants to appreciate years after you are gone.

Taking Notes and Making Photocopies

When you take notes, take your time and be neat and organized. Remember, you can't complete your family history in a day, so don't work as if you had to. It's more important to be able to read your notes when you return home or when you return to the library the next time. I recommend keeping all notes on 8½″ × 11″ sheets of paper. It's a lot harder to lose a large sheet of paper than a yellow sticky note or a small call slip.

Once you start looking at records, you're likely to locate new information on your ancestors. Do not record the information directly on your Pedigree Chart and Family Group Sheets. This destroys the audit trail of where you found the information. You always want to retrace your steps to see when, where, and how you located information. If you do not photocopy the information and prefer to write it down, record it on a sheet of notepaper with the day's date, name of library, author, title, publication date, card catalogue number (or microfilm number), and page number (frame number for microfilm). This keeps the information as a unique document and assists you in finding it again. It also assists others if they have to retrieve the document. Most of this information will also be needed to properly cite sources on your Family Group Sheet.

For many records you'll prefer making photocopies. When you do, you'll want to follow some good research techniques. If you copy several pages, be sure you keep them in order. Book pages are normally numbered, but not everything you copy will contain page numbers. If it does not, be extra careful to keep pages in their original order. If a record was created in chronological order, it might be necessary to keep it in that order to understand and analyze the process of creating the record. If you mix the pages up, trying to figure this out when you return home can be a disaster. If you copy the front and back of a document, it's best to staple the two pages front to back so later you'll know how the document looked when you first saw it.

You'll know the titles of books and records you're researching each day, but will you remember six months later? To prevent that problem, when copying pages from a book, also photocopy the title page and copyright page. The copyright page will give you the date of publication and, for later books, the subject headings determined by the Library of Congress. This will help you locate books on similar subjects. Then staple these pages to the other pages you photocopy, so they will all be together and you'll know what book they came from. It's better to photocopy this information rather that write it down because you'll have everything, bypassing possible transcription errors. Finally, turn the last page over and record the name and location of the library and the day's date. Then whenever you examine the document again, you'll know exactly when and where the information came from. It's not left to your fading memory.

If you make a copy from something other than a book and it does not have a title and copyright page, record the following on the back of each sheet of paper.

Title or description of record
Author and or publisher
Date of publication, filming, or compilation if it exists
Card catalogue number or microfilm reel number
Name and location of library
Date of research

The goal is to record information so you know where it came from, when you copied it, and how someone else can obtain the same record. Elizabeth Shown Mills, in her book *Evidence: Citation and Analysis for the Family Historian,* advocates recording this information on the front of photocopies. Then if you send a copy to someone else, he or she will have the full documentation as to what it is and where it came from. I advocate recording it on the back because I like to keep documents looking as they did when originally created. I don't want to look at a document many years later and have to analyze whether the notes were done by me or the person who created the document. If a copy has to go to someone else, I'll record the proper information or photocopy the back.

Abstracting and Extracting

Sometimes you will not want or be able to photocopy every document you are searching. The record may be too voluminous, copy machines may not be available, or copy charges might be too expensive. In these cases you will need to record the information in your notes or directly into your computer. How you record this information will determine whether you are creating an abstract or an extract. An abstract is a summary of the important details in a document, whereas an extract is an entire copy from an original document.

If you are searching through a mass of marriage records and locate many surnames of your ancestors but don't know if they are related, you may not want to copy all the information in each record. It would take too long and add a lot of unnecessary bulk to your research, especially when they all contain the same legal verbiage. Therefore, you will record the relevant data to distinguish one record from another. This is an abstract.

In other cases it will be important to record all the information in a document, exactly as it appears in the original. This is an extract. If you find a copy of your ancestor's marriage record, you'll want to copy everything exactly as it is on the original document.

It's also important to know when you are looking at an abstract or an extract versus an original document. Most records in genealogical libraries contain abstracts of genealogical documents, even though they may not say so. A book of marriage records or wills that you pull from a shelf (or see a list of similar records on the Internet) does not contain original records or copies of original records. Some researcher looked at the originals in the county courthouse and made abstracts of them to publish. Understanding this, you'll know that there could be errors or omissions in the published version and that you always need to search the original documents or microfilm copies of the originals.

One researcher abstracted many details for a will I was interested in but didn't include all the details I needed. It wasn't until I received a copy of the original will from the county courthouse that I learned it was the document that provided for the freedom of my ancestors when it was written in 1795. I'd say that's a very important detail.

Those of you who take a computer to the library need to be careful to cite the source of your documents with meticulous care. It is so easy to quickly type in the information you are interested in without indicating where it came from or distinguishing between one record and another. If you let this happen, you will destroy your audit trail and not be able to properly cite the source of information on your Family Group Sheets.

Research Strategy

Before you start looking for any records, recall the difference between primary (original) records and secondary records, explained in the chapter "What Is Genealogy?" Most libraries contain secondary records: books, indexes, and compiled records from original records. This is where you need to recognize the difference. If you're still a little foggy, reread that chapter. But the essence is, you don't want to reinvent the wheel, so first check what others have researched and made easy for you. Only after you've exhausted all the compiled sources should you attempt to look for original sources. This will save you time and effort and also reveal new original sources. A good idea is to check the bibliography in the back of books, which will point out additional sources.

! Trap: Doing primary research before secondary research. See what others have done first so you won't reinvent the wheel.

To get a good understanding of what the library might have on your ancestors or on the places where they lived, you'll need to go to the card catalogue and give it a good going over before you start looking at books and records. There will be many items you'll want to examine, but everything will not be of equal importance. Therefore, make a list. Every time you see a book or record in the catalogue you want to examine, add it to your list, noting the title, author, and card catalogue number or microfilm reel number. Only after you compile the list will you determine what you should examine first. So when your list is finished, prioritize it. What would you like to look at first, second, and third? This way you'll spend your time wisely and efficiently. You don't want to waste time on something that may be interesting but of little use in locating your ancestors. You can always come back to it later.

How Segregation, Racism, and Black History Affect Research

Once you're ready to search for records, segregation will become vitally important. Segregation was a major fabric of our ancestors' lives. You'll search many traditional genealogical records, but some will be segregated by race. If you're not aware of segregated records, you'll likely miss locating your ancestors in many records.

In the South segregation affected the compiling and organizing of records. In many locations there were separate docket books containing records for whites and African Americans (referred to at the time as "colored"). In some county courthouses there were even separate rooms, still in existence today, to house white and "colored" records.

In some city directories African Americans are not included in the regular alphabetical listing but at the end of the book. They have a separate "colored" section or "colored department" that looks almost like an addendum. Whites are listed in the front section, and African Americans are listed in the rear, in the "colored section." If you searched for your ancestors in such a directory and got to the end of the alphabet without seeing your ancestor's name, you would probably think they were not in that city and would search elsewhere. But if you knew there was a "colored section," you could search that section or search it first. This happened to me when researching city directories in South Carolina. I had researched unsuccessfully for several hours before I discovered African Americans were listed in a segregated section in the rear of the directory. Then I found the gold mine at the end of the rainbow, so to speak, listing my ancestors.

Whatever was the norm in one southern state or county was not necessarily the norm in another state or county. Also, some records in the same area were segregated in some time periods but not in others. Some cities listed African Americans in the back of the directory, whereas others integrated the names but used abbreviations and notations for African Americans (see lists, pages 247 and 248).

Sometimes African Americans were deliberately kept out of records entirely. This latter situation is why many African Americans haven't traced their family history. I have had countless people come up to me and say, "They didn't keep any records on Black people." Well, that is true in some situations, but there are many records that do include African Americans. A genealogist's job is to find out which records *do* exist.

Genealogists have compiled indexes and transcriptions for many cemetery records, vital records, census records, and other genealogical records to aid fellow genealogists. You will need to see originals eventually to verify these published sources, but indexes and transcriptions can save you invaluable time searching entire books and microfilm reels or traveling to search

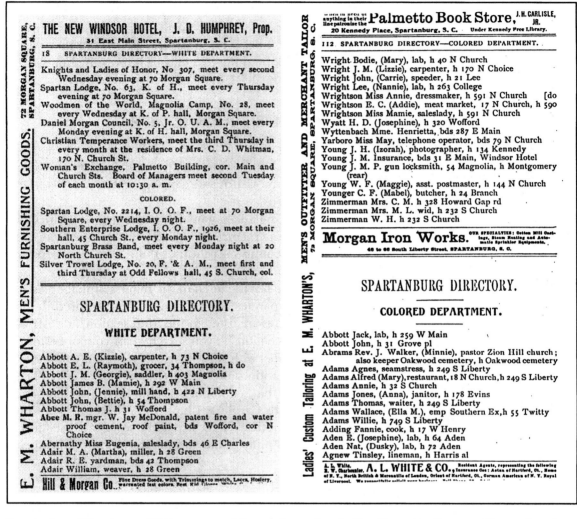

Spartanburg Directory—1899 segregated Spartanburg, South Carolina, city directory illustrating the beginning of the whites-only section and the beginning of the Black listings.

original records. Unfortunately, many indexes and transcriptions do not contain the names of African Americans who were free or slaves. During segregation white genealogists figured they were not related to African Americans and therefore purposely omitted their names.

To further complicate matters, some of these indexes have been put on computer databases by software firms unaware of these omissions. This has duplicated the omission of African Americans. In such a case neither source, the book index or the computer database, is useful for African American genealogy. Unfortunately, many African American researchers may incorrectly think their ancestors were not living in a particular location because their names are not in these indexes. Similar problems occurred in some records that were microfilmed. Sometimes listings of African Americans are tagged onto the end of a microfilm roll.

As you can see, some genealogy records in the library will not assist African American genealogists. Some indexes are misleading and hinder rather than help our research because they lead us astray. You must get a sense of whether or not these records are inclusive. If they are not, you'll have to turn to the original sources. But don't assume either way. Check and make a determination. See if the introduction mentions race and indicates if African Americans are included. Also browse through the book and search for listings of African Americans. If other records indicate African Americans were in the area and there are no listings in the book you are searching, they may have been omitted. Sometimes it's a matter of asking other experienced genealogists or a reference librarian. I recall one sharp librarian who knew that a source of records systematically excluded African Americans in their abstracting process. He refused to purchase their publications for the library. Sometimes it's a matter of knowing the original records and comparing them with published abstracts. Fortunately, many current publications are more inclusive than works done in the 1940s, '50s, and '60s.

It also pays to be knowledgeable of the many different terms that have been used for African Americans through the years. The following terms have all been used at various times and in various places:

TERMS FOR AFRICAN AMERICANS

African	Mulatto
African American	Negro
Afro-American	Negress
Black	Octoroon
Colored	Quadroon
Freedman	Slave
Free person of color	Wench

Abbreviations often appear in records. Sometimes those abbreviations were used in reference to African Americans and are not easily discerned by genealogists. For example, a *c* before or after a name usually stands for "colored." For genealogists this is both a blessing and a curse. Many lists can be skimmed until a *c* is found. But if the *c* was forgotten or misapplied, your ancestor could be overlooked.

ABBREVIATIONS FOR AFRICAN AMERICANS

b	Black
c	colored
col	colored
col'd, col^d, cold.	colored
ed	color*ed*
F.P.C.	free person of color
mu	mulatto
n	Negro
*	denotes colored

When searching records, indexes, books, guides, and microfilms, check all the above designations (read the fine print, the explanations, and the footnotes). Otherwise, you could miss your ancestors.

Historical Research

In addition to searching for your ancestors, you'll also need to study history, geography, law, transportation, politics, wars, and other events in the time periods in which your ancestors lived. You've got to place your ancestors in context to understand their lives and activities. If an ancestor worked on the railroad, you need to know about railroad companies, train routes, mergers, jobs of employees, and job hazards in order to understand your ancestor's life and what he or she did on a daily basis. This will also help you uncover other records.

The library is the best place to begin studying history. In order not to be overwhelmed by the vast field of history, we must focus our study. As in genealogical research, when we study history, we start with ourselves and work backward, one generation at a time. We start at the present and work backward, paralleling the study of history to our ancestors' lives.

The most recent era to study is the Civil Rights period. Depending on your age, either you or your living relatives have directly experienced this period.

The modern Civil Rights period begins in 1954 with the Supreme Court decision outlawing separate but equal in *Brown* v. *Topeka Board of Education,* and runs to 1968 with the passage of the Civil Rights Act of 1968 outlawing discrimination in housing. At least that's what one Civil Rights historian told me. The period is defined by Civil Rights legislation brought about by political agitation. However, the exact dates are not as important as the time frame.

Questions on the Civil Rights struggle should be covered in your interviews of relatives to see what role, if any, they played in this historic era in American history. But in order to ask intelligent questions, a little study is warranted on the subject. You'll need to brush up on picketing, sit-ins, boycotts, demonstrations, and Civil Rights legislation. What did your relatives think of these different events? Were they activists, passivists, militants, or moderates? If your relatives did not play a direct role, you need to know how the Civil Rights Movement affected them because it was a time of great change. Were they against direct action or apathetic? What attitudes did their parents and siblings have, and what role did they play? Were there any heated discussions or frictions within the family?

Prior to the Civil Rights struggle there were two major events that affected African Americans. One was segregation, which was evidenced by a severe period of prejudice, racism, discrimination, and bigotry that brought on the Civil Rights Movement. The other was the great migration of African Americans from the South to the North, escaping segregation and searching for better jobs and a better way of life. We discussed segregation earlier, but researchers need to study it in more detail. You'll discover later that there were investigations of abuses that led to records being created to assist researchers. For example, there were investigations of the Ku Klux Klan and investigations of "peon" farmers in the South by the federal government that created and preserved records.

When you get back to the 1940s, you need to study World War II and how it affected the country at home and abroad. What role did African Americans play, how did the war affect your ancestors and their community, and how did that role shape our nation's history? African Americans served in segregated military units but were well received in Europe. Did your relatives and ancestors serve in World War II? If so, what are their stories? There were also Civil Rights protests for African Americans to gain employment in war-related industries. This period needs to be studied so you can ask other questions of your relatives and place your ancestors in perspective.

Prior to World War II, African Americans served in World War I between 1917 and 1919. Did you have any relatives who served in World War I? If they didn't serve, they probably registered for the draft, and those records are available for research.

African Americans also served in the Spanish American War in 1898 and the Philippine Insurrection from 1899 to 1901. There are books, articles, and original records of theses events, as well as genealogical records for them. But researchers must first study the events before searching for their ancestors in any records.

Continuing backward in time, we come to the Reconstruction period after the Civil War. This period lasted from 1865 to 1877 and created tons of records that historians and genealogists can research. Prior to Reconstruction more than 200,000 African Americans served in the Civil War, which created thousands of records that are useful for genealogists. Between all these wars, thousands of African Americans served in the peacetime army and cavalry as career soldiers. They became known as the Buffalo Soldiers.

Prior to the Civil War, most but not all African Americans were slaves. So we must study slaves, slavery, and slave owners before we can search for our ancestors. Black history was not taught in schools until recently, and even now classes do not cover the explicit detail needed for genealogy.

To easily review major events in African American history, you can refer to books like *The Chronological History of the Negro in America, Timelines of African-American History—500 Years of Black Achievement,* and *The Timetables of African-American History—A Chronology of the Most*

Important People and Events in African-American History. (All are listed under "Black History—Intermediate" in the Bibliography.)

To locate books, articles, and even dissertations on African American history, you can consult published bibliographies, which will quickly turn up thousands of works. Monroe N. Work created a bibliography of African Americans while publishing the first edition of the *Negro Year Book* in 1912 while at Tuskegee Institute. This spawned the *Bibliography of the Negro in Africa and America,* compiled in 1928, which was reprinted in 1965 and 1970 and contains listings of 17,000 books and articles. Dorothy Porter, librarian at Howard University, came along in 1970 and compiled *The Negro in the United States: A Selected Bibliography,* which lists 1,965 books and 31 periodicals. A smaller, singular bibliography is *The Black Family in the United States,* by Lenwood G. Davis, published in 1986, which lists over 500 books, articles, dissertations, and essays. How would you like to learn about all these bibliographies of African American history? There is a book that attempts just that—*Black Access: A Bibliography of Afro-American Bibliographies,* compiled by Richard Newman in 1984. It lists more than 3,000 bibliographies of African American bibliographies in history and other subject areas. (The above titles are also listed under "Black History—Intermediate" in the Bibliography.)

Research Strategy

Much of this new learning will involve researching topics on which you have little prior knowledge. This is what makes genealogy interesting. You learn so many new things. But learning new subjects can be intimidating if you let it be. There is a key to tackling new subjects at your own pace. It involves going from the general to the specific. You'll want to get the big general picture first and then gradually zoom in on the minute details. You do this by using the following resources, which we will illustrate in the case study that follows:

- Encyclopedias
- Sections in general history books
- Chapters in books
- Journal articles
- Books on the subject
- Unpublished manuscript materials

CASE STUDY: RESEARCHING PULLMAN PORTERS—My great-grandfather Morris Burroughs was a Pullman porter. We'll use him as an example in implementing our strategy. A quick, big picture of a new subject can easily be gotten from an encyclopedia. It takes only a few minutes to read a few paragraphs or pages on a subject in an encyclopedia. This will give you an idea of a new topic or refresh your memory of an old topic. However, in genealogy we'll usually need to go deeper than the surface on most topics. Encyclopedias are only meant to scratch the surface.

ENCYCLOPEDIAS—To get a quick picture of Pullman porters, I can turn to the *Encyclopedia of Black America,* which has half a page explaining who the Pullman porters were and how they formed the first African American labor union, the Brotherhood of Sleeping Car Porters. The *Encyclopedia of African-American Culture and History,* which is in four volumes, devotes three pages to Pullman porters. Both of these resources are in many libraries around the country, and it will take only a few minutes to learn about Pullman porters.

The *Encyclopedia of Black America* is very handy, and you might consider adding it to your personal library. Then when an idea develops, you won't have to wait until the next day when the library opens to follow up. Of course, I know that some of you will have forgotten the thought by the next day. I found a copy of the encyclopedia in a used bookstore at less than half price, which is how I built up much of my library collection. Secondhand books are a great way to build an inexpensive library.

SECTIONS IN GENERAL HISTORY BOOKS—Next I can look in a general history book to get more information. In this case I turned to *From Slavery to Freedom,* by John Hope Franklin, and *Before the Mayflower,* by Lerone Bennett, which explore the African American experience from Africa to the present. However, I was a bit disappointed. *From Slavery to Freedom* had only three paragraphs on Pullman porters, and *Before the Mayflower* had only a couple of sentences. Naturally, some topics are covered in greater detail than others. These two classic sources give a good background on the breadth of African American history.

CHAPTERS IN BOOKS—The next sources to check are chapters in books on a broader topic, in this case "African American labor history." This is an area often missed by genealogists. A lot of good information is found in chapters of history books. *The Black Worker: The Negro and the Labor Movement,* by Sterling Spero and Abram Harris, has thirty-one pages devoted to Pullman porters and another thirty-two pages devoted to African Americans working in other capacities on the railroad (as brakemen, switchmen, and so forth).

Eric Arnesen, Julie Greene, and Bruce Lauri edited *Labor Histories: Class, Politics, and the Working-Class Experience,* which contains twenty-five pages on Pullman porters and other railroad workers in the chapter "Charting an Independent Course: African-American Railroad Workers in the World War I Era." *The Black Worker: A Documentary History from Colonial Times to the Present,* edited by Philip Foner and Ronald Lewis, contains thirteen pages on the Brotherhood of Sleeping Car Porters in volume 4, *The American Federation of Labor and the Railroad Brotherhoods.* Volume 6, *The Era of Post-War Prosperity and the Great Depression, 1920–1936,* has 103 pages in three chapters on the Brotherhood of Sleeping Car Porters.

Books like *The History of the Pullman Car,* by Joseph Husband; *Night Trains: The Pullman System in the Golden Years of American Rail Travel,* by Peter T. Maiken; *The American Railroad Passenger Car,* by John H. White, Jr.; and *The Sleeping Car,* by William Dean Howells, may not all mention African American porters, but they provide good background on railroad transportation and passengers, as well as photographs, dimensions, and descriptions of the cars that porters worked in every day. *The Place Car Prince: A Biography of George Mortimer Pullman,* by Liston Edgington Leyendecker, tells us quite a bit about Morris's employer (at least the good side). And books like *The Life and Decline of the American Railroad,* by John F. Stover, and *The Industrial History of the United States,* by Katharine Coman, place the Pullman porters, the Brotherhood of Sleeping Car Porters, and the Pullman Company into the larger picture of American history and transportation history.

JOURNAL ARTICLES—The next area to pursue is scholarly journal articles, which are often written by historians and college students majoring in history. The recently published ones are particularly important because they are often well documented, with sources footnoted. These will lead to original sources where additional information can be obtained.

There are several indexes to periodicals that will point you to good articles on any subject (see "Periodical Indexes" in the Bibliography). The one most people are familiar with is the *Readers' Guide to Periodical Literature.* The *Readers' Guide* indexes about 180 general interest magazines like *Time, Newsweek,* and *Ebony.* But a great source for locating scholarly historical articles is *America: History and Life—A Guide to Periodical Literature.* It comes in four parts: *Part A—Article Abstracts,* which gives a synopsis of each article; *Part B—Index to Book Reviews; Part C—Bibliographies, Books, Dissertations & Articles;* and *Part D—Annual Index.* Also check *Writings on American History: A Subject Bibliography of Articles* and, for older works, *Combined Retrospective Index to Journals in History,* which covers articles written from 1838 to 1974. Also covering history, as well as other fields, is the *Humanities Index.* If you want to broaden your search, you can check articles in the *Business Periodicals Index,* the *Index to Legal Periodicals,* or the *Biography Index.*

Scholarly, in-depth articles on strictly African American history can be located in several sources. Dwight L. Smith extracted 2,274 abstracts of articles from *America: History and Life* from 1953 to 1972 in his *Afro-American History: A Bibliography,* published in 1974. The *Journal of Negro History* has been published regularly since 1915 by the Association for the Study of Afro-American Life and History. There is a good index to the first fifty-three volumes of the *Journal,* covering 1915–68. There's also the *Index to Periodical Articles by and About Negroes, 1960–1970; Black Index: Afro-Americana in Selected Periodicals, 1907–1949,* edited by Richard Newman in 1981, which has 1,000 articles from 350 periodicals in the United States, Canada, and Great Britain; and the *Analytical Guide and Indexes to the Colored American Magazine, 1900–1909,* published in 1974.

"The Brotherhood" is an excellent nineteen-page article about the Brotherhood of Sleeping Car Porters published in the fall 1996 edition of *Chicago History,* the journal of the Chicago Historical Society. We can go back further and locate "The Pullman Porter from 'George' to Brotherhood," a twelve-page article published in *The South Atlantic Quarterly* in 1974. However, Morris Burroughs died in 1903, and the union wasn't formed until 1925. So I searched for older articles and located "The Art of the Pullman Porter," written in the July 1931 issue of *American Mercury,* and "Reminiscences of a Pullman Porter," published in the 1916 issue of *Pullman Porter Review.* They weren't very long articles, but they concentrated on the porters' job duties instead of their union.

BOOKS ON THE SUBJECT—Then we can search specific books on our subject. This is the area that most researchers pursue but often prematurely. They look at the card catalogue in the library to find a book before they know very much about the subject. They often get deep into details and become bored before they know much about the subject. They may even get discouraged and never return to learn more. You only have to read an entire book if your curiosity is not satisfied by the above resources and you still need more information. If we stopped to read books on every subject, we wouldn't get very far. We must be selective. For some subjects you'll need to read entire books; for others you will need to read only a chapter or two.

Since Pullman porters are very important to my research, I have accumulated several books on the subject. The latest book on Pullman porters was written in 1996, *Those Pullman Blues: An Oral History of the African American Railroad Attendant,* by David. D. Perata. It gives a good idea of what the men did on a daily basis, but the oral histories are relatively recent.

A similar work, *Miles of Smiles, Years of Struggle: Stories of Black Pullman Porters,* by Jack Santino, was published in 1991. A 1977 book on A. Philip Randolph, *Keeping the Faith: A. Philip Randolph, Milton Webster and the Brotherhood of Sleeping Car Porters,* by William H. Harris, gives a lot of information on Pullman porters, in spite of the fact Randolph was not a porter himself. He organized the porters and was not vulnerable to being fired by the Pullman Company.

UNPUBLISHED MANUSCRIPT MATERIALS—After you exhaust all published sources and you still need more information, and you often will, you can turn to unpublished manuscript materials. You can see what authors have not yet discovered or have not yet published. You can examine original records and interpret them yourself. We all know how many racist and biased words have been written (and omitted) about African Americans. By examining original records, genealogists can set the record straight. However, original records should be examined only when published sources are exhausted. Published sources will have answered most of your historical questions.

In our case study, published sources will give us a good idea of the daily duties of being a sleeping car porter; what the working conditions were like; who the key players were, from management to labor to the government; where the company locations were for manufacturing and administration; where the train routes went. If we read the footnotes, introductions, acknowledgments, and appendixes in our published sources, we'll learn other important details, like what other books, articles, newspapers, and dissertations to consult; who the experts are; and where the resources are located. This is called "Doing our homework." Then when we go to a repository with original records, we can talk intelligently with the librarian, curator, or archivist.

Manuscript collections contain records like newspapers, personal papers, correspondence, diaries, dissertations, government documents, court records, and other original documents. The original records for the Pullman Company are housed at the Newberry Library. They consist of 2,500 feet of company records, including 693 cubic feet of employee records, 17 cubic feet of payroll records, and 25 cubic feet of scrapbooks. However, in spite of the vastness of the collection, we don't stop there. The Library of Congress has an additional 45.2 linear feet (41,000 items) of records for the Brotherhood of Sleeping Car Porters; the Chicago Historical Society has 16 linear feet of records for the Brotherhood in 137 boxes; the Smithsonian Institution has 2.6 linear feet of records; the Schomburg Research Center for Black Culture has 2.6 linear feet of records and 141 oral histories for the Brotherhood. This does not include court records and dissertations, which are way beyond beginning genealogy.

So we see we have access to massive amounts of information. I used Pullman porters in the above strategy, but you can use it for any occupation or topic—domestic workers, automobiles, World War I or II, or the Civil Rights Movement. This strategy starts you off with no knowledge of a subject and takes you to a point where you'll know quite a bit about the subject. You can go as far as you want and stop anywhere along the journey. Along the way you'll probably meet experts in the field who can assist your search and sometimes become lifelong friends.

Migrations and Transportation

When I learned my ancestors came from South Carolina having never lived in South Carolina myself, I had to study its history and geography. Then when I traced them to Tennessee, Virginia, and Maryland, I had to do the same thing again for these other states. I also had to learn about Pennsylvania, where my mom was born. I had visited the state many times as a kid, but I knew very little of its history. Then I learned that a couple of ancestors were buried in a Quaker cemetery, and I was off studying Quakers.

Once you see how mobile your ancestors were, you understand the need to study migrations and transportation. It's important to know if your ancestors traveled during a major migration period, along a migration route, or against the trend. The first may help locate where they came from; the last may illustrate their independence. The president of the African-American Genealogical and Historical Society of Chicago, Belzora Cheatham, was able to locate a log belonging to the former slave owner of her ancestors, which chronicled their 1,027-mile migration from South Carolina to the Republic of Texas in 1840. The log recorded every day of the trip—where they stopped, how far they traveled, how long they stayed at a location—and mentioned visits with friends and relatives along the way. Cheatham published excerpts from the log in "A Trip from South Carolina to the Republic of Texas," *Journal of the Afro-American Historical and Genealogical Society* (vol. 14, nos. 3 & 4 [Summer 1995], pages 163–165).

Local History

After you get a look at the big picture, you'll need to zero in and learn what was happening in the local community where your ancestors lived. You need to study the area and time period in which your ancestors lived. Histories were written for many counties in the United States. There is most likely one for the county where your ancestors lived. Many county histories mention only prominent people, but they may be key to some of your future research. The history will usually mention military veterans, politicians, historic events, places, businesses, schools, churches, newspapers, transportation, and migrations to the area.

Blacks and slaves were rarely mentioned in county histories, but often enough to make them required reading. In 1976 I interviewed Aunt Illa, a distant cousin who appeared to be in her eighties. A beginner's mistake I made was not asking when she was born. But an even bigger mistake was talking to her only twice. I now have a million questions I'd like to ask her.

In one interview she told me about her great-grandmother Hannah. Aunt Illa said Hannah was the mistress of Dr. Wheeler from England. His wife couldn't have children, and Hannah bore him ten to twelve children. As I listened intently and scribbled down notes, she suddenly said the magic words: "It's written in the history of Washington County."

I went to the public library in Washington, Pennsylvania, and located a copy of the *History of Washington County, Pennsylvania, with Biographical Sketches of Many of Its Pioneers and Prominent Men,* edited by Boyd Crumrine in 1882. Page 986 stated Dr. Charles Wheeler was one of the first settlers in the territory, arriving around 1774. It later referred to a church history that said Dr. Wheeler was an Englishman and surgeon by profession and served in Dunmore's War. But it wasn't until I got to the next page that there was any mention of slaves. It said, "Dr. Wheeler was the owner of several slaves, all of whom he remembered in his will. Hannah Young was the latest survivor of these slaves, she living until after 1870." The excerpts of the will, executed in 1808, indicated "£50 to black Samuel, £50 to black Benjamin, £50 to black Hannah, £25 to black Lydia, £50 to black Daniel, and £25 to black Rachel. The above named black people were raised under my roof."

Genealogist Eunice Pressie read *Life by the Roaring Roanoke: A History of Mecklenburg County, Virginia,* by Susan L. Bracey, which covers the area where her ancestors lived. She was very fortunate to learn the name of the slave owner who owned her ancestors, as well as the name of the plantation.

> One of Mecklenburg's former slaves became quite prominent. James Solomon Russell, founder of St. Paul's College in Lawrenceville, Virginia, was on December 20, 1857, born a slave on the Buck Hendrick Plantation ("Logsdale") near Palmer Springs.

In addition to county histories, check for histories of cities and towns. These are often smaller volumes, pamphlets, or articles in journals or newsletters. I located the history of a small town in Fayette County, Pennsylvania, where my great-grandmother was born, called Perryopolis. The town history didn't mention my ancestors, but there was a photograph of the "Livery Stable Gang" taken in 1916. The caption indicated one was Jess Truman. My great-grandfather had a cousin named Jessie Truman I'd identified in census and court records. Interviews with older family members said many of the Trumans were musicians. When I saw the black-and-white photograph of the Livery Stable Gang, I knew it was the Jessie Truman I'd been tracking. There was only one African American in the photograph of nineteen men. He was standing in the doorway of the livery stable playing the fiddle while the other men were posing for the camera.

There are several guides to locating local histories. There's the *Bibliography of American County Histories,* by P. William Filby; *Local Histories in the Library of Congress,* by Marion J. Kaminkaw; and *Consolidated Bibliography of County Histories in Fifty States in 1961,* by Clarence Stewart Peterson. In addition, Kory Meyerink compiled *Genealogical Publications: A List of 50,000 Sources from the Library of Congress* on a CD-ROM. (In the Bibliography, see "Local History" for the books and "Genealogy Reference Guides" for the CD-ROM.)

Indexes in Local Histories

Many county histories were written in the late 1800s. Because of the increased interest in genealogy, some are being reprinted. Some reprint editions are reindexed to include every name and location mentioned in the text. Original editions often contained abbreviated indexes of a few prominent persons. Genealogists not wanting to read an entire book normally check the index, don't see their ancestor's name, and think they were not mentioned.

Genealogists tend to read books from the rear instead of the front. If the name they are looking for is not in the index, they set the book aside and proceed to the next one. However, rarely are all the names listed in a book also listed in the index.

! Trap: Reading only the index and not the book.

The original *History of Fayette County, Pennsylvania,* edited by Franklin Ellis in 1882, contained 841 pages without an index. The table of contents was four pages long and included a list of eighty-eight prominent white men in the county. Naturally, none of them were related to me. In the late 1970s I searched all through the book and learned a lot about Fayette County but nothing about my ancestors.

In 1995 I discovered that the *History of Fayette County* by Ellis was reprinted in 1986 with an index. It appears the Connellsville Area Historical Society prepared the new index. I guess I wasn't the only one who couldn't find their ancestors in Fayette County. The new index has 80 pages of listings of local histories, biographies, businesses, cemeteries, churches, schools, newspapers, battlefields, military units, and geographic features and 152 pages of names! What an index. This time I found a listing for one of my ancestors, Charles Smothers.

> Christian Tarr, the potter, lived on the present J. S. Elliott place, and for many years made earthenware there. He was elected to Congress in 1817 and 1819, and served, it is said, with a good deal of credit. Mr. Tarr had on his place a colored man named Charles Smothers, who fought with Perry on Lake Erie, and for whom Mr. Tarr succeeded in obtaining an allowance of prize money for his share in the capture of the enemy.

I almost screamed when I read this. I had been tracking Smothers's son, Oliver Perry Smothers, and wondered to no end why he got the name Oliver Perry. I knew he was too young to fight in the Battle of Lake Erie, which was in 1814, and didn't realize his dad had fought in the battle and named Oliver after the famous Commodore Oliver Perry.

I located many of Charles Smothers's military records in the National Archives, as well as records for Congressman Tarr, but never found any assistance he gave Smothers. Official records indicate Smothers received his share of the prize money personally, along with many other servicemen.

My Smothers ancestor was listed in the new index, but the original county history had no index. So before you fall into the trap, examine the entire book, in addition to the index. If I'd been more diligent, I could have discovered this gem twenty years before I did. Also check for newer editions of older books to see if they have new indexes.

Another problem with relying on indexes is they are often riddled with errors. I located a list of published school records from Spartanburg, South Carolina. The indexer couldn't make out the spelling and recorded "Banrough" instead of Burroughs. So Burroughs was not in the index. Other errors occur in indexes because of typos, transposed letters, and misinterpreted letters. In early American handwriting, a double *s* looks like *fs* and is a common error for untrained indexers.

Church and Labor History

We must also study history specific to our ancestors' lives. I discovered cousins and great-grandparents who were members of the A.M.E. (African Methodist Episcopal) Church. Being born and raised an Episcopalian, I had to study A.M.E. beliefs, history, organization, and publications. When I found my great-grandfather was a Pullman porter, I started studying the Pullman Company, the Pullman Strike, the railroad industry, railroad accidents, individual railroads, African American porters, and the Brotherhood of Sleeping Car Porters.

When I learned several female ancestors were laundresses and domestics, I began studying the subject. I located books and articles on laundresses and domestics (*Living In, Living Out: African American Domestics in Washington, D.C., 1910–1940,* by Elizabeth Clark-Lewis, and "The Negro Washerwoman, A Vanishing Figure," by Carter G. Woodson, in the *Journal of Negro History* [vol. 15, no. 3, July 1930]). I learned that working as a domestic was almost the only job an African American woman could get in the nineteenth century and most of the twentieth century. It was a carryover from jobs held in slavery and discrimination in the workplace. I also learned a woman listed on census records as a "housekeeper" worked in someone's house for wages, whereas a woman "keeping house" was unemployed and took care of her own house.

I knew my grandfather Asa Burroughs was a lawyer, but I got very excited when I found a book on Black lawyers that had several mentions of him (*Emancipation: The Making of the Black Lawyer, 1844–1944,* by J. Clay Smith and Thurgood Marshall). After Grandma and I went through his brother Robert's trunk and saw the vehicle licenses for owned cars I'd never heard of (Kessel, Liberty, and Stearns), I began studying the cars and the auto industry. I discovered the National Automotive History Collection at the Detroit Public Library, which is an archive of the auto industry. It has files on all the cars Robert owned and any others you'd want to research. I found plans, photographs, advertising brochures, and newspaper articles. It really put me in touch with Robert's time period when I saw photographs of the cars he owned, which reminded me of Model T Fords. Unfortunately, the Model T is the only old car we hear about.

So the trip to the library is an excellent place to learn history needed for genealogy. You'll need to study the circumstances of your ancestors' lives. This is why genealogy is so fascinating. You learn so many new things. In addition to the historical references listed thus far, consult others in the Bibliography.

Geography Research

Studying geography and finding the location of towns and counties are very important. Before you can do much research on your ancestors, you have to know where they lived because that's where the records were created. It will be difficult to find records if you can't locate the communities. Many records used in genealogy were created at the county level. So towns and villages must be located and then placed in counties so you can access the records. This will save you agonizing frustration because you won't find records for ancestors in Washington County if they were living in Fayette County. The library is a good place to locate maps and study the geography of the areas where your ancestors lived.

Purchasing Maps

In the chapter "The Family Archives," I mentioned locating the town your ancestors lived in. I suggested you start with a highway road map. If you do not have maps for the states where your ancestors lived, you can obtain them inexpensively from several sources. If you are a member of a motor club like AAA, you can often get free highway road maps. You can also purchase maps from bookstores, drugstores, Rand McNally map stores, and The Map Store. Larger, local county maps can usually be obtained from the state highway department, the county courthouse, or the local chamber of commerce. Sometimes these government maps are free.

More detailed than your local highway map is the excellent *Rand McNally Commercial Marketing Atlas and Marketing Guide,* available in many libraries. It is very large, very detailed, and has clearly defined county boundaries.

If the town is not listed on one of the above maps, you'll have to do more sophisticated research. In addition to current maps, there are historical maps. These may show small towns no longer in existence, or you may find the boundary lines for counties were different when your ancestors lived in the area. In addition to maps, you'll also need atlases, which are books of maps; gazetteers which are geographical dictionaries; and travel guides that describe localities.

Locating Map Collections

Some large libraries have special map or cartography departments. Cartography is the design, production, and reproduction of maps. If the library you use does not have a strong map department, you'll probably have to visit a university library or private library that has one.

The Library of Congress in Washington, D.C., has the largest map collection, with 4 million maps, 51,000 atlases, and 8,000 geographical reference works. Slightly smaller is the National Archives, also in Washington, D.C. The Cartographic and Architectural Branch of the National Archives has 2 million maps, but they are rather specialized, including postal maps, census enumeration maps, general land office maps, and military maps. Smaller but still large collections are in places like the University of Wisconsin, which has 250,000 maps, and the Newberry Library in Chicago, with 70,000 maps.

Okay, so you say you don't live in any of those cities. There are two excellent reference works for locating map collections all over the United States. *Map Collections in the United States and Canada: A Directory* lists and describes collections of maps, and *The Map Catalogue* describes sources of new and old maps worldwide. (See "Geography Research" in the Bibliography.)

Atlases

Atlases are often overlooked by genealogists. I mentioned the *Rand McNally Commercial and Marketing Atlas,* but Rand McNally began creating atlases in 1876. They have thousands of atlases. Their collection is housed in the Newberry Library.

For use with census records, the *Township Atlas of the United States* lists subdivisions within each county. Several genealogists have told me they found their ancestors listed on the census as living in "Beat Four" or some other number. They wanted to know what that meant and where it was. A "beat" is a political subdivision and was an enumeration district that defined the boundaries census takers used to record names. Counties are subdivided into smaller areas, often called townships. The *Township Atlas* outlines these smaller subdivisions.

Also used with the census is the *Map Guide to the U.S. Federal Censuses, 1790–1920,* by William Dollarhide and William Thorndale. It lists county boundary lines for each of the ten years the census was taken. Since many counties were subdivided, the atlas shows the overlapping boundary lines to indicate earlier county boundary lines. However, there were many more boundary line changes than when a county was split into two or three.

We know from segregation that many political boundaries were changed in small or very clever ways to prohibit African Americans from voting or to create majority voting blocks. This was called gerrymandering. A more sophisticated work that attempts to record each and every small boundary change is the *Historical Atlas and Chronology of County Boundaries, 1788–1980,* edited by John Long. It is a massive, multivolume project.

There were also atlases created for individual states. They began being published after the Civil War. Be sure to check for a state atlas in your library map collection for the state you're researching.

Gazetteers

If the town is too small, too old, or perhaps changed its name, you'll have to consult even more sophisticated sources. You will probably have to check a gazetteer or geographical dictionary. These list geographical place names in alphabetical order and are similar to dictionaries. For hard-to-find places, gazetteers should be consulted before detailed searches for maps that may be nonexistent. The map curator at Newberry Library estimated that 50 percent of locality problems can be solved with gazetteers versus maps. Gazetteers also help locate places of the same name or with different spellings than what you're used to.

Three good gazetteers are *Webster's Geographical Dictionary,* which lists 40,000 places; *American Places Dictionary,* which lists 45,000 places; and the *Columbia-Lippincott Gazetteer of the World,* which claims to list every incorporated place on the 1950 U.S. Census.

A very interesting gazetteer is the *Gazetteer of the United States, Showing the Population of Every County, City, Town, and Village According to the Census of 1890,* by George Franklin Cram. It has towns so small the population was only twenty-five people. This work is extremely valuable because most of the 1890 U.S. Census no longer exists, but this index was created before the census was destroyed in a fire.

This book went out of print, and Gilbert S. Bahn edited a reprint version, wrote an introduction, and titled it *American Place Names of Long Ago: A Republication of the Index to Cram's Unrivaled Atlas of the World, as Based on the Census of 1890.* Published in 1998, it is more widely available.

There are also statewide gazetteers. An example is *A Gazetteer of Virginia and West Virginia,* published in 1904. There are also statewide gazetteers for the southern states of Georgia, Maryland, North Carolina, and West Virginia. Statewide gazetteers are found in genealogy and college libraries, but more often are located at a state archives or a state historical society library.

Post Office Directories

If you still can't find the town, you can try post office directories. Remember the phrase "The mail must go through"? The post office had to know where all these little places were in order to deliver the mail. The U.S. Postal Service publishes an annual directory of post offices that is similar to a gazetteer, *Table of Post Offices in the United States.* I located one for 1851, which is organized alphabetically by city. Once you locate the city, it indicates the name of the state the town is in. It even gives the name of the postmaster.

There is also a shippers' guide that is useful for locating small towns. *Bullinger's Postal and Shippers Guide for the United States and Canada* has been published annually since 1897. These postal and shipping directories are not available everywhere. They are found mainly in major genealogical libraries or in government documents departments at larger public and university libraries. You can have your reference librarian conduct a computer on-line search (OCLC) to locate these directories for you.

Historical Societies

If the name of the town is *still* not found, there are two additional sources to consult. One is the county historical society if you have narrowed the location to one or two counties. Historical societies usually pride themselves on knowing the small towns in their county. They sometimes maintain card files listing towns and villages in their area. Consult the *Directory of Historical Organizations in the United States and Canada,* by Mary Keysor Meyer, or *The Source: A Guidebook to American Genealogy* (revised edition), by Loretto D. Szucs and Sandra H. Luebking, to locate historical societies in the counties you are researching. (See "Genealogy Reference Guides" in the Bibliography.)

I was searching for the site of a battle in the War of 1812—the Battle of Conjockta Creek—which was near Buffalo, New York. I checked my highway maps, atlas, and geographical dictionary at home without success. I then ventured to the University of Illinois map department and consulted with Marsha Selmer, the map librarian. She is great at solving geography-related questions. She tried to locate Conjockta Creek with all the resources in the university and also couldn't solve the mystery. However, she sent out a query via e-mail, and the response pointed me in the right direction. There were creeks in the Buffalo area, but none named Conjockta. I needed to contact sources in the area and research the local history.

I had a speaking engagement in Rochester, New York, and traveled to Buffalo to research my War of 1812 ancestor. I stopped at the Buffalo Public Library and checked the local history department. They had a local history card file that included geographic entries. One of the researchers who had responded to Selmer's query mentioned Scajaquada Creek, which was near the area where the battle occurred. I checked the cards for Scajaquada Creek, and one listed an article on the variations in spelling. The creek was named for Philip Kenjockety, a Native American Indian. Everyone in the area had difficulty pronouncing Indian names, and the article said there were *seventy-six* different spellings! I located another article, written in 1911, listing the spellings, including Conjockta.

United States Geological Survey

Your last resort is the United States Geological Survey (USGS), which has a service for locating small forgotten towns, called the Geographic Names Information System (GNIS). Its database contains approximately 2 million place and geographic feature names, mostly for towns and features on USGS maps, many of which were created in the 1930s and '40s. However, the GNIS is adding historical data to the database every day and updating its directories and software databases.

The database categorizes sixty-four geographic features on USGS maps, including such things as locales, populated places (cities, villages, settlements, and towns), lakes, streams, schools, cemeteries, and churches. The *Omni Gazetteer* is a published version of 1.5 million place names from USGS maps. Comprising ten volumes, it is found in larger public and academic libraries.

The USGS publishes topographical maps that are available for research in libraries, often in map departments, cartography departments, or government documents departments. Topographical maps have lines indicating whether the terrain is flat or hilly. There are two different size USGS maps, a 15-minute map and a 7½-minute map. The 15-minute map has a ratio of 1 to 63,360, with 1 inch equal to 1 mile. Each map covers 207 to 280 miles. The 7½-minute map has a ratio of 1 to 24,000, with 1 inch equaling only 2,000 feet. Each map covers 49 to 64 miles, so it's much more detailed than the 15-minute map. This is the one that's good for genealogy because it lists all the small details we're looking for.

I tried to find a place called Honey Hill in South Carolina, where my ancestors fought in the Civil War. One died in the battle preparing for General Sherman's famous "March to the Sea." I couldn't find Honey Hill on a map or in an atlas or gazetteer. I had the hardest time trying to locate where it was. I finally found it in *The Official Atlas of the Civil War* by Thomas Yoseloff. The atlas is a companion volume to the *Official Records of the War of the Rebellion.* I discovered Honey Hill was not a city after all. It was only a hill where the battle was fought. I then went to a USGS topological map and located Honey Hill and the site of the battle.

If the USGS can't locate your town over the telephone, they will do more extensive research and get back to you. The USGS has a toll-free telephone number (1-800-USA-MAPS or 1-800-872-6277) for general information and ordering materials. The Branch of Geographic Names does not have a toll-free number, but you will obtain more extensive assistance by directly contacting them. The USGS has also produced a database of towns and geographic features that is available for an economical price on CD-ROM. Consult the "Electronic Genealogy" chapter for this and other geographic sources on CD-ROM and the Internet.

The USGS also has maps available for sale to the public. Once the town you are looking for is located, the USGS will give you the geographical coordinates so you can pinpoint the town on the map. If you want to use these maps, it is a good idea to order their guide, *Using Maps in Genealogy* (formerly *Maps Can Help You Trace Your Family Tree*).

To summarize, there are many ways to locate the place where your ancestor touched the ground. In libraries or archives, you can search maps, atlases, gazetteers, postal and shipping directories, and card files. In addition to the name of the location, also use such topics as cities, towns, villages, travel, and descriptions. With a little luck, you'll be able to find the place where your ancestor lived.

Why Some Places Are Hard to Find

Some towns were too small to survive; others were never towns. Some places were merely the names of tracts of land recorded on original patents when the land was purchased from the federal government by private individuals. These are often evidenced on land ownership maps and warrant tract maps. I researched land ownership maps for Fayette County, Pennsylvania. Recorded on them were names no longer used that appeared only on original land patents. These included such names as Goesburg for land owned by William Goe; Copenhagen for land owned by John Cope; Magrudie's Farm, which was owned by Hezekiah Magruder; Hutton's Fancy, which was owned by Margaret Hutton; and Clarksbury, which was owned by George Clark.

Some places were locales, places where people once gathered but never lived. The locale developed a name and people continually referred to it. They included places like junctions, battlefields, and geographic features. Then there were the plantations, which were not towns, but people often referred to the name of the plantation as if it were a town.

In other cases the federal government changed the names of towns. There were many problems with towns having the same name, with inconsistent spelling, and with townspeople using one name, the post office using another name, and the railroad using still another for the same town. The government rectified this in 1890 when the Board of Geographic Names began to standardize town names. Their report was published and is available for checking town name changes: *Report of the United States Board on Geographic Names, 1890–1891*. Be glad your ancestor didn't live in Yeehaw Junction, Florida; Whorehouse Meadow, Oregon; Tightwad, Missouri; Wide Awake, Colorado; or Flush, Kansas. Or did they?

Genealogy Reference Guides

There are hundreds of genealogy reference guides, those large, expensive directories best afforded by the library. They give the addresses of every place related to genealogy you'll want to find, covering many aspects of genealogy you'll need to learn. The following are industry standards you need to be familiar with:

- *The Researcher's Guide to American Genealogy,* by Val D. Greenwood (2000)
- *The Source: A Guidebook of American Genealogy,* by Johni Cerny and Arlene Eakle (1984); revised by Loretto D. Szucs and Sandra H. Luebking (1997)
- *Printed Sources: A Guide to Published Genealogical Records,* by Kory L. Meyerink (1998)
- *The Handy Book for Genealogists,* by George Everton (1999)
- *Ancestry's Red Book: American State, County & Town Sources,* by Alice Eichholz (1992)

! Trap: Not being familiar with and reading standard genealogy reference works.

A good library genealogy department will also subscribe to many magazines, newsletters, and quarterly journals published by genealogical and historical societies.

If you want to take a class in genealogy, and I'd recommend it, the genealogy department should be able to direct you to places where they are taught. They also usually have flyers and announcements on upcoming seminars, workshops, and institutes, which are like a week-long class in genealogy. (See also "Genealogical Institutes and Conferences" in the appendixes.)

At some point you'll want to network with other genealogists and perhaps join a genealogical society. The genealogy library has directories of genealogical societies on the local, state, and national level. Even if you don't want to join right away, you'll want to review society newsletters and quarterly journals, which will be jam-packed with information. Good genealogy libraries have back issues from the national organizations, state societies (usually from the state where the library is located, but sometimes from neighboring states), and local and ethnic societies in the surrounding area. (See also "African American Genealogical Societies" in the appendixes.)

Guides to States and Counties

In addition to learning the methods and techniques of genealogy research and the sources of records, you also need to learn how resources differ in the state your ancestor lived in. There are three resources to check: general reference guides, books, and articles. General reference guides have sections for different states and the genealogical resources in each. Consult guides like *The Handy Book for Genealogists*, edited by George Everton; *Ancestry's Red Book: American State, County & Town Sources*, edited by Alice Eichholz; and *Genealogical Research: Methods and Sources*, edited by Milton Rubincam.

The Handy Book is organized alphabetically by state and then alphabetically by county. Because it provides details on every county in every state, it is one of the first books you should consult. Each section begins with a brief history of each state and gives the years of vital records. It then lists major books, articles, and bibliographies for researching the history and genealogy in each state. You can search for these items in the library, which will tell you how genealogy research in one state differs from that in another state. *The Handy Book* includes a directory of major genealogy libraries, archives, and genealogical societies. It also lists printed indexes for early census records. Every county is listed with address and phone number and the years of vital records, probate, and land records. There are color maps of each state with outlines of the counties, regional migration trails, and an 1860 railroad map. If you have some extra cash, this is a nice reference book to add to your personal library. I often consult it in the wee hours of the morning.

Ancestry's Red Book is also organized alphabetically by state. It lists guides for researching each state in a section titled "Background Sources." Similar to *The Handy Book*, it begins with a brief history of each state. Then there are sections within each state describing vital records, census records, maps (and other geographical sources), land records, probate records, court records, tax records, church records, cemetery records, military records, immigration records, periodicals, newspapers, and manuscripts. There are also lists of archives, libraries, and genealogical societies. Then a table for each county lists the beginning dates for the county's formation and the earliest vital records, land records, probate records, and civil court records.

Genealogical Research: Methods and Sources is a two-volume set. In addition to discussing genealogical methods, it gives brief histories of individual states along with the county formations and government structure. It's organized by region of the country. It also lists printed and manuscript sources for individual states, including census, land, and vital records, as well as bibliographies. It's a bit dated and concentrates on earlier records and history (pre-twentieth-century) but is an excellent source.

In addition to these general references, entire books have been written on how to research genealogy in a particular state. Many of these books are mentioned in the above guides. Three examples are *North Carolina Research: Genealogy and Local History,* by Helen F.M. Leary; *Tracing Your Mississippi Ancestors,* by Anne S. Lipscomb and Kathleen S. Hutchinson; and *South Carolina Genealogical Research,* by George K. Schweitzer.

Guides to Genealogy Newsletters and Journals

In addition to reference guides and books, there are articles on doing genealogy research in various states as well as counties. These can usually be found in the card catalogue or in one of the genealogical periodical indexes.

The largest index of genealogical articles is the *Periodical Source Index,* known by genealogists as *PERSI.* It was developed by the Allen County Public Library Foundation in Fort Wayne, Indiana. *PERSI* indexes the titles of articles appearing in more than 5,000 genealogical journals and newsletters. Before *PERSI,* several genealogical indexes were published, but they only scratched the surface. *PERSI* covers all genealogical periodicals from 1847 to the present and is carried by most genealogical libraries.

The topics in *PERSI* are divided into five categories. Basically, you can search a state and/or county, a surname, or a research source such as vital records, cemeteries, census records, or probate records.

- Places—U.S.
- Places—Canadian
- Places—Foreign
- Families
- Research Methodology

Indexing such a vast number of periodicals requires several volumes. The breadth of this index can make it a bit confusing to some researchers. Once you realize how many volumes it takes to cover 5,000 periodicals, *PERSI* becomes less daunting.

The first sixteen volumes all have the same titles, either *Places 1847–1985* or *Families 1847–1985.* They are divided into four retrospective series and a current series (see the following table). The difference in each series is only the articles that were indexed. The library keeps uncovering more periodicals than were previously known. *PERSI* is also available on CD-ROM and the Internet.

PERSI is not the only index to cover genealogical newsletters and journals. The *Genealogical Periodical Annual Index (GPAI),* edited by Ellen Stanley Rodgers and George Ely Russell, indexes seventy-eight periodicals from 1962 to 1969. *GPAI* differs from *PERSI* in that it includes surname periodicals, ancestor charts, and family group sheets, none of which are indexed in *PERSI*. *GPAI* also provides page numbers for articles, making them somewhat easier to find than *PERSI* does.

GPAI stopped publication for five years and was restarted by Laird C. Towle, who indexed 300 major journals. The current edition covers the period from 1974 to the present. However, the published volumes lag behind the time period being indexed. For example, the 1997 edition indexes 1992 periodicals.

The *Index to Genealogical Periodical Literature, 1960–1977,* by Kip Sperry, focuses strictly on genealogy how-to articles and does not include surnames, family histories, and articles on locations.

There are also statewide indexes to genealogical articles. Among the southern states, which affect most African Americans, there are statewide indexes for Georgia, Kentucky, Texas, and Virginia. If you have ancestors in these states, consult "Periodical Indexes" in the Bibliography for the titles.

Genealogy Records

Now that you've got all the reference work out of the way, it's time to look for your ancestors. Since this may take a little work and you don't want to reinvent the wheel, it's wise to see if anyone else has done your research for you. In other words, someone may already have written something about your family. You won't know until you check previous research. I'm not saying that someone may have written your entire family history and you didn't know it, although it's possible. What someone might have done is written a biography of one of your ancestors. Or maybe one of your early ancestors wrote an autobiography of his or her life. Unknown to many people, there are thousands of biographies, autobiographies, oral histories, genealogies, and family histories written by and about African Americans. If you check these sources first, you could save a lot of time and effort.

The mere existence of these records confirms the point I've been making that African American genealogy is *not* the same as any other genealogy until you get back to the slavery period. Most of these records cover the period from the Civil War to the present. Few would be needed if it weren't for racism and segregation. Collective biographies that white genealogists use do not include African Americans, except perhaps as a token here and there. Thus, the African American community had a need to develop its own biographical dictionaries and encyclopedias. These were also created because the history of African Americans was excluded from most history textbooks and therefore whites said African Americans had no heroes. Many of the works that follow were written to dispel that myth.

Autobiographies

An autobiography is the story of a person's life written by the person. It usually has the benefit of contemporary descriptions and explanations. An autobiography can also illustrate why the

PERSI (Periodical Source Index)

1st Series	I	Places 1847–1985
	II	Places 1847–1985
	III	Families 1847–1985
	IV	Families 1847–1985
2nd Series	V	Places 1847–1985
	VI	Places 1847–1985
	VII	Families 1847–1985
	VIII	Families 1847–1985
3rd Series	IX	Places 1847–1985
	X	Places 1847–1985
	XI	Families 1847–1985
	XII	Families 1847–1985
4th Series	XIII	Places 1847–1985
	XIV	Places 1847–1985
	XV	Families 1847–1985
	XVI	Families 1847–1985
5th Series	XVII	Places, Families 1847–1985
Current Series	1986 Annual	
	1987 Annual	
	1988 Annual	
	1989 Annual	
	1990 Annual	
	1991 Annual	
	1992 Annual	
	1993 Annual	
	1994 Annual	
	1995 Annual	
	1996 Families	
	1996 Places	
	1997 Families	
	1997 Places[1]	

[1]1998 and later annual volumes are published on CD-ROM. All years are available on the Web at Ancestry.com, but there is a fee.

writer did certain things in his or her life, whereas a biographer has to analyze and interpret these events. Autobiographies should not be accepted as all truthful. They are subject to a person's lapse in memory, omissions, and exaggerations of events.

While researching in a college library her ancestor founded, genealogist Eunice Pressie located an autobiography written by that ancestor, James Solomon Russell (*Adventure in Faith*, 1936). Eunice was very excited when the autobiography mentioned an earlier ancestor coming from Africa.

> In Mecklenburg County (Virginia), however, the story has been handed down that my mother's grandmother was sold in Palmer Springs shortly after she was brought from Africa. She had a daughter, Seleah, and both of them worked in the "Big House."

Interestingly, Eunice traced Seleah's mother and found records that she was born in America, not Africa. So we must be very careful when collecting oral traditions and other records. We must always solicit corroborating evidence from other, independent sources. There may be some truth to the above story, and the generations might be different because the story had been repeated through several generations. Seleah's mother was James Solomon Russell's great-grandmother. So the story had been handed down for at least four generations.

There are many ways to check for published autobiographies of African Americans. An excellent source is *Black Americans in Autobiography*, by Russell C. Brignano. He describes 710 autobiographies written from 1789 to 1982, along with libraries that have copies.

Biographies

In contrast to an autobiography, a biography is the story of a person's life written and researched by someone else. Information can be gathered from varying sources, which may or may not include interviews with the subject of the biography. What resources were utilized, what resources were available at the time of the writing, and even whether the subject was available or interviewed will determine the quality, comprehensiveness, and reliability of the biography. A biographer must analyze and interpret a person's life and therefore could add biases, prejudices, and inaccuracies. Biographies can be located by searching card catalogues for the names of the individuals.

Biographical Dictionaries

Biographical dictionaries, also called "collective biographies" and "biographical encyclopedias," are like encyclopedias containing the biographies of many individuals. The dictionary may be organized by profession, religion, time period, or some other category.

Good sources of biographies of African Americans can be found in sources like *Dictionary of American Negro Biography,* compiled by Rayford W. Logan and Michael R. Winston in 1982. It contains over 600 biographies of African Americans who died before 1970. *Who's Who Among Black Americans* has been published since 1977 by Gale Research and other publishers and is now titled *Who's Who Among African Americans*. Gale Research also publishes *Contemporary*

Black Biography. Each volume contains about sixty-five biographies, and three volumes have been published per year since 1991.

An excellent source for older biographies of African Americans is *Black Biographical Dictionaries 1790–1950,* edited by Randall K. and Nancy Hall Burkett and Henry Louis Gates Jr. It is a historic effort to combine 290 biographical "Who's Who" dictionaries with encyclopedias containing biographies on approximately 31,000 African Americans. Many of the works are very rare, with only one copy in existence. The volumes have been reproduced on microfiche and are available at larger public and academic libraries. There is a three-volume index to the set titled *Black Biography 1790–1950: A Cumulative Index.* The index shows the name, year of birth and death, place of birth, religion, and occupation of a person with a biography. It also indicates which biographical dictionary the biography came from and where more information can be located. The index is available on the Internet to paid subscribers at http://aabd. chadwyck. com/. (For other sources, see "Biographies" in the Bibliography.)

I was surprised and fortunate to locate a biography of my grandfather Asa Morris Burroughs in *Who's Who in Colored America, 1930–1932.* He was a prominent attorney, and this biography gave me many additional facts about his life, including the names of his clients, the board of director positions he held, and the names of his fraternal affiliations. Through researching *Black Biography 1790–1950: A Cumulative Index,* I learned he was also included in the fourth through the seventh editions of *Who's Who in Colored America,* from 1934 to 1950. These new biographies enabled me to see how his political and legal career evolved.

One might say, "Well, my ancestors weren't prominent. Therefore, these published biographies won't help me." You never know until you look. I never knew my grandfather would be included until I looked.

One of my favorite examples of biographies on common people is from *Cincinnati's Colored Citizens: Historical, Sociological, and Biographical,* by Wendell P. Dabney, published in 1926. Dabney has a small biography and photograph of Mr. J. M. Tadlock, who was a maintenance man with Bell Telephone Company. You can't get any more common than that. If we knew everything about our ancestors, we wouldn't be doing genealogy research. Remember the saying we have in genealogy, "Leave no stone unturned." So check each and every source. Like me, you may be surprised one day.

Black Family Histories and Genealogies

Likewise, there are sources for Black family histories and genealogies. As genealogy becomes more popular, more African Americans are researching their families and publishing the results.

A family history details the story of a family or several families within a lineage. This history could result from only oral history, which many African Americans recite at family reunions, or it could result from extensive research into primary or secondary sources. The history could be merely information on individuals, or it might include social and historical narrative, placing yer, Boston, Mass., 1921-present; Special Assistant Attorney General, Massachusetts, 1925-26; appt. Member, Mass. Board of Parole, 1927 mem. K. of P. (Past Grand Keeper of Records and Seal, Grand Lecturer); Masons; Omega Psi Phi Fraternity; Pol. Republican; Relig. Baptist; Office, Old South Building, 294 Washington St.; Residence, 56 Windsor St., Boston, Mass.

While at Dartmouth he was a member of the football team for three years, track team for four years, Glee Club for four years. He was a member of the Aegis Board (Annual Sophomore publication), Paleopitus (Honorary Senior Society) and Executive, Class Day Committee.

After graduating from college he served as Football Coach at Massachusetts Agricultural College, 1904, 1907 and 1908; Football Coach at Malden (Mass.) High School, 1905 and 1906. He was Athletic Director and Coach at Morehouse College, 1908 to 1912.

During the World War Mr. Bullock served three months as Y.M.C.A. Educational Secretary at Camp Meade, Md., and for fifteen months was Physical Director with the troops in France, being attached to 369th U. S. Infantry (15th N. Y. Regiment) from July, 1918, to January, 1919. He was recommended for Croix de Guerre for service during the September-October offensive on Champagne front.

Because of his work overseas an invitation was extended to him to participate in the burial of the Unknown Soldier at Washington, D. C., as a guest of the nation.

BURLEIGH, HENRY THACKER — Baritone Soloist-Composer.

b. Dec. 2, 1866, Erie, Pa.; s. Henry T. and Elizabeth (Waters) Burleigh; m. Louise Alston, Feb. 9, 1898; one child, Alston Waters, b. Aug. 18, 1899; studied at National Conservatory of Music, N. Y.; A.M. (Honorary), Atlanta Univ.; Mus.D. (Honorary), Howard Univ.; Baritone Soloist, St. George's Church, New York, since 1894; member of the choir of Temple Emanu-El, New York, since 1900; Musical Editor, G. Ricordi & Co., Inc., New York; composer "Deep River," "Jean," "Little Mother of Mine,"; and in all about two hundred compositions; Spingarn Medalist, 1917; Address, 823 E. 166th St., New York, N. Y.

He received the 1929 award in Music, and the Harmon Medal. For the past 37 years he has been the baritone soloist of the aristocratic St. George's Church, in New York City, the membership of which consists of many wealthy white people. The Temple Emanu-El, in New York City, the richest synagogue in America, also engaged him to sing for their services. He sings with amazing facility songs not only in his mother tongue, but also in German, French, Italian, Latin, Hebrew.

He is considered one of the greatest living Colored singers. The genius he has displayed by the compositions of several hundred masterful songs makes him one of the most remarkable musicians in the annals of music in America.

BURNETTE, ALICE C. — International Organzer.

b. Jackson, Miss.; d. E. L. and Jane (Thompson) Erskine; m. William Hallback; second marriage, C. A. Burnette; two children; Blanche Edward Hallback; Aurelia Ida Hallback; educ. Pub. Sch., Jackson, Miss.; Tougaloo College; taught school in Jackson, Miss., until 1916; engaged by Madam C. J. Walker to travel in the interests of her manufacturing Company; has traveled through forty State and Foreign countries; engaged as International Organizer, Madam C. J. Walker Mfg. Company; mem. Elks; Past Matron of Eastern Star City Lodge; Woodman of Union; Relig. A.M.E. Ch.; Address, c/o Madam C. J. Walker Mfg. Co., 617 N. West St., Indianapolis, Ind.; Residence, 1890 7th Ave., New York City, N. Y.

BURROUGHS, ASA MORRIS — Lawyer.

b. Jan. 26, 1893, Chicago, Ill.; s. Morris and Mary J. L. (Williams) Burroughs; m. Alma I. Rice, Jan. 7, 1915; four children, Morris; Leonard; Elmer; Irene Jane; educ. Crane Technical High Sch., 1911; Kent Law Coll., Chicago, Ill.; Lawyer, 1920-present; Attorney, Mid-South Finance Corp.; Attorney, A. B. C. Bond and Investment Co.; Attorney, John T. Wilson Medical Foundation; Attorney, South Park Bank Building Corp.; Attorney, Union Mason Temple Assn.; Attorney, Mid-South Side Property Owners' Assn.; Attorney, Mid-South Side Business League of Chicago; Vice Chairman, Camp Wabash Committee, Y. M. C. A.; Chairman, Board of Directors, Upsilon Sigma Chapter Phi Beta Sigma; mem. Special Shelter Committee, South Side, Joint Emergency Relief Committee, Illinois; Sec., Cook Co. Bar Assn., 1924-26; Pres., 1928-29; mem. Masons; Appomattox Club; Phi Beta Sigma; Pres., Chicago Democratic Lawyers' Club; 4th Ward Community Club; Relig. Methodist; Address, 188 W. Randolph St.; Residence, 4739 Champlain Ave., Chicago, Ill.

BURROUGHS, MISS NANNIE H. — Training School President.

Founded National Training School for Women and Girls, in 1909; instrumental in raising over $350,000 for the benefit of the School; Property vested in Board of Trustees; Secretary of the Woman's Convention Auxiliary to the National Baptist Convention; Address, Lincoln Heights, Washington, D. C.

BURT, ROBERT T. — Physician-Surgeon.

b. Nov. 25, 1873, Kosciusko, Miss.; s. Robert and Silvia A. Burt; m. Emma E. Williams, June 11, 1913; one child, Em Tecumseh, b. Feb. 14, 1915; educ. Kosciusko High Sch., 1884-87; Jackson Coll., Jackson, Miss., 1887-89; Walden Univ., 1889-92; Meharry Med. Coll., Nashville, Tenn., 1893-97; M.D., 1897; Post Graduate, Harvard Univ., 1901-04; Surgeon-in-Chief, Home Infirmary, Clarksville, Tenn., 1900-present; Relig. A. M. E. Church; Business Address, 122 N. Third St.; Residence, 20 Currant St., Clarksvile, Tenn.

Dr. Robert T. Burt has, since 1906, con-

Who's Who in Colored America—1930–31–32 edition of *Who's Who in Colored America*, listing a biography of author's grandfather, attorney Asa Morris Burroughs.

the family in historical context. The quality of a family history must be evaluated by noting the sources used in compiling it. If no sources are cited, the entire work is suspect. It will serve only to provide clues, and you'll have to search for records to prove every name and linkage in it.

A genealogy is the study of family relationships and lineage, the written results of which detail births, deaths, and marriages since the oldest ancestor, the progenitor. The genealogy can be written in several formats used by professional and experienced genealogists and scholarly periodicals (called Register, Modified Register, and Henry Systems). Sometimes genealogies contain narrative material, but sometimes they are merely lists of names, dates, and events. Better genealogies include footnoted sources to prove the relationships of individuals listed. In comparing genealogies with biographies, John R. Totten, editor of the *New York Genealogical and Biographical Record,* put it succinctly: "A genealogy deals with the who and a biography deals with the what."

There are four good sources for published family histories and genealogies. African Americans have been interested in family history for a long time, but it wasn't until after *Roots* was published in 1976 that groups organized to form genealogical societies. One of the early ones was the Afro-American Historical and Genealogical Society, which began in 1977. Three years later they began publishing a quarterly journal of transcriptions of records and articles on African American history, family history, and genealogy. Barbara Walker, widow of one of the founders, James Dent Walker, compiled an index for the first ten years of the journal, *Index to the Journal of the Afro-American Historical and Genealogical Society Quarterly: Issues of 1980–1990.* Researchers need to check the index for their family names to see if any are mentioned.

While working as a librarian in the Genealogy Room at the Library of Congress, Sandra Lawson was familiar with several genealogies and family histories about African American families. However, there was no list of them. She began combing bibliographies to find citations and also went through the stacks in the Library of Congress to find others. When she finished, she compiled a list of fifty-six African American genealogies and family histories. She published the list in a book she edited, *Generations Past: A Select List of Sources for Afro-American Genealogical Research.* Most were written between 1971 and 1986, but the earliest one was written in 1913. The update for *Generations Past* is on the Library of Congress Web site and is titled *African American Family Histories and Related Works in the Library of Congress (http://lcweb.loc.gov/ rr/genealogy/big_guid/aframer/).* There could possibly be more African American family histories in the Library of Congress collection because not all use the terms *Black, colored,* or *African American* in the title. The Library of Congress didn't add the subject heading "Afro American—Genealogy" until the early 1980s, so it's difficult to locate the early ones. Sandra also said there are undoubtedly other African American family histories that are never sent in to the Library of Congress.

The *Negro History Bulletin,* the journal of the Association for the Study of Negro Life and History, published over thirty family histories between 1942 and 1978. Most range from three to five pages, but one ran as long as sixteen pages. Most include photographs of family members, and a few include genealogy charts. Each *Negro History Bulletin* indexes family names and subjects. However, I haven't seen sources footnoted in it and surmise that most of the information came from oral histories.

Marie Taylor, working in the Family History Library in Salt Lake City, followed a route similar to Sandra Lawson's at the Library of Congress by comparing genealogical and historical bibliographies of African Americans and then searching the catalogue of the Family History Library to see if they owned the titles. Marie then compiled a bibliography project similar to *Generations Past*, titled *Family History Library Bibliography of African American Sources*. It has two chapters with biographies and family histories, titled "Biographies, collected/oral histories" and "Family History/Genealogy." The library realized they had many more African American family histories than previously thought because a book title like *The Jones Family History* would not indicate whether the family was African American. The bibliography is located in the Family History Library in Salt Lake City in a binder at the second-floor information booth, and it can be borrowed on microfiche by a Family History Center.

PERSI

Many other African American family histories, genealogies, biographies, autobiographies, and oral histories have been published in newsletters and journals. Researchers should check the "surname" section as well as the locality section in the *Periodical Source Index (PERSI)* and other periodical indexes.

I once used *PERSI* to research a white family I was tracking, which illustrates the importance of looking for published articles. I traced one family line to early nineteenth-century Pennsylvania. I found a mention in an article that indicated the family migrated to western Pennsylvania from Prince George's County, Maryland. I had traveled to Maryland but never researched their records. As it was a new state for me to research, I had to start from scratch.

I started with *PERSI*. I grabbed *Volume I: Places, 1847–1985*. I photocopied all the pages for Maryland, which totaled four pages. Then I grabbed *Volume V: Places, 1847–1985*, which indexed articles not included in Volume I. This gave me an additional three pages for Maryland. I repeated the process for Volumes IX and XIII. I photocopied twenty-six pages from these four volumes, which covered all 5,029 periodicals but only for 1847 to 1985.

Next I copied the annual supplemental volumes for 1986 through 1994 (the only volumes out at the time). When I finished, I had forty-four pages totaling 1,416 articles on Maryland. At that point I knew of all the articles published in a genealogical newsletter or journal for 147 years covering the state of Maryland! I repeated the routine for the county, Prince George's. This search located an additional 180 articles. When I finished, the list had grown to 1,596 articles. The articles can be found in many genealogical libraries. However, the Allen County Library in Fort Wayne, Indiana, has them *all*, and will gladly photocopy any article and mail it to you for a small fee. (To contact them, see "Miscellaneous Addresses" in the appendixes.)

After copying the last supplement, I reviewed each photocopy. I went down the list of articles and marked a pencil dash next to each one that had the potential of listing an ancestor or giving me important new information. Then I reviewed the marked list and placed a cross through the dashes of articles having the highest potential. I wanted to read those first.

The next day I returned to read the articles. I placed a check next to each one I read. Before the day was over, I located a key document, a 1937 family history published in the *National Genealogical Society Quarterly*. It linked three families completing the connection that brought my enslaved ancestors to western Pennsylvania from Prince George's County, Maryland, in 1773. I'll follow the same procedure for all the surnames I'm researching.

I could have searched for years and never run across this family history nor been able to make the connections through searching individual records. Checking for published materials is called "doing your homework."

Once you locate information on an ancestor in a biographical work, remember it is a secondary source and the information should be verified if possible. Always check to see if the compiler included the source of the information. Many early biographies came from interviews with the subject and word of mouth from others. Much of the information was embellished and is not verifiable. Therefore you should take it with a grain of salt. Many a tall tale has been gleaned from these biographies.

Vital Records

After you do a thorough search for published works on your ancestors, you're ready to look for new information. In the "Vital Records" chapter I covered sending for copies of original birth, death, and marriage records from the vital records office. The next strategy is to search for vital records and "finding aids" to vital records in the library. These include guides, inventories, descriptions, indexes, transcriptions, and sometimes copies of original records.

Where to Write for Vital Records, which lists the addresses of every state vital records office, dates of records, and current fees, can be found in many libraries. It will be in either the genealogy section or the government documents section, since it was published by the U.S. Department of Health and Human Services. Other guides that include vital records information include: *The Handy Book for Genealogists,* by George Everton; *Ancestry's Red Book,* by Alice Eichholz; and the *United States County Courthouse Address Book,* by Leland Mertzler, give addresses and phone numbers for all county courthouses in the United States. You should also check the *International Vital Records Handbook,* by Thomas J. Kemp, which has copies of forms for applying to state vital records offices.

WPA

During the Great Depression of the 1930s, a federal government agency was created to hire unemployed people. It was initially called the Works Progress Administration, later changed to the Work Projects Administration, but quickly became known as the WPA. One of the divisions of the WPA was the Historical Records Survey (HRS). The HRS hired unemployed teachers, librarians, archivists, researchers, and clerks to inventory government records, church records, school records, books, newspapers, paintings, photographs, maps, and manuscripts. In addition, some individual states indexed, transcribed, and microfilmed records. Two publications of the WPA Historical Records Survey that are very important for genealogists are the guides to vital records and the inventory of county records.

WPA GUIDES TO VITAL RECORDS—One WPA Historical Record Survey project was to inventory state records. This resulted in guides to vital records for most states. The guides are arranged by vital record, then alphabetically by county, and include the name of the county seat. Then each group of records within each county is listed. The entries detail the years records began, the number of volumes of records, how the records are arranged, if there is an index, the cost of copies at the time, and where the records were housed.

Many birth certificates, death certificates, and marriage records were segregated by race. This varied from state to state, from county to county within a state, and even by time period within the same county in a state. The only way to know for sure is to research inventories of vital records in the states and counties you are researching. The state guide to vital records in Mississippi revealed three groups of marriage records: Marriage Records (white), Marriage Records (colored), and Certificates of Marriages returned. Below is a list of the vital records guides published for southern states.

Alabama	*Guide to Public Vital Statistics Records in Alabama: Preliminary Edition,* March 1942
Arkansas	*Guide to Vital Statistics Records in Arkansas*—Vol. 1, Public Archives, 1942
Florida	*Guide to Public Vital Statistics Records in Florida,* February 1941
Georgia	*Guide to Public Vital Statistics Records in Georgia,* June 1941
Kentucky	*Guide to Public Vital Statistics Records in Kentucky,* February 1942
Louisiana	*Guide to Public Vital Statistics Records in Louisiana,* December 1942
Mississippi	*Guide to Vital Statistics Records in Mississippi*—Vol. 1, Public Archives, April 1942
Missouri	*Guide to Public Vital Statistics Records in Missouri,* July 1941
North Carolina	*Guide to Public Vital Statistics Records in North Carolina,* August 1941
Tennessee	*Guide to Public Vital Statistics Records in Tennessee,* June 1941
Texas	*Guide to Public Vital Statistics Records in Texas,* June 1941
West Virginia	*Inventory of Public Vital Statistics Records in West Virginia: Births, Deaths, and Marriages,* March 1941

Naturally, there are guides for other states. A complete list is published in *The Researcher's Guide to American Genealogy,* by Val Greenwood, and the complete list of these and the other 1,800 HRS publications are included in *Bibliography of Research Projects Reports: Checklist of Historical Records Survey Publications—WPA Technical Series, Research and Records Bibliography No. 7,* edited by Sargent B. Child and Dorothy P. Holmes in 1943 and reprinted by the Genealogical Publishing Company in 1969. Unpublished WPA records are detailed in *The WPA Historical*

- 31 -

Marriages

GEORGE COUNTY   (Lucedale)

1932-- Marriage Notices, 1 vol. Chron. by date of notice. No
index. Certified copy 80¢. Circuit Clerk, Lucedale.
1910-- Marriage Record (white), 6 vols. Chron. by date issued.
Index alph. by first letter of surnames. Certified copy
80¢. Circuit Clerk, Lucedale.
1910-- Marriage Record (colored), 3 vols. Chron. by date issued.
Index alph. by first letter of surnames. Certified copy
80¢. Circuit Clerk, Lucedale.
1928-- Marriage Certificates, 1 f. b. Chron. by date returned. No
index. Certified copy 80¢. Circuit Clerk, Lucedale.

GREENE COUNTY   (Leakesville)

1930-- Notice of Application for Marriage License, 1 vol. Chron.
by date issued. No index. Circuit Clerk, Leakesville.
1874-- Marriage Record, 14 vols. Chron. by date issued. Index
alph. by first letter of surnames. Certified copy $1.
Circuit Clerk, Leakesville.
1912-- Certificate of Marriage, 2 f. b. and 5 pkgs. Chron. by
date returned. No index. Certified copy $1. Circuit
Clerk, Leakesville.

GRENADA COUNTY   (Grenada)

1870-- Marriage Record (white), 7 vols. Chron. by date issued. No
index. Certified copy $1. Circuit Clerk, Grenada.
1880-- Marriage Record (colored), 15 vols. Chron. by date issued.
No index. Certified copy $1. Circuit Clerk, Grenada.
1908-- Certificates of Marriage Returned, 6 f. b. Chron. by date
issued. No index. Certified copy $1. Circuit Clerk, Grenada.

HANCOCK COUNTY   (Bay St. Louis)

1853-- Marriage Record, 29 vols. Chron. by date issued. Index alph.
by first letter of surnames. Circuit Clerk, Bay St. Louis.
1853-- Marriage License Certificates (colored), 2 f. b. Chron. by
date returned. No index. Circuit Clerk, Bay St. Louis.
1882-- Marriage License Certificates (white), 10 f. b. Chron. by
date returned. No index. Circuit Clerk, Bay St. Louis.

HARRISON COUNTY   (Gulfport)

1841-- Marriage Record, 51 vols. Chron. by date issued. Index alph.
by first letter of surnames. Certified copy $1. Circuit
Clerk, Gulfport.
1846-- Marriage Certificates, 41 f. b. Chron. by date returned. No
index. Circuit Clerk, Gulfport.
1869-78 Marriage Bonds, 1 vol. Chron. by date of Bond. No index.
Circuit Clerk, Gulfport.

Vital Statistics Guide—WPA *Guide to Vital Records in Mississippi* describing
marriage records in various Mississippi county courthouses in 1942.

Records Survey: A Guide to the Unpublished Inventories, Indexes and Transcripts, by Loretta L. Hefner.

WPA COUNTY INVENTORIES—Another WPA Historical Record Survey project was to inventory the records in each county courthouse. At the time there were 3,066 counties in the United States. Inventories were completed for 90 percent of them, listing the birth certificates, death certificates, marriage records, and divorce records that existed in each county courthouse from about 1936 to 1942, when the inventories were conducted and published. Only about 20 percent of these inventories were published. Others exist in manuscript form in various institutions. Locations of the unpublished inventories are in the above-mentioned guide by Loretta L. Hefner.

The descriptions of vital records in the county inventories are more detailed than those in the state vital records guides. They detail the year the records began, the number of volumes, the different types of records (e.g., marriage license, marriage certificate, marriage application, affidavits, parental consent forms, notices mailed to parents), full description of each type of record, manner of recording, number of pages, and dimensions. They also describe changes at different time periods. If there is an index, it is described in a separate entry.

Two examples of descriptions of vital records from the WPA inventories are from Georgia and Mississippi. The WPA inventory for Chatham County, which includes Savannah (*Inven-*

```
                    Vital Statistics
               (See also entries 85, 425-427)

Births

    720.  BIRTH RECORD (White and Colored), 1889.  1 vol.
Shows name, sex, date of birth, residence, name of parents, nationality,
name of physician or midwife, remarks.  Arr. chron.  No index.  Hdw.  150 pp.
19 x 13 x 1.  C.H., bsmt. strm.

    721.  REGISTER OF BIRTHS (City of Savannah), 1890-96.  4 vols. (White,
          2 vols.; Colored, 2 vols.).
Shows date of birth, name of parents, sex, race, nationality, residence, date
reported, and by whom.  Arr. chron.  No index.  Hdw. on pr. fms.  400 pp. 17
x 14 x 2.  Off. va.

    722.  BIRTH RECORDS WHICH OCCURED PRIOR TO 1890, THE ORIGINAL BEING
          FILED AT THE STATE BUREAU OF VITAL STATISTICS ACCORDING TO THE
          LAW CONCERNING OLD RECORDS NOT REPORTED, 1843-90.  1 file box.
Copies of birth certificates, showing name of infant, name of parents, race,
sex, nationality, date of birth, oaths, and signatures of witnesses.  No
arr.  No index.  Hdw. and typed on pr. fms.  13 x 4 x 14.  Off. va.

    723.  BIRTHS (Certificates, City and County), 1890-1919.  28 file
          boxes (dated).  Title varies: Births and Deaths, 1890-1900,
          12 file boxes.
Original certificates, showing name of infant, race, sex, date of birth, and
where born, parents' names, nativity of parents, and physician's signature.
Also contains: Deaths (Certificates, City and County), 1890-1900, entry 729.
Arr. chron.  No index.  Hdw. and typed on pr. fms.  10 x 4½ x 14.  Off va.

    724.  BIRTH CERTIFICATES (City and County ), 1919--.  35 vols.
Duplicates of certificates, showing registration number, militia district or
ward, address, name of infant, sex, whether legitimate, whether born dead or
alive, date and hour of birth, whether multiple birth, maiden name of mother,
name of father, race, birthplace, profession, number of other children born,
```

WPA Georgia Births—WPA *Inventory of the County Archives of Chatham County, Georgia (Savannah),* describing birth records in the county courthouse in 1938.

Marriages

125. MARRIAGE RECORDS WHITE, 1870--. 7 vols. (A-G).
Record of marriages of white persons, including original applications for
marriage licenses, original affidavits made by male applicants, original
consents given by parents, guardians, or next of kin to marriage of persons
under statutory age for marriage, and abstract records of marriage licenses
issued and of certificates of marriage returned. Since 1930 includes also
original applications and affidavits of female applicants and record of notices
mailed to parents, guardians, or next of kin of applicants under statutory age
for marriage. Applications to 1930 show names of applicants, affidavit of male
applicant, signature of male applicant, signature of clerk as officer taking
affidavit, and date affidavit made. Applications since 1930 show names, race,
ages, and addresses of applicants, names and addresses of parents, guardians,
or next of kin of applicants, affidavits of applicants as to their ages, signatures of applicants, affidavit of male applicant that no legal cause exists
to obstruct the marriage, signature of male applicant, signature of clerk or
officer taking affidavit, date affidavits made. Consents show name of person
under statutory age for marriage, statement of consent to marriage, signature
of parents, guardians, or next of kin, signatures of subscribing witnesses or
of officer taking proof, date of proof. Record of notices mailed to parents,
guardians, or next of kin shows names and addresses of parents, guardians, or
next of kin notified, names, ages, race, and addresses of applicants, for license, statement that license will be issued within five days from date if no
legal objections are made, date notices mailed and date license will be issued,
clerk's signature as attestor. Record of marriage licenses issued shows names
of contracting parties, signature of clerk as licensor, date license issued,
and clerk's certification of dates licenses issued and dates certificates of
marriage returned. Record of certificates of marriage returned shows names of
contracting parties, date ceremony performed, name of person performing ceremony, dates certificates received for filing and dates recorded; and signature of clerk in attest. Arr. chron. by date affidavits made. No index. Hdw.
on ptd. form. 640 pp. 18 x 13 x 3.

126. MARRIAGE RECORD COLORED, 1880--. 15 vols. (A-O).
Record of marriages of colored persons. For description of contents, arrange-
ment, indexing, manner of recording, number of pages, and dimensions, see entry 125.

**WPA Mississippi Mar-
riages**—WPA *Inventory
of the County Archives of
Grenada County, Missis-
sippi,* describing segre-
gated marriage records
in the county court-
house in 1940.

tory of the County Archives of Georgia, No. 25. Chatham County [Savannah], March 1938), indicates one volume of segregated birth records for white and "colored" for 1889, two volumes of white birth records for Savannah from 1890 to 1896, and two volumes of "colored" births for the same time period. Later birth records appear to be integrated.

The WPA inventory for Grenada County, Mississippi *(Inventory of the County Archives of Mis-sissippi, Grenada County),* shows seven volumes of white marriage records beginning in 1870 and fifteen volumes of "colored" marriages beginning in 1880.

In addition to determining if the records were segregated by race, you can search the inventories to see what years birth and death certificates and marriage and divorce records existed in the counties where your ancestors lived. You'll be able to tell when the county began keeping birth and death certificates or at least determine the dates of the earliest records. The inventory will also indicate things like whether the county had marriage applications, marriage bonds, or marriage returns in addition to marriage licenses. When you applied to the county courthouse for an ancestor's marriage record, you may have received only a copy of the marriage license. In this case you'll want copies of the other marriage records.

The WPA inventory for Grenada County, Mississippi, indicates they have marriage licenses, marriage certificates, marriage applications, affidavits, and consents given by parents or next of kin for underage marriage applicants. Some consent records show ages, race, and addresses of applicants and parents, as well as notices mailed to parents, guardians, or next of kin for underage applicants.

It's also a good idea to study the WPA guides and inventories because you may find other gems you didn't know existed. For example, the *Guide to Vital Statistics Records in Mississippi* indicates there are records for "Marriage license(s) issued but never cancelled and no returns made showing that marriage was never consummated." That is a real gem. Can you imagine finding out your ancestor applied for a marriage license but never went through with the marriage? And also learning who the spouse was supposed to be? I bet that could rattle some skeletons in the closet.

Keep in mind that some records that existed in the 1930s and '40s may no longer exist when you search for them. Amazingly, some records were destroyed. Workers in Maine had trouble locating a library to store the records and eventually dumped them into the bay. In larger cities some records may have been shipped to warehouses and no one knows about them.

These WPA guides and inventories are available in genealogical and academic libraries, as well as on loan from the Family History Library. Check card catalogues and ask reference librarians if they have any WPA guides to vital statistics and county inventories from the Historical Records Surveys. Sometimes they are in the government documents department of the library. If you cannot locate a WPA vital statistics guide for the state you're researching or a county inventory for the county you're researching, check with the local county clerk in the state to determine if the records were segregated for the time period you are researching.

Another useful guide is *Marriage Laws in the United States, 1887–1906,* by S.N.D. North. It's a condensed version of a U.S. Census Bureau study of each state's marriage laws. It details legal age requirements, consent needed for underage marriages, prohibited, voidable, and criminal marriages, who may perform marriages, what records must be kept, and many other useful details for genealogists.

Microfilm Copies of Original Vital Records

We stated that vital records began around the turn of the century, some before. Hopefully, by now you've applied for and received vital records for the ancestors listed on your Family Group Sheets. Some of these vital records, or at least indexes to them, have been microfilmed and some indexes have been published. It's a good idea to double-check for those you don't have. Perhaps a record exists for your ancestor, but the county clerk couldn't find it.

Some libraries have microfilm copies of original vital records. The New Orleans Public Library is the repository for the city archives and maintains older death records. They have board of health death certificates from 1804–1915 and indexes for 1804–1916. They have no birth certificates or indexes to births. In some cases you might have to go to the state archives in the area where your ancestors lived to find microfilmed copies of vital records.

You can also check for microfilm copies of original vital records at the Family History Center. Check the card catalogue "locality" section for the state and county where your ancestors lived. Once you get to the section, check the subject headings for vital records, birth records, death records, coroner's records, marriage records, and divorce records. Following is a chart showing examples of vital records and indexes to vital records for a few Southern states.

VITAL RECORDS AND INDEXES FOR SOUTHERN STATES

	Birth Indexes	Birth Records	Marriage Indexes	Marriage Records	Death Indexes	Death Records
Alabama	1917–1919		1936–1959	1936–1992	1917–1919	
Florida			1927–1909		1877–1969	
Kentucky	1911–1954	1874–1878 1907–1910	1972–1990	1874–1875 1906–1914	1911–1986	1874–1878 1904–1910
North Carolina					1901–1967	1906–1977
Tennessee	1908–1912	1908–1912	1838–1987	1919–1938	1908–1912	1908–1912
Texas	1900–1945				1900–1945	

Notes: These records are for a limited number of states and for sporadic years, from the Feb. 25, 1995, Family History Library (FHL) Catalogue on microfiche. There are indexes and records for other states, but because the vast majority of African Americans have southern roots, this chart was created to aid that research. These indexes, records, and dates are subject to change as records are added to and withdrawn from the FHL collection. In addition, some of these records have restrictions. Always check the FHL Catalogue to see what is current. These records are for the state level only. There may be additional vital records and indexes at the county and city levels, so check for each one of the ciites and counties you're researching.

You'll recall that in the chapter on "Vital Records" I couldn't find the marriage record for my great-grandparents Morris Burroughs and Mary Jane Lillie Williams. I thought they were married in 1888, the year before their first child, Robert, was born. However, I didn't know where they were married. I contacted the county clerks in Cook County, Illinois, where they lived and where Robert was born; in Spartanburg County, South Carolina, where Morris was from; and in Hamilton County, Tennessee, where Mary was raised. I even wrote to Rossville, Georgia, and they had no record. Many Chattanooga, Tennessee, couples were married in Rossville, Georgia. Genealogists who aren't familiar with that geographic area are surprised to learn that Rossville is across the street from Chattanooga.

In 1993 I traveled to Salt Lake City to research in the Family History Library. The card catalogue revealed they had copies of marriage returns for Hamilton County, Tennessee. Even though the Hamilton County clerk wrote me and said there was no record, I decided to take a

Marriage Return—1888 marriage return, obtained from the Hamilton County (Chattanooga, Tennessee) clerk, listing a marriage license issued to Morris R. Burroughs and Mary J. L. Williams, which is the same as was obtained at the Family History Library in Salt Lake City, Utah.

look myself. Much to my surprise, I found the marriage record. Morris and Mary were married in 1888, just as I had thought. It seems as if whoever looked for the record didn't do a thorough job. That's what happens sometimes with old records. Nobody likes to go through them but us crazy genealogists.

When I examined the marriage record, I even found something new. Morris had a middle initial, *R*. I never knew that. However, when I looked back at other records in his file, I realized I should have known. There was a middle initial on one of the listings for him in the Chicago city directory. From now on, I'll pay much closer attention.

Having proved the marriage, the record told me a few other things. One, Morris and Mary were married a year before their first child, Robert, was born. It wasn't a shotgun wedding, like others in the family tree. Two, they were married while Mary was still in school at Spelman Seminary in Atlanta. The record also led me again to think Morris may have lived in Chattanooga before he moved to Chicago to work as a Pullman porter in 1887. He and Mary had to meet somewhere. This theory was first introduced when I located the affidavits of Morris's death certificate and the original death certificate, which indicated erroneously he was born in Tennessee. These two confirming indicators give me the incentive to search for him in Chattanooga.

After I located the marriage record in Salt Lake City, I decided to write the Hamilton County clerk a second time. I now had the exact date of their marriage, May 24, 1888. I paid the five-dollar fee again, and this time they located Morris and Mary's marriage record and sent me a copy. When I examined it, I saw it was the exact same record I had found at the Family History Library, with one exception—the price. The one from the Hamilton County clerk cost five dollars, whereas the copy from the Family History Library cost twenty cents for the microfilm machine.

This goes to show you, you can't give up. You can't say, "They didn't keep records of Blacks." You have to check every source and keep on trying. Remember, "Leave no stone unturned."

Fortunately, some vital records offices have transferred their older vital records to the state archives. This is good for genealogists because it gives us better access to the records. Many vital records offices and county courthouses prefer servicing current records, not historical records. In addition, state archives are more experienced and qualified in caring for older records and have preservation supplies and equipment, which is why they are in business.

After getting experience at your local genealogical library, you'll want to contact the state archives where your ancestor lived to see if they have copies of original vital records or at least indexes of them. Another important microfilm record often found at state archives or city archives is coroner's records. Original coroner's inquest records for Cook County, Illinois, from 1872 to 1911 were deteriorating and subsequently were microfilmed by the Illinois State Archives. These are not available through interlibrary loan and can be viewed only at the Illinois State Archives in Springfield. However, whenever you locate a microfilmed record, always check to see if it is available through interlibrary loan to your hometown library. The New Orleans Public Library has New Orleans coroner's inquest records from 1844 to 1904.

The American Genealogical Lending Library also has copies of original vital records you can borrow to view at home. But remember, you must have a microfilm reader to view the microfilm. You might be able to take it to your local library to view, but I recommend checking with the librarian first to obtain permission and to make it clear it's your film, not theirs.

Microfilm Indexes of Originals

Some libraries have copies of indexes of vital records without copies of the original records. For example, I mentioned the New Orleans Public Library's city death certificates records, as well as the indexes. The library also has a Louisiana state death index from 1971 to 1976 without the death certificates. The indexes are still valuable without the actual records because you can determine when an ancestor died and then send for the certificate. This will sometimes save you money paying for records you're not sure actually exist.

Published Indexes of Vital Records

Many genealogists have created indexes and abstracts of vital records and published them. Because vital records are so important for genealogy, genealogists have almost re-created vital records for the time periods before vital registration was a legal requirement. They've done things like combing newspapers for death and marriage notices and then publishing lists of the people mentioned. The lists are invaluable for genealogists. You'll find them by checking the card catalogue under terms like births, marriages, deaths, divorces, vital records, and "registers of births, marriages, and deaths." You can also find many listings in *PERSI*. Look under the name of the state and then "vital records," as well as under the name of the county and then "vital records."

Genealogist Desmond Walls-Allen transcribed original indexes of the Arkansas death records from the board of health and published two volumes, *Arkansas Death Record Index, 1914–1932*, and a sequel, *Arkansas Death Record Index, 1934–1940*. They include the deceased's name, date of death, and the county where the death was reported. Unfortunately, these indexes do not indicate race.

The original index was created in the 1970s, and not all of the deaths that were reported to the state were indexed, and not all of the records in the index have death certificates. Some were lost through poor record keeping. Desmond found about one in twenty or thirty death certificates were nonexistent (that's 3 to 5 percent, not a small percentage). Arkansas death records less than fifty years old are not open to the public. She said there were actually more Blacks than whites in many of the records for some areas.

Transcriptions of Vital Records

Transcribing and publishing vital records have been done by genealogists for years. In the 1980s this practice began for African Americans. There isn't much published material in libraries, but the practice is growing. Most of the transcriptions cover the nineteenth century, but some are useful for beginners.

Gwendolyn Tippie self-published birth and death records of African Americans from Kentucky counties in the 1850s and 1860s. Most of these individuals were born slaves. If any of them lived to be sixty or seventy years old or older, they would have died between 1910 and 1930 or later. They could possibly have been one of your great-grandparents. One example of her publications is *Afro-American Births of Adair thru Bath County, Kentucky 1852–1862*, published in 1980.

In 1988 Robert A. Hodge published "colored" birth records from Fredericksburg, Virginia, from 1900 to 1940 in *Birth Records, Fredericksburg, Virginia A–Z (Colored), 1900–1940.*

There have also been marriage records of African Americans transcribed and published. David Thornton Ray published *Black Marriage Records, Hart County, Georgia: Vol. I, 1866–1923* in 1994, and Freda Reed Turner published *Henry County, Georgia, 1821–1894: Marriages, Colored/Freedmen; Record of Sales, Inventory and Wills* in 1995. (For all of these transcriptions, see "Vital Records" in the Bibliography.)

Many other transcriptions are of earlier periods that won't be of much help to you until you gain more experience and advance your family tree well into the nineteenth century. But always check card catalogues for transcriptions of vital records for African Americans. Many are self-published and will mainly be found in the states and counties where the events occurred, but larger genealogical libraries are collecting them when they find them.

Omissions

If you don't find your ancestors in an index or transcription for the local area where they lived, that doesn't mean they are not in the records. Because of segregation and racism, African Americans were sometimes omitted from indexes and transcriptions of vital records. When searching books of vital records in a genealogy library, carefully read the introduction and scrutinize the book to determine if the editor included the "colored" records or transcribed the notices of vital records in the African American newspapers in that town. All too often these were omitted. In many cases African American genealogists search these books, do not find their ancestors, and think they were not in these locations. They often were in the area, but the genealogists who transcribed and indexed the records failed to include them in the book. I didn't realize why my searches in genealogy books were so unsuccessful until years later when I realized the genealogists had excluded African Americans and slaves.

Cemetery Records

The next records to look for in the library are cemetery records. You may have contacted or visited cemeteries in the area where you live after reading "Records in Cemeteries." The records from some cemeteries have been microfilmed, and some have been transcribed and published and are available in genealogical libraries.

The Cemetery Record Compendium, by John and Diane Stemmons, lists cemetery records available at the Family History Library in Salt Lake City, as well as those in genealogical journals and the DAR Library in Washington, D.C. This book is available in many genealogical libraries, but a more up-to-date list of cemetery records in the Family History Library is available in their card catalogue. Remember to check for both the state and the county.

The New Orleans Public Library has copies of records of several cemeteries in New Orleans from 1815 to 1974. These are not African American–owned cemeteries, but they include many burials of African Americans. The Mississippi Department of Archives and History has cemetery records on microfilm from 1862 to 1938, which include African Americans.

Cemetery Transcriptions

Individual genealogists and genealogical societies regularly record names from cemetery grave markers and sextons' records. These records are published as books or as articles in genealogical newsletters or journals. To find them, check in card catalogues under terms like cemeteries, tombstones, tombstone inscriptions, gravestones, and sextons' records to see if any exist in the counties where your ancestors lived. Also check *PERSI* and other periodical indexes for the state and county where your ancestors lived. *PERSI* has a category listing for cemetery records.

Genealogist Belzora Cheatham compiled an index of names of interments from her family cemetery, which earned a Texas historical marker. The book, *Index to Whittaker Memorial Cemetery*, will help many genealogists and historians researching African Americans in Cass County, Texas.

Certified genealogist Paul E. Sluby has written histories and published records for many cemeteries in the Washington, D.C., area. Some are predominantly African American cemeteries, while others contain African Americans in segregated sections. Along with Stanton L. Wormley, he published records from Payne Cemetery, a predominantly Black burial ground that started sometime before 1880. The records comprise five volumes of photocopies of the original records from 1907 to 1952. The records are arranged by date, but there is a surname index at the end.

Sluby and Wormley have also published records for Holmead Cemetery in Washington D.C., which began in 1794. It contained whites, free blacks, and slaves. A fence separated white and nonwhite graves. However, the fence was later replaced by a ravine, and eventually the demand was so great for space the cemetery stopped segregating and began burying in any space available.

Former ambassador Ronald Palmer discovered ancestors who served in the Civil War and located them in a Pennsylvania cemetery. He published a list of African American Civil War veterans buried in the county in the *Journal of the Afro-American Historical and Genealogical Society,* under the title "James Palmer and Other African American Civil War Soldiers Buried in Fayette County, Pennsylvania."

Dentist J. Harlan Buzby published a list of 116 burials in the Mount Pisgah A.M.E. Church in Salem, New Jersey, in the *Salem County Historical Society Newsletter* (vol. 40, no. 1 [March 1995]).

These are just a few examples. If you locate published cemetery records, they will probably not be all-inclusive. Many published transcriptions of cemetery records come from reading grave markers. Since many graves did not have markers, there will be burials not included in the transcriptions. Check to see if the published records indicate where the information was obtained. If it came only from grave markers and did not include the names of your ancestors, you may be able to contact the sexton and locate additional records.

You should also be very skeptical when seeing statements like "All cemeteries in the state have been indexed." Because there have been so many cemeteries over time, no one has listed all the cemeteries in a given location. For example, there are 110 cemeteries listed on the 1991 *Chicago Tribune* map for the greater Chicago area, which covers seven counties. The Geographic Names Information System of the U.S. Geological Survey lists 357 cemeteries in those same counties. However, by searching historical maps, rare books, and manuscripts, cemetery researcher Helen Sclair has identified over 800 burial sites in the same area since Chicago was incorporated in 1833. Sites she includes that others usually omit are columbariums, abandoned cemeteries, missing cemeteries, and churches that accept ashes. Don't forget the African Burial Ground and others that are no longer listed on current maps. How many times have construction crews been alarmed when they struck bones that shouldn't have been there?

If you don't find your ancestors in books listing transcriptions of grave markers, that does not mean your ancestors were not buried in the particular cemetery. All it means is that the names of your ancestors were not in the *index* to the cemetery. Many times our ancestors were buried in the segregated section of a white-owned cemetery. When local genealogists recorded information from the gravestones, they sometimes neglected to record African American cemeteries in the town or neglected to record the names in the African American section of a white cemetery or made no indication in their publication there was a "colored" section in the cemetery. Check the introduction to see if there is any mention of race.

Funeral Home Records

To search for existing funeral homes, check the *Blue Book of Funeral Directors,* which is sometimes found in genealogy libraries. The Newberry Library has the 26th edition of the *Blue Book,* which covers 1982–83. It has been published every even-numbered year since 1932. It is excellent for searching small towns. The directory is divided alphabetically by state and then alphabetically by city. The 1982 edition lists the name and address of the funeral home but no phone number. However, several ran advertisements that listed phone numbers, and you can always get the number from directory assistance. African American funeral homes were indicated by a *B* for Black, but browsing the listings reveals not all African American funeral homes used the *B.* Since it was probably a sensitive issue, the introduction says the designation was requested by both races. Listings also indicate if owners are members of NFDA, the National Funeral Directors Association.

Many African American funeral homes have gone out of business. Their records have either been handed down through the family, taken over by the new funeral home, deposited in a library, archive, or historical society, or thrown in the trash. Hopefully for your ancestors, it's not the latter. If the funeral home you're looking for is no longer in business, try contacting one of the existing homes to see if they know what happened.

It is also worth the effort to check card catalogues in libraries, historical societies, and archives for records of funeral homes. The Dallas Historical Society acquired ledgers of autopsy records from Crawford Funeral Home, an African American funeral home in the city. Donald Payton, an African American historian at the society, found the records in the basement before the building was demolished. The African American Interest Group of the Dallas Genealogical Society is now indexing the records. Also found in the funeral home were insurance records from the local Knights of Pythias, which contained the names of beneficiaries of the deceased. These are usually relatives. Another place to check for funeral home records is the card catalogue at the Family History Center.

Transcriptions of Funeral Records

There are records from funeral homes that have been transcribed and published in books and genealogical journals. The best source for these is *PERSI* and the *Index to the Journal of the Afro-American Historical and Genealogical Society*. One of the most fascinating funeral home records I've seen is for the Sellers Funeral Home in Chambersburg, Pennsylvania. Sellers is a white-owned and -operated funeral home, and Chambersburg is predominantly white. However, they handled most of the African American burials prior to 1915. Reverend C. Bernard Ruffin III extracted records of the African American burials at Sellers Funeral Home and published extracts from 1866 to 1933 in three volumes of the *Journal of the Afro-American Historical and Genealogical Society* in 1982 and 1983. They include the deceased's name, date of funeral, and other details that sometimes include date of death, cause of death, cemetery, age, cost of funeral, and place of funeral, which was sometimes an African American church.

Certified genealogist Paul Sluby, along with Stanton Wormley, published records from the Joseph F. Birch Funeral Home in Washington, D.C., from 1847 to 1938 (*Register of Burials of the Joseph F. Birch Funeral Home*). Birch was a cabinetmaker who occasionally made coffins. In 1841 demand was so great he abandoned his cabinet business to exclusively make coffins and arrange funerals. White and "colored" burials are listed separately in the first three volumes and integrated in the fourth volume. The original records are housed at the Daughters of the American Revolution (DAR) Library in Washington, D.C.

In addition to original records and transcriptions of funeral home records, check for histories of funeral homes. There are several ways to research a known funeral home or search for the names of funeral homes. Histories of funeral homes are often found in the history department of the library instead of the genealogy department. *African American Entrepreneurship in Richmond, 1890–1940: The Story of R. C. Scott* is the story of a funeral director and other Black businesses in Richmond, Virginia. You can also check local newspapers to find advertisements of funeral homes and often get the names of owners. You can then locate them in census records (discussed later) to determine the owner's age, race, and children. If the home was in a city or town, and most were, you can track it in city and telephone directories (discussed later) to learn when it may have ceased operation or changed hands.

Other funeral records to search for are funeral programs. More and more African American genealogists are collecting these and beginning to publish them. Bell Cheatham donated her collection of more than 560 funeral programs mentioned in the "Family Archives" chapter to the Cass County, Texas, Public Library. She also created a separate index of names of the deceased *(Funeral Programs/Obituaries of 579 African Americans).*

Records of Lynchings

Another record of death that can be found in the library is for lynchings. After the Civil War and throughout the wretched period of segregation, African Americans were hanged from trees throughout the South, as well as the North. Estimates have placed lynchings and brutal murders of African Americans at well over 5,000. This history can't be forgotten, overlooked, or ignored. In fact, sometimes when African American genealogists run into roadblocks during oral interviews, and older relatives do not want to talk about the past, it is because one of the ancestors was lynched or brutally murdered in a hate crime. As long ago as it may have been, such an event is often too painful for relatives to discuss. The difficulty of obtaining oral history while navigating the pain of reliving these experiences requires unique skills.

The record of a lynching is not the same as a death certificate, but it will provide vital information needed to obtain a death certificate. Genealogists can access records of lynchings. The NAACP, which was founded in 1909 in response to a race riot in Springfield, Illinois, in which eight African Americans were killed, researched and investigated lynchings to file lawsuits and influence Congress to pass a federal antilynching law. This research will likely include additional information for a genealogist whose ancestor was lynched. The NAACP papers are available for research in the Manuscript Division of the Library of Congress. Fortunately, University Publications of America microfilmed over 400 reels of records from the NAACP collection, 65 of which concern lynching. This microfilm may be at a library in your area or available through interlibrary loan.

Tuskegee Institute also has records of lynchings. Students at the institute, in Tuskegee, Alabama, under the direction of Dr. Monroe Nathan Work, regularly clipped newspaper articles mentioning Blacks from America, Africa, and other parts of the world. Fortunately for African American genealogists, the bulk of the collection has been microfilmed as *Tuskegee Institute Newspaper Clipping Files.* African American tennis great Arthur Ashe based much of his heralded series, *African Americans in Sport,* on information obtained from the Tuskegee clipping files.

The Tuskegee microfilm collection totals 252 reels of film and includes 15 reels of lynchings of African Americans from 1899 to 1966. This microfilm collection is not found in most genealogy collections. However, it is available in some larger public libraries, academic libraries, and collections specializing in African American history.

Ralph Ginsburg chronicled 5,000 lynchings in America from 1859 to 1959 in his book *100 Years of Lynchings.* Each lynching is listed alphabetically by state. So even if you've never heard of an ancestor being lynched, you can look up the names of your ancestors alphabetically in the book to see if one is listed. The book also contains almost 300 newspaper articles about some of the events.

In addition to Tuskegee and the NAACP, Ida B. Wells Barnett, students, and scholars have researched lynchings. Many people believe that Black men were lynched because they raped or whistled at white women. Studies have shown this is a myth. In fact, white women organized the Association of Southern Women for the Prevention of Lynchings to expose the falsity that lynching was necessary to protect white women.

The 1964 and 1952 editions of the *Negro Year Book* listed "accusing a person of homicide" as the main cause of lynching. This occurred in 41 percent of lynchings between 1882 and 1951. Homicide was twice as likely as rape, the second leading accusation at 19 percent.

The most common reason African Americans were lynched was in order to intimidate other workers during labor disputes or when whites feared losing their status of racial superiority. Terrence Finnegan, professor of history at William Paterson College, studied 800 lynchings and found that the number of lynchings increased as the demand for labor increased and also at the end of harvest time.

If you find a record of a lynching, you should then check several other sources. Research newspapers for any possible details. If you don't find any articles in *100 Years of Lynchings* or the *Tuskegee Institute Newspaper Clipping Files,* you should check the papers in the area where the event occurred. There's not always something published in the paper, but you must do the search. Remember, *100 Years of Lynching* included 300 newspaper articles. Then check the NAACP's lynching investigations.

If you find a record of a lynching, apply for a death certificate. Since a lynching was a death due to unnatural causes, investigate records from the county coroner or medical examiner. Finally, search for criminal court records and jail records. Search from the side of the perpetrator, if known, as well as the victim. Many African Americans were pulled from jail cells and lynched. In addition to state and county court records, check federal government records of cases involving law enforcement officers denying persons' Civil Rights. Of course, many records of lynchings do not exist because government authorities often protected those committing the crime and witnesses were reluctant to testify, so only indictments were brought in many cases. However, you never know if a record exists until you conduct a search. There might also be older people living in the community who remember the incident. This is another dark period of our history that must not be forgotten.

Obituaries

A genealogist once complained to me about her frustration in researching an ancestor. She knew he was a physician in Arkansas. His daughter refused to give her any information, and she didn't know where to go. He died around 1948. I asked if she'd looked for an obituary for him. She said she didn't know where to look.

In the chapter on "Family Records," I discussed obituaries that were found among the family papers. If an obituary for a particular ancestor was not saved by family members, researchers can still obtain a copy. If the date and place of death are known, an obituary can be obtained directly from an old newspaper in the library. You never know if an obituary exists for an ancestor until you search the newspapers.

Finding an obituary for an ancestor may sound like finding a needle in a haystack, but if you have a strategy, your search can be productive. Below is a five-point strategy for locating obituaries for African Americans.

Start by noting the deceased persons on your Family Group Sheets. Then conduct a thorough search to locate an obituary for each one of these ancestors. The date and place of death must be known and can be determined from death certificates, cemetery records, funeral home records, insurance and pension records, Social Security death records, and sometimes military records. Search daily newspapers for an obituary for up to ten days after the death, and weekly papers for several weeks after the death. It's also a good idea to check several weeks before the death because the person might have been sick and mentioned in the paper.

Contact the public library in the town where the death occurred and see if they have copies of the local newspaper for the time period when the death occurred. If you know where the person was born and raised, also check there. Obituaries were often published in the deceased's "hometown" newspaper. Old newspapers are usually preserved on microfilm and may also be found in historical societies, archives, and university libraries.

I searched for an obituary for my great-grandfather Morris Burroughs, who died in Chicago in 1903. Much to my surprise, there was a notice in the *Chicago Tribune*. Unfortunately, it was not actually an obituary. It was merely a "death notice" compiled from data received from the board of health. But it was another piece of evidence I was able to collect verifying his date and place of death.

The average person may not know there were thousands of newspapers published by African Americans. Fortunately, someone has assembled a list of them. Barbara Henritzie compiled a list of more than 5,000 African American newspapers (including some magazines) in *Bibliographic Checklist of African-American Newspapers*. It identifies newspapers published in hundreds of cities dating back to 1827.

If you identify a newspaper from the *Bibliographic Checklist* you can check several sources for locating copies of the newspapers. First, ask the reference librarian at your local library (or the periodicals librarian) if the library has a copy of either *Newspapers in Microform, United States 1948–1972*, which lists 34,289 titles held by 843 libraries and 48 corporations, or *American Newspapers, 1821–1936: A Union List of Files Available in the United States and Canada*, edited by Winifred Gregory, which lists the newspaper holdings of 5,700 depositories. These directories will list the location of thousands of newspapers that may be available on interlibrary loan.

Additionally, the State Historical Society of Wisconsin has been identifying, collecting, microfilming, and cataloguing all known copies of African American newspapers that exist in the United States. Their directory, *African American Newspapers: A National Bibliography and Union List*, by James P. Danky, identifies the location of all known copies of African American newspapers (see "Obituaries and Newspapers" in the Bibliography).

In 1953, under the direction of Armistead Scott Pride, director of the Lincoln University School of Journalism (Jefferson City, Missouri), the Library of Congress microfilmed more than 400 African American newspapers. The microfilmed set, titled *Negro Newspapers on Micro-film,* is available at many major libraries and research institutions around the country. If it is not available in the library in your area, ask the reference librarian to conduct an OCLC search to determine the nearest location. The collection might be available at a nearby college or university library.

Obituaries can serve another function. If an exact date of death is not known for an ancestor, but a general location and approximate time frame are known, sometimes the exact date and place of death can be revealed in an obituary. In this case the obituary is used not only to obtain personal information on the deceased but to determine the exact date and place of death.

Locating an obituary for an ancestor without the exact date and place of death is sometimes not as hard as it sounds, especially if you have an index. And we know all genealogists *love* indexes!

Many indexes of local newspapers have been created, and they are a gold mine for genealogists. There are indexes of local newspapers and African American newspapers. Ten current African American newspapers are indexed in *Black Newspapers Index,* edited by Beth Haendiges. It covers 1985 to the present. Prior to 1985 the index was titled *Index to Black Newspapers* and covered 1977 to 1984.

Mary Mace Spradling's *In Black and White* references over 21,000 African American individuals and groups appearing in newspapers, magazines, books, and other publications. Although it consists primarily of people making notable contributions and obituaries are not cited specifically, it is well worth a look.

Early newspaper indexing of African Americans was conducted by James de T. Abajian, a San Francisco librarian, when he edited *Blacks in Selected Newspapers, Censuses, and Other Sources: An Index to Names and Subjects.* This three-volume set indexes African Americans appearing in forty-three newspapers and thirteen periodicals from 1842 to 1948. Abajian lived in San Francisco, California, and most of the newspapers were published in the West, but a few eastern publications are included. I found two Pennsylvania ancestors listed from the *Cleveland Gazette.* These were deaths occurring in Pennsylvania but reported in an Ohio newspaper! So there didn't even have to be a newspaper published in the town or area your ancestor lived in to have an obituary in a newspaper. A two volume supplement to Abajian's index was published in 1985.

To go back even further, Donald Jacobs indexed four Black newspapers from 1827 to 1841 in *Antebellum Black Newspapers: Indices to NY Freedom's Journal 1827–1829, The Rights of All 1829, Weekly Advocate 1837, and The Colored American 1837–1841.* Of course, most of these are so early they won't be of current help for most people. But some African American lineages with free northern roots before the Civil War are easily extended into this period. The *Kaiser Index to Black Resources, 1948–1986* indexes a few obituaries, but most are of prominent persons.

In addition to general newspaper indexes, there are also indexes exclusively of obituaries in newspapers. Lori Husband, an African American genealogist in Chicago, indexed obituaries of African Americans appearing in the *Chicago Defender* from 1910 to 1920. This is a tremendous source, and now work has begun on the next ten years of the *Chicago Defender.* Researchers are needed to index obituaries in other African American newspapers. The work is not difficult,

NEBRASKA STATE HISTORICAL SOCIETY
1500 R STREET, BOX 82554, LINCOLN, NE 68501
DIRECTOR: JAMES A. HANSON   (402) 471-3270

FT. ROBINSON MUSEUM
BOX 304
CRAWFORD, NE 69339

<u>Crawford (Nebr.) Tribune</u>   Aug 18, 1905

Preston Brooks, who died at his home here on Thursday of last week, was buried at Fort Robinson the next day, having been a member of D Troop, 9th Cavalry. The deceased was a member of the Masonic Order, which had charge of the funeral affairs and engaged Undertaker Cleland and the hearse from Crawford, and also the Tenth Cavalry Band to furnish music for the occasion.

Mr. Brooks was engaged as manager of the water works and saw mill at Fort Robinson for about fifteen years and had a large circle of friends in the vicinity, who respected him for the honorable and upright manner in which he transacted his business affairs. The bereaved family have the sympathy of community and the them we publish the following:

Card of Thanks

We wish to express our sincere thanks to our friends of Crawford and Fort Robinson for their kindness shown and assistance rendered during the sickness and death of our beloved husband and father. Also for the beautiful flowers contributed.

Mrs. Brooks and Family

AN EQUAL OPPORTUNITY/AFFIRMATIVE ACTION EMPLOYER

Preston Brooks's Obituary— Transcript of the obituary for Preston Brooks, which appeared in the Crawford, Nebraska, *Tribune* on August 18, 1905; obtained from the Fort Robinson Museum.

just time-consuming and meticulous. But it will make a wonderful contribution to the field of genealogy and will assist many genealogists and historians beyond our lifetime.

The *Journal of Negro History* also published obituaries of people they called "Leaders of the Negro race." An index of 200 obituaries of these African Americans was published in volume 57 (October 1972, pages 447–454).

Betty M. Jarboe compiled a list of hundreds of published obituaries, divided by states, in *Obituaries: A Guide to Sources*. Although not all sources listed are obituaries (she includes marriages and biographies), she frequently mentions obituaries for African Americans. And Anita Check Milner edited a three-volume set titled *Newspaper Indexes: A Location and Subject Guide for Researchers*. It is a state-by-state listing of newspapers that have been indexed and gives the location of the index files. For these and other books on obituaries, see "Obituaries and Newspapers" in the Bibliography.

You can also find obituaries by researching lynchings (see "Records of Lynchings," pages 287–88). Although many of the articles are not actually obituaries, they are newspaper records of deaths, and many list relatives' names and describe the circumstances of the lynching.

A fourth source for obituaries is "newspaper clipping files." Some libraries, archives, and historical societies created files of newspaper clippings. The librarians or volunteers searched newspapers and clipped obituaries and general news items and then placed the clippings in files or in scrapbooks. Sometimes these clippings were microfilmed.

The largest African American clipping file is the *Tuskegee Institute Newspaper Clipping Files*. In addition to the records of lynchings discussed earlier, there are four reels of film containing obituaries from 1912 to 1966 in the "Necrology File."

Hampton University in Virginia also created a clipping file (*Index to the Hampton University Newspaper Clipping File*, edited by Nicholas Natanson), and the Schomburg Center for Black Culture, a branch of the New York Public Library, also maintained a clipping file (*Index to the Schomburg Clipping File*). There are many subjects in the index to the clipping files, but unfortunately, none are titled obituaries, deaths, or necrology.

Finally, obituaries can be obtained directly from some libraries, archives, museums, historical societies, and genealogical societies. Many of these institutions index and clip obituaries mentioning people in their local communities. So it is always wise to consult the local institution in the area where your ancestors lived to see if they maintain an obituary file or index of the local paper.

One of my great-grandfathers was a Buffalo Soldier. After he mustered out of the service, he worked at Fort Robinson in Nebraska. When I contacted the curator at Fort Robinson, I learned they had an obituary file. He checked the file and located an obituary for my ancestor, published in the local paper in 1905. Even though I already knew a lot about this ancestor (from family members, census records, tax records, and military records), this obituary gave me plenty of new information found nowhere else.

I also contacted the public library in Uniontown, Pennsylvania, when I learned of their obituary file index. Fortunately, they had a listing for my great-great-great-grandfather's brother, who was said to have lived to be more than one hundred years old. They called him "Old Uncle Davie." I had calculated he died between 1900 and 1910, and the obituary confirmed he died in 1903. But the amazing thing was that the obituary stated he was the "oldest man living in Pennsylvania at 107"!

Obituaries will often lead to other genealogical sources. When things like occupation, religion, military service, and similar details are mentioned, be sure to follow up with research in these new areas.

Obituaries can add life to your ancestors and sometimes provide a wealth of information. They can be a lot of fun, and they're not hard to research. But you must make a concerted and exhaustive effort to look for them. And don't just look in the African American newspapers and indexes. Your ancestor could be listed in the local newspaper, as some of mine were. There are also religious newspapers that should be consulted. The *AME Christian Recorder* is an excellent source. I also located an excellent obituary index for *The Southern Christian Advocate* at Wofford College in Spartanburg, South Carolina. It contained obituaries for the slave-owning families I'm researching.

To summarize, five sources for locating obituaries for ancestors are:

1. Family records
2. Newspapers (local and African American)
3. Newspaper and obituary indexes
4. Newspaper clipping files
5. Obituary files in libraries, historical societies, and museums

Not all the information located in an obituary will be accurate and true. As with any genealogical source, details must be verified with other records. Usually the informant for the source of the information is not given, so an obituary, by definition, is a secondary source, not a primary record.

Directories

Tracing African Americans in cities and towns using telephone and city directories is fun and easy. Anyone can do it. I love to use directories. They don't always give the names of parents or dates of birth and death, as vital records do, but they can help you locate other records and hold valuable clues to family history and personality. Try to locate each and every one of your ancestors in a telephone directory and city directory for every year of their life. You never know what you'll find until you start looking. And, as the television commercial says, "Pull out the book and let your fingers do the walking."

In addition to telephone directories and city directories, there were county directories for rural areas. They often listed farm ownership and agricultural information. There were also business and professional directories and ethnic directories.

Telephone Directories

A fun and easy source for genealogists is old telephone directories. Many back issues of telephone directories have been preserved on microfilm and are available to research in public and academic libraries. Unlike today, when many people have unlisted telephone numbers, in days past most people had telephone numbers listed in the directory. Whether your ancestors lived in large cities or small towns, they can be tracked in the telephone directory from year to year, back through time.

I grew up across the street from Washington Park on the south side of Chicago. We lived in a two-story apartment building at 505 E. 60th Street until I was eight years old. I was curious as to when my family moved into that building, and turned to old Chicago telephone directories. I began with the 1948 directory, the year I was born, and found the following listings:

Burroughs, AM Lwyr 188 W Randolph	CE ntrl 6-5277	page 249
Lwyr 505 E 60	PL aza 2-5505	
Burroughs, Elmer 505 E 60	PL aza 2-8469	
Burroughs, Morris 9337 S Vernon	CO modor 4-5364	

A. M. Burroughs is my grandfather Asa Morris Burroughs. The first listing is his law office in downtown Chicago, and the second is his residence, where we lived. My grandparents lived on the first floor, and we lived on the second floor. Elmer is my dad and Morris is his brother, who was married and living in a house farther south.

When I saw the listings, I was struck by the old telephone numbers. We're so accustomed to dialing seven digits and often eleven (including the one and the area code), we tend to forget it wasn't always like that. It seemed as if my grandparents had the Plaza 2-5505 telephone number forever, and it always rung in my mind. When I saw the number, it brought back memories of my grandparents' living room and Grandma taking care of my brother and me after school. When Grandmother died, I went by the house and took the heavy metal telephone, which still had the Plaza 2-5505 number on the rotary dial. Today that telephone sits in my living room as an antique and a memento of my grandparents and my childhood.

I next looked in the 1947 telephone directory and there was no listing for my dad, so I figured he didn't have a telephone. He married in 1946, and neither he nor my mom are around for me to ask about their living arrangements or when they first got a telephone. Uncle Morris is listed at 505 E. 60th, so he obviously moved from home in 1947 or 1948.

I traced the listings for 1946 and 1945, which were the same for my grandfather. Then the 1944 directory revealed a different address and answered my question about when the family moved to 505 E. 60th Street. Neither Dad nor Uncle Morris was listed, perhaps because they were in Europe during World War II and had just returned home by 1946.

Burroughs, AM Lwyr 188 W Randolph	CEN tri 5277	page 209
Lwyr 4739 Champln	OAK ind 2747	

The house at 4739 South Champlain Avenue was the one I'd always heard my dad discuss and the address I'd seen on envelopes addressed to my grandparents during World War II. I then traced the family forward into the 1950s.

1952	Burroughs, AM lwyr 188 W Randolph	CE ntrl 6-5277	page 259
	lwyr 505 E 60	PL aza 2-5505	
	Burroughs, Elmer 505 E 60	HY dpk 3-4496	
	Burroughs, Leonard—505 E 60	PL aza 2-8692	
	Burroughs, Morris—1516 S. Albany	RO ckwl 2-7731	
1953	Burroughs, AM lwyr 188 W Randolph	CE ntrl 6-5277	page 260
	lwyr 505 E 60	PL aza 2-5505	
	lwyr 188 W Randolph	FR ankin 2-0465	
	Burroughs, Elmer 505 E 60	BU trfld 8-5702	
1955	Burroughs, AM lwyr 505 E 60	PL aza 2-5505	page 258
	lwyr 188 W Randolph	FR ankin 2-0465	
	Burroughs, Elmer rl est 188 W Randolph	FR ankin 2-0465	
	residence 505 E 60	BU trfld 8-8747	
	Burroughs, Morris ins 188 W Randolph	FR ankin 2-0465	
	residence 4506	DR exl 3-0289	
	S Oakenwald		

The 1952 directory picks up my Uncle Leonard, and it appears my Uncle Morris moved to the Westside. I've never located any other Morris Burroughs in Chicago, so I assume that was him.

The 1955 telephone directory was the most revealing. It listed my father as working in real estate and his brother Morris working in insurance, all in their father's office. It appears they were all using the same telephone number. However, I'm not so sure Grandfather sacrificed calls from his law practice to his two sons' beginning businesses. The telephone might have merely been in his name. He obviously helped his sons get into business by sharing office space.

Office Photograph—Photograph of attorney Asa Morris Burroughs (center) and his two sons, Elmer (left) and Morris (right), in their office at 188 West Randolph Street in Chicago.

The three of them listed in the same office triggered my memory of a family photograph I have showing the three together in an office. It had no captions or labels on it, but now I know where and approximately when it was taken. I knew my father was in real estate for a while and my Uncle Morris sold insurance, but now that I know about the office building and their telephone number, the photograph is more real.

I never found any telephone listings for grandfather's brother, Robert. That's not too unusual because telephone service was expensive. I checked the telephone directory for 1916, which indicated the basic rate for a single line phone service was thirty-six dollars a year, a two-party line was twenty-four dollars a year, and a four-party line was eighteen dollars a year. Of course, the amount people paid was always higher depending on how many calls they made.

City Directories

The telephone was invented in 1876 but was not in widespread use until after 1900. Before the telephone was invented, people found out where friends and neighbors lived and where businesses were located through city directories. A city directory is an alphabetical listing of people, businesses, and institutions in the community, similar to today's telephone directories and yellow pages (business directories), but without a telephone number. The city directory listing often includes a name, address, sometimes an occupation, sometimes an employer, and sometimes a spouse or widow's name, or whether a woman was the head of a household. City directories are still maintained in some cities for business marketing.

Ancestors can be searched backward through telephone directories until the point when they did not own a telephone. Then they can be picked up in the city directory and continued backward. I continued tracing my grandfather Asa Burroughs in this way. The 1916 Chicago city directory was the first one showing him living on the south side at 45th and St. Lawrence Avenue.

1916	Burroughs, A Morris clk 1306 155 N Clark	page 304
	h 4526 St. Lawrence	
	Burroughs, Robt chauffeur h 5312 S Wabash av	
	Burroughs, Robt E brklayr h 255 N Hoyne	
1915	Burroughs, Asa M porter h 255 N Hoyne ave	page 281
	Burroughs, Robt E brklayr h 255 N Hoyne ave	

The 1915 Chicago city directory showed brothers Asa and Robert living at the same address, 255 North Hoyne, which was on the westside. In 1916 they both moved to the South-side but to different residences. They had both been living at home with their mother, who died in 1914. Now they appeared to be venturing on their own into manhood. Robert was twenty-seven years old and Asa was twenty-three in 1916.

This was probably not the first sign of the family split, which had probably been brewing for a while. But it was the first outward manifestation of it. Both brothers also changed jobs—Asa from porter to law clerk in a downtown skyscraper, and Robert from bricklayer to chauffeur. They would go on to lead completely different lives.

I also traced their father, my great-grandfather Morris Burroughs, and found out when he came to Chicago, which was about 1889.

1893	Burroughs, Morris M porter h. 848 W. Madison	page 305
1892	Burroughs, Morris M porter h. 848 W. Madison	page 273
1891	Burroughs, Morris M porter h. 848 W. Madison	page 415
1890	Burroughs, Morris porter h. rear 723 W. Madison	page 405
1889	Burroughs, Morris—not listed	
1888	Burroughs, Morris—not listed	

Since 1890 was the earliest date I found him in the Chicago city directory, it indicates the approximate year he moved to Chicago from another city or state. I compared this with information on his death certificate from 1903, which indicated he lived in Illinois for twelve years. That would have been 1891.

The numbering system in Chicago changed in 1908, so 723 W. Madison today is not where it was in 1890. However, directories included tables converting old addresses to new ones. I learned 723 W. Madison is close to the United Center, where the Bulls play basketball. Always check to see if there have been any changes in street names, numbers, or addresses in the city you're researching.

In addition to learning migration dates, you can use old telephone directories and city directories to help pinpoint deaths and marriages, learn occupations and employers, further census research you're doing, and begin to locate other relatives and ancestors.

We see Morris Burroughs is listed as a porter. This confirms other records from family papers, vital records, census records, and employee records. When a woman is first listed as a widow, it's an indication her husband recently died. However, be sure you trace her back as far as possible, because sometimes women carried this title for several years. When a man is first listed outside his parents' home, it's often an indication he recently married. If you've lost track of a distant relative, one of the first steps might be to check the telephone directory at the time you last knew of his or her whereabouts. Then start tracing them forward, picking up new numbers and addresses. As long as his name wasn't John Smith, you shouldn't have a difficult time.

REVERSE DIRECTORY—In addition to the regular city directory, there are reverse directories, sometimes called "criss-cross" directories. Instead of listing all the names in alphabetical order, a reverse directory lists everyone by address. These are extremely valuable, because once you have an ancestor's address, you can change over to the reverse directory and locate everyone else who lived in the building, on the block, around the corner, and in the neighborhood. As you might suspect, this can easily lead to other relatives living nearby. Unfortunately, reverse directories were not published every year. In many areas you'll be lucky to find them.

BUSINESSES AND INSTITUTIONS— Since directories also listed businesses and institutions, other searches will assist your research. Looking at the names and addresses of black restaurants and stores gives life to the community where your ancestors lived.

When an occupation and employer is listed for your ancestor, locate that business in the directory and you'll learn where the ancestor probably traveled to work. Then locate an advertisement for the business to learn what kind of company it was and what kinds of products and services it offered. Later on you might be able to locate business records and photographs for the business that have been donated to a library, an archive, or a historical society. This process will make your ancestors' lives more complete.

I checked the listings for railroad stations in the Chicago city directories and learned the Chicago and Alton train departed from Union Station. Since my great-grandfather Morris Burroughs was a Pullman porter on the Chicago and Alton, this told me where he went to work. Union Station is still operational, and now when I go there, I have a whole new feeling and appreciation for it, thinking of my great-grandfather each time.

Directories also list churches. If you know what religion your ances-

---

32   TELEGRAM'S CAIRO GUIDE.

office 541 Rookery. Memphis office 336 Randolph building. Yards at Cairo, Mississippi Levee and Big Four Track. Arthur A. Maclean, president; Maxwell A. Kilvert, secretary; Henry Wells, treasurer. All of Chicago.

CHURCH DIRECTORY.

BAPTIST.

First Baptist Church, northeast corner Poplar and Tenth streets. Rev. W. B. Morris, pastor.

Missionary Baptist Church, (colored,) 2814 Poplar street.

First Missionary Baptist Church, (colored,) southwest corner Walnut and Twelfth streets. Rev. Henry Allison, pastor.

Mount Moriah Missionary Baptist Church, (colored,) corner Twenty-sixth and Poplar street. Rev. J. H. Knowles, pastor.

Free Will Baptist Church, (colored,) north side Thirty-second street, between Commercial avenue and Poplar street. Rev. William Kelley, pastor.

First Free Will Baptist Church, (colored,) southwest corner Walnut and Fifteenth streets. Rev. Nelson Ricks, pastor.

CHRISTIAN.

Christian Church, north side Eighteenth street, between Washington avenue and Walnut street, Rev. E. W. Symmonds, pastor.

LUTHERAN.

German Lutheran Evangelical Church, 415 Douglas street.

METHODIST EPISCOPAL.

Methodist Episcopal Church, northwest corner Walnut and Eighth streets. Rev. S. P. Groves, pastor.

African Methodist Episcopal Church, north side Seventeenth street, between Washington avenue and Walnut street. Rev. A. J. Burton, pastor.

PRESBYTERIAN.

Presbyterian Church, north side of Eighth street, between Washington avenue and Walnut street. Rev. C. T. Phillips, Pastor.

PROTESTANT EPISCOPAL.

Church of the Redeemer (P. E.), northeast corner of Washing-

Church Directory—Cairo, Illinois, city directory listing churches in town, with African American churches (other than the African Methodist Episcopal Church) denoted by "(colored)."

---

tors practiced or what church they attended, search for it in the directory to see where the church was located. The name of the minister or pastor will often be listed. If you do not know what church they attended but you know the name of the minister who performed the marriage of your ancestors, you can locate him in the city directory. If his listing does not indicate his church, check all the church listings to see which one he's affiliated with. You can also check a reverse directory and see what churches were in the community where your ancestors lived. They most likely attended one of them. The church might still be in existence, older members might still be around, or the records or photographs may have survived. Church records could be in a library, historical society, church archive, or older member's house.

The city directory also lists schools. By locating the ones closest to your ancestors' house, you can surmise that's where their children most likely went to school.

Clubs and fraternal organizations are listed in city directories, usually in a front or rear section along with other institutions. These organizations usually list the officers and sometimes when and where meetings were held. African Americans have participated in clubs and fraternal organizations for a long time and may be included in the listings.

The advertisements in directories can be helpful in understanding the community and times in which your ancestors lived. My paternal grandmother's mother and aunts lived in Memphis, Tennessee, before migrating to Cairo, Illinois, and eventually Chicago. In the Memphis city directory I saw ads for steamers traveling the Mississippi River from Memphis to Cairo, with prices and travel times. I suddenly realized that's the mode of travel they probably took when they moved from Memphis to Cairo. The Illinois Central Railroad went from Chicago to New Orleans, passing through Cairo. They probably traveled from Cairo to Chicago on the train.

Black Directories

African Americans felt a need to develop their own city and business directories to communicate with the African American community. After researching the local city and telephone directories, see if there was a "Black" or "colored" directory in the city you're researching.

The *Colored People's Blue Book and Business Directory* of Chicago for 1905 listed my great-grandmother Mrs. M. Burroughs under the business listings for "Confectionery and Ice Cream." This was consistent with the Chicago city directory. However, I was surprised to see a

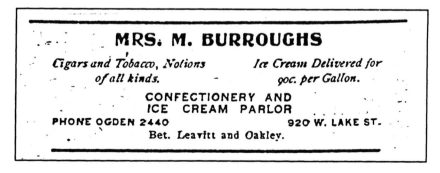

Mary Burroughs Ad—Advertisement for Mary Burroughs's confectionery business, which appeared in the 1905 *Colored People's Blue Book and Business Directory of Chicago* and was later found in the *Chicago Defender* newspaper.

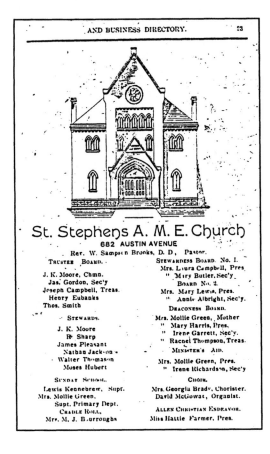

St. Stephens Ad—Advertisement for St. Stephens A. M. E. Church, on Austin Avenue in Chicago, which appeared in the 1905 *Colored People's Blue Book and Business Directory of Chicago*. Ad lists Mrs. M. J. Burroughs under "Cradle Roll."

quarter-page ad she placed for her confectionery and ice cream parlor. It looked like a business card and indicated she sold cigars, tobacco, and notions of all kinds, and delivered ice cream for ninety cents per gallon. The ad also listed her telephone number.

I knew the Burroughs family attended St. Stephen's A.M.E. Church on the west side of Chicago. I searched the *Colored People's Blue Book* and saw a full-page ad for St. Stephen's Church. It included a nice drawing of the church building, which has since been demolished. Many church members' names were listed. Under Sunday School it listed "Cradle Roll, Mrs. M. J. Burroughs." This verified oral history that Mary started a cradle society at the church, which was a program for young kids.

Locating Directories

Telephone and city directories are normally found in local and county public libraries, academic libraries, and historical societies in the area that the directories served. Larger collections of directories for multiple cities can be found in genealogical libraries, state archives, the Library of Congress, and the Family History Library in Salt Lake City.

For African American business, professional, social, and city directories, also consult major public libraries, especially major Afro-Americana collections, such as the Schomburg Collection at the New York Public Library and the Vivian Harsh Collection of the Chicago Public Library. In addition, traditionally Black colleges and university collections, such as the Moorland-Spingarn Collection at Howard University, will have Black directories for selected cities.

Determine and record the first and last years that directories are available for the city you are researching. Determine if the library has a complete run of those directories. Ask the reference librarian what years were not published and for what years no copies have survived. Then ask where other issues can be obtained. Some libraries may have selected years for some cities, and collections at other libraries can fill in the gaps. Find out if any reverse, criss-cross, county, telephone, business, professional, ethnic, or social directories exist and what years they were published and are available.

Recording Your Ancestor

Once you locate the right directories, determine the approximate years your ancestor lived in a particular location. Start from a year you know your ancestor was in the city. Obtain the city directory for that year or the closest year available, then check the alphabetical listing for your ancestor's name.

Once you locate the listing, record his or her name, address, occupation, and any other information exactly as it is recorded, along with the page number. Be sure to record any misspellings if they are listed in the directory. Make notes of what you think is the correct spelling. Then make a photocopy of that page if it is permissible. (Many of the directories are old and fragile and are not permitted to be photocopied. However, microfilm copies can be photocopied.) Next, photocopy the title page, which shows the name of the directory and year of publication. If the publication date is not on this page, write the date on the title page of the photocopy. If the ancestor is not located, note that he or she was not listed in that directory.

While you're there, make sure you check for the names of other ancestors who lived in that city, not just your direct ancestor, but brothers, sisters, aunts, uncles, cousins, and in-laws.

See if there is a reverse or criss-cross section in the rear of the book or in a separate volume. Locate your ancestor's address and also photocopy that page. This will show the neighbors and the other heads of the household who lived in the building if it is an apartment building. Also determine the street names at the end of the blocks and photocopy those pages. These will be the neighbors, friends, and sometimes relatives who lived around the corner. To be very thorough, you can also photocopy the blocks on either side of the street where your ancestor lived.

Note the names of schools, churches, businesses, cemeteries, and other institutions in the neighborhood. Your ancestor probably attended these institutions. Then look for the preceding year's directory and follow the same procedure. Use this process for each and every year backward until your ancestor does not show up in the directory. Then continue searching for another five to ten years. The ancestor's name may be omitted from some directories, or he or she may have moved and then returned.

Return to the first year you located the ancestor and follow the same process forward until the ancestor is no longer listed. Then trace another five to ten years forward. If the city directories run out, switch over to the telephone directories.

I mentioned in the chapter on "Family Archives" that my grandfather had a long-lost cousin my grandmother hadn't seen in sixty years. There was a business card in Robert's trunk with a full name, Earl P. Gaither, along with an address, telephone number, and occupation (see page 113). I went to the 1915 Chicago city directory and found President Gaither at the same address as Earl. I figured they were related. I went to the 1914 directory and found President again. Then I traced him every year to 1910 and also located him on the 1910 U.S.

Census. This verified President was Earl's father. Next I traced President backward every year in the city directories until I couldn't find him anymore.

I traced President Gaither in Chicago all the way back to 1888, about the same time my grandfather's father, Morris Burroughs, came to Chicago. But then I continued to trace backward and realized he was not in the directory for 1887 but he was for 1886 and 1885. I traced another five years until I was sure he wasn't in Chicago. When I had trouble locating a marriage record for him, I decided to look elsewhere. Through obtaining death certificates for his children, I learned his wife, Annie, was from Washington, D.C. I decided to check city directories for Washington and found President there in 1887, the one year he wasn't listed in the Chicago city directory. I decided to check for a marriage record in Washington and easily found it for 1886.

I also discovered President was from Spartanburg, South Carolina, the same town my great-grandfather was from. I then traced the Gaither family and their children in 1916, 1917, and forward until the city directories ran out, then switched over to the telephone directories. I traced Earl until he died in 1958 and then traced Joseph Gaither, at the same address, until 1968, when he no longer had a listed telephone number. At that point the telephone operator confirmed he had an unlisted number and could not give it to me. I asked for Mr. Gaither's address and was again denied. I couldn't think of what else to do at that point. I told the operator we'd lost contact with these relatives for sixty years and recounted all the hard work I'd done in the library to try to locate them. She said she still couldn't give out the information. I finally told her not to give me his phone number or his address and pleaded, "Just give me the block he lives on." She finally relented and gave me the block. I searched every house and apartment building on the block and finally located him. For me it was a very emotional meeting. All this had started from vague oral history and a small business card! It again illustrates how we're searching for bits and pieces of a puzzle to reconstruct. Unfortunately, Mr. Gaither did not know as much about his family history as I did. There was a family Bible, but it had burned in a fire. So I wasn't able to find out how we're related.

Later I traveled back to Spartanburg, South Carolina, and continued researching the city directories there for the Burroughs and Gaither families. However, I could not locate either family in the directory. After a while I discovered that, because of segregation, African Americans were not listed with everyone else. They were listed in the back of the book, just as Blacks were forced to ride in the back of the bus in the South.

There was a section in the front of the city directory marked "White Department" and one in the rear marked "Colored Department." If I weren't diligent, knowing my ancestors lived in this town, and had had no understanding of segregation, I probably would have missed locating my ancestors.

As I continued to search, I discovered that in other years African Americans were listed with everyone else. However, beside each "colored" name was an asterisk (*). The introduction in the front of the directory listed notations and abbreviations. It explained this asterisk indicated the person was "colored." I learned that in other years African Americans were denoted with a c next to their name for "colored." I also realized that not all the African

Americans had an asterisk or *c* beside their name. So I couldn't totally rely on the code and ignore the names that did not have an asterisk or a *c* beside them. If an African American had a very light complexion, he or she was sometimes mistaken for white. In other cases, as a defense mechanism, these persons pretended to be white (passed for white). They married a white spouse, moved into a white community, and broke off all communication with African Americans and the African American community. Therefore, some of the people who were listed as white actually had mixed parentage.

Analysis

Take a sheet of paper (or use your computer) and make a chronological list of the information in each directory for one ancestor. If you searched for more than one name, make separate lists. List the year, name, occupation, wife (if listed), address, and page number in the directory.

When this list is finished, sometimes patterns can be drawn for entering and leaving the city, moving from one house to another, purchasing property, changing jobs, getting married, and sometimes dying (when the spouse is listed as "widow of . . ."), as well as other interesting facts.

On another sheet of paper (or computer), take the information from the reverse directory. List in numerical order all residents on one side of the street. Below that, list all the residents of the other side of the street. This will give you a picture of the block and who were your ancestor's neighbors.

Next, alphabetize the neighbors' names. Without a computer, the names can be alphabetized more easily by writing them on 3″ × 5″ cards. Then compare the names with the signatures of witnesses on your ancestor's marriage license, real estate transactions, or other court documents. You'll then know if neighbors signed as witnesses. You may also be able to tell if they came into the area at the same time as your ancestor. If so, when you get stumped looking for your ancestors, look for their neighbors and your ancestors will probably be around the corner. If you're lucky, you might be able to locate other relatives and ancestors.

Hard-to-Find Books

You will often learn of books or records you want to research but cannot find in the library. With so many millions of books in print, this is not unusual. No library can buy all the books that have ever been printed. Other times you'll see a reference to a book or record that is supposed to be in a library or an archive, but you won't find it in the catalogue. Fortunately, there are ways of locating these hard-to-find items.

After exhausting the card catalogue, the next best step is to consult the reference librarian or archivist. He or she will become your best friend. Librarians and archivists can tell if the item is in the collection but for some reason is not in the catalogue. If the item is not in the collection, they can do a computer search to locate it in the nearest library. They use a computer system called OCLC (Online Computer Library Center), which is subscribed to by thousands of libraries around the country. If none of the libraries in your area have the item you need, the reference librarian can search across the country in the OCLC system, locate it, then place an interlibrary loan request so the item can be transferred to your neighborhood library. Not all items are available through interlibrary loan, but enough are that the search is worth it. Some computer searches can be done from your home computer, which will be covered in the chapter on "Electronic Genealogy."

However, the OCLC system is not infallible. We searched for a Catholic newspaper, and the OCLC system said it was in only one library. We then checked individual libraries and found four other copies of the newspaper. Because computers are a recent invention compared to books and newspapers, not all records are in the OCLC system. A librarian has to enter the item into the OCLC system, and most enter only current acquisitions. A few libraries are returning to enter older items. The predecessor to OCLC is the *National Union Catalogue,* developed by the Library of Congress. It is an attempt to list all published books (over 12 million) and the repositories where they can be found. So if the item you're looking for is not found in the OCLC system, check the *National Union Catalogue* if it is available at your library. You may have to visit a larger library in the area to find one. The companion to the *National Union Catalogue* is the *Union List of Serials in the United States and Canada,* which catalogues pre-1950 periodicals. More recent periodicals are catalogued in *New Serial Titles: A Union List of Serials Commencing Publication after December 31, 1949.* For specific genealogical periodicals, Michael Clegg edited the *Bibliography of Genealogical and Local History Periodicals with Union List of Major U.S. Collections.* It lists 5,400 genealogical newsletters and journals along with their locations in eleven libraries with major genealogical collections.

To locate specific titles of family histories and genealogies, Marion J. Kaminkow's *Complement to Genealogies in the Library of Congress* lists 23,000 titles and indicates which of twenty-four libraries holds each one.

Another good source is the *Family History Library Catalogue,* which is not included in the Kaminkow *Complement.* The Family History Library in Salt Lake City holds over 78,000 family genealogies, which are listed in their catalogue. Many of these are on microfiche and available on loan to one of their 1,500 Family History Centers around the country for a small fee. A more comprehensive listing of sources for locating published family histories and genealogies can be found in *Printed Sources,* by Kory Meyerink.

Before You Leave the Library

Before you leave the library, there are several things you need to do to increase the success of your trip. These are best done before you walk out the door, while things are fresh in your mind. So if you plan to spend the day at the library, stop researching half an hour to an hour before the library closes. Unfortunately, many genealogists frantically try to cram every minute into research and even hold up employees trying to leave for the day. If this is you, you'll neglect important organizational tasks, and it's not the way to make a good impression on librarians.

First, record in your Research Calendar where you stopped researching so you can pick up where you left off on your next trip. Also, make notes on items you want to research on your next trip to the library.

! Trap: **N**ot documenting your research. Sources should be cited on
• the back of each document.

Update your Research To Do and Things To Do forms as ideas come to you. Then make some descriptive notes to yourself that will help you on your next trip. Record descriptions of the records and what you found in them. Record what you liked, what problems you had, what tips you'll want to use next time, and the names of key people who helped you.

Next, review all your research notes. Fill in those that may be spotty and rewrite all illegible items. You may know what they are in the heat of the moment, but will you know a few months from now? If you "accidentally" wrote any notes on small scraps of paper, transfer them to 8½″ × 11″ sheets of paper or transfer them to the proper genealogy form.

Examine all photocopies for proper source citations on the reverse. If any are missing, this is the best time to add them, while they are fresh in your mind. You don't want to fall behind in your work.

After You Return Home

After you return home, check for photocopies made on thermofax paper that had to dry, because the ink will smudge and fade over time. It's best to rephotocopy these sheets onto more stable paper. If you discovered any new ancestors or located new dates and places of birth, marriage, or death, update your Pedigree Charts and Family Group Sheets. Don't forget to cite the source properly.

Study and analyze your new research findings. Determine new sources to research, writing new ideas on your Research To Do form. Many genealogists come home after a trip to the library and put their work on the desk. It will sometimes sit there for weeks and months, sometimes years. When they return to research again, the information is stale and they can't remember significant finds, problems solved, and where to look next. The best time for review is right after a trip to the library.

! Trap: **N**ot reviewing research findings and notes right after a
• research trip.

After you make out your new Research To Do list, prioritize it. Determine some logical order for your next research steps. Then put the photocopies you made at the library into their proper folders. If any copies are legal size, don't fold them; place them in legal-size file folders. If any document is particularly voluminous, you may consider putting it in a folder by itself. If you picked up any new brochures or finding aids from the library, you may need to start a new file folder for that library. If the trip was out of town and you picked up any maps or brochures on the city, county, or state, you may want to start a new folder for that city, county, or state.

! Trap: Not filing, organizing, and updating findings after research trips.

Finally, make a bibliography of important books and articles, including the author, title, publication city, publisher, and date of publication. This way you'll be able to easily refer to them in the future.

Then sit back and relax from a successful trip to the library.

No Library in Town

Let's say you live in a small town and there is no library, or there is a small library without a genealogy collection. Or worse yet, perhaps you're homebound and can't get to a library or don't have enough money to travel. Are you out of luck? Do you have to wait until you can travel to a sizable city to research? No, you have several alternatives.

There are libraries that will lend their genealogy books and microfilm. Some will send books and microfilm to your home; others will send them to your local library; and still others will send them to a nearby Mormon church library. There is also a company that tapes genealogical lectures on all kinds of topics. You can order these through the mail or on the Internet, and they will be sent to your home for your listening pleasure. So you can research your family history no matter where you live.

Mid-Continent Public Library
15616 East 24 Highway
Independence, MO 64050
http://www.mcpl.lib.mo.us

The Mid-Continent Public Library was begun in 1926 by a local chapter of the Daughters of the American Revolution (DAR). The library established the Genealogy Circulation Collection in 1984 that now has over 5,000 volumes. They send books through interlibrary loan to local libraries in the United States and Canada. There are no fees for borrowing books unless your local library charges an interlibrary loan fee. Because the collection is relatively small and is available to all libraries here and in Canada, there can be a six- to twelve-month wait for some of the more popular books. The types of materials include microfilmed U.S. Census records, genealogies, local histories, and reference works. Some materials are available only to Missouri institutions, and others are available to all libraries. A catalogue was published in 1992, with supplements published in 1994, 1996, and 1998. Plans are to publish an update every two years. The collection has also published a guide for genealogy materials available from other institutions *(Interlibrary Loan Sources: A Guide for Librarians and Genealogists)*. Borrowers should request the catalogues and supplements or view them on the Internet. Then they can place orders through their local library's interlibrary loan service (not OCLC).

National Genealogical Society (NGS)

4527 17th Street, North
Arlington, VA 22207-2399
http://www.ngsgenealogy.org/

The NGS library collection contains 30,000 volumes, not all of which are available on loan. Books are lent only to members in the United States (excluding Alaska and Hawaii) and are not available through interlibrary loan. There is a one-time fee to start service, then postage costs for shipping books. Two books may be borrowed at a time for two weeks. The collection contains genealogies, local histories, published indexes, and genealogy reference works.

New England Historic Genealogical Society (NEHGS)

101 Newberry Street
Boston, MA 02116
http://www.NewEnglandAncestors.org

NEHGS is the oldest and largest genealogical society in the United States. It began in 1845 and has more than 18,000 members. The society is located in Boston, Massachusetts, and has members around the world. Many do not have New England roots but benefit from the library holdings. NEHGS has a library in Boston as well as a circulating library. Member borrowing has existed since the founding of the society, but mail service to out-of-town members began around 1925. So in addition to being the oldest genealogical society, it also has the distinction of having the first genealogy lending collection. As of 2000, the circulating library collection had more than 20,000 volumes, including family genealogies, local histories, genealogical reference works, and vital records and tax records from New England.

Members can borrow three books at a time for a small fee and keep them for two weeks. Books are sent through regular mail throughout the United States and Canada, and rush service is available for an extra fee. Borrowers must take out a membership to utilize the service and then purchase a book loan catalogue. The catalogue will eventually be on the Internet.

National Archives Microfilm Rental Program

P.O. Box 30
Annapolis Junction, MD 20701-0030
http://www.nara.gov/publications/microfilm/micrent.html

Selected microfilmed records of the National Archives can be inexpensively rented directly from the National Archives. They lend copies of all the U.S. Census records from 1790 to 1920, as well as all Soundex records from 1880 to 1920. They also rent microfilmed records from the Revolutionary War, but that is for more advanced researchers. There is a small life-time start-up fee that includes National Archives guides, census catalogues, a discount on publications, and a couple of free microfilm rentals. Microfilm can be sent to your home if you own a microfilm reader, or to your local library through interlibrary loan if you do not. Microfilm is loaned for thirty days and can also be purchased.

Heritage Quest (formerly American Genealogical Lending Library—AGLL)
P.O. Box 329
Bountiful, UT 84011-0329
http://www.agll.com

AGLL began in 1989. It is the largest genealogical lending library, with a collection exceeding 250,000 volumes. It includes microfilmed U.S. Census records from 1790 to 1920, as well as microfilmed Soundex records from 1880 to 1920, military records, ship passenger lists, local histories, vital records, and surname, ethnic, and special collections. There is a multivolume catalogue available on CD-ROM, microfiche, and paper. Because much of the collection is on microfilm and microfiche, users must purchase or have access to a microfilm and microfiche reader. Prices of machines have fallen, and many genealogists purchase inexpensive ones for their homes. AGLL also sells machines. Film is loaned for thirty days and can also be purchased, with rental fees applied toward the purchase price. There is an annual membership fee to borrow film, which includes a newsletter and other privileges.

Family History Library
35 West North Temple
Salt Lake City, UT 84150
http://www.familysearch.org

The Church of Jesus Christ of Latter-day Saints, known as the Mormon Church, has more than 1,600 branch libraries around the world that are free to use for nonmembers. The library has the largest genealogy collection in the world, including more than 2 million reels of microfilm. There are genealogies, family histories, local histories, census records, military records, vital records, church records, and others, which can be borrowed on microfilm or microfiche and sent to a Family History Center near you. Most records date from before 1910, but there are some that are later. Costs amount to postage, and the records can be viewed for several weeks. You must locate materials from their card catalogue and then place an order at a Family History Center, which is usually attached to a Mormon Church.

Interlibrary Loan

Many public and academic libraries in the United States will lend books to each other through an interlibrary loan cooperating service. To see if your local library participates, ask if they have an interlibrary loan department. If they do, ask if there are any fees. Then all you have to do is locate a book at another library (often through OCLC) that also has interlibrary loan, and they can send the book or microfilm to your local branch. The interlibrary loan department at your branch must place the order for you.

Lecture Tapes

There are also audiotapes of lectures delivered at genealogical conferences available for purchase online. A company called Repeat Performance has been taping national and some regional conferences for a number of years (see "Miscellaneous Addresses" in the appendixes).

Social Security Records

My dad was twenty years old and a senior at Englewood High School in Chicago when he applied for a Social Security card on March 6, 1940. His Social Security application lists his father's name and his mother's maiden name. I'd have been ecstatic had I not already known their names. Nothing else on the card added new information, but it did verify his address in 1940 as well as his date and place of birth.

Just as I received a photocopy of my dad's original Social Security application, you can get a copy of your ancestor's application. Social Security began under President Franklin D. Roosevelt, during the Great Depression. Public Law 271 was enacted on August 14, 1935, by the 74th Congress (P.L. 74-271), "to provide for the general welfare by establishing a system of Federal old-age benefits, and by enabling the several states to make more adequate provision for aged persons, blind persons, dependent and crippled children, maternal and child welfare, public health, and the administration of their unemployment compensation laws; to establish a Social Security Board; to raise revenue; and for other purposes." Workers who retired at age sixty-five were entitled to old-age pensions, and their widows qualified when they turned sixty.

Between 1935 and 1996, 383 million people registered with Social Security. So for genealogical research, this government agency has the largest body of records of Americans, other than census records.

Social Security Benefits

Social Security is a vast and complicated system. We are accustomed to having a Social Security card because employers require it for employment. Once we retire, we're eligible for benefits based on the amount of money we earned and the Social Security credits we received. Other provisions of the program provide medical coverage (Medicare and Medicaid) to pay hospital expenses. Another feature provides disabil-

Social Security Application for Elmer Burroughs—Copy of original Social Security application (Form SS-5) for Elmer Burroughs in 1940, obtained from the Social Security Administration.

ity payments for workers injured on the job and unable to return to work. Another element provides benefits to dependents of workers on Social Security.

The original Social Security Act provided only retirement benefits, and only to the worker. Two amendments in 1939 made fundamental changes in the Social Security program, adding two categories of benefits. Payments called dependents' benefits could be made to the spouse and minor children of a retired worker. The other category was survivors' benefits, which were paid to families when a worker covered under Social Security died before retiring and obtaining Social Security payments. These changes transformed Social Security from a retirement program for workers into a family-based economic security program. They also created additional records that can be used for genealogy research.

Unfortunately, many African Americans did not benefit from the new Social Security law. The traditional jobs of African Americans, such as farmer, domestic worker, and federal employee, were not covered by the original Social Security Act. That means that 65 percent of employed African Americans were not covered in 1935. This is another case in which white genealogists can utilize a tremendous group of records but African Americans have limited usage. That's not to say African American genealogists should not search for these records, only that our job is much harder because of limited resources. The Social Security Act was amended in 1951 (P.L. 82-78) to cover these occupations.

Almost everyone else is covered by Social Security. I say almost everyone because I have to think of my self-employed Uncle John, who never fit into corporate America. He developed skill as a plumber after World War II and could always find work. He never joined the plumbers' union and was always able to get work, underbidding high union rates. Uncle John survived well past retirement but never applied for Social Security. He stashed away a little nest egg under his mattress, still leery of banks because of the Depression. I'm sure we all have an Uncle John in our family tree.

The Social Security Number

The first Social Security numbers were issued in November 1936. Employers were to register their employees by January 1, 1937. The first applications were handled by post offices while Social Security offices were being established. By June 1937, 151 Social Security offices were open and 30 million employees were registered for Social Security. By 1998, 386 million Social Security numbers had been assigned and about 6 million numbers are added every year.

The Social Security number itself seems like a mystery, and some of the mystery is justified. The Social Security number consists of nine digits divided into three parts (000-00-0000). Only the first three digits are useful for genealogists. They are called the "area number" and refer to the state or U.S. possession in which the original application was issued. (The 700 to 728 series was originally reserved for railroad employees, but this practice was discontinued in 1963.) The first three numbers of my Social Security number are in the 300 series, and so are those of my siblings, my father, and his Uncle Robert. We were all born in Chicago. However, my mom, her sister, and her mother are all in the 200 series because they applied in Pennsylvania. However, Mom's brother also applied in Pennsylvania and his area number is 192. That's because Pennsylvania was assigned numbers from 159 to 211. Some genealogists erroneously think these three numbers refer to the state of birth for the applicant. Although this is not true, employees often applied for a card in the same state where they were born.

This state indicator is not static. As the population grows and shifts, the Social Security Administration assigns more numbers to states. So whereas a block of numbers may have been reserved for one state, some of those unassigned numbers may be shifted and assigned to states with growing populations. The Social Security Administration continually updates this information, which can be viewed on its Web site (http://www.ssa.gov).

The middle two numbers are called the "group number" and are coded by the Social Security Administration. Some researchers say they relate to when the card was applied for, but the Social Security Administration says the middle two numbers have no special significance. A rumor spread on the Internet that even group numbers were assigned to African Americans and could be used to discriminate against people of color. However, this is not correct. I checked numbers for my ancestors and found eight had even group numbers and six had odd numbers, statistically even. The last four numbers are called the "serial number" and are a straight numerical progression of assigned numbers.

000-00-0000
area-group-serial

In reviewing Social Security numbers for my ancestors, I was amazed to see my maternal grandmother, Lydia Brooks, and her eldest daughter, Margaret Ann, had sequential Social

SOCIAL SECURITY AREA NUMBERS

001-003	New Hampshire	425-428	Mississippi	580	Virgin Islands
004-007	Maine	429-432	Arkansas	581-584	Puerto Rico
008-009	Vermont	433-439	Louisiana	585	New Mexico
010-034	Massachusetts	440-448	Oklahoma	586	Guam
035-039	Rhode Island	449-467	Texas	586	American Samoa
040-049	Connecticut	468-477	Minnesota	586	Philippines
050-134	New York	478-485	Iowa	586	Northern Mariana Islands
135-158	New Jersey	486-500	Missouri	587-588	Mississippi
159-211	Pennsylvania	501-502	North Dakota	589-595	Florida
212-220	Maryland	503-504	South Dakota	596-599	Puerto Rico
221-222	Delaware	505-508	Nebraska	600-601	Arizona
223-231	Virginia	509-515	Kansas	602-626	California
232	North Carolina	516-517	Montana	627-645	Texas
233-236	West Virginia	518-519	Idaho	646-647	Utah
237-246	North Carolina	520	Wyoming	648-649	New Mexico
247-251	South Carolina	521-524	Colorado	650-653	Wisconsin
252-260	Georgia	525	New Mexico	654-699	unassigned
261-267	Florida	526-527	Arizona	700-728	Railroad workers to 1963
268-302	Ohio	528-529	Utah	729-749	unassigned
303-317	Indiana	530	Nevada	750-751	Hawaii
318-361	Illinois	531-539	Washington	752-755	Mississippi
362-386	Michigan	540-544	Oregon	756-763	Tennessee
387-399	Wisconsin	545-573	California	764-899	unassigned
400-407	Kentucky	574	Arkansas	900-999	not valid
408-415	Tennessee	575-576	Hawaii		
416-424	Alabama	577-579	District of Columbia		

Information as of May 1997. Some Area numbers will be added as population grows and shifts. Some Area numbers are shown more than once because they have either been transferred from one state to another or divided for use in other geographic locations.

Security numbers. They obviously went to the Social Security office in Pittsburgh together when Margaret Ann was eighteen years old.

Social Security Applications

The Social Security Administration, having covered millions of Americans, is an important source for genealogists. Researchers can obtain a copy of an ancestor's original Social Security application, Form SS-5. These forms have been microfilmed and are available to researchers upon request and fee payment.

This application has changed over time but contains valuable personal information for genealogists. It shows the applicant's full name, sex, race, date and place of birth, home address, employer's name and address, father's name, mother's maiden name, and applicant's signature. Unfortunately, like many government records, the forms weren't always filled out fully, so you may not get all this information.

My grandma Lydia Brooks was forty-four years old when Social Security began. Her Social Security application revealed she worked as a maid at the Webster Hall Hotel in Pittsburgh in 1937. When I mentioned this to her daughter, my Aunt Doris, she remembered her mother going to work at the hotel when she was a kid. A close examination of her Social Security application indicates she worked there only from February 4 to February 6, 1937. I couldn't make out the handwriting to see why she left the job, but most of the spaces on the form were blank. The hotel's name was on the line where she was supposed to sign, so it appears she didn't fill out the information. It had only her name, address, date of birth, and dates of employment.

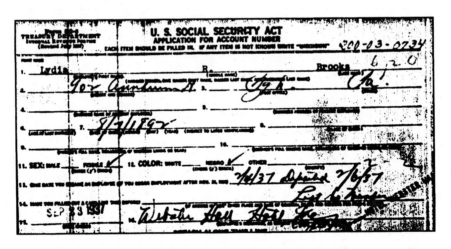

Social Security for Lydia Brooks—Copy of original Social Security application (Form SS-5) for Lydia R. Brooks in 1937, obtained from the Social Security Administration.

How to Obtain Copies of Social Security Applications

To obtain a copy of the original Social Security application (Form SS-5), request a copy of Form SSA-L997, "SSN Social Security Number Record—Third Party Request for Extract or Photocopy," from the Social Security Administration (Social Security Administration, Office of Central Records Operations, Baltimore, MD 21201). Then you'll need a copy of your ancestor's death certificate because privacy laws prohibit information being released for living persons. The Social Security number is not mandatory to receive a copy of the original application, but the request will cost extra without it.

Because of the volume of applications, the original application forms were microfilmed and the information entered into computers. The original applications were then destroyed. A printout of the information in computer format is called a "numident printout." The numident printout contains:

First name, middle initial, and last name
Social Security number
Date of birth
Place of birth (city and state)
Date of death
Sex
Mother's first name, middle initial, and maiden name
Father's first name, middle initial, and last name

You should request a photocopy of the microfilmed Social Security application (Form SS-5), as well as the numident printout. The original application contains more information, as well as the applicant's signature. As good genealogists, we always prefer copies of original documents to computer printouts, which are secondary documents. However, the computer printouts sometimes contain information not found on original applications. If a widow remarries, both surnames will appear on the computer printout but not on the original application. There will be a fee for the copy of the original application but not the computer numident printout.

You should record the Social Security numbers of all your deceased ancestors and send for their original applications. Be prepared to wait, though—the last one I received took three months to come back from Social Security.

Where to Find Your Ancestor's Social Security Number

The first place to check for an old Social Security number is an old wallet. Most people kept their Social Security cards in their wallets for identification. If the Social Security card is not found, look for the person's driver's license, which often contains the Social Security number. Other records that may contain the Social Security number are:

- Correspondence from the Social Security Administration
- Death certificates
- Funeral home records
- Employment records
- Hospital records
- Veterans Administration records
- Military discharge certificates
- Tax returns
- Bank records

Social Security Death Index

The Social Security Administration maintains data on deceased persons whose Social Security survivors were paid benefits. As a result of the Freedom of Information Act, the Social Security Administration created a Death Master File of these individuals on magnetic tape and CD-ROM. The data is not cheap, but it is available for a fee on an annual or quarterly basis. It is purchased by vendors who repackage it on CD-ROMs and sell it to institutions and individuals for genealogy research. Vendors give their products various names, such as "Social Security Death Index," "Social Security Benefits Death Index," and "Social Security Death Master File." They're all the same thing, but the name, data, search capability, and look and feel of each product will differ from vendor to vendor.

The first CD-ROMs contained over 50 million names. Ninety-eight percent of the entries were for individuals who died between 1962 and 1988. Only 2 percent of the entries were for people who died between 1937 and 1962. The Social Security Administration releases this data on a quarterly basis, and later editions from vendors have additional names.

Information on the Death Master Index includes the following items: last name, first name, Social Security number, date of death, date of birth, zip code of the last residence, and zip code to where benefits were sent. Some zip codes will refer to more than one city, but they will put you in the ballpark if you know where the ancestor should have lived when he or she died.

Where to Find the Social Security Death Index

The Social Security Death Index of names is available on CD-ROM and on the Internet, and can be located in libraries with genealogy departments. However, not all databases are the same in content, quality, or ease of use. It's up to individual vendors to process and package the data as they see fit. So not every database looks the same, has the same format, offers the same features, or contains the same number of names. Some are easier to use than others; some have different search capabilities than others; and some are faster to use than others. I have had the experience of not finding a name on one index but locating it on another by a different vendor.

The Social Security Death Index can also be purchased on CD-ROM for home computer. But remember, you will not be getting the quarterly updates or the changes from Social Security. Several vendors have also placed the database on the Internet, some charging subscription fees.

Once you locate the Social Security Death Index on CD-ROM, you can search for your ancestor's Social Security number and also pinpoint dates of birth and death. It is a nationwide index, and there may be many people with the same name. However, those with the same name will probably not have the same dates of birth and death. So if you know your ancestor's approximate date of birth, this will help you identify the person in the index and provide the date of death. If you think a distant relative died but you're not sure, the Social Security Death Index can help verify it and give you the exact date of death. One of the advantages of using the CD-ROM versus the Internet is you can browse names. On some of the Internet search engines, if you don't locate the name you're looking for, you can't browse a list of similar names.

Caveats or Weaknesses

Social Security provides a list of corrections to the main database. Yes, they admit they make errors. Once the master file is created, Social Security estimates 4,000 to 8,000 records each month need to be changed or deleted. The question genealogists need to determine is if the product they are using is being updated by the vendor.

You may not locate the ancestor you're searching for in the Social Security Death Index. Remember, not everyone is included. Farm laborers and domestic workers were not covered until July 12, 1951. And even if a person was registered with Social Security, in order to be included in the database, their death had to be reported to Social Security and someone had to receive survivors' benefits. Other ancestors might not be located because some state Social Security offices restrict data for six to eight years before they release it for inclusion in the Death Master File.

In addition, from 1937 to 1962 many railroad employees were covered under the Railroad Retirement Act, not Social Security. So those ancestors working on the railroad and dying in this period might not be in the database.

Also remember that the place indicated on the index is the place where benefits were sent, not the place of death. A survivor could easily live in a different state than the deceased. The date of birth given to the Social Security Administration may be different from that found on death certificates, birth certificates, cemetery records, and census records.

Where to Go Next

After an ancestor's name is located on the Social Security Death Index, you have an exact date of death if you did not have it previously. You can now apply for a death certificate. Once you get the death certificate, it will usually indicate the cemetery and the funeral home, sources of additional records. Next, look for an obituary in the newspaper for the person. After the death certificate or the obituary is obtained, you'll then be able to apply for a birth certificate if it is available for the time period. Refer back to previous chapters for these sources if you need a refresher. With this newfound Social Security number and death certificate, you can also apply for a copy of the original Social Security application for the lower fee.

Railroad Retirement Board

At the time Social Security was created, the railroads already had pension plans. However, the coverage was inadequate, and many workers never received benefits. The Great Depression also imposed financial hardship on many railroad retirement plans. These factors led to creating the Railroad Retirement Board around the same time Social Security was created.

Railroad Retirement records began in 1937 and are similar to Social Security records. There are no records for persons who died prior to 1937, but there may be records for those who worked prior to 1937. Unfortunately, many older records were routinely destroyed under federal guidelines. Railroad Retirement records include last job title, years of rail service, and name of employer. Older records may have place of birth and parents' names. If the worker received a pension, there might be additional substantial information. Records are organized by Social Security number.

Those genealogists with ancestors who worked for the railroad can contact the U.S. Railroad Retirement Board (Office of Public Affairs, 844 North Rush St., Chicago, IL 60611-2092) for a search of the records. They ask that you supply the worker's first, middle, and last names, Social Security number if known, date and place of birth if known, and date of death. They will not provide information on living persons without their consent. The board can verify railroad employment and will sometimes have a pension file for retired workers. There is a hefty nonrefundable fee to search for records, and it takes sixty to ninety days to receive a reply.

I located a receipt in Robert Burroughs's trunk from his optometrist, dated October 20, 1944. I had looked at the receipt many times over the years and never paid much attention to it. Then one day I saw something I had not noticed before. It said "c/o The Pullman Company." I knew Robert's father, my great-grandfather Morris Burroughs, worked for the Pullman Company, but I never thought about Robert working for them.

I wondered if Robert really worked for Pullman and decided to contact the Railroad Retirement Board. They didn't charge search fees at the time I did the research. I called on the telephone, and the board verified that Robert worked for the railroad in 1944. However, he did not get a pension and therefore they did not have a file for him.

I then researched the Pullman records at the Newberry Library in Chicago. The library has one of the largest genealogical collections in the United States and received the bulk of the Pullman records from throughout the country. I located an employee registration form that listed Robert's first and last names, his signature, date of hire, and occupation. Robert was not a Pullman porter but an electrician. It also listed his place of employment, Social Security number, address, date and place of birth, father's name and mother's maiden name. This was another document that verified Morris and Mary as Robert's parents and Mary's maiden name as Williams. A tremendous find, all starting from a seemingly insignificant receipt for eyeglasses. Thank goodness for his poor eyesight.

Optometrist Receipt—Receipt for eye examination of Robert Burroughs done for the Pullman Company in 1944; found among family papers.

U.S. Census Records

I was giving an all-day genealogy workshop one day at the Allen County Public Library in Fort Wayne, Indiana. Halfway through the program I got to census records, and all of a sudden I heard a loud noise from the first row. It was a lady gasping for breath and slapping her face. I couldn't imagine what was wrong. I stopped my explanation in midsentence and asked her if she was OK.

She said yes. It had just dawned on her why she could never find her ancestors on the census records. She hadn't realized she was supposed to look for all the records we've been discussing (oral history, family records, cemeteries, funeral homes, vital records, obituaries, and previous research) before looking at census records. She said it makes perfect sense. Census records used for genealogy are eighty years old, and the more records you exhaust in that period, the more successful you'll be in researching the census. Now she's going to start all over again and do it right.

One of the most popular records for researching genealogy are U.S. Census Population Schedules. You've probably heard of people going to the National Archives or seen pictures of researchers with their heads buried in microfilm readers. I recall Alex Haley's anticipation when he first visited the National Archives in Washington, asking for the microfilm rolls for Alamance County, North Carolina, after the Civil War. Then after tedious searching, the excitement that followed when he found "Tom Murray—blacksmith," who was his great-grandfather, and his great-aunt Liz, who used to sit on the porch telling Alex stories of their ancestors in Henning, Tennessee. I had the same excitement when I first found Morris Burroughs, my great-grandfather, and I've experienced the glee and joy of countless others who found their ancestors in census records while taking my classes or workshops. I have heard people scream, shout, gasp, and even cry when locating their ancestors on the microfilm. This is particularly true if it took a long, hard struggle to find them.

Purpose of the Census

The census was not taken for genealogists, but the records can greatly aid genealogical research. Conducted every ten years, the census is a count of all the people in the United States. It was established in Article 1 of the U.S. Constitution to determine how many representatives are sent to the United States Congress from each state. Since this number varies according to population, it was decided to take it every ten years. Article 1, Section 2, paragraph 2 of the U.S. Constitution reads:

> Representatives and direct taxes shall be apportioned among the several States which may be included within this Union, according to their respective numbers, which shall be determined by adding to the whole number of free persons, including those bound to service for a term of years, and excluding Indians not taxed, three-fifths of all other persons. The actual enumeration shall be made within three years after the first meeting of the Congress of the United States, and within every subsequent term of ten years.

The first meeting of Congress was in 1787, and the first U.S. Census was taken in 1790. Interesting in this paragraph are the words "three-fifths of all other persons." Without calling them by name, this phrase refers to enslaved Africans. The Constitution provided for enumerating slaves, but unfortunately, they are not listed by name on census records. This is yet another stumbling block that other genealogists do not have to hurdle.

Fortunately, census records after the abolition of slavery contain the names of African Americans, as well as other valuable family information. This information varies from census to census but generally includes names, ages, sex, race, marital status, relationships, parentage, addresses, occupations, places of birth, parents' places of birth, literacy, education, home ownership, naturalization, and military service. Early census records had scant information, but as years progressed they tended to include more personal information.

Accuracy

As diligent genealogical researchers, we must ask the question, How accurate is the genealogical information found in census records? There is no simple answer. Sometimes the information is accurate, and sometimes it's very inaccurate. Just envision the task census takers (called enumerators) had to accomplish. They had to count every man, woman, and child in the United States. It was an awesome task, even in the beginning. In 1790 the population of the United States was 3,929,214, and there's no time when everyone in the United States is home. The 1920 census was taken in January, when many people had gone south for the winter.

If a person was not home, the enumerator still had to record information for every household. In 1920 census enumerators were paid between one and four cents for every name recorded (depending on whether they had a rural or an urban district), and enumerators could be fined or imprisoned for falsifying or omitting names. Therefore they did not skip households because residents were not home. Instructions to enumerators guided them when residents were not home: "Obtain the required information as nearly as may be practical from the family or families or person or persons living nearest to such place of abode who may be competent to answer such inquires."

The enumerator would normally ask a neighbor about the person next door. And even though people knew their neighbors much better than we do now, how well did the neighbor know things like full names, ages, places of birth, and parents' places of birth? Neighbors usually guessed at the answers, and enumerators were not required to record the source of the information they were collecting. So the information on census records could be obtained from a child, a neighbor, a landlord, or a janitor who couldn't give accurate answers.

It's amazing how many researchers I run into say, "My ancestor lied about his age to the census enumerator." That may have been true, but we have no way of knowing if the ancestor was even home when the census enumerator knocked on the door. Therefore we must take the information on census records with a grain of salt. The information could be true or false. The picture is more accurate when several census records are compared with each other and even better when the information is compared with documents from other sources.

! Trap: Accepting the information in census records as gospel.

Questions have been raised as to whether African Americans were included on the census or not. Many skeptics have said Blacks were undercounted and missed on census records. They often use this skepticism as an excuse for not doing genealogical research or looking at census records. My experience has shown African Americans are more likely recorded on the census records than not. I've found my ancestors on almost every census enumeration. I've learned that when I did not find them, there was something I wasn't doing right or my ancestors were listed in a way I hadn't expected—for example, under a nickname or a middle name instead of their given name—or they had moved or were living with a different family.

Organization and Restrictions

Census records are not listed alphabetically by last name. But there is a method to the madness. First, they are organized by census year (every ten years). Then they're arranged alphabetically by name of state, alphabetically by name of county, then by enumeration district, and thereafter block by block, house by house, household by household, and finally by name of the head of the household in the order the enumerator visited the dwellings.

There are statistical reports from the census bureau that are available for all census years. However, the census records genealogists use are the Census Population Schedules, which include personal information used for genealogy. Because Census Population Schedules contain personal information, their use is restricted. To protect people who are living, researchers can access only the U.S. Census Population Schedules that are seventy-two years old and older. Currently the 1920 through the 1790 U.S. Census records are available for research. The 1930 U.S. Census will be available for research for the first time in 2002. About 99 percent of the 1890 U.S. Census was destroyed sometime after a fire in 1921 in Washington, D.C. Many researchers think the entire 1890 census was destroyed, but, in fact, their ancestors could be among the 1 percent of surviving schedules.

Where Can You Research Census Records?

U.S. Census records were created by a federal agency called the Bureau of the Census. Older records that can be researched for genealogy have been transferred from the Bureau of the Census to the National Archives. Microfilm copies of the originals can be researched at the National Archives in Washington, D.C., as well as the thirteen regional branches of the National Archives around the country (see "National Archives Branches" in the appendixes). They can also be researched at some public and genealogical libraries, university libraries, historical societies, and state archives that have purchased census microfilm from the National Archives. However, whereas branches of the National Archives contain census microfilm from every state for every census year, many other institutions purchase only limited geographical areas or selected years of census microfilm. For example, a public library in Alabama may purchase census microfilm for the state of Alabama and possibly its surrounding states.

Census microfilm can also be borrowed from several different places. The National Archives rents and sells census microfilm. The Family History Library in Salt Lake City, Utah, loans film to its thousands of branches called Family History Centers for a modest fee. The American Genealogical Lending Library (a division of Heritage Quest) rents census microfilm to be viewed in your home, but you need a microfilm machine to view it. They also sell the machines (see "Genealogical and Archival Vendors" in the appendix for details).

Which Census Should You Research First?

Because you want to follow the sound genealogical principles of starting with yourself and proceeding backward, one generation at a time, and proceeding from the known to the unknown, you begin with the latest census available and the closest to you in time. Presently that would be the 1920 census, which is available on microfilm. The Bureau of the Census microfilmed the 1920 census in 1945 and 1946 and transferred the microfilm to the National Archives in 1949. Unfortunately, they destroyed the original records in 1953, and all that remains is the microfilm.

The names you should look for on that 1920 census are your relatives and ancestors who were living in 1920. Genealogist Carolyn Grant lives on Hilton Head Island, South Carolina, as her ancestors have for over a hundred years. She knew her great-grandfather's name and began looking for him and his relatives on the 1870 U.S. Census. She found plenty of Grants, but none of the names were familiar to her. I suggested she start with the 1920 census and work her way backward, which she did. She was pleased and excited to see several names she could recognize on the 1920 census. Seeing her ancestors on this census also solved a puzzle about one relative. The family always called this relative Blossom, but on the census she was listed as Charlotte. Carolyn talked with Blossom, who was in her eighties, and was told she never liked the name Charlotte and therefore never used it. So begin from the known and work back to the unknown. Start with the 1920 census and work your way back to earlier records.

Preparation for Researching U.S. Census Records

If the steps outlined in the first part of the book are completed, census research will be much more successful. A review of those steps are:

- Complete oral interviews with family members.
- Research family papers and documents.
- Research cemeteries where ancestors are buried.
- Research funeral home records that buried ancestors.
- Fill out Family Group Sheets, including all ancestors.
- Document sources of all data on Family Group Sheets.
- Fill out a Pedigree Chart, including all direct ancestors.
- Obtain birth, death, marriage, and divorce records for all ancestors.
- Research published biographies, autobiographies, family histories, and genealogies.
- Search for obituaries for all ancestors.
- Research telephone directories and city directories.
- Research Social Security records.

There is some basic information you need to know before researching census records. Completing the above steps will help provide the following information.

NAMES—It will be helpful to know the full names of all your relatives and ancestors who were living in 1920. This includes their first names, last names, and middle names if known. Nicknames are also very helpful. Sometimes people went by their nicknames more than their given names (remember Blossom). Men were often listed under their initials instead of their names. My grandfather always signed his name A. M. Burroughs instead of Asa Morris Burroughs. There is no telling how your ancestors' names will be listed on the census, and it could be either of the above.

Many beginners never consider dates of women's marriages. If a woman married within a few years before or after the date the census was taken, the date of marriage will tell you whether she was listed on the census under her maiden name with her parents or under her married name with her new husband. Hence the importance of obtaining marriage records before census records.

RESIDENCE—Since census records are organized by state, you'll have to know what state your ancestor was living in in 1920. This might seem obvious but is more subtle than what meets the eye. For African Americans 1920 was a time of great migration from the South to the North. Many people were on the move, and if they moved from Mississippi to Illinois during that time, you need to know when the move took place and if they were in Mississippi or Illinois at the time the census was taken.

It is also advisable to know the county and city where the relatives and ancestors lived. The index to the census is a statewide index, and there may be many people with the same name. The county of residence is listed on this index and differentiates two people with the same name.

If the family lived in a city versus a rural area, knowing the street address can be very helpful. Street addresses can be obtained through old letters, envelopes, postcards, city directories, and other records. If your ancestors are not found in the census index, the street address will lead you directly to the location on the census, so you can bypass the index.

HEAD OF THE HOUSEHOLD—Census records are grouped under the "Head of the Household," and therefore the index is also listed by "Head of Household." If you are not intimately familiar with the family makeup in 1920, it is good to know if your known ancestor was a child or a parent and possibly the head of the household. It also helps to know who was living in the house at the time of the census. The census will list everyone living in the house at the time the census was taken. African Americans often lived in extended families comprising grandparents, aunts, uncles, nephews, nieces, cousins, and even friends of the family. If this was the case, there's no telling if the head of household was the father, grandfather, or some other family member.

AGES—It is helpful to know the ages of your ancestors in 1920. This can also help you differentiate between people with the same name. It can also help you determine who was the head of the household. Knowing the ages of the other members of the household is also helpful. They will be listed on the census in birth order, oldest to youngest. Therefore it is helpful to know the birth order of siblings.

The 1920 census was taken the first week in January to reflect the population as of January 1, 1920. The enumerators had two weeks to finish in the city and thirty days for rural areas. So any ancestors born in 1920 will not be listed on the census.

How to Research U.S. Census Records

When you prepare to go to the archive or library that houses U.S. Census records, there are a few things you should take with you.

- Research Calendar
- Family Group Sheets and Pedigree Charts (up to date)
- Biographies, chronologies, and other family information

- Soundex abstract forms (blank forms created to look like the index to the census, for accurately recording information in the right columns)
- Census extract forms (same as above, but for the census)

Likewise, there are certain things you should not take with you. As was stated in the "Going to the Library" chapter, you should not carry around original, rare, or valuable documents and photographs. If you think you need the information in the documents, make photocopies and take the copies with you. You don't want to lose, soil, or damage original documents. Most of them should remain at home in your acid-free containers or in your safe deposit box.

Name Problems

Because of a lack of formal education, many people in the nineteenth and early twentieth centuries spelled names as they sounded. So names may have been spelled several different ways, like Stewart, Stuart, and Steuart. In fact, one trap beginners fall into is ignoring names that are spelled differently.

I hear many genealogists say, "We didn't spell our name with an *s* on the end," or "We spelled our name with an *e*." Many researchers miss their ancestors for precisely this reason. Nettie, an experienced genealogist, located her ancestor's name on the 1900 census spelled Mazique. On subsequent census records it was Mazsck in 1880 and Muski in 1870. She realized it was the same family because the names of the other family members were the same.

My surname, Burroughs, is sometimes spelled Boroughs, sometimes Burrows, and sometimes Burrowes. In fact, I've found it spelled over thirty different ways. I made a list of the different spellings, alphabetized the list, and now I carry it with me when I research. I'd be hard-pressed to miss a variant spelling. A few of them are:

Borough	Buroughs	Burrough
Boroughs	Burow	Burroughs
Borroughs	Burows	Burrow
Borrow	Burrells	Burrowes
Borrows	Burrill	Burrows
Bouroughs	Burrills	

And the problem is not limited to surnames. Genealogist C. Bernard Ruffin III reported in the *National Genealogical Society Quarterly* (vol. 81, no. 2 [June 1993]) that he located his ancestor Ottaway Ruffin under Ottoway, Otway, Otto, Ordway, Ordaway, and Oliver.

The problem with names is an important one. We are very attached to our names. They are very personal. We want to know where our surname came from and how to trace it backward. It therefore goes against all conventional thought to suddenly change and say the spelling of the name is unimportant. At first it's hard to imagine, but the sooner you can get over it, the better researcher you'll become and the more successful you'll be. When you get to more advanced African American genealogical research, names will become an even bigger problem. You'll quickly learn that the name is not as important as you thought. We have to learn to trace people, not names. There are many characteristics of people that determine who they are, other than their name. Then when the name is different but the person is the same, you will still be able to recognize the person.

The Soundex

Now that you've done all your homework and you've gotten all your supplies together, the next thing to decide is which family to research. It will be either your mom's side of the family (maternal) or your dad's side of the family (paternal). If your grandparents or older relatives are alive on only one side of the family, choose that side to research first because you have living people to help you with the names, dates, locations, and events. If no one is alive on either side, try to pick the side for which you have the most information. You want to improve your chances of success the first time out.

Once you've determined which side of the family to research and you've identified who the probable head of the household is, you must know how to find that person in the index to the census, called the Soundex.

The Soundex is not an alphabetical name index like we're used to seeing in the backs of books. The Soundex is based "loosely" on the sound of the last name of an individual. Education in the early years of this country was not as widespread as it is today (although sometimes I question if we are now more educated). So the Soundex was developed to compensate for the difference in spelling variations discussed earlier. Surnames are coded on index cards used by Census Bureau employees in locating individuals in census records who needed proof of age when applying for Social Security in 1936. Creating an index to the census was one of President Franklin D. Roosevelt's WPA (Works Progress Administration) projects.

The Soundex uses a code consisting of a letter and three numbers to represent an individual's surname. The letter is always the first letter of the last name. Numbers are assigned to the remaining letters of the surname according to the Soundex Coding Guide, as follows:

SOUNDEX CODING GUIDE

The Number:	*Represents the letters:*
1	B P F V
2	C S K G J Q X Z
3	D T
4	L
5	M N
6	R

The letters *a, e, i, o, u, w, y,* and *h* are not coded.

Determining a Soundex Code

Step 1   Write the surname of the relative or ancestor you will be researching.

Step 2   On the line below it, record the first letter of the surname.

Step 3   Except for the first letter, cross out the letters *a, e, i, o, u, w, y,* and *h.*

Step 4   Names with double letters: If the surname has any double letters, treat them as one letter. Thus, in the surname Burroughs, the second *r* should be crossed out.

Step 5   Names with letters side by side that have the same number on the Soundex Coding Guide: If the surname has different letters that are side by side and have the same number on the Soundex Coding Guide, the second letter should be crossed out. For example, the name Jackson has *c, k,* and *s* next to one another, and each letter corresponds with the number 2 in the Soundex Coding Guide. Therefore the *k* and s should be crossed out. In the name Scott, both *S* and *c* are coded 2, so the *c* should be crossed out.

Step 6   If two letters with the same code are divided by an *h* or *w,* treat them as one letter. For example, Burroughs has an *h* that divides *g* and *s,* both representing the number 2 in the Soundex Coding Guide. Therefore the last *s* should be crossed out. (Some instructions omit this rule.)

Step 7   Names with prefixes: If the surname you're researching has a prefix like Mc, Mac, Van, Von, De, Di, or Le, and you don't find it on the Soundex cards, try coding it without the prefix.

Step 8   Determine the next letter that is not crossed out. Locate it on the preceding Soundex Coding Guide. Record the number opposite the letter on line 2 next to the first letter of the last name.

Step 9   Repeat this for the remaining two letters. If no letters remain, add zeros to your Soundex code. Once you have a letter and three numbers, disregard any remaining letters.

(Tip: Many states use Soundex codes in driver's license numbers. Check yours to see if it includes your Soundex code.)

In our Burroughs example the first character is a *b,* the *u* is crossed out, the second *r* is crossed out because it's a double letter, the *o* and *u* are crossed out, the number 2 is recorded for *g* and the last *s* is not coded because it is the same code as *g* and is separated by an *h.* So our Soundex code for Burroughs is B620.

| Line 1 | Burroughs | 4 = 6, g = 2 |
| Line 2 | B620 | |

In our Stewart, Stuart, Steuart example, the code would be S363 for all.

| Line 1 | Stewart | Stuart | Steuart | t = 3, r = 6, t = 3 |
| Line 2 | S363 | S363 | S363 | |

Line 1	J~~ackso~~n	c = 2, n = 6
Line 2	J260	
Line 1	S~~cott~~	t = 3
Line 2	S300	

Selecting the Microfilm Roll

You've now determined the Soundex code. Next you have to determine what state and county your ancestors lived in because the Soundex is a statewide index. The *1920 Federal Population Census Catalogue* will tell you which roll of microfilm your ancestors should be listed on. The front of the book lists Soundex microfilm, and the rear of the book lists census microfilm.

Turn to the Soundex section, then locate the state where your ancestor was living. You'll see an *M* number next to that state. This is part of the National Archives system of numbering microfilm, so record that number. Next, locate your Soundex code within that state. The codes begin with A000 and progress to Z999. However, many codes were put on more than one roll because there were too many names for one. The way you determine which roll your ancestors should be listed on is by the first name of the head of household. The Soundex code represents the last name, and first names are listed opposite each code in alphabetical order. If your roll is split, look for the first name of the head of household and to determine which roll the family is located on.

Record this roll number after the *M* number on your Research Calendar, along with the name of the state you are researching. You should have a number such as M1559-45 or M1559, roll 45. (Your entry should look something like "1920 U.S. Census Soundex—Illinois—M1559-45." It's also a good idea to record the surname being searched and the resultant Soundex code. You should have already listed the date and name of the library where you're researching.) That is the complete microfilm roll number. You will need it to retrieve the roll of film and also to document what you've researched and what you've found, if you find anything. You'll also need it once you have to return to look at the Soundex again. And you'll more than likely have to look at this roll of microfilm again, so don't forget it.

Next, retrieve the Soundex microfilm roll from the cabinet and load it on the microfilm reader. Instructions for loading the film will be on the machine.

Next, locate the Soundex code on the left side of the microfilm roll. If there is more than one Soundex code on the roll, you'll have to turn the roll until you get to your code. Once you're sure you're in the right Soundex code, there will be different surnames, but many will sound the same. The cards are now arranged alphabetically by first name of the head of household. Some codes that have few names are sometimes mixed on a roll. If this happens, you'll see a sign that says "Mixed Codes." The next section may contain several Soundex codes, like M210, M211, and M212, but the first names will be in alphabetical order.

Now proceed alphabetically down the list to your ancestor's first name. If you're lucky and the gods are with you, the head of household will be right where you expect him. However, if you don't find him right away, don't panic and don't give up and say the family was missed. There are many other possibilities to investigate.

Didn't Find Your Ancestors

First, go back and check the initial of the first name. Many men during this time went by their initials instead of their first names. So David Truman would be listed as D. Truman instead of David Truman. If you know the ancestor's middle name, check for it.

Also check for the person's nickname if you know it. If it's a nickname you are using, try to determine the first name. Remember the book *Nicknames: Past and Present,* by Christine Rose, which I mentioned in the chapter on Family Group Sheets? Check your names and you'll be surprised by the nicknames you've probably missed. As you can see, you don't know how the name will be listed until you find it.

If the family is still not found, you may have the wrong head of household. Look for other family members' names (brothers, sisters, aunts, uncles, cousins, grandparents). If a family member was living outside the immediate family and had a surname different from that of the head of household, he or she will have a separate Soundex card. So it pays to look for other family members who were living in 1920.

Many researchers record all the people with the same surname who were living in the county where your ancestors resided because there is the possibility they could be related. This will save time in having to repeat your steps if you discover later they were related. Of course, this may not be feasible if the surname you are researching is Smith or Williams or your ancestors lived in a large metropolitan area like New York or Chicago. I'd also caution against trying this for all the surnames in the state. I started doing this for South Carolina when I began census research. That's when I realized Burroughs may not be a common name in Illinois, but it sure is in South Carolina. There were dozens, if not hundreds, all over the state. I realized not all of these names were related.

If you do record individuals with the same name, be sure to indicate you are not sure if they are related. Otherwise, months or years later you may review your records and think they are ancestors.

Examples of Problems

One of my students named Susan had an ancestor named Dr. Jones. She couldn't locate him on the 1920 census but wasn't sure where he was. Susan didn't know when Dr. Jones got his medical degree, when he returned to school for advanced studies, or when he moved from one city to another. A lot of these questions could have been answered in a published biography, which is not hard to obtain on physicians. I suggested she check for published biographies and obituaries.

Research Susan had completed revealed Dr. Jones was born in Springfield, Illinois, in 1899 and married in New York in 1921. His first child was born in Chicago in 1922, and he was listed in the Chicago city directory in 1918. He lived for a while in Memphis, Tennessee, and went to Meharry Medical School in Nashville sometime around 1920. I suggested contacting Meharry Medical School to verify the years he attended school and when he earned his degree. She then could make detailed searches of telephone directories and city directories in Chicago, New York, Memphis, and Nashville to pinpoint when he was in each city.

Another student named Larry was looking for his dad in the 1920 Soundex without luck. I reviewed Larry's Family Group Sheet and Pedigree Chart and realized his dad was only sixteen years old in 1920. Larry's dad would not have been the head of his household at that age. I suggested Larry search for his grandfather and he found him right away. His dad was in the household as a sixteen-year-old kid.

Another student, Mary, kept confusing her Soundex code with the microfilm number. Each time she couldn't find her ancestors, I realized she'd been retrieving the wrong box and therefore was looking in the wrong Soundex code.

John's ancestor was Robert L. Walker. He found a lot of Robert L. Walkers on the 1920 Soundex for Georgia, but none from Atlanta who fit the description of his ancestor's family. It never occurred to him to look under the list of Roberts without the middle initial, L. Once he did, he found the right family.

Another student started looking on the Soundex and got confused because the last names were not in alphabetical order. I had to remind her that the Soundex is in "sound" order for the surname and that first names are in alphabetical order.

Solving Soundex Problems

If you still cannot find the family, check to see if you are in the right state and the family didn't migrate from one state to another. Then check to make sure you have the right Soundex code. I hate to tell you this, but there are weaknesses in the Soundex code. If the first letter of the surname has the same sound as another, there could be two different Soundex codes. If, for example, the name is Kant and the census enumerator spelled it with a *C*, the code could be C530 instead of K530. Therefore the researcher must check under both codes.

If the census enumerator had bad handwriting (like mine) and the person who Soundexed his name misinterpreted it, the name could be misfiled in the Soundex system. For example, if the name is Lee and it looked like See to the person who created the Soundex card for the name, the Lee family would be on a Soundex card with S000 instead of L000.

In addition, depending on the sounding of the name, it could come under several Soundex codes. I mentioned my surname Burroughs is spelled several different ways. I found out not all of them come under the same Soundex code. Burroughs is B620, and this code picks up four other spelling variations. However, Burrells is coded B642. Some people don't pronounce the *s* at the end, and Burrow is coded B600 and Burrill is B640.

Burrells	Burrow	Burrill
B642	B600	B640

Therefore I should look under four different Soundex codes. In our example of Mazique, Mazsck, and Muski, the first and second are coded M220, but the last one is M200.

Mazique   Mazsck   Muski

M220   M220   M200

If spelling variations of your surname are coded differently, you have a lot more work to do. So check different spelling variations for your name and see if they are Soundex coded the same way.

Tips

As you can see, there are many reasons you may not find your ancestors on the Soundex. It doesn't mean they weren't recorded, so don't get discouraged. Take your time and don't rush. Rushing is the best way to make mistakes and miss your ancestors. Some names on the census were missed by the Soundex indexer, which means you'll have to go directly to the census. Also be aware that some African Americans may be listed as whites. If they were very fair skinned, they may have been mistaken for white or they may have been passing for white. So don't just go by the color column in the census. If you still do not find your ancestors, try the following:

- Check your Family Group Sheets to see they are up to date and accurate.
- Check the addresses of your ancestors.
- Check marriage dates.
- Check maiden names, nicknames, and middle names.
- Make a chronology of your ancestor to track his or her movement from year to year.
- Make sure you checked with the cemetery and the funeral home of the ancestor.
- Make sure you obtained vital records for the ancestor.
- Check for an obituary for the ancestor.
- Check the entire Soundex code and look at every name for clues.
- Search the whole city in the census, then the county.

If the exact address is known, you can bypass the Soundex and go straight to the census. Look for the state, then the county, then the city, then the street, or look at every name in the city or town. Then if you still don't find the family, check the 1910 Soundex and hope they lived in the same location.

When you finally locate your ancestor on the Soundex, it will be very exciting. I always get thrilled when I find new ancestors in the census. At this point in my research, I've found all the easy ones. For each additional one I find, it is a very long, hard struggle of analysis and trial and error. So finding one is like a reward for persistence, struggle, and correct analysis. Many researchers let out an emotion similar to that of athletes winning the big game, the Super

Bowl, the World Series, the Final Four, or the Olympics. Finding our ancestors in the records is like winning the Olympics, only we don't have to wait another four years to find another one.

When you find your family on the Soundex, you'll see a synopsis of the information that is on the actual census. It will show the head of household; his or her race, age, birthplace, state, county, and city of residence; and others living in the household. For other members in the house, it will indicate each individual's name, relationship to the head of household, age, and state of birth.

Soundex Search—Asa Morris Burroughs and Family

We'll try to locate my paternal grandfather and grandmother, Asa Morris and Alma Burroughs, on the 1920 Soundex. I first turn to the Soundex section of the *1920 Federal Population Census Catalogue* and locate Illinois and its *M* number, which is M1559. I then look down the list of codes and see that the B620 Soundex code for Burroughs is split on four rolls.

ROLL	SOUNDEX CODE, ALPHABETICALLY BY FIRST NAME
43.	B610 Carl—B620 Charlie
44.	B620 Charles—B620 James
45.	B620 James—B620 Quirk
46.	B620 R.—B622 Ksoveri

Morris Burroughs's Soundex Card—Copy of 1920 Soundex card for Asa Morris Burroughs, listing him by his middle name, and all the members of his family.

The names are first names of heads of household, so Asa should be on roll 43. I record this information on my Research Calendar, "1920 U.S. Census Soundex—Illinois—M1559-43."

Next I retrieve the Soundex microfilm roll from the cabinet and load it on the machine. Since there is more than one Soundex code on the roll (B610 thru B620), I have to turn the roll until I get to B620. I proceed alphabetically down the list to my grandfather's first name, Asa.

Wouldn't you know it, he isn't there. I go back and check the initial of the first name. As I've mentioned, Asa went by A. M. instead of Asa Morris. I look under the initials A. M. and he isn't there either.

I could check for his nickname if I knew it. My brother named Asa goes by Ace sometimes, but I don't find grandfather under that name either. Next I decide to check Asa's middle name, Morris. It would be on another roll, so I go back to the cabinet and retrieve roll 45. What do you know? I find him and the family.

I never would have guessed he was listed under his middle name instead of his first name. If I'd thought about all the different ways Granddad could have been listed on the census, I would have come up with seven ways. Few of these would have been next to each other on the Soundex cards, and as you saw, they were not even all on the same roll of microfilm. If you don't find your name, you need to be very careful to check under each variation of the full name.

Mr. Burroughs
Mr. A. Burroughs
Mr. A. M. Burroughs
Mr. Asa Burroughs
Mr. Asa Morris Burroughs
Mr. Ace Burroughs
Mr. Morris Burroughs

In this instance I can be sure Grandma was home when the census taker came by. Granddad's age and hers are exactly right, which I know because I have both birth certificates. And the ages of their three children are almost exactly right, down to the month. She's the only one who would have known that information. The little two-month-old infant with no name listed is my father, Elmer. It must have been rough going for two months without a name. I still can't understand that one. Perhaps that's why his birth certificate was filed three months late.

The relationships listed are to the head of household. So *W* is for wife and *S* is for son. However, these abbreviations are not always obvious. Below are some of the abbreviations used on Soundex cards:

ABBREVIATIONS FOR RELATIONSHIPS TO HEAD OF HOUSEHOLD

A	Aunt		First C	First cousin
Ad	Adopted		Fo.B	Foster brother
Ad.Cl	Adopted child		Fo.Si	Foster sister
Ad.D	Adopted daughter		Fo.S	Foster son
Ad.Gcl	Adopted grandchild		God Cl	Godchild
Ad.M	Adopted mother		Go	Governess
Ad.S	Adopted son		G.Cl	Grandchild
Ap	Apprentice		Gd	Granddaughter
At	Attendant		Gf	Grandfather
Asst	Assistant		GM	Grandmother
Al	Aunt-in-law		Gml	Grandmother-in-law
B	Brother		Gs	Grandson
Bar	Bartender		Gsl	Grandson-in-law
Bo	Boarder		Ga	Great aunt
B.Boy	Bound boy		Ggf	Great-grandfather
B.Girl	Bound girl		Gni	Grandniece
Bl	Brother-in-law		Gn	Grandnephew
Bu	Butler		Ggm	Great-grandmother
C	Cousin		Gggf	Great-great-grandfather
Cap	Captain			
Cha	Chambermaid		Gggm	Great-great-grandmother
Cl	Child			
Coa	Coachman		Gu	Great uncle
Com	Companion		Gua	Guardian
Cil	Cousin-in-law		H.Si	Half sister
D	Daughter		H.Sil	Half sister-in-law
Dl	Daughter-in-law		Hb	Half brother
Dla	Day laborer		Hbl	Half brother-in-law
Dw	Dishwasher		He	Herder
Dom	Domestic		H.Gi	Hired girl
Emp	Employee		HH	Hired hand
En	Engineer		Hm	Hired man
F	Father		Hlg	Hireling
Fa.H	Farmhand		Hk	Housekeeper
Fa.L	Farm laborer		H.Maid	Housemaid
Fa.W	Farmworker		Hw	House worker
Fl	Father-in-law		I	Inmate
Fi	Fireman		L	Lodger

ABBREVIATIONS FOR RELATIONSHIPS TO HEAD OF HOUSEHOLD

La	Laborer	SiL	Sister-in-law
Lau	Laundry	Sl	Son-in-law
M	Mother	Sb	Stepbrother
Man	Manager	Sbl	Stepbrother-in-law
Mat	Matron	Scl	Stepchild
Ml	Mother-in-law	Sd	Stepdaughter
N	Nephew	Sdl	Stepdaughter-in-law
Nl	Nephew-in-law	Sf	Stepfather
Ni	Niece	Sfl	Stepfather-in-law
Nil	Niece-in-law	Sgd	Stepgranddaughter
N.R.	Not reported	Sgs	Stepgrandson
Nu	Nurse	Sm	Stepmother
O	Officer	Sml	Stepmother-in-law
P	Patient	Ssi	Stepsister
Pa	Partner	Ssil	Stepsister-in-law
Ph	Physician	Ss	Stepson
Por	Porter	Ssl	Stepson-in-law
Pri	Principal	Su	Superintendent
Pr	Prisoner	Ten	Tenant
Prv	Private	U	Uncle
Pu	Pupil	Ul	Uncle-in-law
R	Roomer	Vi	Visitor
S	Son	W	Wife
Sa	Sailor	Wt	Waiter
Sal	Saleslady	Wai	Waitress
Se	Servant	Wa	Warden
Se.Cl	Servant's child	Wkm	Workman
Si	Sister		

Source: 1910 Federal Population Census: A Catalogue of Microfilm Copies of the Schedules, Appendix II (Washington: National Archives Trust Fund Board, 1982), and *1900 Federal Population Census: A Catalogue of Microfilm Copies of the Schedules*, Appendix II (Washington: National Archives Trust Fund Board, 1978).

When we closely examine Morris Burroughs's Soundex card, we see the coders didn't agree on the Soundex code for Burroughs. B622 is recorded, then crossed out and changed to B620. This may have resulted from not following the instruction that says if *h* or *w* comes between letters with the same number in the guide (in this case *g* and *s* are both 2), only one letter is coded. That means I have an additional Soundex code to check for my Burroughs ancestors.

Recording the Information

Once the excitement has subsided, there are several steps you should take. First, record the information exactly as you see it on the microfilm. There are Soundex extract forms that can be used for this purpose. There is key information on the right of the form needed to find your family in the actual census:

Vol.   34   E.D.   138

Sheet   2   Line   17

Vol. (volume) refers to the original census schedules, which were bound into volumes, and is not used for genealogy. *E.D.* refers to the enumeration district assigned to the census taker (enumerator) to record residents' names. *Sheet* refers to the census page where the information is recorded, and *Line* refers to the row on the census page where the head of household is listed. These last three items (E.D., sheet, and line), along with the state and county, are needed to locate the household on the actual census microfilm—so be sure to record it accurately. In your excitement you may have thought it was just statistical information and neglected it. If so, go back and record it.

After recording everything on the Soundex card on paper exactly as you see it (or on your Soundex extract form), print a photocopy of the microfilm page if your facility has a machine that prints photocopies. Some do not and everything will have to be recorded by hand. When I first started genealogy in the mid-1970s, very few facilities had microfilm printers. Now many do, but there are still some that do not. Then turn the photocopy over and on the back record key information such as the microfilm *M* number and roll number, Soundex state and year of the Soundex, county, township, town or city, name of ancestor being researched on the Soundex, the day's date, and the name of the library or archive where the Soundex was obtained.

This is called documenting your source. After you photocopy many dozens, if not hundreds, of pages, this will help to refresh your memory of when and where you obtained this document and whom you were researching. It will also help you locate the records again and document your Family Group Sheets, noting where you obtained the information.

The Census

Up to this point, you have looked only at the Soundex, which is the "index" to the census. Now we need to research the census itself.

You'll return to the *1920 Federal Population Census Catalogue*. This time you'll check the back of the book, which lists the census microfilm rolls. Instead of the *M* catalogue numbers the Soundex had, the 1920 census rolls use *T* catalogue numbers. For the 1920 census, all rolls have the same *T* number, which is T625.

Now locate the state you are researching, then the county, and then look for the E.D. number you found on the Soundex card. This will determine the census microfilm roll number.

The complete roll number will contain the *T* and the roll number (for example, T625-312). Record this information on your Research Calendar, along with the name you are researching. Now you can obtain the census microfilm roll from the cabinet and load the film on the microfilm reader.

After the microfilm is loaded, make sure you are in the right state and county. If the E.D. you need is not at the beginning of the roll, turn the film until it shows up in the upper right corner of the page. Once you're in the right E.D., keep turning until the sheet number you need is in the upper right corner of the page. Once the sheet is located, look down the left side of the page for the line number found on the Soundex card, and your ancestors should be right there.

Most of the information will already be known from the Soundex card. However, the additional information will reveal if the head of household owned the home or rented it, if members were married or single, citizenship status, if children attended school, if persons could read and write, the states of birth of every member's mother and father, as well as the native language they spoke, their occupation and industry, if each was an employee or employer, and if they were on a farm schedule. However, the majority of the farm schedules no longer exist.

In addition to this personal information, you will see the neighbors and their personal information. You won't see all the neighbors, though, only the ones living on the same side of the street as your ancestor. You'll have to go forward or backward to pick up neighbors on the other side of the street. But it will give you an idea if the block was all African American, predominantly white, or a mixed-race community. If your ancestor was in an institution, such as a hospital, prison, school, or military service, you will be able to recognize it right away because all the other patients, inmates, students, or servicemen will be there together. Census records for these institutions are sometimes placed at the end of the enumeration section, not in the actual location in the community.

Burroughs Family on the Census

When I went from the Soundex to the census, I obtained additional information for the Burroughs household. It indicated Granddad rented his apartment at 627 Bowen Avenue and two other African American families lived in the building. In fact, everyone on his side of the street was African American except one white couple who were sixty-one and fifty-eight years old. They were undoubtedly the last whites on the block, who had not moved out after the neighborhood changed.

The census indicated that both Morris and Alma could read and write and both were born in Illinois. Both things are correct. However, when I read the next columns, I began to wonder whether the enumerator really spoke to someone in the household. The census listed Granddad's mother and father as being from Alabama. That contradicts numerous pieces of evidence I've collected saying his father was from Spartanburg, South Carolina, and his mother from Chattanooga, Tennessee. The census page listed Grandma's mother and father as from Tennessee. Grandma's mother was from Tennessee, but her father was from Missouri, which she told me many times. I substantiated her stories by obtaining his death certificate and census records, all indicating Missouri. So we really have to question the reliability of places of birth of parents on census records. Too many genealogists put faith in them and start researching those states based on this thin evidence.

Usually we're so excited about finding our ancestors, we don't even realize there were other people on the block. In fact, you'd be wise to look at everyone on the block because they probably knew your ancestors. You also might find other ancestors who lived on the block, around the corner, or down the road.

ROBERT BURROUGHS—Once we turn to Granddad's brother, Robert Burroughs, we get a different picture. If you recall, Robert and his buddies robbed Illinois Tool Works of $5,700 in 1917. When I located him on the Soundex, he was on an individual Soundex card as opposed to a family card like the one for his brother. An individual card shows whom the individual is enumerated with and what his or her relationship is to the person or institution enumerated with.

Robert is listed as an inmate in Illinois State Penitentiary in Joliet, Illinois. The census sheet shows all the other inmates incarcerated along with him. It shows him as a thirty-year-old married man. His parents are correctly listed as being born in South Carolina and Tennessee, and his occupation is listed as chauffeur. Since the census enumerator had a captive audience, Robert definitely talked with him directly.

PRESTON BROOKS—Let's look at the profile of my maternal grandparents from Pennsylvania, Preston Clyde Brooks and Lydia Rae (Terrell) Brooks, at the time of the 1920 census. I obtained death certificates, a marriage license, and a marriage application for them. No birth

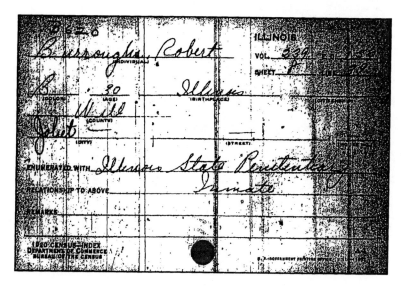

Robert Burroughs's Soundex Card—Copy of 1920 Soundex card for Robert Burroughs, living in the Illinois State Penitentiary in Joliet, Illinois.

Robert Burroughs on Census Schedule—Copy of 1920 U. S. Census Population Schedule for the Illinois State Penitentiary in Joliet Township, Illinois, which lists inmate Robert Burroughs on line 39.

certificates were located for either, but I determined the date and place of birth for Preston through his father's military pension application from the National Archives. Preston Sr. was a Buffalo Soldier stationed at Fort Riley, Kansas, from 1882 to 1885. He would have supplied the information about his son when he applied for a pension in 1891, and therefore the information is judged highly reliable.

Preston and Lydia's first child, Margaret Ann Brooks, was born in Pittsburgh on November 6, 1919. This was verified through oral interviews, as well as her birth certificate, death certificate, and Social Security application. Therefore, in 1920 Preston and Lydia should have been living in Pittsburgh, Pennsylvania, with a two-month-old daughter.

PROFILE

Preston Clyde Brooks

Born	4 June 1882	Fort Riley, KS
Married	6 November 1918	Elizabeth, PA
Died	13 August 1954	Pittsburgh, PA
1920—38 years old		

Wife—Lydia Rae Brooks

Born	7 August 1891	Fayette City, PA
Died	10 October 1964	Chicago, IL
1920—29 years old		

Child—Margaret Ann Brooks

Born	6 November 1919	Pittsburgh, PA
1920—2 months old		

The Soundex code for Brooks is B620. The last *s* is crossed out because it is next to the *k* on the Soundex guide. There are no more letters, so we add a zero.

Line 1   Brooks   r = 6, k = 2
Line 2   B620

However, we see B620 is split on five rolls because there are too many names for one roll.

58.   B616 E. Annabeil—B620 Cyprizian
59.   B620 D.—B620 Irwin S.
60.   B620 Isaac—B620 Martin
61.   B620 Mary—B620 Vulkert
62.   B620 W.A.—B622 Otto G.

The Soundex codes represent the last names, and opposite them are first names in alphabetical order. So Preston, being head of household, would be on roll 61.

I located three men named Preston Brooks in Pennsylvania in the 1920 Soundex. None of them appeared to be the one I was looking for. None was with a wife named Lydia and a two-month-old daughter named Margaret. The first was living in Pittsburgh at 636 Watt Street, but he was living alone and was born in Arkansas, not Kansas. This Preston was thirty-five years old, and my grandfather was thirty-eight. Only three years off isn't too bad.

The Soundex card with Preston Brooks's name is an individual card like the one Robert Burroughs is on. Preston is listed as a lodger, which means a person who rents a room but eats on his own. You'll often see people living with a family listed as boarders. These are people who are supposedly not related but rent and eat there. It was very common for people to rent out rooms and others to have room and board.

The second Preston Brooks found on the 1920 Soundex was living in Chester, Pennsylvania, clear across the state. He was forty-nine years old, born in Georgia, and the wife and children didn't match. The

Preston Brooks's Soundex Card—Copy of 1920 Soundex card for Preston Brooks, lodging in the residence of Flora Ader in Pittsburgh, Pennsylvania.

third Preston Brooks was white. That didn't throw me because I've found ancestors listed both ways on records, depending on their complexion. However, this Preston Brooks was living in Fayette County, and his wife and kids didn't match either.

I didn't think my Preston Brooks was on the 1920 census until I reviewed other research I'd done on him. When I checked his file, I realized the research I'd done in the Pittsburgh city directories listed him in 1920.

1948	Brooks, Preston	2948 Webster
1941	Brooks, Preston	2917 Orbin
1937	Brooks, Preston	920 Anahiem
1935	Brooks, Preston	512 Junilla

1931	Brooks, Preston	621 Conkling
1927	Brooks, Preston	621 Conkling
1924	Brooks, Preston	621 Conkling
1920	Brooks, Preston	636 Watt
1918	Brooks, Preston	none
1915	Brooks, Preston	none

I realized I had an exact address where he should be listed on the 1920 census. It was 636 Watt Street, the first one I found in the Soundex. Of course, there could have been two in Pittsburgh and I'd have to look at the census to see if this was indeed my grandfather.

Preston Brooks on Census Schedule—Copy of 1920 U. S. Census Population Schedule for Pittsburgh, Pennsylvania, listing Preston Brooks with his wife, Lida (Lydia), daughter, Margaret, and other people in their building.

When I discussed this with my aunt Doris, Preston's other daughter, she almost screamed. She remembered the apartment building at 636 Watt Street and she knew Flora Ader, the landlady who owned the building. Aunt Doris said her family lived upstairs and Flora Ader lived on the first floor and also ran a candy store. My aunt and her sister attended Watt School across the street and would buy pickles in the candy store after school. She said they were the best pickles she'd ever eaten. Aunt Doris said she hadn't thought about Mrs. Ader since she was a kid.

When I finally saw the actual census page, I realized this Preston was definitely my grandfather. I scrolled down the page and saw Grandma listed under her nickname, Lida, and their two-month-old baby, Margaret, listed with her age as 2½. However, they were both listed as lodgers, just as Preston was. For some reason the census enumerator listed the landlady as the head of household and everyone in the apartment building as lodgers.

This verifies the Brookses were not home when the census taker came knocking on the door. The three years' age difference is the first tipoff. A young man of thirty-eight doesn't miss his age by three years. Preston definitely would have told the enumerator he had a wife and baby. The Arkansas place of birth was undoubtedly an estimate when the landlady probably heard him say he was born out west. Ironically, Kansas is part of the name Arkansas.

Record the Information and Make Photocopies

After you get over the excitement, there are several things you should do. First, record all the information for your ancestors just as you see it on the microfilm. Again, this is best done by using a census extract form, which has preprinted columns and rows.

Next, photocopy the census page if the library or archive has a microfilm printer. Your extract will have information on your family, and the photocopy will get everyone on the page. It's always good to have a photocopy because months and years later you might discover something new, or additional research might make insignificant information significant.

Sometimes you will not be able to photocopy the entire census page on one sheet of paper. It's important to copy the heading, which gives the state, the date the census was taken, and the sheet and enumeration district number. Those are very important for locating the page again, as well as documenting your Family Group Sheets. Also, if your family is at the bottom of a page and split between two pages, make a couple of photocopies. If you can get the entire page on one sheet of paper, fine. But you can also roll the film a bit so you get the bottom of one page and the top of the other on the same photocopy.

Be sure to record key information on the back of the photocopy (microfilm *T* number and roll number, census state and year, county, township, town or city, E.D. number, sheet and line number, name of ancestor on census, the day's date, name and location of repository).

BACK OF PHOTOCOPY

T625-61—1920 U.S. Census, Pennsylvania
Allegheny County, Pittsburgh
Preston Brooks
E.D. 27, Sheet 8, Line 54
May 30, 1992
National Archives, Great Lakes Region—Chicago

Some of this information will appear to be redundant because it is on the front of the photocopy. However, you will record most of this information on your Family Group Sheet as your source documentation.

Census Research Follow-up

Once you locate your ancestors on the census, there are some follow-up chores to keep you on track.

1. If the photocopies you made are on fragile facsimile-type paper, it will tend to smudge and fade. To preserve it longer, photocopy it onto regular paper or sheets of acid-free paper.
2. Check the back of each photocopied sheet to ensure the source documentation is recorded.
3. Check to see your Research Calendar is up to date. It should have the following information:
   a. Date research was conducted.
   b. Location (e.g., National Archives—Chicago).
   c. A list of each source searched, such as:
      (1) 1920 Soundex—state, surnames
      (2) 1920 Census—state, surnames
      (3) 1910 Soundex—state, surnames
      (4) 1910 Census—state, surnames
   d. Microfilm roll number of each film you viewed.
   e. If you found something, number the census record copies consecutively.
   f. If you did not find something, list *nil* or *none*.
   g. If you did not finish searching, note where you stopped.
4. Make notes on what went right and what went wrong. Then your next trip might be more successful. Place these into your National Archives file or a census file.
5. Fill out your Research To Do form with items like:
   a. Where to continue researching the census or Soundex.
   b. Notes to recheck any census or Soundex.

c.   Notes to research the next census in order. For example, if you researched the 1920 Soundex and census, make a note to research the 1910 Soundex.

d.   Notes to check other sources, such as relatives, vital records, cemeteries, etc.

6.   If you found new names of ancestors, new dates of birth, or new places of birth on the census records, update your Family Group Sheet and Pedigree Charts, footnoting the 1920 census as your source. Never footnote the Soundex because it is only the index, not the original record. A proper census footnote citation will read like this:

> [1]Morris Burroughs household, 1920 U.S. Census, Cook County, Illinois, Population Schedule, City of Chicago, Ed. 138, Sheet 2, Line 19, dwelling 627, family 27; National Archives microfilm T625, roll 312.

7.   Start new acid-free file folders for any new ancestors you found.

8.   Start a file on "Census Research," including notes, guides, brochures and other materials on researching census records and/ or using the National Archives. Do not mix these notes and papers with notes and documents about your ancestors.

9.   Talk to your relatives and inform them of your findings. Have your notepad and pencil (and tape recorder) ready. They may tell you something about these ancestors they hadn't mentioned previously. Write this information up as a separate interview.

It's OK to proceed from the 1920 to the 1910 and 1900 census if you're successful. However, I wouldn't recommend going beyond that twenty-year time span. There are many more records to search, and the family could have moved or changed dramatically. Many genealogists get excited when using census records, and rightly so. Genealogy is hard work, and to finally locate the names of your ancestors on old records is always exciting. However, census records are only one source. There are dozens, if not hundreds, of other records to search.

! Trap: Relying mainly on census research.

Research Calendar

File Number
Researcher *Tony Burroughs*
Surnames *Burroughs*

Date	Repository Call No.	Description of Sources	Doc. No.
5/26/92		National Archives – Great Lakes Region – Chicago	
	M1559-43 1920 Soundex – Illinois		
	B620 – Burroughs		
	Burroughs, Asa Morris		Nil
	Burroughs, Asa		Nil
	Burroughs, A.		Nil
	Burroughs, A. M.		Nil
	Burroughs, Ace		Nil
	M1559-45		
	Burroughs, Morris ✓		1
	Note! Return to research Census		
5/27/92		National Archives – Great Lakes Chicago	
	T625-312 1920 U.S. Census – Illinois		
	Cook County, Chicago, ED. 138, Sheet 2		
	Burroughs, Morris ✓		2
	Note! Search for Robert Burroughs on Soundex		

Research Calendar #7—Updated Research Calendar illustrating how to record census research at the National Archives.

Part III
Stepping into the Future

Electronic Genealogy: Computers and the Internet

As discussed in the chapter on organization, the nature of genealogical research means the more successful you are, the more names, dates, events, and data you'll uncover and collect. It doesn't take long for a family history project to become unwieldy with data. This happened to me in 1977 after only two years of research. I collected more information than I could process. I called it "information overload." Personal computers did not exist at the time. That experience gave me more respect for early genealogists. They succeeded without word processors, genealogy software programs, CD-ROMs of data, photocopy machines, fax machines, e-mail, and the Internet. Now electronic processing of genealogy data is almost required. We wouldn't even consider returning to the stone age.

The age of technology and electronics has affected genealogy in many ways. This will undoubtedly continue as long as technology evolves. However, the fundamentals of genealogy research will remain the same. Genealogists will still need to study history, understand genealogical records, search records, collect evidence, evaluate that evidence, verify sources, prove relationships, and construct pedigrees.

So that technology will not cloud these principles of genealogy, researchers must be firm in their understanding and learn how to use technology to their advantage, not let technology control their research. If you understand this from the beginning, you should not be confused or overwhelmed by technology.

In spite of the growth and popularity of genealogy resulting from the explosion of the Internet and other technologies, I have saved this chapter until now so you first get firmly grounded in the fundamental principles and sources of genealogy. Then and only then can you evaluate technology to see if it is helping or hindering your research. There are advantages as well as disadvantages to using electronic technology for genealogy research.

! Trap: Getting on-line too soon.

There are many things beginning genealogists can do on the Internet, but I do not advocate they search for genealogy records on the Internet or other electronic technologies. I hear of too many people going to the Internet to do genealogy research without a clue about what they are looking for. They're merely name surfing without understanding the genealogical process.

Mrs. Smith called one day because her daughter Portia had serious problems with a genealogy assignment in class. Portia's teacher recommended she go to the Internet to "search for her ancestors." Mrs. Smith was frustrated because she and Portia had spent hours on the Internet without results. I informed her that genealogy is not mysterious and is not solved by some magical technology. I suggested Portia write what she remembers about growing up and her experiences with her relatives, some of whom may have passed away. Then I suggested Portia interview her mom and dad, as well as her aunts, uncles, and grandparents to get their life stories. Then if Mrs. Smith could show Portia the names in the family Bible, explain the pictures in the photograph album, and take her to the cemetery to see where her ancestors are buried, she'll have done her genealogy. That's plenty for a class assignment, and none of that information is on the Internet.

Mrs. Smith was relieved and amazed because it all made sense. Portia felt good about it too and developed confidence where she had experienced nothing but frustration before. Unfortunately, Portia's teacher did not give the proper guidance to her students.

The steps we discussed in the beginning chapters—recording oral history, collecting family records, and visiting the family cemetery and funeral home—are not resources you'll likely find on the Internet.

So we start our family history research at home. After these resources are exhausted, there are ways in which electronic technology can assist our research. Below are twelve areas in which electronic technology can aid genealogy research:

- Typing notes, narratives, and correspondence
- Converting manual charts into electronic format
- Communicating with relatives and other genealogists
- Sharing research with relatives and other genealogists
- Searching library catalogues
- Buying genealogy books, software, and supplies
- Reading genealogy news
- Planning genealogy research trips
- Learning genealogy
- Studying history
- Searching for ancestors
- Writing family histories

I'll describe each of these, but because technology changes so rapidly, researchers will have to investigate each on their own to learn the latest technology in each area.

Computers

Personal computers (PCs) came into wide use in the early 1980s. Soon after, genealogists began using them to organize their research. Even though computers change every year, genealogists don't need to buy a new computer every year to do genealogy. If you need to buy a computer, a rule of thumb is to research the software program before you buy the computer. The program will indicate the computer hardware requirements needed to run the program. Then you'll know how much computer to buy, what features and additional equipment you'll need, and if your son's old computer will run the program you plan to buy. Pay attention to the minimum requirements and the recommended requirements. You should always purchase more memory and hard disk space than you need so you'll have room for growth.

Computers perform many genealogy tasks we do manually. Converting these records to digital format often improves efficiency. Before the advent of computers, most genealogists wrote longhand and later used typewriters. Because of the efficiency of computers, no one would think of using a typewriter now. Not only are corrections easier to make, but moving data from one document to another or from one program to another and even adding photos and graphics have become very easy with word processing software, which works like a sophisticated typewriter.

Writing the Family History

One of the best uses of the computer is to write your family history. If you're already typing oral interviews, biographies, and research notes into your computer, you're ahead of the game. Many of these notes can be adapted for the family history. Again, that's the benefit of the computer—once information is in, you don't have to reenter it.

Many genealogy computer programs that create genealogy charts have added the capability to transform the information you've entered into a family history or compiled genealogy. There are other companion programs that can read data in a genealogy software program and transform it into a family history or compiled genealogy.

Word Processing Software

Most computers come with word processing software preinstalled (like Word Perfect or Microsoft Word). It will probably be the most used program for your genealogy. You'll want to type your autobiography as you write it. You'll also want to transcribe tapes of oral interviews and type letters to relatives, researchers, libraries, archives, and county courthouses.

I recommend that whenever you take handwritten notes, transcribe them as soon as possible using your word processor. Then you have a permanent record, as well as several ways of searching for the transcription and searching for names, dates, or locations mentioned in any transcription. You can then easily copy those notes or pieces of them to add to other parts of your research, place in articles to publish, or send to other relatives or researchers. You'll also use your word processor to type research notes, narrative stories, biographies, and histories. I use mine practically every day.

Genealogy Software

Once you complete the research in this book, you'll have detailed information on your ancestors entered onto Family Group Sheets. These should be documented with footnotes indicating the sources where you found the information. In the 1980s genealogy software programs were developed that began managing this data electronically. With a genealogy software program, once you change a name, date, place, event, or relationship, every element of the program is automatically updated. You no longer have to change several different forms, charts, and notes and recalculate every relationship. Genealogy software programs also create Family Group Sheets, Pedigree Charts, and Descendant Charts for anyone in the database and know each relationship.

Naturally, this saves time and effort. However, there are downsides. Not all programs are the same, nor do all of them provide all the features you need as a researcher. You need experience doing the work manually first to judge the capabilities of a software program. One of the most important elements you should seek in a software program is the ability to document your research and footnote your sources as we learned to do in the chapter on Family Group Sheets. The computer program should do it better than you can do it manually. Unfortunately, many programs don't document sources as well as you've been doing it manually. So before you rush off and purchase the program advertised in the newspaper or your favorite catalogue, investigate how the program documents sources. Are there merely general spaces for notes, or does it link a specific source to every name, date, place, and event? The better programs do.

Another feature you should look for is the ability to record multiple and conflicting information. What if you find three different dates of birth for an ancestor? Will your program record those three dates for the same individual, along with where you found them? That's how you research. Or does the program force you to select a date and use only one, forgetting about the others? That doesn't help your research; it hinders it. In this case the program is not as good as recording the information manually. What if you have four names for an ancestor? Sometimes he is referred to by his given name, sometimes by a nickname, sometimes by his initials or even an alias. Does the program have the ability to record these names for the same individual as names, not miscellaneous notes?

These are the features of better programs. Not only will they record your research the way you do it, but they will also help you become a better genealogist. So don't rush out to buy the cheapest program, the most "popular" program, the easiest program, or the one that is the most fun to use. Spend some time investigating programs to get the best one. Look for quality. You can often buy a second program to do other things.

It is difficult to recommend a program because they change so often. The popular programs of today might be passé tomorrow. The best course of action is to look for software directories and unbiased reviews of programs in genealogy journals, magazines, newsletters, and computer publications. The main publications are *Genealogical Computing*, published by Ancestry, *NGS/SIG Newsletter*, published by the National Genealogical Society, and *The Computer Genealogist*, published by the New England Historic Genealogical Society (this publication, as of 2000, has been incorporated into *New England Ancestors*). You have the option of subscribing to these or reviewing back issues in the genealogy department at a library. Some programs have demo versions, and some can be seen at national genealogical conferences. Finally, talk to experienced genealogists who are familiar with different computer programs and visit genealogy computer discussion groups on the Internet.

Once you settle on a program, be sure to make frequent backups of your data and also store backup diskettes off-site (e.g., in a safe deposit box) in case of a fire. It's also a good idea not to destroy your original notes.

Going On-line

In the old days we used the telephone when we wanted to get in touch with friends, relatives, and other genealogists. In the real old days our ancestors kept in touch by visiting friends and relatives close by and wrote letters to those who lived in faraway places. Today many people communicate through the computer via electronic mail (e-mail).

Networking with Other Genealogists

The first genealogical society, the New England Historic Genealogical Society, was organized in 1847, but it wasn't until the 1960s and '70s that these groups started to proliferate around the country. One of the advantages of forming a society is the benefit of networking with other genealogists. Invariably, other genealogists have solved problems you're struggling with, researched the same state or county you need to research, or researched the same surname you're researching. Therefore some societies have new members stand up and recite the surnames they are researching and recite the states and counties they are researching. Then members can connect after the meeting. This is fine if the group is small. If the group is large, it could consume a large part of the meeting. So some societies started posting these names and locations on cork bulletin boards on the wall, where researchers could search for surnames and locations.

Some societies also printed this information in their newsletter along with brief questions from researchers looking for details on their ancestors, referred to as "queries." A query is a very simple question, such as "Does anyone know the whereabouts of Mrs. Jane Doe, wife of John, who lived in Any County, Alabama, between 1900 and 1950?" Then a member researching the same family could connect with the person who posted the query. Some societies also began publishing databases of surnames in "surname directories" in book form.

Once we entered the computer revolution in the 1980s, societies began to adapt the new technology to their research. One of the early uses was to digitize these cork bulletin boards, queries, and surname directories on what were called "electronic bulletin boards."

On an electronic bulletin board, someone has a central computer that stores all the data. Then everyone calls that computer with a telephone modem connected to their home computer to list the surnames and locations they are researching and also to see what surnames and locations other genealogists are researching. It is an electronic form of the bulletin board that genealogy societies used to post surnames and places that members were researching. Genealogists also post queries on the computer, which are read and answered electronically by other members. It is a new way of genealogical networking.

This revolutionized genealogy because researchers could reach larger and wider audiences, the computer could handle a much larger volume of names and places than anyone could manually, and everything was done electronically. Now instead of being confined to your local society of fifty members, you can network with thousands of genealogists across the country and around the world. Genealogists can quickly make valuable connections and save time and effort.

CHAT ROOMS—Another way genealogists can network with others is through a live electronic discussion. When researchers are connected by computer, you can have an electronic discussion group called a "chat." Chat rooms are discussion groups in which all participants can see the same words appear on their screen simultaneously. When one person types, everyone logged on can see the typing. So if one person asks a question, he or she can get several responses, just as in a discussion group. Chats started before the Internet but have become more popular because it.

AFRICAN AMERICAN GENEALOGY CHAT ON AOL—African American genealogists have a chat room discussion group on Tuesday evenings on America Online. Beginning and experienced African American genealogists discuss problems, answer questions, and relay information about lectures, books, and current events in genealogy and African American genealogy. You have to subscribe to America Online to participate.

Sharing Research

Digitizing genealogy data makes it easy to share research with family members and other researchers. When you meet new family members, it's easy to print a new chart to share with them, including only the relatives and ancestors you share in common. If you meet another computer genealogist who has a connection with one of your family lines, it's easier to have your genealogy program import the names into your computer rather than retype everything.

Even if you use different genealogy programs, most software can import and export data from one program to another. However, transporting information isn't always perfect. Sometimes the names, dates, and locations will transfer but not the notes and miscellaneous information. So make sure you read the manual and run a few tests before you do anything important. Also remember to check the source documentation of other genealogists before accepting their data as fact and especially before merging with your database. If their sources are not footnoted and the researcher can't tell you where the information came from, it's not going to help you very much. Import new records into a new file and examine data thoroughly before merging with your database. If you discover major errors, it may be a nightmare deleting the additional names from a merged database.

Mailing Lists or List Serves

One of the early uses of the Internet was another version of the electronic bulletin board called mailing lists or list serves. Whereas the original electronic bulletin boards were a system in which many people could connect to one computer, the Internet is a system in which all computers are connected to each other throughout the world.

An electronic mailing list is an efficient form of conferencing. Many people can contribute to a discussion, and thousands of others can participate or read everyone's else's comments. It is not live like a chat room; everyone receives e-mail messages once or twice a day. It's a good way to learn, either by passively reading comments or by asking questions. However, because there are no qualifications to participate or run a discussion, the quality of information can vary tremendously. The uninitiated cannot always tell who knows what they are talking about and who merely sounds authoritative. Also, some discussions veer off from the topic, wasting everyone's time. The volume of daily e-mail from some groups is so large it takes a great deal of time to keep up every day.

If you'd like to try one, the Afrigeneas Mailing List is the discussion group for African American genealogy. It's an automated system, so to subscribe, send an e-mail message to majordomo@msstate.edu, typing only the words "subscribe afrigeneas" in the body of the text. If you don't want to receive hordes of individual messages but prefer them combined into one e-mail message, type "subscribe afrigeneas-digest" in the body of the text. Both subscription methods will give directions on how to cancel the subscription.

Genealogy News

Several free newsletters are published on the Internet through e-mail to keep you informed about what's going on in genealogy. They discuss conferences, lectures, new products, how-to articles, and current events in genealogy. Two good ones are *Ancestry Daily News* by Ancestry.com and *Eastman's Online Genealogy Newsletter*, published weekly by Dick Eastman. Once you forward an e-mail message subscription, the newsletter comes automatically on a regular basis.

To subscribe to *Ancestry Daily News,* visit http://www.ancestry.com/whatsnew.htm and type your e-mail address in the box provided, or send an e-mail message to ancestry_daily_news@ anclist001.ancestry.com with the word "Subscribe" on the subject line.

Current and past issues of *Eastman's Online Genealogy Newsletter* can be read at http://www.ancestry.com/columns/eastman/index.htm. To subscribe, visit http://rootscomputing.listbot.com.

Buying Books, Software, and Supplies On-line

Many suppliers who sell genealogy books, software, preservation supplies, and historical books have Web sites. You can safely purchase items over the Internet using a credit card and have them delivered overnight. There are also software programs that are free, shareware, or inexpensive that can be downloaded to your home computer.

Searching Library Catalogues

As you study genealogy, attend lectures and classes, and talk with other genealogists, you will run across titles of books and periodical articles you'd like to read. You can visit your local library and see if it has the book or periodical, but what if you get a hot idea at midnight, when the library is closed? Or what if it's snowing outside and you don't want to put on your boots and shovel the snow to get to your car?

In many instances you can turn on your computer and check the library's card catalogue from the Internet. More and more libraries are putting their card catalogues on the Internet so patrons can search authors, titles, and bibliographic citations from the comfort of their home or office. The content of the books is not on the Internet, just the card catalogues. This saves you time and effort, of course, but you may also discover the rare book you want is in only one of six libraries in your area. Wouldn't it be nice to know this in advance instead of going to the library, only to discover the book's not there and you have to go to another library?

If you plan on visiting a major genealogy library in a different city, searching the card catalogue before you depart will make your trip more efficient. In addition, if you plan to visit a city where your ancestors lived, it's a good idea to visit the public and academic libraries in the same area. It's wise to search the Internet for these libraries in advance. Most public libraries, college and university libraries, genealogy libraries, historical society libraries, and manuscript archives have card catalogues on their Web sites. Tom Kemp's *Virtual Roots* (listed under "Electronic Genealogy" in the Bibliography) lists many library Web sites by state. The following are a few sites for major genealogy collections:

National Genealogical Society Catalogue
    http://www.ngsgenealogy.org
Family History Library Catalogue (Salt Lake City)
    http://www.familysearch.org/Search/searchcatalog.asp
New England Historic Genealogical Society Catalogue (Boston)
    http://www.NewEnglandAncestors.org/researchsection/libsearch.asp?search=yes
Allen County, Indiana, Public Library Catalogue (Fort Wayne)
    http://catalog.acpl.lib.in.us/uhtbin/webcat

Newberry Library Catalogue (Chicago)
   http://www.newberry.org/vtls/english/vtls.html
"Guide to Federal Records in the National Archives of the United States"
   http://www.nara.gov/guide
Library of Congress Card Catalogue (Washington, D.C.)
   http://lcweb.loc.gov/catalog/

Remember those difficult searches only reference librarians can do (see pages 303–04) called OCLC? Computer access to the same database is now available in many libraries from patron access computers called "WorldCat from FirstSearch." Your library may also allow you access from your home computer. Check with your reference librarian and listen to Delia Cothrum Bourne's lecture "Bibliographic Sources for Genealogists Starring WorldCat from FirstSearch." (See "Computers and the Internet" in the Bibliography.)

Planning Genealogical Research Trips

Whenever I plan a research trip out of town, in addition to checking library card catalogues, I check the Internet for weather reports, maps, points of interest, and upcoming events. I sometimes surf the net for airfares but sometimes good travel agents and airlines are much more efficient than I am in determining the best travel arrangements. There are always some airlines, airfares, and connections you'd never know about.

I frequently use e-mail when preparing for trips. It's much cheaper than making many long-distance telephone calls. If I know other relatives or genealogists in the area with e-mail, I'll usually drop them a message in advance. E-mail is also good for contacting librarians so you have a contact person before arriving to research. On a recent trip I e-mailed the reference librarian and learned I needed written permission from an estate before photocopying records in a manuscript collection.

Learning Genealogy

There are several classes on the Internet for learning more about genealogy.

Ancestry Academy
   http://www.ancestry.com/lessons/academy.htm
Bellevue Community College
   http://www.conted.bcc.ctc.edu/users/marends/outline.htm
Family Tree Maker
   http://www.familytreemaker.com/university.html
National Genealogical Society
   http://www.ngsgenealogy.org/
   "Introduction to Genealogy: An Online Course"
   Information for home study course, "American Genealogy: A Basic Course"

Studying History

There are many opportunities for studying history on the Internet and on CD-ROM. Most colleges and universities have Web sites, and history departments are continually uploading articles, documents, and discussions. In addition, many historical societies, archives, museums, libraries, newspapers, independent scholars, and history buffs have great sites with historical material. Many historical documents are in the public domain, so researchers are busy placing them on the Web. I encourage you to surf to your heart's content but with my regular caveat. Be sure to look for source citations. Many amateurs transcribe historical documents without citing where the documents came from, and sometimes they do a poor job of transcribing.

CD-ROMs (discussed below) have become a great medium for studying history because of their large storage capacity. Many encyclopedia publishers create CD-ROM versions of their published volumes. Harvard University and Microsoft created the Encarta Africana on CD-ROM, which is a great resource for African American history. However, some CD-ROM encyclopedias are abbreviations of the published versions and lean heavily on photos, sound animation, and video. They are good for starters, but remember the rich historical resources in the "Going to the Library" chapter.

Searching for Ancestors Electronically

The technological revolution has greatly affected the way genealogists search for their ancestors. Currently there are two major sources of electronic data (subject to change in the future, of course). Information can be gathered directly into your computer via the Internet or supplied on a CD-ROM disk.

I'm hoping you aren't reading this section first, but if you are, I'm not surprised. The popularity of the Internet has resulted in a new popularity in searching for ancestors on-line. Unfortunately, many researchers' first introduction to genealogy is from the Internet. The Internet adds many search capabilities that didn't exist in the past, but genealogists also need to be aware of its many weaknesses and minefields.

In spite of the vast resources and richness of the Internet, everything needed for genealogy is not on the Internet and may never be on it. There are more resources in a good genealogical library. Think about the Internet as another tool to supplement your research, not the only tool you use for research.

The Internet is unregulated, and anyone can create a Web site publishing whatever information he or she wants. Just because a site looks very fancy and very official, that doesn't mean the information is true, accurate, complete, or up to date. There are many poor-quality sites full of errors, inaccuracies, and misinformation. Statements, charts, and databases on some genealogy Web sites do not document the source of the information so you can check the accuracy. Many sites are merely links to other sites, sending you in circles. You can waste a lot of time on the Internet, so surf with a purpose. Have a goal in mind and know how to evaluate Web sites before you arrive.

I wish genealogists could use the Internet only in genealogical libraries. Then they could follow up on the indexes they find and go to the original source to verify information and obtain greater detail. Surfing in a good genealogical library would have the additional benefit of seeking expert consultation from good reference librarians. Since that will probably not happen, I've listed several articles published on the Web that discuss evaluating the quality of Web sites. Then I list genealogical standards developed by the National Genealogical Society and the Genealogical Web Site Watchdog. If you begin by surfing these sites, you'll be well armed before pursuing the onslaught of information.

Electronic Documentation

When you search electronic sources, you still need to maintain your Research Calendar, recording positive and negative searches of each source you search. When you print pages from the Internet, CD-ROMs, or e-mail, you still need to document the source as you did for books and microfilm photocopies. Even though many Web browsers and e-mail programs print Web addresses on printouts, I recommend using Elizabeth Shown Mills's *Evidence: Citation and Analysis for the Family Historian* as your documentation guide. Most electronic sources are not original primary records, although some are electronic images of original records. Therefore they should be used as a guide to locate original records or photocopies of original records and to footnote Family Group Sheets and family histories.

Web Sites

Below are a few Web sites that may be of interest to beginners in African American genealogy. There are thousands of other sites, so I encourage you to search on your own. Keep in mind that Web addresses (URLs) change often, so these may not be current. Also, the Internet is unorganized, whereas a library enables you to easily search by clearly defined subjects. I suggest you search by themes of records or methods and avoid the indiscriminate shotgun approach of name surfing.

WEB SITE QUALITY—

"Evaluating Quality on the 'Net," by Hope Tillman, Babson College
http://www.tiac.net/users/hope/findqual.html

"Evaluating Internet Resources," by Medical Radiography (Massachusetts General Hospital)
http://web.wn.net/~usr/ricter/web/valid.html

"How to Critically Analyze Information Sources," by Cornell University Library
http://www. library.cornell.edu/okurerf/research/skill26.htm

"Information Quality WWW Virtual Library," by T. Matthew Ciolek, Australian National University
http://coombs.anu.edu.au/WWWVL-InfoQuality.html

"Internet Source Validation Project," by Faculty of Education at Newfoundland's Memorial University
http://www.stemnet.nf.ca/Curriculum/Validate/ratings.html

"Resource Selection and Information Evaluation," by Lisa Janicke Hinchliffe, Parkland College
http://alexia.lis.uiuc.edu/~janicke/Eval.html

Yahoo category on evaluating Internet resources
http://www.yahoo.com/Computers_and_Internet/Internet/World_Wide_Web/ Information_and_Documentation/Evaluation

GENEALOGY STANDARDS—

National Genealogical Society
   http://www.ngsgenealogy.org/
   Guidelines for Publishing Web Pages on the Internet
   Standards for Sharing Information with Others
   Standards for Sound Genealogical Research (also at
   http://www.genealogy.org/~ngs/standsgr.html)
   Standards for Using Records Repositories and Libraries
   Standards for Use of Technology in Genealogical Research
Genealogical Web Site Watchdog—Members of the Association of Professional Genealogists and the Board of Certification of Genealogists review genealogical Web sites for misinformation.
   http://www.ancestordetective.com/watchdog.htm
The Genealogical Software Report Card
   A guide for selecting genealogy software programs.
   http://www.mumford.ab.ca/reportcard/index.html

ORAL HISTORIES—

Interview Questions—http://www.rootsweb.com/~genepool/oralhist.htm

Tips—http://www.lib.berkeley.edu/BANC/ROHO/rohotips.html

One Minute Guide—http://www.lib.berkeley.edu/BANC/ROHO/1minute.html

CEMETERY RECORDS—

African American cemetery records
   http://www.prairiebluff.com/millenium/aacemetery/

African American Cemeteries in Orange County, Indiana
   Lick Creek Settlement Cemetery, also known as Little Africa Cemetery
   http://www.rootsweb.com/~orange/lcsettlement.htm

Knights of Pythias Cemetery
http://www.rootsweb.com/~orange/kop.htm

Newberry Cemetery (has "Colored" section)
http://www.rootsweb.com/~orange/newberry.htm#colored

US Genweb Tombstone Transcription Project
http://www.rootsweb.com/~cemetery

Cemetery Junction
http://www.dadezio.com/cemetery/index.html

VITAL RECORDS—Most state and county vital records offices and boards of health receive significant income from selling vital records. They are not in the business of giving them away or incurring the tremendous expense of placing them on the Internet. However, isolated states and counties have placed limited records and indexes on the Internet. Keep in mind many of these records and indexes are not complete and if you do not find your ancestor, apply to the vital records office.

U.S. Department of Health and Human Services—National Center for Health Statistics,
"Where to Write for Vital Records" (Washington: U.S. Government Printing Office, 1990)
http://www.medaccess.com/address/vital_toc.htm

THE CALIFORNIA DEPARTMENT OF HEALTH SERVICES
California Births 1905–1995
http://userdb.rootsweb.com/ca/birth/search.cgi

California Deaths 1940–1997
http://userdb.rootsweb.com/ca/death/search.cgi

ILLINOIS STATE ARCHIVES
Illinois Marriages, 1763–1900
http://www.sos.state.il.us/depts/archives/marriage.html

INDIANA STATE LIBRARY
The Indiana State Marriage Index up to 1850
http://www.statelib.lib.in.us/www/indiana/genealogy/mirr.html

MAINE STATE ARCHIVES
Marriage Indexes 1892–1966 and 1976–1996
http://thor.ddp.state.me.us/archives/plsql/archdev.Marriage_Archive.search_form

Death Indexes 1960–1996
http://thor.ddp.state.me.us/archives/plsql/archdev.death_archive.search_form

MICHIGAN DEPARTMENT OF PUBLIC HEALTH
Death Records 1867–1882
http://www.mdch.state.mi.us/PHA/OSR/gendis/search.htm

OHIO HISTORICAL SOCIETY
Ohio Death Certificate Index, 1913–1937
http://www.ohiohistory.org/dindex/

TENNESSEE STATE LIBRARY
Partial Index to Deaths 1914–1925
http://www.state.tn.us/sos/statelib/pubsvs/death.htm

TEXAS DEPARTMENT OF HEALTH
Births 1926–1949
http://userdb.rootsweb.com/tx/birth/general/search.cgi

Births 1950–1995
http://userdb.rootsweb.com/tx/birth/summary/search.cgi

Deaths 1964–1995
http://userdb.rootsweb.com/tx/death/search.cgi

Marriages 1966–1997
http://userdb.rootsweb.com/tx/marriage/search.cgi

Divorces 1968–1997
http://userdb.rootsweb.com/tx/divorce/

UNIVERSITY OF KENTUCKY
Kentucky Death Index, 1911–1992

Kentucky Marriage Index 1973–1993

Kentucky Divorce Index 1973–1993

http://ukcc.edu/~vitalrec/

HILLSBORO COUNTY, FLORIDA
Marriage Records 1878–1884
http://www.lib.usf.edu/spccoll/gene.html

OBITUARIES—

African American obituaries—Christine's Genealogy Web site
http://ccharity.com/cgi-local/aagenealogy/Obituaries/

"Obituaries for African Americans," by Tony Burroughs, Family Tree Maker On-line, February 5, 1997
http://www.familytreemaker.com/12_obits

PUBLISHED SOURCES—

Black Biographies—fee-based Web version of Chadwyck-Healey's published volumes of *Black Biographical Dictionaries 1790–1950*
http://aabd.chadwyck.com/

PERSI—Periodical Source Index
http://www.ancestry.com

QUERIES—

Afrigeneas Surname Database
http://members.aol.com/afrimgene/surnames/

Roots Surname List Name Finder
http://searches.rootsweb.com/cgi-bin/Genea/rsl

Usenet Newsgroups (like bulletin boards)
soc.genealogy.african

SOCIAL SECURITY—

Social Security Administration
http://www.ssa.gov/

Social Security History
http://www.ssa.gov/history/brief.html

Social Security Numbers by Geographic Region
http://www.ssa.gov/history/geonumb.html

SOCIAL SECURITY DEATH INDEX—

Ancestry.com	http://ancestry.com/search/rectype/ vital/ssdi/main.htm
Everton	http://www.everton.com
Family Tree Maker	http://www.familytreemaker.com/ fto_ssdisearch.html
My Trees.com	http://www.mytrees.com/cgi-bin/ genealogy/navf?-1+0+S+English
Ultimate Family Tree	http://www.uftree.com/UFT/Nav/ familytracersearch.html

MAPS AND GEOGRAPHIC INFORMATION—In addition to the Web sites listed below, many geography departments of colleges and universities have Web sites displaying maps, gazetteers, and other geographical information.

U.S. Geological Survey
http://mapping.usgs.gov

United States Geographic Names Information System
http://mapping.usgs.gov/www/gnis/gnisform.html

Map Quest
http://www.mapquest.com

Getty Thesaurus of Geographic Names
http://www.gii.getty.edu/tgn_browser

U.S. Census Bureau Gazetteer
http://www.census.gov/cgi-bin/gazetteer

CENSUS RECORDS—As of 1999, the National Archives had 120,000 documents on-line. That may seem like a lot, but they have 4 *billion* pages of records in their holdings. That's one page on the Internet for every 34,000 documents in the collection! At seven dollars a page to digitize records, one regional administrator said the National Archives doesn't plan on digitizing very many records, and that includes census records. The National Archives Web site states, "Because of the sheer size of our holdings, it will be many years before electronic access to a significant portion of our genealogical records is possible." The National Archives has estimated the cost of digitizing the 1930 census to place on the Internet would be $30 million. Therefore they have no plans on putting it or any other census records on-line. However, in 2000 both Heritage Quest (www.HeritageQuest.com) and Ancestry.com announced plans to put the entire census population schedules from 1790–1930 on-line.

Most census records on the Internet are indexes and transcriptions, not images of original population schedules. Other than small samples of selected counties, most of these are not for 1920, 1910, or 1900 census records. One site, GenealogyLibrary.com, has over 200,000 images of actual census population schedules for selected states on the Internet. However, they are very early records, not useful for beginners and with little use for African Americans. They are images from the 1850 U.S. Census, which does not give names of slaves.

There are also sites that generate Soundex codes after you enter a surname. Be careful in using these sites. Some use different coding rules without stating the rules they use. Therefore some generate different codes for the same name.

Genealogy at the National Archives
http://www.nara.gov/genealogy/geindex.html

The Federal Population Censuses—Catalogs of National Archives Microfilm
http://www.nara.gov/publications/microfilm/census/census.html

US Genweb Archives Census Project
http://www.usgenweb.com/census/

"Census Schedules and Black Genealogical Research: One Family's Experience,"
  by Debbie Hollis
http://www.colorado.edu/libraries/govpubs/debbie/cover.htm

U.S. Census Bureau
http://www.census.gov

AFRICAN AMERICAN GENEALOGY WEB SITES—Several African American genealogical societies have Web pages that list addresses, membership information, activities, and officers. Consult the appendixes for their names and addresses. There are many sites that cover African American history and culture. They can easily be found using search engines and Internet guides. Below are a few Web sites that concentrate on African American genealogy. They typically have articles, news, transcribed records, surname registries, and links to other African American sites. Many topics and links will be on more advanced topics and records, which may be frustrating until you complete beginning and intermediate research.

Afrigeneas
www.afrigeneas.com

Afrigeneas News
www.afrigeneas.com/news.html

Christine's Genealogy Web site
www.ccharity.com

Lest We Forget
http://www.coax.net/people/lwf/data.htm

Major Sites

There are a few genealogy Web sites with large searchable databases, extensive records, or large numbers of links that get thousands of visitors a day.

Family History Library
http://www.familysearch.org

The biggest genealogy phenomenon to hit the Internet lately has been the Mormons' Family History Library Web site. In May 1999, the first week the site was launched, 400,000 users per day logged on and delivered up to 40 million hits a day! Another 60 million hits couldn't get through. The site immediately catapulted into the top ten Web sites on the Internet.

The three main features on the Web site are the library catalogue and two databases, the International Genealogical Index (IGI) and the Ancestral File. The IGI consists of names extracted from births, christenings, and marriages by church volunteers. The Ancestral File consists of names contributed by genealogists, linked in family groups and pedigrees. Read *Understanding Genealogy in the Computer Age: Family Search,* by Elizabeth L. Nichols, to learn details about the computerized IGI and Ancestral File (see "Electronic Genalogy" in the Bibliography).

Researchers used to using Family History Centers around the country are very excited about being able to access the catalogue, IGI, and Ancestral File from home. Many of the centers are small and have a waiting list to use the computers. Now this time can be spent at home and you can go to the center just to order and view microfilm.

Other features of the Family History Web site include a database of other genealogists' research (the quality of this data will vary by submitter), a guide to learning about genealogy resources (primarily found at the Family History Library), and links to other Web sites.

In spite of all the activity, this Web site doesn't have genealogy records on-line. Researchers still have to go to the Family History Library or one of its branch Family History Centers to order and research actual records on microfilm.

Ancestry.com
http://www.Ancestry.com

Ancestry.com began as a genealogical publishing company and then developed a Web site consisting of articles, maps, a search engine you can use to search their genealogy databases for your ancestors' names, and books and software for sale. The March 6, 1999, issue of *Eastman's Online Genealogy Newsletter* reported Ancestry. com was the most popular genealogy Web site, surpassing other genealogy sites with 953,000 total unique visitors during the month of January. Of course, that was before the Mormons launched their site, so Ancestry.com is now number two.

Ancestry.com says they have over 240 million names in 1,610 databases and are adding a database every day. They also have a free genealogy class in which you can learn about genealogy. Ancestry charges fees based on different packages but also has free databases and articles.

Family Tree Maker
http://www.familytreemaker.com

Family Tree Maker began as a genealogy software program and evolved into producing CD-ROMs with genealogical indexes and databases. They now have databases on their Web site in which you can search for your ancestors' names. They also have articles and free genealogy classes in which you can learn about genealogy and products. It is also a fee-based system with free areas.

Cyndi's List
http://www.CyndisList.com

Cyndi Howells began keeping a list of genealogy Web sites and realized other researchers could use her list. She put it on the Web, and it kept growing and growing until it became the largest list of genealogy Web sites on the Net. As of 2000 she had links to more than 70,000 other sites. Some researchers begin their searches with Cyndi's List.

You won't find genealogy records on Cyndi's List, only links to other Web sites. You may not find all the categories you're looking for, but she does have a category for African Americans (http://www.CyndisList.com/african.htm). Using the list is sometimes frustrating because some of the links are merely links to other links. Because she includes everything, not all sites have useful, accurate, complete, or updated information. So use Cyndi's List, but with caution.

USGenWeb

http://www.usgenweb.org/statelinkstable.html

To access state pages, then access county pages from state pages

USGenWeb began as an effort to seek a volunteer from each county in the United States to coordinate uploading indexes and transcriptions of records for their county. It quickly spread and is very popular among genealogists. You can search for your state and see if records are listed for your county. Not all counties have coordinators, and some have only a few records. Like most genealogy records on the Internet, most are older records that are in the public domain.

Some records are very exciting, thoroughly researched, and add sorting and searching capabilities lacking in published sources. Some even have digitized versions of original records. These truly enhance genealogy research. However, USGenWeb is another Web site lacking quality control. What you find varies with the quality of the genealogist who posted the information. Many links are to records that are undocumented or poorly documented. Always look for complete source citations that lead you to original records.

Internet Database Weaknesses

The quick and easy method of searching huge Internet databases is exciting if you find your ancestor's name. Some resources previously found only in libraries are now on-line. I've heard some great stories about family lines being extended several generations from links found on the Internet. I found one of my ancestors in an on-line database. It said his name appeared on a census index. I could purchase the index and scanned images from the census on a CD-ROM for $79.95. That might have been economical if I did not have ready access to the same material at my library, where I'd have to pay for only a couple of photocopies.

Internet databases have limitations. Searching most Internet databases relinquishes control from the genealogist to the Web site. The question becomes, What happens if you don't find your ancestor's name? Do you get a list of all the databases that were searched? If not, how will you know what index has your ancestor listed and which ones don't? What if you merely spelled a name wrong? What if the index in the database spelled your ancestor's name differently? What if the database included every state but your ancestor's state in the database? Which indexes include African Americans and which don't? There are an awful lot of questions you need answered to do intelligent research and track and analyze your sources.

Browsing

You don't get to browse a list of names in many search engines as you would in a book. If all you do is enter a name in a box and receive results back that your search was successful or unsuccessful, you lose the capability of browsing through a list of names. Browsing is a part of the valuable genealogical experience. It stimulates the mind, which does not happen when waiting for someone else (or some machine) to search a list for you. As your eyes gaze down a list of names, you may see spelling variations and realize the spelling you're used to might be a little different. By browsing you may find the name you're looking for but spelled differently.

By browsing you may see other names you've forgotten or didn't realize were in a location. It's often stimulating to browse for the names of other siblings, relatives, neighbors, and friends of the family. The point is, it's the *process* that's important, not just the results. The process of researching is a learning process, and as a result we become better genealogists. If someone else or some database does all the searching for you, you'll never learn to research on your own and therefore will not increase your research skills. In order to become a better genealogist, you must learn skills and techniques and build upon them for future research. Databases are beneficial after you have gained experience, researched all the records you can think of, and hit a brick wall. In this case a database might turn up something you've missed or something that would have been difficult to know, like an unexpected migration pattern.

Privacy

Many genealogists are now creating Web pages or putting their Pedigree Charts on the Web. This way genealogists who are researching the same ancestors can easily connect with one another. If you decide to put your ancestors on the Web, remember to be careful about living relatives. Your relatives reserve their right to privacy, so it's prudent to put only the names of deceased relatives on the Web. You also don't want unscrupulous people gaining women's maiden names, birth dates, and birthplaces.

CD-ROMs

Because of their large storage capacity and multimedia capability (pictures, sound, video, and text), CD-ROM disks have become very popular for delivering genealogical books, indexes, images, and databases. CD-ROMs are also inexpensive to produce and are widely distributed. Many companies are now publishing data directly on CD-ROM without first publishing in book form.

There are advantages and disadvantages for genealogists researching with CD-ROMs. They are inexpensive, convenient, easy to use, and store large amounts of information. This enables genealogists to do plenty of research at home, whereas just a few years ago they had to go to libraries, archives, and county courthouses for all their research.

The disadvantages of CD-ROMs are several. Many essential resources for genealogy are not on CD-ROM, some of which you should research before searching for data on CD-ROM. The content of many CD-ROMs is of poor quality, with no indication of the source of the records on the disk. When using electronic sources (or any sources, for that matter), it is important to determine the source of the records. Knowing where the information came from will help you determine the quality of the images, data, indexes, and transcriptions. The source of the data is not the CD-ROM; it only carries the information. You need to evaluate the information on the CD-ROM, just as you evaluate other books in the library. If the publisher of the CD-ROM does not indicate the source of the information or cite sources fully and properly, you're wasting your time and money using it.

Once you know the source, you can tell if you've searched that source before, which is indicated on your Research Calendar. You also need to record that you are searching a source on a CD-ROM.

Some CD-ROMs omit records in their category. I once looked at a CD-ROM of mortality records. When I didn't see any Burroughs on the entire disk, I became suspicious. Only after an inquiry to the developer did I learn the disk did not contain records from South Carolina.

Even worse, some CD-ROMs reproduce errors and omissions from the published works they are duplicating. If there are errors or omissions in a published book or database, transferring that work to a CD-ROM reproduces the errors and omissions.

Many unsuspecting genealogists are using CD-ROMs, unaware of the errors and omissions. In his chapter, "Censuses and Tax Lists," in *Printed Sources* (edited by Kory Meyerink), G. David Dilts does an excellent job explaining errors in early published census indexes and how these errors were copied onto CD-ROMs. Tests showed the CD-ROM census records from 1790 to 1850 have a 12.8 percent error or omission rate. This early period doesn't affect beginners who are using census records from 1900 to 1920, but it's important to understand potential problems with electronic sources. These same census records have now been transferred to the Internet, with the same errors and omissions.

Several records on CD-ROM were copied from published records that omitted African Americans. Unless there was a concerted effort to add them to the electronic record, African Americans do not appear on the CD-ROM version. Researchers need to investigate the source to see if there is any mention of African Americans, as well as test the CD-ROM by comparing it to original records.

These errors and omissions create problems because beginning researchers often use CD-ROM records to do their initial research and don't locate their ancestors. Then they look elsewhere instead of checking printed and original records.

Some companies encourage genealogists to submit their research to be included on a CD-ROM. This is good in theory because genealogists working on the same lines can connect with each other. However, most of the data on these CD-ROMs is undocumented research that is of little real value.

There are, nevertheless, some exciting products on CD-ROM. Heritage Quest has digitized images from U.S. Census records from National Archives microfilm for all years and states.

Each CD-ROM disk corresponds with a National Archives microfilm copy of the original population schedules. Now researchers can view these census records at home from their computer. An added benefit is higher-quality images than on the original microfilm because they have been digitally enhanced.

A companion product is CD-ROM indexes to census records, also by Heritage Quest. They claim their indexes have the lowest error rate in the industry. They capitalized on mistakes made by early indexing projects, and their published census indexes are very highly regarded. Their CD-ROM census indexes are outstanding because they take advantage of the power of the computer by allowing you to search by columns in census records, which you cannot do with any printed sources. For example, if you want a list of all the African American Trumans listed on the 1870 census in Fayette County, Pennsylvania, who were between twenty and forty years old and born in Maryland, it will create a list. This will revolutionize the way genealogy research is done.

Another exciting CD-ROM product is the Genealogical Library Master Catalogue, developed by Rick Crume at OneLibrary.com. It combines the titles of 300,000 family histories, local histories, and genealogical sources from eighteen major libraries with genealogical collections.

There are other useful CD-ROM disks. Consult genealogical vendors for catalogues and genealogical newsletters for reviews of CD-ROMs.

Printed Versus Electronic Records

Books have been around for hundreds of years. Printing began in China in 868, and the Gutenberg Bible was printed in 1456. The first printed genealogy was published in 1771, *The Genealogy of the Family of Mr. Samuel Stebbins, and Mrs. Hannah Stebbins, His Wife,* and still exists for genealogists to research. Kory Meyerink, editor of *Printed Sources,* estimates there are 90,000 genealogies and family histories in print. Microfilming genealogy records began in the late 1930s when the government began to microfilm census records for preservation. On the other hand, electronic genealogy data has been around only since the 1980s. So printed genealogies and family histories have been around for over two hundred years, microfilm about seventy years, and electronic records about twenty. Obviously the longevity of electronic data is yet to be known. This, coupled with the rapid rate of technological obsolescence, places electronic genealogy data at severe risk. It is hard to imagine that many computers manufactured in 2000 can't read data from software developed just twenty years ago.

Future Technologies

Like electronic bulletin boards, the Internet, and the World Wide Web, new technologies will continue to be invented in the future. Sometimes a new technology can assist our research, and sometimes it can hamper our research. We have to be as critical in judging technology as we are in judging genealogical sources of evidence. In spite of changes in technology, the principles of research will remain the same. If you remember this and always operate by principle, new technologies will not distract you with razzle-dazzle and hype. We must make the crucial decisions of when to use technology and when to override it with our instincts, infinite wisdom, analytical thinking, creativity, and common sense. We must not become slaves to technology and think it will answer all our questions. By always turning to computers to solve problems, we limit our ability to recognize other solutions. Clifford Stoll, author of *Silicon Snake Oil: Second Thoughts on the Information Highway,* said, "When the only tool you know is a hammer, everything looks like a nail."

The challenges of genealogy in the future will not be a lack of records. Quite the opposite, it will be too much data, which causes other problems, like "information overload." Solving that problem is learning how to get the right information efficiently.

I contend that genealogy is *not* easier with the Internet and will not be any easier in the future than it was in the past. Some resources are more convenient, but genealogy will still be challenging. Genealogy in the future will be very different. Researchers will have so many choices from such an abundance of records created from indexing, abstracting, publishing, microfilming, digitizing, the Internet, and future technologies that they will be overwhelmed with records and choices. Their work will double or triple. Even now the Internet is filled with information, but using it efficiently to find what you need is not what we call easy.

Electronic Research Versus Genealogy Research

No matter how much data they make available, electronic sources will never be able to replace genealogy research. Many genealogy sources are not available electronically and may never be available electronically. Electronic sources should supplement your research, not be your research.

Genealogy research requires human skills computers will never be able to duplicate. Computers will not be able to survey the research you've done, analyze the quality and thoroughness of your research, discover incorrect conclusions you've made, set priorities for future research, retrieve new data from non-digitized sources, tell you which records are not in the published inventories, or connect you with the experts in the country who are not on the Internet. Neither can computers analyze the results of your work, prepare a circumstantial evidence case, and then repeat this entire process at a higher level. Only a genealogist can do that. I use every bit of technology that exists, but I will always enjoy analyzing my research, consulting with other genealogists, traveling to new locations for research, leafing through exciting original documents, meeting new and interesting people, and traversing the ground my ancestors walked on.

Information Versus Knowledge and Intelligence

Unfortunately, too many people are buying the hype and being overwhelmed by the Internet and new technology. They do not solve all our problems. There is a big difference between information and knowledge. Information is merely a collection of data or facts that may be true or false. People often use words, phrases, and even records (i.e., information) without knowing what they are talking about.

CD-ROMs and the Internet will not solve your genealogy problems any more than walking into a library with thousands of books will solve your problems. The Internet is just an electronic room filled with information.

When you know something, you are aware of certain information and understand it, but not necessarily thoroughly. You can tell when the information is true or false. You can explain it from different perspectives and apply it to different situations, not merely regurgitate it as if memorized.

Intelligence is applying knowledge to solve problems. Problem solving is a human process involving problem recognition, analysis, hypothesis, application, and evaluation. Each step requires human intervention, skill, and ingenuity.

In genealogy this means understanding genealogy sources and methodology to locate sources, solve genealogical problems, and build a pedigree based on evidence that could stand up in a probate court or persuade a jury of genealogical peers (i.e., becoming a certified genealogist, being admitted to a lineage society, or becoming published in a genealogy peer review journal). Information does not guarantee knowledge, understanding, or intelligence.

Help!

Since technology is constantly changing, there will always be a need to adapt it to genealogy research. Questions will always be raised, such as, What products and services do I use? How does this relate to my research? How can I properly use technology to do genealogy research?

To answer these questions and others, I suggest looking to genealogical authorities and professionals. There are large national organizations of intelligent, experienced, and respected genealogists, including the National Genealogical Society (NGS), the Federation of Genealogical Societies (FGS), the Board for Certification of Genealogists (BCG), the Association of Professional Genealogists (APG), and GENTECH (genealogy and technology).

These organizations examine the positives and negatives, advantages and disadvantages, and strengths and weaknesses of using technology for genealogy research. They also set standards for quality research. Most have journals, newsletters, Web sites, and conferences at which experts lecture and write on different aspects of technology and genealogy. You should seek their counsel and follow their leadership. You will then be able to take advantage of new technology instead of letting it take advantage of you.

Writing the Family History

I know many genealogists who have researched for years, amassing dozens of notebooks, or several file cabinets full of research, and still the information is in raw form. I've heard horror stories about genealogists researching for many years and after they died their research was thrown in the garbage. I've also listened to genealogists complain of libraries not wanting their research. All of these problems are solved by writing and publishing your research as a genealogy or family history. This a library will gladly accept.

So what is the difference between a genealogy and a family history? You will recall that in the chapter "What Is Genealogy?" we discussed their similarities and differences. Genealogy deals with lineage, whereas family history is broader and tends to have more narrative. It combines history, biography, and sometimes sociology to place the family into historical context. A family history takes more time but is more valued by family members, historians, and the general public, as well as other genealogists.

I've seen genealogists place copies of all their research notes, documents, and charts in an inexpensive spiral binding, add a title, and call it a family history. That is not a family history. It is your research in a binder. It is not interesting reading, nor will other readers who are not genealogists understand your research. It's a poor excuse for not taking the extra step to learn how to turn your research into an interesting and readable family history. In this chapter I'll show you how to do it.

When to Publish

Every time you find another ancestor, that person has two parents. This means, theoretically, that genealogy research never ends. So after you've spent a lot of time researching, the question becomes "When do I publish?"

This question is answered by many genealogists in many different ways. When you have completed the steps in this book, you'll have enough information to write the *first edition* of your family history. Then no matter what else you do, you've published some of your research. After it's in print, you can search for more information and come out with a *second edition*.

This way, whenever you stop or no matter how long you research, you and others can benefit from what you've done. Your work is not in vain. Other than interviewing and recording your relatives' stories, writing the family history is the most important thing you can do. I encourage all genealogists to publish their research; otherwise, it never gets done.

Before you get too excited about publishing the family history, I offer a few words of caution. Some researchers make big mistakes publishing their family history before they are ready. I recall a famous vintner saying, "We shall sell no wine before its time." In other words, if things are going to be done right, they take time.

One of the first mistakes some genealogists make is to rush their work into print. They start in the spring to have it ready for the family reunion in the summer. I know because many of them have said so in my classes. Some family histories are written by senior citizens who think they have only another year of life left and they must get their work done before they die. Still others set their own deadline and want to get their work published no matter what the finished product looks like. They are not concerned about quality, which takes time. This is what is known as the "rush to publish." Many a poor book has come off the press that hasn't been edited, proofread, or reviewed by knowledgeable authors, editors, or genealogists. So if you want a quality publication that will be respected by your family and peers, take the time and do it right.

Where to Publish

Unfortunately, many genealogists get frightened away from publishing. One reason is that they feel they cannot write well. This is sometimes true, but more often than not, it is mere phobia. You are not expected to be a Pulitzer Prize–winning writer, an English teacher, or a grammar expert. After you finish writing, someone else with editing skills can review your work to ensure it is grammatically correct. That's the editor's responsibility, not the writer's.

Another reason genealogists never publish is because they fear it will be impossible for a publisher to accept their manuscript. Again, we are not writing the great American novel. Most genealogies and family histories are self-published. That means the genealogist types the manuscript (or has someone else type it) and then sends the manuscript to a printer who turns it into a book. The genealogist then pays for the printing (or has family members chip in for the costs) and then sells books (mostly to other family members) and distributes copies to libraries, historical societies, and other useful places where researchers can find it.

Few genealogists worry about rejection slips from commercial book publishers. However, some genealogists are very good writers, some have unique stories, and others are well-known genealogists who've had their family history research published by commercial and academic presses. Some African American family histories that come to my mind are *Roots*, by Alex Haley; *Somerset Homecoming*, by Dorothy Spruill Redford; *Living In, Living Out: African American Domestics in Washington, D.C., 1910–1940*, by Elizabeth Clark Lewis; *We Were Always Free: The Maddens of Culpepper County, Virginia, a 200-Year Family History*, by T. O. Madden; *Once Upon a Time When We Were Colored*, by Clifton Taulbert; *The Sweeter the Juice: A Family Memoir in Black and White*, by Shirlee Taylor Haizlip; *Free Frank: A Black Pioneer on the Antebellum Frontier*, by Juliet E. K. Walker; and *Having Our Say*, by the Delaney Sisters. (For these and other titles, see "Black Family Histories and Genealogies" in the Bibliography.) So don't discount commercial publishers altogether, but remember that it's rare for them to accept a family history.

Once you are ready to publish, there are many books on self-publishing that can guide you through the mechanics of getting your manuscript into print. One of the best is *The Publish It Yourself Handbook*, by Bill Henderson, now in its twenty-fifth anniversary edition. Author and certified genealogist Pat Hatcher's book, *Producing a Quality Family History*, is specifically geared toward genealogists and covers many of the mechanics. (See "Publishing Your Family History" in the Bibliography.)

When most researchers think about publishing their family history, they think about writing a book. However, there are other forms for publishing, especially to start off. Many genealogical societies around the country publish newsletters four times a year. Many of these accept short family histories or biographies of single ancestors society members are researching. Writing an article before writing an entire family history is a good way to ease into publishing. You've probably completed a lot of research on one or two ancestors and can write a short article on your research. This is a way to get initial publishing experience, get your research into print, and get feedback from your peers on your research and writing.

In addition to newsletters, which are the easiest place to get your story into print, many societies have quarterly journals that publish genealogical research. Journal articles are longer and more detailed than articles in newsletters and require sources to be properly footnoted. The advantage here is that with the larger publications, your work is sometimes reviewed by a peer group of genealogists who judge the quality of your work and give you feedback before it goes into print. So if you get accepted in a peer-reviewed journal, you can feel proud that your work has passed rigorous standards.

Preparing a Compiled Genealogy

You may want to begin with a compiled genealogy, which is quicker, easier to do with a computer program, and gets your research out to the public. A compiled genealogy will be valued by other genealogists who are researching the same family lines or areas of the country. Some genealogy software programs can produce a compiled genealogy from the data you've already entered.

Genealogists have struggled for ages on how to organize and number a genealogy so that many generations are included and readers can distinguish between one generation and the next. This becomes particularly important when a family is large and several generations have common given names. My maternal line has five direct descendants named Preston Brooks. The fifth Preston Brooks recently got married, and guess what name he's decided on for his first son?

Types of Systems

If a genealogist uses his or her own system, it may be difficult for others to understand. Therefore it's best to use one of three major systems for compiled genealogies that are used in publishing: the Register System, the Modified Register or NGSQ System, and the Henry System. There are strengths and weaknesses in all systems. Each of them starts with the earliest known ancestor and lists all his or her known descendants. Children are listed in the order of their birth, from the oldest to the youngest. Basic facts of birth, marriage, and death are included.

The Register System gives an identifying number only to those children who are known to have had children and are carried forward in the genealogy. You can see many examples by reading past issues of the *New England Historical and Genealogical Register.*

The Modified Register or NGSQ System gives a number to all children and averts renumbering when new ancestors are discovered. Children who are continued forward in the genealogy sometimes have a plus sign in front of their number to alert readers that there is more information. You can see many examples by reading past issues of the *National Genealogical Society Quarterly.*

The Henry System issues a unique number for each individual, adding a digit for each successive generation. It is not used as frequently as the Register and Modified Register Systems.

Before you decide on a system or blindly accept a format from a computer program, it's best to study the systems to see which one you prefer. A brief explanation of these systems is provided in *Printed Sources,* edited by Kory Meyerink, and three good publications that explain them in detail are *Guidelines for Genealogical Writing: Style Guide for the New England Historical and Genealogical Register, with Suggestions for Genealogical Books,* by Margaret F. Costello and Jane Fletcher Fiske; "Numbering Your Genealogy: Sound and Simple Systems," by certified genealogist Joan Ferris Curran; and *Guidelines for Authors of Compiled Genealogies,* by Thomas Kozachek (see "Writing Your Family History" in the Bibliography).

The following is an example of a two-generation compiled genealogy with supporting documentation.

Compiled Genealogy of Ellen Burroughs
Modified Register System

Generation number   *Source footnotes*

Generation One

1. Ellen[1] Burroughs; born March 1835 in South Carolina;[1, 2] died 3 August 1910 in Spartanburg, South Carolina, at age 75.[3]

Children of Ellen[1] Burroughs and an unknown spouse, both born in Spartanburg, South Carolina:

+2   i.   Charlotte[2] Burroughs, born 1862.
+3   ii.   Morris R. Burroughs, born December 1864; married Mary Jane Lillie Williams.

Identifying number   *Birth order number*

Generation Two

2. Charlotte[2] Burroughs (Ellen[1]); born 1862 in Spartanburg, South Carolina; married George Clemons 1880 at Spartanburg;[4] died 6 July 1932 at Spartanburg, South Carolina, at age 70.[5]

Children of Charlotte[2] Burroughs and George Clemons, all born in Spartanburg, South Carolina:

4   i.   Anna[3] Clemons, birth date unknown.[6]
5   ii.   Andrew Clemons, born 6 November 1885.[7]
6   iii.   Harold Clemons, born November 1890.[8]
7   iv.   Nelly Clemons, born March 1893.[9]
8   v.   Herbert Clemons, born July 1895.[10]
9   vi.   Morris Clemons, born 1896;[11] died 4 August 1931 in Spartanburg, South Carolina, at age 35.[12]
10   vii.   St. Lawrence Clemons, born July 1897.[13]
11   viii. Pearl Louise Clemons, born 9 July 1900;[14] died 9 September 1978 at Tuskegee Institute, Alabama, at age 78.[15]

3. Morris R.[2] Burroughs (Ellen[1]); born December 1864 in Spartanburg, South Carolina;[16, 17] married Mary Jane Lillie Williams, daughter of Martha Williams, 24 May 1888 in Chattanooga, Tennessee;[18] died 15 December 1903 at Chicago, Illinois.[19, 20, 21]

Children of Morris R.[2] Burroughs and Mary Jane Lillie Williams, both born in Chicago, Illinois:

12   i.   Robert Elliott[3] Burroughs, born 13 May 1889;[22, 23] married Jessie Young 1915;[24] he and Jessie Young were divorced 1919;[25] married Malvina Holman 18 October 1929;[26] died 28 January 1958 in Chicago, Illinois, at age 68.[27]
13   ii.   Asa Morris Burroughs, born 26 January 1893;[28] married Alma Irene Rice[29]; died 22 December 1971 in Chicago, Illinois, at age 78.[30]

Endnotes

[1] 1910 Funeral home record for Ellen Burroughs from J. F. Floyd Mortuary; P.O. Drawer 1530; Spartanburg, South Carolina 29304.

[2] 1900 U.S. Census—Spartanburg County, South Carolina, George Clemons household, town of Spartanburg, E.D. 108, Sheet 24, National Archives microfilm T623, reel 1542.

[3] 1910 Funeral record for Ellen Burroughs from J. F. Floyd Mortuary.

[4] Based on 1900 U.S. Census for Spartanburg, South Carolina.

[5] South Carolina Death Certificate No. 11260 for Charlotte Clemons.

[6] Oral interview with Georgianna Rutherford by Tony Burroughs on August 24, 1980, in Cincinnati, Ohio.

[7] 1900 U.S. Census—Spartanburg County, South Carolina, George Clemons household.

[8] Ibid.

[9] Ibid.

[10] Ibid.

[11] Ibid

[12] Spartanburg, South Carolina, Death Certificate, File No. 14065 for Morris Clemons, filed August 8, 1931.

[13] 1900 U.S. Census—Spartanburg County, South Carolina, George Clemons household.

[14] John A. Andrew Hospital, Tuskegee Institute, Alabama, Medical Records.

[15] Ibid.

[16] Little Red Book of notes owned by Asa Morris Burroughs, n.d. Date of birth written by son Asa Morris Burroughs.

[17] 1900 U.S. Census—Cook County, Illinois, Morris Burroughs household, City of Chicago, E.D. 405, Sheet 9, family no. 199, National Archives microfilm T623, reel 261.

[18] Hamilton County, Tennessee, Marriage License No. 3779, page 464.

[19] City of Chicago Death Certificate No. 12908 for Morris Burroughs, filed 17 December 1903.

[20] Chicago Tribune newspaper Death Notice, 18 December 1903.

[21] Little Red Book by Asa Morris Burroughs listed Morris's death as 15 December 1903.

[22] Cook County, Illinois, Delayed Birth Certificate No. 16058/260288 for Robert Elliott Burroughs, filed 2 November, 1943.

[23] 1900 U.S. Census—Cook County, Illinois, Morris Burroughs household.

[24] Little Red Book, notation by Asa Morris Burroughs.

[25] Ibid. Divorce from Jessie Young noted by Asa Morris Burroughs.

[26] Crown Point Indiana Marriage Certificate for Robert E. Burroughs and Malvina V. Holman, found among family papers in Robert's trunk.

[27] Cook County, Illinois, Death Certificate No. 4192 for Robert E. Burroughs, filed 3 February 1958.

[28]Illinois Birth Certificate #680 for Asa Morris Burroughs, filed in Chicago, Illinois, on 1 July 1893.

[29]Cook County, Illinois, Marriage License #686175 for Asa Morris Burroughs and Alma Irene Rice, dated 7 January, 1915.

[30]Illinois Death Certificate #635952 for Asa Morris Burroughs, filed in Chicago, Illinois, on 24 December 1971.

Beginning a Family History

When you are ready to begin writing, decide which families and individuals you want to cover. It's good to concentrate on one individual at a time. You may have only sketchy information on some ancestors and detailed information on others. While you are doing this exercise, have your Research To Do sheet handy because ideas may pop into your mind that you will not want to forget.

Review Documents

Take out the file or files you've created for this ancestor. Review the research you've done, the documents you've collected, and all the notes you've created for this one individual. Check to see if you've transcribed tapes from relatives you've interviewed some time ago. This is where you will need the additional information not recorded on your Family Group Sheets to add details and interest to your story. If you haven't transcribed them, refer back to the chapter on "Oral History" to review how to do it and what to do with the information.

Create a list of all the records you've researched (relatives' memories, books and records in libraries, archives, and courthouses). You might want to refer to your Research Calendar. List each source checked and also note negative research (when you did not find something).

RESEARCH—ROBERT ELLIOTT BURROUGHS

Family records	WWI draft registrations
Chicago telephone directory, 1917–1926, 1956, 1958	WWII draft registrations
	1920 Soundex
Chicago city directories, 1914–1928	1920 U.S. Census
Chicago Board of Education elementary student records—none for Robert	1910 Soundex
	1910 U.S. Census
Cook County birth records	1900 Soundex
Cook County divorce records	1900 U.S. Census
Oak Ridge Cemetery records	U.S. Railroad Retirement Board—no file
Jones Funeral Home—out of business	Pullman Company employee service records
Cook County death certificates	Pullman Company employee payroll records
Social Security applications	Palmer House—no early employee records

RESEARCH—ROBERT ELLIOTT BURROUGHS

Chicago Historical Society, Palmer House
 employee records—none
Newspaper articles—*Chicago Tribune* and
 Chicago American

Cook County Criminal Court records
Parole Review Board records—Illinois State
 Archives

Now you're going to take the documents you've obtained and make a list of each of these documents for the ancestor you're concentrating on.

DOCUMENTS—ROBERT ELLIOTT BURROUGHS

Family records (see separate list)
Cook County Delayed Birth Certificate
 No. 16058 (260288), filed 2 Nov. 1943
1920 Soundex—Illinois
1920 U.S. Census—Chicago
1910 Soundex—Illinois
1910 U.S. Census—Chicago
1900 Soundex—Illinois
1900 U.S. Census—Chicago
Chicago city directories—1914, 1915,
 1916, 1928
Newspaper articles—*Chicago Tribune*, 1917,
 and *Chicago American*, 1917
Cook County Criminal Court records, 1917
1921 Parole Review Board record—Illinois
 State Archives

1929 Marriage Certificate to Malvina
 Holman—Crown Point, Indiana
1937 Social Security application
WWI draft registration card—1917
WWII draft registration card—1942
1944 Pullman Company employee service
 record
1944 Pullman Company payroll records
1944 U.S. Railroad Retirement Board
 registration
Cook County Death Certificate No. 4192—
 1958
Oak Ridge Cemetery sexton's records for
 Lot 487, Section 11

Make sure you know what each document is and where you obtained it. This source documentation should be on the back of each sheet of paper. While checking these documents, see if your Family Group Sheets and Pedigree Charts are up to date. Be sure they reflect all the documents you've obtained. If you've missed any, update the chart and remember to footnote new names, dates, and locations on your Family Group Sheets with this source information.

Resolve Discrepancies and Conflicting Evidence

One of the reasons for writing the family history is to finalize the research we've done and put it all together. Up to now we've been collecting information and haven't made many value judgments on what's true and what's false.

As genealogists, we must sift through all the research we've done, compare information from different sources, analyze the records, and determine which record is most likely correct, given the sources we've uncovered thus far, but recognizing this reality is subject to change in the future. In this process we'll want to let our readers know when we "don't trust the sources" or when we haven't located definitive information to prove our case conclusively.

In preparation for writing a history of your ancestors, you'll find conflicting evidence you'll want to resolve first. It doesn't take much research to locate two records that contradict each other. They might give different ages or different dates of birth for the same individual.

An article in the summer 1984 issue of the *Journal of the Afro-American Historical and Genealogical Society* (vol. 5, no. 2) described several examples of elderly African Americans with different ages reported in different records. You can expect one or two years' difference, but these were pretty extreme.

Thomas Wilson was listed as a "63 year old Black laborer" on the 1850 census of Herkimer County, New York. On the 1860 census he was listed as seventy-seven years old. Wilson died five years later. His obituary in the *Little Falls Journal* said, "He (Thomas Wilson) reached the ripe old age of 96 years and was universally known and respected." So in the fifteen-year period between 1850 and 1865, Mr. Wilson aged thirty-three years!

Another example is Sarah Pugsley, listed as a "52 year old Black housewife" on the 1850 census of Herkimer County, New York. She was listed as sixty-two years old on the 1860 census, which was just right. However, on the 1870 census she had aged eighteen years instead of ten and was listed as eighty years old. She died six years later, and a mention in the *Little Falls Journal* a week after her death in 1876 said, "Mrs. Sarah Pugsley, the old colored woman whose death was reported last week, is said to have been over 100 years old."

Now do you believe all those stories of your ancestors who supposedly lived to be one hundred years old? Admittedly, the stories above are extreme examples. However, your ancestors don't have to have such wide divergences to throw off your research.

Compare Sources

Genealogist Stan Beck compared ages at death in three different sources in Alpena County, Michigan, in the 1870s and found few correlations. He looked at records in the Death Book located in the county courthouse, death notices in the county newspaper, and ages on cemetery grave markers. His results were published in an article in *Family Trails* titled "Documenting Your Research."

1. Records in the courthouse and newspaper agreed 50 percent of the time.
2. Records in the courthouse and cemetery agreed 41 percent of the time.
3. Records in the cemetery and newspaper agreed 32 percent of the time.
4. Records recorded in all three sources agreed 25 percent of the time.

It's amazing none of the sources agreed more than 50 percent of the time. Beck accurately stated that genealogists should not rely on only one source to prove genealogical events. This also implies we should not believe everything we see or read. Beck's theory is that when three sources agree, the statement is most likely true. However, there is another scenario Beck didn't consider. Take the situation in which the informant at the time of death does not know the exact age of the deceased. That informant fills out information for the death certificate, pays for the cemetery gravestone, and provides information to the newspaper for the obituary. Here you have all three sources agreeing, yet none of them are correct. It's better to have corroboration among different sources of independently supplied information.

The problem of age discrepancies is not only historical. Research has shown age discrepancy continues well into the twentieth century. A study by demographers of age discrepancies published by Harvard University Press found only 44.7 percent of African American males and 36.9 percent of African American females had the same age reported on death certificates as on the 1960 census.[1]

Another demographic study compared the consistency of ages among elderly African Americans on death certificates with the Social Security records. It found only 63 percent of African Americans over the age of sixty-five having the same age reported on both the death certificate and the Social Security record. However, the differences were not great. Seventy-nine percent of the records differed by one year or less. But in 8.1 percent of cases they differed by more than four years. The study found age reporting in Social Security records superior to that found on death certificates.[2]

This is consistent with the genealogical theory that records created closer to the time of the event by someone knowledgeable of the event are usually more accurate. Social Security applications were normally created when a person was young and applying for a job. The information was supplied by the individual applicant. Information on death certificates was created at the end of a person's life by the next of kin, or friends or associates, depending on who was around at the time of death. The informant may or may not have known the deceased's actual age. However, even Social Security data for older African Americans was found to be very inconsistent. Demographers found lax procedures used to verify age for Social Security prior to 1965. The Social Security Administration didn't verify proof of birth for people born near or before the turn of the century, and many African Americans did not have birth certificates.

Another study published in a 1992 edition of *Demography* compared the accuracy of informants listed on death certificates. They found an individual's spouse is more likely to know

---

[1]E. M. Kitagawa and P. M. Hauser, *Differential Mortality in the United States: A Study in Socioeconomic Epidemiology* (Cambridge, Mass.: Harvard University Press, 1973).

[2]Irma T. Elo, Samuel H. Preston, Ira Rosenwaike, Mark Hill, and Timothy P. Cheney, "Consistency of Age Reporting on Death Certificates and Social Security Records Among Elderly African Americans," *Social Science Research* 25 (1996): 292–307.

the decedent's correct age than any other death certificate informant.[3] So check your death certificates to see who were the informants.

Create Discrepancy Charts

Understanding that the genealogical data you have collected may contain contradictions, you've probably wondered how to resolve them. They're resolved by developing Discrepancy Charts. A Discrepancy Chart is a matrix comparing conflicting dates and analyzing the quality of the sources. The questions we ask are, Is the source primary or secondary? How close was the data supplied to the occurrence of the event? Did the person supplying the data have direct knowledge of the event? Did the person supplying the information have a motive for lying?

I found no birth certificate for my maternal grandmother, Lydia Rae (Terrell) Brooks. However, I located many records that gave her year of birth—five different years! Lydia's death certificate indicated she was born in 1894; her marriage application indicated she was born in 1890; her Social Security application and her cemetery headstone both indicated she was born in 1892; the 1920 U.S. Census indicated she was born in 1895; and the 1900 and 1910 census schedules indicated she was born in 1891. Which one is correct? To analyze these sources in trying to resolve the contradictory evidence, I created a Discrepancy Chart.

Fundamental analysis of genealogy says we should seek primary records, those created at or close to the time an event occurred by someone who had knowledge of the event. In this case none of the evidence obtained was created when Lydia Terrell was born. The closest record to her birth is the 1900 U.S. Census indicating she was nine years old, which means she would have been born in 1891. Since the census enumerator did not indicate who supplied him with the

DISCREPANCY CHART—LYDIA RAE (TERRELL) BROOKS

Year of Birth	Record	Date Created/Age	Primary or Secondary—Informant
1891	1900 U.S. Census	1900/9	Secondary—Enumerator
1891	1910 U.S. Census	1910/19	Secondary—Enumerator
1890	Marriage Application	1918/28	Secondary—Person
1895	1920 U.S. Census	1920/25	Secondary—Enumerator
1892	Social Security Application	1937/45	Secondary—Person
1892	Cemetery Headstone[4]	aft 1952/60	Secondary—Other
1894	Death Certificate	1964/70	Secondary—Daughter

[3]B. Kestenbaum, "A Description of the Extreme Aged Population Based on Improved Medicare Enrollment Data," *Demography* 29 (1992): 565–80.

[4]Headstone is for a three-grave lot and was created before the death of Lydia Terrell Brooks. The exact date is not known, but is sometime after 1952.

information, we have no way of knowing if it came from Lydia, her parents, a friend, or a neighbor.

Two sources appear to come from Lydia Terrell herself. The closest to the date of her birth is her marriage application in 1918 (reproduced on page 215). It indicates she was twenty-eight years old, being born in 1890. She would have supplied that information herself, so you'd think it was reliable. However, many people lie on their marriage application, usually to put their age up because they are underage. At twenty-eight, Lydia would appear not to have had a motive for lying about her age to get married. Neither was she of the age to say she was younger than she really was. We'd judge this source to be fairly reliable. However, since a person's memory does not go back to birth (three to four years old is the best I've seen), no one can vouch for his or her own birth. We've all heard stories of people saying they didn't know when they were born, particularly those born in slavery.

Lydia also appears to have supplied the information for her Social Security card (application reproduced on page 314), which says she was born in 1892. However, upon close examination and analysis, this may not be the case. She did not sign the application (the hotel's name was on the line where she was supposed to sign), and key personal information is conspicuously missing, like date and place of birth and her parents' names. It appears she'd left the job by the time the application was filed and her previous employer supplied the information.

The 1900 U.S. Census was the closest one taken to Lydia's birth. It indicates she was nine years old, being born in 1891. This is a year before the year of birth on the Social Security application and a year after the date on the marriage application. It is in the ballpark, but we don't know who supplied the information to the census enumerator and therefore have to question its reliability. However, the 1900 census also shows the month of birth, which is correct in Lydia's case. The oldest female in the household, listed as a cousin, has no occupation and therefore could have been at home when the enumerator arrived.

The cemetery headstone presents a very interesting dilemma. It is a three-grave marker, placed sometime after 1952 when another relative died. Lydia's name and year of birth were inscribed when the stone was installed. They planned for Lydia's date of death to be inscribed on the headstone after she died. In 1952 Lydia was still living and supposedly sixty years old. She probably attended the 1952 burial and knew about the stone. The year of birth, 1892, is consistent with the Social Security application. What we don't know is if there was an error in the date on the stone and Lydia complained about it.

The other records have serious concerns for reliability. Lydia's death certificate was the last record created, and traditionally death certificates are the least accurate sources for dates of birth. They are the furthest removed from the ancestor's birth. Lydia's daughter was the informant, and spouses are statistically the most accurate.

The 1920 U.S. Census indicates she was born in 1895. It is the furthest distance from her birth of the three census records available. It is also the extreme of the five years of birth. We don't know who supplied the information and therefore have to question its reliability.

Therefore, based on the evidence, I conclude Lydia Rae Terrell was probably born between 1890 and 1892. The strongest evidence appears to come from her marriage application indicating she was born in 1890. In second place is the 1900 census, taken when Lydia was nine years old and the closest record to her birth. It indicates she was born in 1891 and is consistent with the 1910 census.

In genealogy we can come to conclusions based only on the evidence we've collected, understanding these conclusions are subject to change in the future if additional evidence is collected, particularly more credible and convincing evidence. Of course, the above analysis is also subject to a jury of my peers, and it would be interesting to see if their analysis differed from mine.

So when you get conflicting evidence, create a Discrepancy Chart and analyze sources of evidence to determine which date is the most likely to be correct.

Build a Chronology

Next you are going to build a chronology of your ancestor's life. A chronology is a tabular list of the events in a person's life. It includes the dates those events occurred and the sources, in chronological order. Make a list of the documents in the ancestor's folder in chronological order of when the events occurred, not when you obtained the documents.

Sorting records in chronological order not only prepares you for the next exercise but is another analysis tool. When you are researching, you're looking for specific records mentioning your ancestor. But looking for specific records is only one exercise in the genealogical process. After obtaining documents, you must review, evaluate, and analyze them. By placing them in chronological order, you begin to see what you know about a person's life and what obvious events are missing. You should be able to see if the person's life makes sense.

This analysis can lead to logical questions and assumptions. Certain predictable events occur in the average person's life, such as birth, baptism, elementary school, high school, work, marriage, children, and death. There are a number of others, but these are pretty basic. These events also normally occur at average ages.

After arranging this chronology, simple questions arise, such as, Did the person marry before he died? Did the woman have a child at eighty years old? Was the man in the military at six years old? This is when you learn if you are researching one individual or you've confused someone else with the same name. The story has to make sense.

After you've compiled a chronology, you have the ancestor's life in front of you. It helps you see travel patterns and will help you identify research gaps in the ancestor's life. Sometimes a person is living in one location at an early age and another location later in life. If you have major gaps, there may have been intermediate stops along the way. These are clues to other research possibilities.

Another task is to parallel an ancestor's life chronologically with a chronology of history—U.S. history, local history, and African American history. Once you parallel the known historical events that occurred during a person's life, you get additional clues for sources to check. For example, World War I occurred between 1917 and 1919. If you have a male ancestor who was between the ages of eighteen and forty-five during that period, there is a possibility that

CHRONOLOGY FOR ROBERT ELLIOTT BURROUGHS

Date	Event	Record	Age
May 13, 1889	Born in Chicago, IL	Delayed Birth Certificate	
1900	In school	1900 U.S. Census	11 yrs. old
Dec. 1903	Father died	Birth Certificate (M. Burroughs)	14 yrs. old
April 21, 1910	Chauffeur	1910 U.S. Census	21 yrs. old
April 11, 1914	Mother died	Death Certificate (M. J. Burroughs)	25 yrs. old
1915	Married Jessie Young	Little Red Book	26 yrs. old
1915	Living at 225 N. Hoyne	Chicago City Directory, pg. 281	
1916	Living at 225 N. Hoyne	Chicago City Directory, pg. 304	
March 31, 1917	Registered for the draft	WWI Draft Registration	28 yrs. old
	Living at 3022 State Street	WWI Draft Registration	
	Chauffeur for Wallace Bryant	WWI Draft Registration	
May 9, 1917	Robbed Illinois Tool Works	*Chicago Tribune* newspaper article	28 yrs. old
May 18, 1917	Indicted for robbery	Criminal Court of Cook County	
May 28, 1917	Convicted of robbery	Parole Review Board record—Illinois St. Archives	
	Sentenced—1 year to life	Parole Review Board record—Illinois St. Archives	
July 26, 1917	Received in Joliet State Prison	Parole Review Board record—Illinois St. Archives	
1919	Divorce from Jessie Young	Little Red Book	30 yrs. old
Jan. 8, 1920	In Joliet State Prison	1920 U.S. Census	30 yrs. old
May 17, 1921	Paroled after serving 5 years	Parole Review Board record—Illinois St. Archives	
April 18, 1922	Discharged from Joliet State Prison	Parole Review Board record	32 yrs. old
1928	Living at 5031 S. Michigan	Chicago City Directory, pg. 695	38 yrs. old
Oct. 18, 1929	Married Malvina V. Holman	Marriage certificate	40 yrs. old
1930	Groom at Washington Park & Cicero Park	Payroll stubs in family papers	41 yrs. old

Date	Event	Age	Source
1931/32	Reliable Auto Parts		
1932	Arlington Park racetrack	43 yrs. old	Claim in family papers
Nov. 22, 1933	Filed for unemployment	43 yrs. old	Badge found in family papers
1936	Groom—Hawthorn Racetrack	45 yrs. old	Cook County Welfare application
1937	Lincoln Fields Jockey Club	48 yrs. old	Stable badge found in family papers
	Wife admitted to mental hospital	49 yrs. old	Payroll stubs in family papers
June 4, 1937	Registered for Social Security	49 yrs. old	Court records in family papers
July 7, 1937	2nd wife, Malvina, died	49 yrs. old	Social Security application
1941	Filed for unemployment	49 yrs. old	Court records in family papers
April 27, 1942	Registered for the draft	52 yrs. old	Family papers
	Living at 60 E. 36th Place	53 yrs. old	WWII Draft Registration
Nov. 2, 1943	Applied for a birth certificate		WWII Draft Registration
1943	United Beverage Co. Repairman	55 yrs. old	Delayed Birth Certificate
Sep. 21, 1944	Started as an electrician		Tax return found in family papers
Oct. 20, 1944	Eye examination	56 yrs. old	Pullman Co. Employee Service Record
Dec. 15, 1944	Resigned from Pullman		Optometrist receipt c/o Pullman Co.
	Living at 3410 South Wabash		Pullman Co. Employee Service Record
Feb. 16, 1951	Self-employed TV repairman	56 yrs. old	Letter from brother in family papers
1954	Renting part of store & garage	62 yrs. old	Bankers Life Insurance policy
1955	at 1135 W. 59th Street	65 yrs. old	Illinois Bell telephone bill
		66 yrs. old	
Jan. 28, 1958	Died in Chicago	69 yrs. old	Death certificate

he fought in World War I or at least registered for the draft. You would therefore check records of the war to see if he was listed. World War I service and draft records are at the National Archives. (See *Locating Lost Family Members and Friends,* by Kathleen W. Hinckley, under "Genealogy Reference Guides" in the Bibliography.)

Writing a Biography

Sorting data chronologically will help you write an ancestor's life story. You will transform the chronology into a biography by weaving a logical narrative into it. This biography is then another preliminary step to writing the family history. For what is family history but a collection of individual biographies?

An advantage of writing a biography of an ancestor is that it gives you another form of analysis. In writing a biography of my grandfather Asa Morris Burroughs, I discovered a naming pattern in my family. Asa named his first son after his father, Morris Burroughs. Asa's son, my father, named his first son after his father, Asa Morris Burroughs. My father and grandfather are both deceased, so I cannot ask them if this was done consciously. However, if it is a pattern, it means my great-grandfather Morris Burroughs named his first son, Robert, after his father. That would mean my great-great-grandfather's name was Robert Burroughs.

Based on this theory, I checked the Spartanburg, South Carolina, city directory where Morris lived. I found two African Americans named Robert Burroughs and one R. B. Burroughs in the 1889 directory. This could be a coincidence, but other evidence makes the theory even stronger. I discovered Morris's middle initial is R, which I found on his marriage license and in the Chicago city directory.

Next you'll add cultural and historical research that places your ancestor in context and also adds interest. Remember all the research you did in the history department of the library, not the genealogy department? This is where you put it to good use. If you haven't been to the history department yet, you'll want to read local history, U.S. history, and African American history for the time period of the ancestor's life. Remember to check for books, magazines, journals, and newspapers to get a good, diversified picture.

I've included a short biography of Robert Burroughs as an appendix. Often when you write out the information in this form, you evoke a lot of questions about your ancestor. When these questions arise, write them down. You may want to go back to your relatives and seek answers to these new questions. Give everyone a chance to fill in a small piece of the puzzle. Hopefully you listed new research ideas on your Research To Do sheet as you wrote. When you return to researching, you'll need this list. But before you use it, prioritize the list, then check off items as you complete them.

Completing the Family History

There are several basic components of all good books, and they are the same for good family histories. They include:

- Title page with title, author, date, and publisher (author if self-published)
- Copyright page
- Table of contents
- Acknowledgments (thanking those who helped you)
- Introduction
- Text
- Illustrations, photographs, and maps (optional)
- Conclusion
- Index

Most of these are self-explanatory, but you can refer to books in the Bibliography for further help. The index is probably the most important component and the one most often neglected by genealogy hobbyists. Most genealogists read books from the back to the front, first checking the index for their ancestors' surnames. If your book is to be respected and read, it must have an index, a good one. In genealogist Pat Hatcher's book *Producing a Quality Family History,* she states: "Quality research is not accessible unless it has a quality index." Your research could be the best in the world, but if it does not have a quality index, researchers will not use it.

Follow her guidelines for your family history, and examples in genealogical journals and newsletters for a shorter article. After you complete the first draft, put it down for a while; then return and write a second draft. Keep doing that until you think it is perfect. Next, have genealogists whom you respect critique it. Finally, seek out someone with good grammatical skills, like a former English teacher, to suggest editorial improvements. Once you pass his or her standards, you're ready to publish.

Family History Competitions

Some of you may love to write and think you write well. You may think you have written a great family history, and I'm sure some of you have. Fortunately, there are contests for the best family stories. If you would like to participate, I encourage you to send in what you've written. Even if you don't participate, it's a good idea to read award-winning family histories so you will recognize quality writing and research when you see it.

The National Genealogical Society Family History Writing Contest began in 1984. It is held once a year for a three- or four-generation family history of 4,000 to 10,000 words (about eight to twenty pages). Winners are published in the society's quarterly journal, so genealogists can research past winners. Winners receive an expense-paid trip to the next National Genealogical Society conference, which includes airfare, hotel accommodations, the conference registration fee, and a ticket for the banquet at which the award plaque is presented. You'll be the star of the show. (See "National Genealogical Organizations" in the appendixes for address.)

The National Genealogical Society also gives an award for the best article published in their quarterly journal. In 1998 Del Alexa Egan Jupiter, an African American genealogist, won for her article, "From Agustina to Ester: Analyzing a Slave Household for Child-Parent Relationships" (*National Genealogical Society Quarterly* 85, no. 4 [Dec. 1997], pages 245–275).

The Colorado Genealogical Society began sponsoring a "Black Sheep Contest" in 1987 for articles on ancestors who may have done less than honorable deeds. It is based on genealogists' original stories about their families or stories found in their research. The society says that the purpose is to "promote high quality documentation while having a little fun." First-, second-, and third-place winners receive engraved trophies. The Colorado Genealogical Society sells an inexpensive book containing previous winning entries.

Where to Distribute Your Family History

After you finish writing and publishing your family history book, you must get it into the hands of the public. The main people who will be interested are family members. Many of them will already know you've been researching and are probably waiting impatiently for the book. If you have family reunions, there will probably be many people there who want to purchase copies. You might solicit orders in advance to get an idea of how many books to print.

After getting books to your immediate and extended family members, you'll want to send copies to libraries in the local area where your ancestors lived. That will be the city or county public library, the county historical society, the state archives, and the state historical society. There may be other major libraries in the region where your ancestors lived that would be interested in a copy. If your ancestor attended college, the college library will be another good place to send a copy. When other genealogists visit the area researching their ancestors, they'll likely visit the local library and state archives to see if there are any books on families that lived in the area.

Next, you'll want to have copies in several of the major genealogical libraries in the country. The two largest collections of family histories are in the Family History Library in Salt Lake City, Utah, and the Library of Congress in Washington, D.C. Other major libraries with large collections of family histories are the Allen County Public Library in Fort Wayne, Indiana, the Newberry Library in Chicago, and the New England Historic Genealogical Society in Boston. The Schomburg Research Center for Black Culture, which is a branch of the New York Public Library, is another good place to have a copy. Finally, the local public library in the area where you live might be interested because you are a local author and may have relatives in the book who live in your town.

I Can't Stop Now: Continuing the Search

Your family history is written, and I know you're wondering where you go from here. It's like the last day of class, when my students are ready for the next course. I try to tell them they're not ready for another course, but they won't listen. Genealogy is more than listening to lectures or reading books—you have to do it. That's when it really develops and you really learn genealogy. It's a participatory activity. So I suggest going through every step in this book and completing each one for all the relatives and ancestors on your Family Group Sheets. You're not really ready for the next phase until you complete these exercises.

Genealogy cannot be done in one afternoon at the library. While at the National Archives recently, a man approached me and said, "I just can't get past slavery," obviously referring to the slave census schedules, which don't list the names of slaves, only the names of slave owners. I asked him, "What other records have you checked besides census records?" He replied, "None!" Herein lies the answer to his problem. There are dozens of other records to research besides the census records, many of which will give information and clues to slavery and slave owners. Don't ever get hung up on any one record.

! Trap: Relying too heavily on one source. Leave no stone unturned and research any and all records.

What About Slave Ancestors?

By now many of you have probably uncovered ancestors you think were slaves or have heard stories from relatives about certain ancestors who were slaves. I'm sure you're eager to start researching them and getting your genealogy back to the motherland, perhaps identifying a tribe or ethnic group for your ancestors. I'm sorry to disappoint you, but for now I suggest holding off. You've been successful up to now, following the fundamental steps of African American genealogy. Don't blow it with impatience and uncontrolled enthusiasm. If you are serious and diligent and lucky, you might get there. But there are many other steps leading back to slave research.

After completing the beginning class, everyone wants to go to the advanced class, looking for slaves. I am reminded of some public school systems that move kids ahead another grade instead of making them pass the class. How many of you would move on if I tested you on your knowledge of this book and completion of the lessons?

Once you have thoroughly mastered and completed all the techniques and sources in this book, you've finished only the beginning phase of African American genealogy. There is an intermediate phase of genealogy lying ahead of you. Slave research is *advanced* genealogy. To be successful, you must understand advanced genealogical techniques, but only after mastering intermediate methods and sources. The documents you collect during the intermediate phase will assist you when researching slaves and slavery.

Slavery ended over 135 years ago. You first need to catch up on 135 years of U.S. history and African American history to understand what your ancestors went through *after* slavery, let alone *during* slavery.

If you are successful enough to trace your family history back to 1870, you'll find that the research methods, techniques, and records begin to change. The vast majority of African Americans before the Emancipation Proclamation was issued in 1863 were slaves. Slaves were treated as property, not human beings. Many records of slaves were kept, but they are different from records of free citizens. You must understand these differences. However, don't assume your antebellum ancestors were slaves. There were more than 200,000 free Blacks in the North and another 200,000 free in the South prior to the Civil War. I know one "experienced" genealogist who assumed his ancestors were slaves prior to the Civil War. I suggested he check the 1860 census schedules of free inhabitants, and he not only found his ancestors were free in the South but also found them free in 1850! Remember, genealogy is based on evidence, not on assumptions.

Before you trace slave ancestors, you need to understand slavery. That can only be done by a lot of reading because slavery wasn't taught in school, at least not in the detail needed for genealogy. You must also study the local history of the community where your ancestors lived, as well as visit the area. You even have to study early American handwriting to be able to read documents created during the slavery period. You also have to study the laws that governed slavery because these affected your ancestors and will lead to other records. You have to become an expert at advanced genealogical methods and sources, including estates, probates, taxes, federal and military records, and church records, as well as develop the ability to solve problems when no records exist. There are no easy answers around any of these obstacles.

! Trap: Trying to trace slave ancestors prematurely.

I recommend if you have an ancestor you think was enslaved, create a file folder for him or her. As you collect information on this ancestor, place it in this folder. Remember, you will need to collect a lot of information *after* slavery to be successful tracing the ancestor *during* slavery. Then when you've progressed through the intermediate phase, traced the family line through to the slavery period, and thoroughly studied the history of slavery, pull the file out and you'll be ready to deal with it.

What Should I Do Next?

Now that the beginning phase has been covered, you're probably wondering what to do next. After you master the techniques and sources in this book, there are several things you can do before you proceed to the next phase.

Read Other Genealogy Books and Articles

After you finish reading this book, I suggest reading other genealogy books and articles. The chapter on "Fundamentals" lists beginning, intermediate, and advanced steps. This book covers only the beginning ones. There are books, articles, and lectures that mention other records and methods you need to study. But before embarking on new records, methods, or techniques, properly prepare before researching for your ancestors by learning these new areas. The books and articles in the Bibliography will cover some of the other items in detail. In addition to books and articles on African American genealogy, you need to read standard genealogy reference guides. I also recommend reading as much literature as you can on how other genealogists are solving their problems. It's a good idea to develop your own library of genealogy books and articles so you can refer to them when ideas and problems arise. However, if these beginning steps are not done properly and thoroughly, you will have limited success with future research.

Read History Books and Articles

You should begin reading articles and books on United States history, African American history, and local history in the areas where your ancestors lived. You need to start from the present and work your way back to the antebellum period. If you study history before researching genealogy, the records will make better sense. You'll also have a better feel for your ancestors' lives and know what to look for and what records to research.

Join a Genealogical Society

I also recommend teaming up with other genealogists. Contact the African American genealogical society closest to where you live. There is a directory of societies in the appendixes. They have members who have experience researching African American genealogy. The societies usually have meetings, classes, and workshops. Many produce newsletters and journals listing activities, upcoming conferences, book reviews, techniques, and research findings. Joining a genealogical society is a good way to locate a researcher familiar with the state or county you are researching. If there is not an African American genealogical society in your area, start one. An inexpensive guide to starting a genealogical society is available from the Federation of Genealogical Societies, called *Organizational Handbook: A Guide for the Organization and Management of Genealogical Societies.*

There's also a national African American genealogical society, the Afro-American Historical and Genealogical Society, based in Washington, D.C. There are several chapters around the country, but you don't have to belong to a chapter to be a member. The society publishes a newsletter every other month, a journal twice a year, and hosts an annual genealogy conference.

You should also consider joining local genealogical societies that are not African American. I belong to several and have learned a lot I'd never have known otherwise. There are state, county, and local genealogical societies in every state and in many local areas. Try to find one in the city, county, or state where your ancestor lived. Check *Meyer's Directory of Genealogical Societies in the United States and Canada,* the *Encyclopedia of Associations,* or other genealogical directories. Joining a local genealogical society is a way of keeping up with the latest research in the area where your ancestors lived and knowing who the key players are.

You should also consider joining the National Genealogical Society. It has thousands of members and publishes a newsletter, a computer newsletter, a journal, and other publications. It also has a library and sponsors conferences.

Attend Genealogy Conferences

There are several annual genealogy conferences at which you can learn a lot of genealogy in a short period of time. Some are on the national level, and many on the state level. Experts give presentations on varied topics, which are usually visually enhanced by overhead transparencies, 35mm slides, or computer slide shows. Some conferences include hands-on workshops and computer labs. Not only do they offer a way to learn genealogy, but the experts often give lectures on new techniques that are not yet published in books or articles. Besides being educational, a conference is a lot of fun because you meet other people involved in genealogy.

There are annual conferences on African American genealogy sponsored by the Afro-American Historical and Genealogical Society, usually held in Washington, D.C.; the Afro-American Genealogical and Historical Society of Chicago, held in Chicago; and the Cleveland African American Genealogical Society, among others. They usually comprise one to three days of lectures and are attended by hundreds of African American genealogists.

! Trap: Attending only conferences and lectures labeled "African American."

I have learned a tremendous amount of genealogy by attending lectures and conferences that are not labeled "African American." There are many aspects of genealogy, and I encourage you to attend all types of lectures and conferences. The National Genealogical Society (NGS) has an annual conference that draws from 1,000 to 2,500 genealogists, historians, and librarians every year. It is a four-day affair with over a hundred lectures, computer workshops, and genealogy software demonstrations. There is an exhibit hall with dozens of vendors selling all kinds of genealogical products. But I must warn you. If you go, take your wallet and your plastic. For a genealogist, going into the vendor exhibit area at a national conference is like going to a candy store as a kid. You'll find everything imaginable in the area of genealogy, including books, charts, forms, software, artwork, clothes, souvenirs—anything that's remotely related to genealogy. You'll also learn about the latest research techniques, see the top speakers, browse the latest books, find out-of-print books, and see new software releases. Once you go, you'll never forget it.

The Federation of Genealogical Societies (FGS) also conducts a national conference every year with a similar number of participants, lectures, and vendors. The Federation is the umbrella group of all the genealogical societies in the country. The first day of their conference is devoted to managing genealogy societies. There are sessions for presidents, secretaries, treasurers, program chairmen, newsletter editors, public relations people, fund-raisers, and boards of directors. FGS also publishes a newsletter called *The Forum* and other publications for managing a genealogy society.

The Association of Professional Genealogists (APG) teamed up with FGS and began a one-day conference in 1998 at each FGS conference. Lecture topics are geared toward professional genealogists and those planning to become professional genealogists.

GENTECH is a nonprofit organization devoted to using technology with genealogy. GENTECH has an annual conference with topics on using computers, software, scanners, the Internet, video, telecommunications, and other forms of technology with genealogy. So if you want to see the latest technology, and talk to the vendors and experts in the field, go to GENTECH.

Many state genealogical societies also have statewide conferences every year. They are usually smaller and more intimate, drawing anywhere from 100 to 800 people and having smaller vendor exhibit areas.

Going to a conference is also a good way to see other parts of the country and visit new research facilities. Many conferences are held close to major genealogy research libraries and offer tours of local points of interest. They're also a place to meet new friends. I always have a lot of fun at the conferences and renew old acquaintances.

If you can't make it to a national conference, you can still benefit from one. Most of the lectures at national conferences are tape-recorded, and the tapes are available for sale, as well as tapes from past conferences. You can buy them from Repeat Performance, as well as find lists of past lectures on the Internet. This is an additional way to learn how to do genealogy. The National Genealogical Society and the Federation of Genealogical Societies have compiled a list of lectures and speakers from past conferences, *Index to NGS & FGS Conferences and Syllabi*, edited by Joy Risenger.

Go to History Conferences

In addition to genealogical conferences, there are historical conferences that are very interesting and educational. They differ somewhat from genealogical conferences in that historians, history professors, and graduate students usually read papers that are then commented on by other historians. There are rarely graphics to accompany their presentations.

The American Historical Association, the Organization of American Historians, the Southern Historical Association, and the Association for the Study of Afro-American Life and History all have annual conferences in different cities around the country. You can find out about these conferences from your local library, on the Internet, or by contacting the association directly.

Take Seminars and Workshops

There are many genealogical seminars and workshops given by local genealogical societies and libraries around the country. These are often half-day or full-day programs without vendors but sometimes have displays of research by members. You should seek out societies and libraries in the area where you live and others where your ancestors lived. You can find out about them in the genealogy department of your library or by joining a society, reading *The Forum*, searching the Internet, or reading society newsletters.

Enroll in Courses and Institutes

There are many other educational opportunities for learning genealogy. There are courses at community colleges and adult education centers, and some colleges offer undergraduate courses. Brigham Young University in Provo, Utah, offers an undergraduate program in family history. The National Genealogical Society has a beginner's course on the Internet and an extensive home study course. Several members of the Afro-American Genealogical and Historical Society of Chicago have taken the NGS home study course in groups, with members studying and researching together.

You can also attend a genealogy institute. An institute is a week or more of genealogical instruction. It's like attending a conference every day for five days or longer, but with much smaller class sizes and more personal instruction. Conferences may be attended by 100 to 500 or more people who gather in a lecture hall, whereas institutes normally have from 25 to 45 in a class. There is the Genealogical Institute of Mid-America in Springfield, Illinois; the National Institute of Genealogical Research in Washington, D.C.; the Institute of Genealogy and Historical Research in Samford, Alabama; the Institute of Genealogical Studies in Dallas, Texas; and the Salt Lake Institute of Genealogy in Salt Lake City, Utah. (See "Genealogical Institutes and Conferences" in the appendixes for details.)

The bottom line is, if you like genealogy and want to learn more, there are many educational opportunities. But in order to master the field, you must study not only African American genealogy but also American genealogy, U.S. history, and African American history.

As you see, there is a whole world of genealogy out there. Some have said it is the most popular hobby in America. Some say stamp collecting is the most popular, but I know thousands of genealogists and only one or two stamp collectors. OK, I might be prejudiced.

Putting It All Together

Now that you've almost finished the book and you've successfully completed all the steps for all your ancestors, I recommend you reread the early chapter "What Is Genealogy?" It will then make more sense to you. You know a lot more than when you first read it, and once you complete all the steps, you'll be a lot more experienced, as well as more knowledgeable. Then if you reread the chapter on "Fundamentals," you'll know what records to research next.

Genealogy Is a Game

I've talked a lot about how to do genealogy and the rules that govern it. I've also related genealogy to a puzzle in which you find bits and pieces of information and connect them together. But genealogy is also a game. It's like a game of hide and seek. Your ancestors are hidden, and you're trying to find them. It requires a lot of work, study, ingenuity, and luck, but it's a fun game. And like many games, the thrill is in the hunt, not necessarily in the end result. You think you can find your ancestors, but you really don't know until you get there. Along the way you'll have trials, tribulations, successes, and failures. Some theories will pan out and others will peter out. Sometimes when you least expect it, ancestors will jump right out in front of you. It will be very exhilarating.

And as in the story of the hare and the tortoise, the race does not always go to the swift. It usually goes to the person who is methodical and prodding, thorough and calculating. Because in the end it's not a race at all. You won't win a prize if you finish before someone else. You win when you do a good job, a complete job, answer the questions of your family and peers, and leave a legacy for those who follow after you.

Keys to Success in Genealogy

There are several keys to success in genealogy. You should seek help when you need it, study the theory of genealogy and then put it into practice, understand that ancestors were human beings, research your entire family, prove your research, and don't give up.

Ask for Help

Don't be afraid to ask for help when you run into problems or get stuck. There is help all around. Especially ask experienced genealogists you respect. You can save years of work and frustration by asking someone with good experience. However, if the person you consult has years of experience but is not a good genealogist, he or she might hinder your progress more than help it.

I'm amazed at some of the basic questions people seem to be afraid to ask. I once talked to a teacher who was wondering where to get records from the Civil War. She had a book that covered the area of the country where her ancestors lived during the Civil War. The book was very well written and footnoted by the historian who wrote it. I realized the footnotes in the book answered all her questions. When I asked if she had checked the sources in the footnotes, she replied, "No, I didn't know what they meant." The sad thing was that these were the answers to all her questions and all she had to do was ask for help. Any reference librarian in the library, particularly in the history department, would have gladly and quickly explained what each footnote meant and how to obtain each original source.

The reference librarian should be your best friend. I have many of them. Whenever you have a question about finding a source or interpreting a source, always check with the reference librarian. If unable to answer your question, he or she will usually point you in the right direction. Those questions the reference librarian can't answer, a history professor in a college might be able to answer. You can also seek out the author of a book or an expert in the field to get your question answered. You'd be amazed at how open people are to helping others and answering their questions. At lectures and conferences, don't be afraid to approach the experts and get their opinion on your questions. This is the best opportunity to discuss genealogy with the best minds in the business.

Theory Versus Practice

I've been an athlete all my life, born and raised on baseball and running. I ran to school every day, played running games during recess and lunch, and played baseball every day after school. I was on the track team in high school, played a little football, and played in tennis tournaments after college. I majored in physical education in college, before changing to Black American Studies. After college I coached high school basketball and track. I attended numerous coaching clinics with some of the best basketball minds that were involved in the game.

I've participated in athletics from both sides of the bench, player and coach. I know there are different aspects to sports. I think they are similar to genealogy. In tennis the first thing to learn is how to hold the racquet, how to spread your feet and bend your knees, how to swing the racquet, and how to follow through. Then there are the rules of the game, what you can and cannot do. Next is understanding what are called "the X's and O's," the basic strategies of offense and defense.[1] These are technical details needed in every sport to accomplish the physical mechanics to participate at a comfortable level. These "X's and O's" exist for every sport and can be found in books in the library.

After these essentials are learned, the next important question is, Do you have the physical attributes to enjoy the game or to participate at a high level of competition? Some of these attributes people are born with; others can be developed with training.

The next aspect is the psychological side. Do you have the mental toughness to do what it takes to be the best you can be in a sport? Are you willing to sacrifice and pay the price to be the best? Or do you want to merely be a weekend recreational player? All that is in your head.

The intellectual side of all of this is being able to understand all these dimensions. Do you know the role each one plays and can you manipulate each one to your advantage and change tactics when necessary?

You might ask, "What does this have to do with genealogy?" From my viewpoint, everything in the world. We're talking about theory versus practice. Some people play sports through trial and error, never taking lessons but having a good time. Others take lessons all the time but are scared to walk on the court or play a match.

I believe that in any game in life you should learn the theory that makes the game work, but you can never understand it or master it until you play. Once you play, you can only improve so much without understanding more theories and strategies of the game. This new information is then put into practice, which in turn improves your game. The result of this synergy between theory and practice produces success.

It is the same in genealogy. Anyone can get genealogical information by talking to relatives at a family reunion and then going to census records and have good results. But that researcher will not accomplish much more without knowing the theories and strategies of proven genealogical research. They need to know about the dozens of records that exist, how to solve genealogy problems, and how to construct pedigrees. Likewise, those of you who have read this book but have not consulted the sources and implemented the methods, theories, and strategies will have limited success. You must learn the theories, put them into practice, and then analyze your results to see what went right, what went wrong, and what to change when you return to research.

You also have to learn other theories by reading other genealogy books and periodicals, attending lectures and conferences, and talking to other genealogists, and then practice what

---

[1] For the nonplayers out there, X's are used to illustrate one team, and O's are used to illustrate the opposing team in diagramming plays on a chalkboard.

you learn. Go to your relatives, the library, the courthouse, the National Archives, and other places where records exist. Find out if what was in the book was right for you. See if what the author or lecturer said worked for you. If not, examine the theories and determine how to make adjustments so you can win.

I advocate keeping notes to yourself on *how* you made genealogical discoveries, *when* you made the discoveries, and *where* you made them. They will help you refresh your memory in the future and help to solve other problems, in other lines, and with other ancestors. You can learn from your own experiences.

More Than Names

Being successful in genealogy requires more than knowing about records and finding names, dates, and places. Genealogy is not about collecting names. Not everyone with the same name is related. I gave a talk in New Orleans and showed a slide with the name Smothers on it. A lady came up afterward and said we were related. Her Smothers ancestors were from Louisiana, but mine had never set foot in Louisiana. I traced my Smothers family in Pennsylvania for over 200 years and found they had migrated from the East Coast. Genealogists waste so much time searching for names.

! Trap: Assuming everyone with the same surname is related. Some surnames are rare in some communities and common in others.

Genealogy is not about names; it's about people. Ancestors were human beings. You must identify families and characteristics of families and individuals. Then the name becomes insignificant. So don't rush off looking for everyone in the country with your surname. You'll waste your time.

Research the Entire Family

Many genealogists don't get very far because their search is too narrow. They start tracing back another generation before obtaining information on collateral lines. They want to research only their parents, grandparents, great-grandparents, and so forth. Who's to say one of those persons will leave more records than their brothers or sisters? Each sibling may have a small piece of the puzzle you're putting together. They're all part of the same family and will help to lead the trail backward. So you've got to trace them all.

> ❗ Trap: Tracing only direct ancestors, not their brothers and sisters.
> These are your collateral lines or collateral ancestors (aunts, uncles,
> great-aunts, great-uncles, cousins, second cousins, etc.), and they
> have the same parents who are your direct ancestors.

Lack of discipline and patience are the two most difficult hurdles to overcome in genealogy. We get so excited, we want to finish all at once. There's a tendency to be impatient, to jump back in time before laying a strong foundation with the current generation. The fear of getting old and dying inspires many people's interest in genealogy. They fear they don't have much time left. But unfortunately, that is a trap that sometimes prevents them from doing good-quality work. They fear their time is running out and use it as an excuse for trying to go back too far too fast rather than dotting their *i*'s and crossing their *t*'s.

Having patience does not mean doing nothing. There's plenty of research to do, so there's no reason to fear sitting idle, waiting to receive information. Having discipline and patience means setting priorities and doing the most important things first, not jumping the gun.

> ❗ Trap: Being impatient and lacking discipline.

Prove Your Genealogy

Remember, genealogy is a science (the suffix *-ology* means "science of"). It is not based on assumptions—it requires evidence and proof. After you collect and evaluate the evidence, you must come to conclusions and present your case to others to prove it. This is very helpful because others can often see things we overlook. We're so close to the trees, we sometimes miss the forest.

There are several ways of proving a genealogy. In court, evidence must be ruled upon by a jury of your peers. In genealogy, the jury of peers is other genealogists—but not just any genealogists. They should be experienced and knowledgeable. One example is submitting your research to a peer-review journal, discussed in the chapter "Writing the Family History."

Another example is being admitted to a lineage society, sometimes called a hereditary society. This is an organization made up of individuals who can trace their genealogy back to a common event, such as the Civil War, the American Revolution, or the pioneers who first settled in an area. They are divided into categories of a particular war, colony, ship, family, or nationality.

A patriotic society is an organization that includes members who can trace their genealogy to a patriotic event. For example, the most well-known patriotic organization is the Daughters of American Revolution, commonly known as the DAR. It consists of females who can trace their lineage to a soldier who fought in the American Revolutionary War or served in the government or aided the cause. Even though tens of thousands of African Americans fought in the Revolutionary War, the DAR used to deny membership to African American women with Revolutionary War ancestors. Nearly twenty-five years ago, Black women who had done excellent research and documented their sources were able to win admittance. Karen Farmer was the first recognized African American woman admitted to the DAR, in 1977. She faced slight resistance in getting admitted. Lena Ferguson was admitted to the national chapter in 1984 but was denied admittance to a local Washington, D.C., chapter. Karen Sutton was admitted in 1993.

The lineage societies have forms to fill out, guidelines on how to submit evidence, and trained lineage specialists who review applications. Once you think you're ready, the society will give you help, or you can seek out another member who can tell you how he or she did it.

Another method of proving your genealogy is to apply for a pioneer certificate. Many states recognize genealogists who can document their lineage back to the early settlers of a state or region. The state genealogical society usually establishes guidelines, rules upon applications, and issues certificates.

Another way of proving your genealogy is applying for certification to the Board for Certification of Genealogists (BCG). This was discussed briefly in the chapter "What Is Genealogy?" Becoming a "certified genealogist" is more difficult than obtaining a pioneer certificate or joining a lineage society. BCG developed *The BCG Genealogical Standards Manual,* a comprehensive guide to help you organize, document, and present your research findings. It contains guidelines for evaluating evidence with examples of proof summaries and numbering systems. There are also sample reports to help professionals present their findings succinctly, which can also help in hiring a professional genealogist.

The International Commission for the Accreditation of Professional Genealogists (ICAP-GEN) also tests genealogists' skills and awards the credentials of Accredited Genealogist (AG). I encourage every African American to seek certification. Many have done the research but not obtained the credit.

African American Genealogists Who Have Done It

More and more African American genealogists are doing good genealogical research and proving it. They are joining lineage societies, becoming certified, and applying for pioneer certificates.

The following list is dedicated to those African American genealogists who have done it.

Daughters of the American Revolution
(DAR)
Karen Farmer
Lena Ferguson
Karen Sutton

Sons of the American Revolution (SAR)
Alvin Collins

First Families of Texas
Bell Cheatham
Jamie Harris

First Families of Oklahoma
Joann Page
Rudy Tolbert

Daughters of Civil War Union Veterans

Laura Blanchet
Cordelia Brown
Dolores Brown
Jocelyn Bush
Hazel Caldwell
Evelyn Cox
Vivian Dorsey
Karen Fox
Sarah Fox
Juanita Hammond
Mildred Harvin
Celestine Hollings
Sara Hunter
Jane Johnson
Cleopatra Jones
Bennie Latimer
Helen Lewis
Cordella MacRae
Ada Maxwell
Lisa McNeal

Carol Muse
Particia Perry
Jessie Pinder
Maia Porche
Vivian Porche
Ruth Reynolds
Jeanette Secret
Phyllis Stone
Elizabeth Turner
Cherly Watson
Thelma Watson
Martha Williams
Peggy Williams
Joan Yates

Certified Genealogists
Paul Sluby

Certified Genealogical Record Specialists
Curtis Brasfield
Jacqueline E. Alexander Lawson

I'm sure there are others, and I apologize for not including them. I hope this list will encourage others to document and prove their genealogy.

Don't Give Up

When driving home one evening after taking my class to the National Archives to research census records for the first time, I made a startling discovery. I realized our best genealogy is done when we don't find our ancestors, not when we find them. It's the problem-solving process that leads to discoveries and new information.

One student, Judy, could not find her ancestors on the 1920 census. She looked on both her maternal side and her paternal side without success. Judy then wanted to give up and look at the 1910 census. I looked at her Family Group Sheet and realized she had not completed her fundamental research. There were birth certificates and marriage records she should have researched that would have shed more light on her family's whereabouts in 1920. If Judy had done this, she probably would have found her ancestors on the 1920 census.

George, another student, wanted to research a great-grandfather without first researching his parents and grandparents. George readily admitted this great-grandfather was fixated in his mind and he couldn't get him out of it. When he started to look for his parents, who were living with aunts and uncles, he couldn't locate them on the 1920 census. Then it dawned on George that the aunt had remarried and he did not know her new surname. I recommended he talk to other relatives and locate marriage records for his aunt to determine her married surname.

Some researchers don't find their ancestors and they give up. Some start to research other years, other records, other ancestors, or leave genealogy altogether. But it's solving these problems that leads to great discoveries, new circumstances, realities different from our simplistic assumptions, and a realistic understanding of history and our ancestors.

Success in genealogy is similar to winning teams that don't have the best players and secret plays. The winning teams are the ones that have great players who are *motivated* to play beyond their potential and have the psychological will to win. Michael Jordan and the Bulls beat many basketball teams that were better than them but didn't have the experience or the unstoppable desire to win that the Bulls possessed. Researchers not wanting to do things that are "hard" are hindered more by their psychological hangups than by a lack of records.

My most important discoveries, and leaps in genealogical methodology, have come when I initially ran into roadblocks and my ancestors were not living where I thought they were. This once led to a revolutionary discovery of African Americans in the 1870 census, which affected all African American genealogists. It then led me to create a new method for researching African American genealogy in 1870. So don't give up, and don't run away from problems—try to solve them. Your tenacity will eventually pay off. Gerald Richard, my high school track coach, had a saying he drilled into our young minds: "A quitter never wins and a winner never quits." He said it so often we memorized it. Now when I run into my old track buddies and we start reminiscing about the old days, it's the first thing we say.

The Family Historian—The Chosen One

Why do we do genealogy? Are we doing it to satisfy our own curiosity and gratification? Or are we responsible to our family and our communities to discover, uncover, and report our findings back to our community? Is it *your* genealogy or *our* genealogy?

By purchasing this book, mastering the subject of genealogy, and tracing your family history, you are now the family historian for your family. Most families have only one. They didn't choose you, but you were chosen. Charles Blockson, a bibliophile, collector of African

American memorabilia, and author of *Black Genealogy,* once said, "Genealogists are chosen people." I believe that and feel we were chosen by some force beyond our control. We have a burning desire to seek the unknown and to discover and uncover hidden ancestors. It flows in our blood and it's driven by our ancestors speaking to us.

Now that you have assumed the position of family historian, remember that it comes with responsibilities. You are entrusted with the responsibility to trace your family history thoroughly and accurately. You are required to report back to the family your findings, both verbally and in writing, for all to see and have. That means you are required to consult your family about your findings and publish the family history. That family history includes all the family, not just your direct ancestors, those you like, or those you honor. You also have the responsibility to place copies of your family history in the library. Along with that awesome responsibility, you are allowed to take pride in your accomplishments.

Now the onus is on you. You know what to do. Now, do you have the discipline to do it? I have tried to give you a good beginning and a strong foundation upon which to start your genealogical research. This is much more than I had when I began. If you follow these basic steps, you'll be off to a good start in uncovering your ancestors. You might not find everything you're looking for, but you will have success. Genealogy is a lot of fun. You never know what or who you'll find. It's like playing detective. When you've been searching high and low for someone and finally find him, it's one of the most exciting feelings in the world!

Good luck, happy hunting, and have fun!

APPENDIXES
Glossary

abstract—a brief synopsis of essential information in a longer document.

African American history—the study of people residing in America whose distant ancestors were born in Africa.

ancestor—a deceased direct relative from whom one is descended, such as a great-grand-mother or great-great-grandfather.

ancestry—the study of older deceased relatives.

ahnentafel system—a system of numbering ancestors on a Pedigree Chart, which starts with the subject being number one, then assigns males even numbers and their wives that number plus one; German for "ancestor table."

archival quality—acid-neutral products with a long lifetime.

archive—an institution that stores original documents or copies of originals to organize and preserve them for research.

archivist—the person in charge of an archive or a professional specializing in organizing or preserving old records.

aunt—a parent's sister or the wife of a parent's brother.

autobiography—the story of a person's life, written by that person.

Black history—the study of people of African descent, including those born in Africa and those dispersed to North and South America and other parts of the world.

biographical dictionary—a book containing biographies of many individuals, sometimes called "collective biographies" or "biographical encyclopedias." The dictionary may be organized by profession, religion, time period, or another category.

biography—the story of a person's life, written and researched by someone else.

bloodline—a direct line of descent.

burial site—any place where human remains are interred, including cemeteries, tombs, mausoleums, columbariums, backyards, churchyards, and floors of churches.

cartography—the study of maps and mapmaking.

census—an enumeration of inhabitants. The U.S. Census is taken every ten years; state and local censuses are taken periodically.

cemetery—land devoted to burying the dead.

circumstantial evidence—indirect evidence that implies facts.

closed stack collection—a library with books behind closed doors. Patrons use the card catalogue to identify books, which are retrieved by library staff members.

collateral ancestor—a deceased relative of a direct ancestor, for example, a great-grandfather's brother.

columbarium—a vault containing spaces for urns with cremated remains.

conservation—the safe repair and restoration of soiled or damaged artifacts.

coroner—the person who determines cause of death when from other than natural causes; often a political appointee and not necessarily a physician.

county courthouse—the government office that conducts county (or parish in Louisiana) business and stores county records.

cousin—a child of one's aunt or uncle.

descendant—an offspring of an ancestor.

direct ancestor—a deceased person related by blood (versus marriage) who follows the lines on a Pedigree Chart, such as parents, grandparents, or great-grandparents.

discrepancy chart—matrix comparing conflicting genealogical records to determine which is most accurate.

disinter—to remove a buried body from the ground.

document—any record relied upon to prove a point.

documentation—a record of the sources of factual information; references.

evidence—items presented to establish a point, including testimony, records, and objects.

extract—an exact transcription of an original document.

fact—something that actually occurred or something that is true.

Family Group Sheet—a genealogy form displaying dates and places of birth, marriage, death, and sometimes burial for a mother, father, and their children.

family history—the detailed story of a family or several families within a lineage.

finding aid—a guide that tells patrons or archive staff what items are in the collection and sometimes their size, quantity, age, or other description and location.

first cousin—the relationship between the children of aunts and uncles.

first cousin once removed—the relationship between a first cousin and the child of another first cousin.

gazetteer—geographical dictionary.

genealogical society—an organization comprising individual genealogists with common interests, usually with a geographical or ethnic interest.

genealogist—a person who studies the history of his or her own family or others people's families.

genealogy—the study of family relationships and lineage, the written results of which detail births, deaths, and marriages from the oldest ancestor. Better genealogies provide evidence to prove these relationships.

given name—a person's first name, usually given at birth.

grandaunt—the sister of one's grandparent; also called great-aunt.

granduncle—the brother of one's grandparent; also called great-uncle.

grave goods—items placed upon a grave in a cemetery, such as dishes, clocks, beds, and lamps, to appease or ward off evil spirits.

hearsay—a story, used to prove a fact, repeated by someone who did not witness the event.

hereditary society—an organization in which members can trace their lineage to a common event. Prospective members usually submit genealogy charts and evidence to prove this lineage, which is ruled upon by a lineage specialist.

historical society—an organization dedicated to collecting and preserving a facet of history. Can be of a geographical area, such as a state, county, or city, or of an organization or industry, such as a railroad historical society. Sometimes has a library or book collection, as well as museum and public programs.

history—a branch of knowledge that deals with accounts of past events.

home funeral—a funeral service held in the home of the deceased rather than a funeral home. Someone in the family cleans and prepares the body.

in-law—a person related to another by marriage (other than spouse or children).

inter—to put a body into the ground or a tomb.

Jim Crow—a period of segregation in the United States marked by laws and practices of dividing people, institutions, and facilities by race. There are several stories of the origin of the name; one refers to a tune and dance called "Jump Jim Crow," performed at minstrel shows.

library—a collection primarily of books and other published materials.

lineage—a single bloodline of a family from one ancestor to a descendant.

lineage society—*see* hereditary society

local history—stories of a limited geographical area, such as a city, town, or county.

maiden name—the surname of a woman before marriage.

manuscript—a handwritten document or an unpublished writing.

maternal—relatives of the mother's side of the family.

mausoleum—a large vault or tomb for the dead.

medical examiner—a physician responsible for determining cause of death when other than natural causes.

memorabilia—personal family collectibles that preserve memories of the family.

microfiche—4″ × 6″ sheet of film containing reduced copies of records for preservation, space saving, or both.

microfilm—a roll of film (usually 16mm or 35mm) containing reduced copies of records for preservation, space saving, or both.

microform—microfilm or microfiche.

microtext—documents that have been reproduced on microfilm or microfiche.

mulatto—a person with interracial parents, but definition varied by state and time period, some defining mulattoes as 50 percent "Negro" blood and some as little as one-eighth. In early periods, referred to a person of white and Native American Indian parents.

necrology—a list of dead people.

nephew—the son of a sister or brother.

nickname—a casual first name different from a person's given name; sometimes a derivative of their first name, such as "Sue" for Susan, sometimes descriptive, such as "Shorty," and sometimes with no connection, such as "Butch."

niece—the daughter of a sister or brother.

obituary—a brief story of a deceased person's life, usually published in a newspaper or funeral program.

octoroon—a person with one-eighth Black blood, that is, one ancestor of African descent and seven white great-grandparents.

open stack collection—a library with books on open shelves, enabling patrons to browse shelves.

oral history—the story of a person's life and perhaps the person's family and ancestors, as told to another person, which may or may not be recorded.

oral tradition—stories that have been verbally handed down from generation to generation.

paternal—relatives from the father's side of the family.

patronymic—naming system in which a child's given name is the same as the father's surname.

pedigree—the direct ancestors of an individual.

Pedigree Chart—a diagram illustrating the direct ancestors of an individual.

periodical—a publication appearing periodically (daily, monthly, quarterly, or annually), such as newspapers, newsletters, and journals.

preponderance of the evidence—the standard of proof in civil court cases when sufficient evidence establishes at least a 51 percent likelihood that allegations are correct. This used to be the standard of proof in genealogy until professionals realized genealogy requires higher standards.

preservation—protection to enable documents and artifacts to last.

primary evidence—that created at the time an event occurred, by someone with direct knowledge of the event; original records.

primary record—*see* primary evidence.

primary source—*see* primary evidence.

progenitor—the earliest known ancestor.

proof—sufficient, credible evidence to certify an allegation is true.

public domain—belongs to the public and is unrestricted by copyright or patent.

query—a brief genealogical statement and question to see if other genealogists have any knowledge of a particular family or ancestor.

quadroon—one-fourth Black; person with three white grandparents and one of African descent.

record—an account of an event preserved on paper, film, tape, or other medium.

reinter—to bury a previously buried body. This occurs when remains are transferred from one grave to another, from one cemetery to another, or are exhumed for examination.

relative—a person related to another by blood.

repository—an institution storing records.

second cousin—the relationship between the children of first cousins.

secondary evidence—that created after events occurred or by someone not having direct knowledge of the event; not original records.

secondary record—*see* secondary evidence.

secondary source—*see* secondary evidence.

segregation—separation of people based on race, religion, ethnic or national origin.

sexton—person in charge of records and maintenance of a cemetery.

soundex—a phonic index to the census, based loosely on the sound of surnames.

surname—a person's last name, which identifies him or her with a family.

tertiary sources—information reported from secondary sources, for example, thirdhand.

tradition—the way things have been done or understood for a long time.

transcription—a word-for-word copy of a document or tape.

uncle—one's parent's brother or aunt's husband.

vital records—government documents recording births, deaths, marriages, and divorces.

vital statistics—dates and places of birth, marriage, and death.

Acronyms

AAGHSC—Afro-American Genealogical and Historical Society of Chicago
AAHGS—Afro-American Historical and Genealogical Society
ACPL—Allen County Public Library (Fort Wayne, Indiana)
AG—Accredited Genealogist
AHA—American Historical Association
ALA—American Library Association
APG—Association of Professional Genealogists
APGQ—Association of Professional Genealogists Quarterly
ASALH—Association for the Study of Afro-American Life and History
BCG—Board for Certification of Genealogists
BYU—Brigham Young University (Provo, Utah)
CALS—Certified American Lineage Specialist
CG—Certified Genealogist
CGC—Council of Genealogy Columnists
CGL—Certified Genealogical Lecturer
CGRS—Certified Genealogical Record Specialist
DAR—Daughters of the American Revolution
FASG—Fellow, American Society of Genealogists
FGS—Federation of Genealogical Societies
FHC—Family History Center
FHL—Family History Library (Salt Lake City, Utah)
FNGS—Fellow, National Genealogical Society
FUGA—Fellow, Utah Genealogical Society
FWP—Federal Writers Project
CG—Genealogical Computing

GEDCOM—Genealogical Data Communications
GPAI—Genealogical Periodical Annual Index
GSU—Genealogical Society of Utah
IGHR—Institute of Genealogical and Historical Research (Samford University, Birmingham, Alabama)
IGI—International Genealogical Index
LC—Library of Congress (Washington, D.C.)
LDS—Church of Jesus Christ of Latter-Day Saints (Mormons)
LOC—Library of Congress
NAACP—National Association for the Advancement of Colored People
NARA—National Archives and Record Service
NEHGS—New England Historic Genealogical Society
NGS—National Genealogical Society
NGSQ—National Genealogical Society Quarterly
NIGR—National Institute of Genealogical Research
NUC—National Union Catalogue
NUCMC—National Union Catalogue of Manuscript Collections
OAH—Organization of American Historians
OCLC—Online Computer Library Center
PERSI—Periodical Source Index
SAR—Sons of the American Revolution
SASE—Self-Addressed, Stamped Envelope
SHA—Southern Historical Association
WPA—Works Progress Administration; later Work Projects Administration

Biography of Robert Elliott Burroughs

Robert Elliott Burroughs was born on May 13, 1889, in Chicago, Illinois.[1] He was the first child born in the North of a family that migrated from the South just a couple of years before his birth.[2] His father, Morris Burroughs, was born in the small town of Spartanburg, South Carolina, at the end of the Civil War.[3] He migrated to Chicago to take a job with the Pullman Company, reportedly the largest employer of African Americans at the turn of the century.[4] Morris worked as a Pullman porter, on the Chicago and Alton Railroad, carrying luggage, making beds, shining shoes, and waiting on train passengers. His route began at Union Station in downtown Chicago and ended at Alton, Illinois, near East St. Louis.[5] Morris frequently took his two sons, Robert and Asa, on train rides.[6]

Robert's mother, Mary Jane Lillie Williams, was born in Chattanooga, Tennessee, in 1868.[7] She left Chattanooga in 1885 for Atlanta, Georgia, to attend Spellman Seminary, an all-Black female college.[8] Mary majored in nursing.[9]

Morris and Mary married in Chattanooga while she was still in school, on May 24, 1888.[10] She enrolled for the fall term but never completed it.[11] She moved to Chicago to be with her husband and start a new way of life in the North. Little Robert was born in Chicago the following May.

Photo of Robert Elliot Burroughs—Photograph of Robert Burroughs taken around 1950.

The Burroughs family lived on the west side of Chicago in an integrated neighborhood, probably in a two-story brick walk-up.[12] At the time African Americans were only 1.3 percent of Chicago's population.[13] Morris and Mary were pioneers, as the great migrations of African Americans to Chicago and other northern cities didn't occur until World War I, lasting to the 1960s.[14] Morris was active with the Pullman porters, and Mary was active in the A.M.E. church.

Robert's parents worked hard and had bright hopes for Robert. They named him for a famous African American, Robert Elliott. Elliott was an attorney who served in the South Carolina House of Representatives during Reconstruction and was later Speaker of the House in the state legislature.[15] He was the first African American commanding general of the South Carolina militia (National Guard). In 1869 Elliott formed the state militia, often called the Black Militia because it contained so many African Americans. Their duty was to protect white and African American citizens from the murderous, fast-growing Ku Klux Klan.[16]

Morris and Mary were undoubtedly proud of their first child, Robert. They traveled to Mary's hometown of Chattanooga to show the family the new baby and posed for a family photo (see page 126). Robert cherished this first photograph and kept it all his life.[17]

But Morris and Mary's hopes were not to be. Robert dropped out of school in the seventh grade.[18] Little known to anyone, this was the beginning of a downward spiral that would haunt him for the rest of his life. His father developed tuberculous and died two years later, when Robert was only fourteen years old.[19]

It is not known how Robert was employed from fourteen to twenty years of age, but then he worked as a bricklayer and chauffeur.[20] Family legend said Robert drove fast cars and had lots of women.[21] Driver's licenses and vehicle registrations left in his wallet, however, reveal that he owned a couple of new cars when he was young but drove nothing but old beaters that were nine to fourteen years old as he got older (see page 115). Many were cars long out of production and unknown to people today. He owned a Cadillac, which is still in production, and a Graham Page, which became a classic. He also owned a Kissel, a Liberty, and a Stearns. He saved vehicle registrations all the way back to 1917, which may have been when he purchased his first car at twenty-eight years old. At the time Henry Ford's Model T Ford had been in production for only nine years. Also found among personal belongings in his trunk were highway maps from 1929, 1936, 1940, and 1941. Robert had a love affair with cars and driving.

Robert's mother died in 1914, when he was just twenty-five years old. It had to have been rough losing both parents when just becoming an adult. Robert married Jessie Young the following year.[22] He had lived at home with his brother until then at 255 North Hoyne on the Westside. In 1916 Robert and Asa relocated from the Westside to the Southside but to different residences. They were both grown, Robert was now married and living in his own residence, and the brothers would go on to lead completely different lives.

Robert registered for the draft for World War I on March 31, 1917, but was never drafted.[23] Unfortunately, he took his chauffeur job to heart when he got involved with the wrong crowd. They drove out West and had too good a time. They lost all their money and began to steal to make ends meet. They returned to Chicago, and on May 9, 1917, Robert drove the getaway car when he and four others robbed the Illinois Tool Works at 145 East Erie. Two of the other men were African American and two were white. The heist was planned by the two white men, one a cashier and the other a bookkeeper at the company they robbed. The five made off with the $5,700 cash payroll, but not for long. Robert was arrested later in the day while walking down the street.[24]

Getting caught was a tremendous embarrassment, as his name was splattered in newspapers all over the city. Robert pleaded guilty, and his misdeeds netted him a year to life in the state penitentiary at Joliet. He went to prison on July 26, 1917, and his wife, Jessie Young, divorced him two years later.[25] He became remorseful for his criminal behavior and began writing poetry. Below are three stanzas from an untitled poem Robert wrote while incarcerated and lamenting his misdeeds.

That night as I lay on my plate of straw,
I vowed there, again I would never break the law,
I tasted life's pleasures found them bitter as gawl,
They placed me in a dungeon behind the stone wall.
Come all of you fellows take a warning from me
You will lose all in life when you lose *Liberty,*
Be on but your mother to see your down fall,
You are dead to this world behind the stone wall,
When I was successful the world was at my feet,
And friends by the million would make life complete.

In Chic fair city where I first saw the light,
Raised up by find parents in the path way of right,
I was left an orphan at the age of ten years,
Over the grave of my mother I have shed many a tear,
I had scarcely reached manhood when I left my good home,
With an other young fellow the west for to roam.
We tasted life's pleasures full of sin and ashame,
Lost all of our money also our good name.
The sharp pains of hunger we were seen made to feel,
Lost all of our money and driven to steal.

In Chic fair city my fate I did meet,
It was there I was arrested while walking the streets.
It happened in the merry month of may,
Which has been many, many a day
My charges were robbery but my feat it was small,
They said it would place me behind the stone wall.
On the morning of my trial I was down cast and sad,
I pleaded for mercy for me none they had.
Through experience and time I had sincerely repented,
While thinking of the day I was first presented.

Robert was released from prison on April 18, 1922, after serving five years. Afterward he hustled low-paying jobs. He returned to being a chauffeur and also worked as an auto mechanic, electrician, and radio repairman.[26] In 1925 he bought a four-year-old Liberty touring car, which he kept until 1928, when he bought a Sterns K.[27]

Robert remarried on October 18, 1929. He and fiancée, Malvina Holman, traveled to nearby Crown Point, Indiana, probably in his Stearns K automobile. Crown Point was known for its marriage mill because there was no waiting period and couples didn't have to get a blood test.

Robert kept the Sterns K until 1930, when he bought a two-year-old Kissel roadster. The Great Depression hit Robert hard. When he wasn't on welfare, he groomed horses at Arlington Park Racetrack and Hawthorn Stables near Chicago. His groom license cost just a dollar, but he earned only sixty-eight cents an hour.[28]

Robert applied for a birth certificate in 1943 and realized there was none on file. He ordered a delayed birth certificate and brought in his brother, Asa, to verify his birth.[29] Ironically, Robert was four years old when Asa was born.

In 1944, in another twist of irony, Robert got a job working for the Pullman Company, just like his dad. However, Robert was not a Pullman porter; he worked as an electrician. He worked at the Santa Fe Yard on the Westside of Chicago for $1.05 an hour.[30] He kept the job for only three months and resigned because of poor health.[31]

Robert bought a nine-year-old Mercury sedan in 1949 that lasted three years. At fourteen years old, it had had enough. He next purchased an eleven-year-old Dodge panel truck that he kept for a couple of years.

When times got rough, Robert applied for welfare and unemployment compensation three or four times.[32] It was difficult for him because he had three strikes against him—he was an ex-convict, had only a seventh-grade education, and was an African American in the Jim Crow segregation era.

Robert's personal life was just as bad. His first wife divorced him when he was in prison, and his second wife was admitted to a mental hospital in 1937. She died in the hospital a couple of months later.[33] His brother, Asa, was a prominent attorney who'd run for political office and not only didn't want the world to know about his ex-convict sibling, but forbade his children to have anything to do with his brother.[34]

During the winter of 1958, Robert suffered from pneumonia and was admitted to Cook County Hospital. Three days later he died a pauper on January 28, 1958, at sixty-nine years old. Before his death he had been living just a block from his brother, at 6021 South Vernon.[35] Ironically, I lived in the same apartment building, upstairs from my grandfather, until 1956 and never knew of Uncle Robert. He's buried in an unmarked grave in the family cemetery lot at Oakridge Cemetery, west of Chicago.[36]

It is through genealogy that Robert's life has been resurrected. A person who was little known to his nephews and niece and nonexistent to the third generation. By telling his story, I hope not only that genealogists will see how family history is resurrected and reconstructed but that adolescents will learn a lesson about life, a lesson Robert learned the hard way.

Through poetry Robert tried to tell others not to follow his errant ways. But perhaps if his brother had given him more support, he might have made more of his life.

1. Illinois Delayed Birth Certificate No. D.S. 16058 for Robert Elliott Burroughs, filed in Cook County on 2 November 1943.
2. Chicago Illinois Death Certificate No. 12908 for Morris Burroughs indicated in 1903 he'd been a resident of Illinois for twelve years. The Chicago city directory listed him in 1889, and Pullman Company payroll records listed him in 1887.
3. Little red book with relatives' dates of birth and death, owned by Asa Morris Burroughs, now deceased. Book is in possession of Tony Burroughs; death certificate for Morris Burroughs, 15 December 1903.
4. These claims are made in *Keeping the Faith: A. Philip Randolph, Milton Webster and the Brotherhood of Sleeping Car Porters, 1925–1937*, by William H. Harris (p. 2); *Those Pullman Blues*, by David D. Perata (p. xvii); and *Miles of Smiles, Years of Struggle: Stories of Black Pullman Porters*, by Jack Santino (p. 7), but none provide supporting evidence.
5. *Rhea's New Citizens' Directory of Chicago, ILL. and Suburban Towns, Also Other Towns and Cities*, ed. by H. W. Rhea, p. 137; Chicago and Alton Railroad timetables, 1912.
6. Interview with Alma Burroughs by Tony Burroughs in February 1976. Mrs. Burroughs is now deceased, and transcript in possession of Tony Burroughs.
7. Little red book owned by Asa Morris Burroughs.
8. Letter to Tony Burroughs dated 4 June 1986, from Jeanne H. Allen, registrar at Spellman College.
9. Spellman Seminary student bulletins, 1885–1887.
10. Hamilton County, Tennessee, marriage return for Morris R. Burroughs and Mary Jane Lillie Williams.
11. Letter dated 4 June 1986 from registrar at Spellman College.
12. 1910 U.S. Census records indicate 848 West Madison Street is an integrated block and Burroughs family is in a multifamily dwelling. Existing structures from the time period are two stories.
13. *Black Metropolis: A Study of Negro Life in a Northern City*, by St. Clair Drake and Horace Cayton, p. 9.
14. *The Encyclopedia of Southern History*, by David C. Roller and Robert W. Twyman, pp. 890–892; *Black Chicago: The Making of a Ghetto, 1890–1920*, by Alan Spears, p. 12; U.S. Census Reports, 1890.
15. *Encyclopedia of Black America*, by W. Augustus Low and Virgil A. Clift, p. 354.
16. *Tour Black Chicago News* 1, no. 4 (February 1997), p. 3.
17. Photograph found in Robert's trunk of Morris, Mary, Martha, and two others when Robert was less than one year old.
18. Untitled poem by Robert Burroughs found in his trunk.
19. Illinois death certificate for Morris Burroughs, 1903.
20. 1916 Chicago city directory, p. 304; Mamie Burroughs household, 1910 U.S. Census, Cook County, Illinois, Population Schedule, City of Chicago Enumeration District 699, Supervisor's District No. 1, Sheet 7A, dwelling 93, family 147, National Archives microfilm publication, T-624, reel 256.
21. Interview with Elmer Burroughs by Tony Burroughs on 29 December 1975. Elmer Burroughs is deceased and transcript is in possession of Tony Burroughs.
22. Little red book.
23. World War I draft registration card, Chicago, Illinois Draft Board No. 3, National Archives microfilm publication M1509, reel 656.
24. *Chicago Tribune*, 10 May 1917 and 11 May 1917; *Chicago American*, 10 May 1917 and 11 May 1917.
25. Little red book noted Robert and Jessie Young divorced in 1919.
26. Business cards found in Robert's trunk; 1944 Pullman Company Employee Service record for Robert Burroughs.
27. 1925 City of Chicago Vehicle License for a Liberty touring car and 1928 State of Illinois Vehicle Registration for a Stearns K, both registered to Robert Burroughs, found in Robert's trunk and in possession of Tony Burroughs.

28. Payroll stubs from Lincoln Jockey Club and Hawthorne Stable; 1937 receipt for Illinois grooming license, both found in Robert's trunk.
29. Cook County, Illinois, Delayed Birth Certificate No. D.S. 16058 for Robert Elliott Burroughs.
30. 1944 Pullman Company Employee Service record for Robert Burroughs.
31. Ibid.
32. Family papers from Robert's trunk, which included driver's licenses, business cards, and welfare applications.
33. "Order Setting Case for Trial" in the matter of alleged insanity of Malvina Burroughs, 8 September 1936, found in Robert's trunk.
34. Interview with Elmer Burroughs by Tony Burroughs on 29 December 1975.
35. Cook County, Illinois, Death Certificate No. 4192 for Robert E. Burroughs.
36. Oakridge Cemetery (Hillside, Illinois) sexton's records for Lot 38, Section 11.

Traps

1. Going back too far too fast. Once genealogists find new ancestors, they immediately want to search for their parents instead of learning as much as they can about that new ancestor.
2. Many novice genealogists hear they are related to some famous person a few generations back and immediately start researching that famous person. Unfortunately, many of them find out there is no connection to that person, and they've wasted years of research. So work backward; don't try to reach back and tie the person into your family. If there is some kind of connection, you'll see how it links up along the way.
3. Not knowing Black history. You must study it to be a successful genealogist.
4. Not keeping files, notes, and papers organized.
5. Not creating a Research Calendar logging places you've been and sources you've checked and keeping it up to date.
6. Not seeking out relatives we haven't met before or those we haven't seen in a long time.
7. Asking only for the names of parents and grandparents.
8. Not getting biographies from Mom and Dad, thinking that we already "know" them.
9. Not tape-recording Mom and Dad, thinking they will be around for years.
10. Waiting to travel to see distant older relatives instead of interviewing them over the telephone.
11. Not transcribing tape recordings.
12. Getting stuck on myths of oral history.
13. Neglecting living relatives by researching in libraries, archives, and county courthouses before all of the relatives have been thoroughly interviewed.

14. Not encouraging Mom, Dad, and other relatives to label their photographs. This can lead to unidentified ancestors in the future.
15. Not keeping genealogy charts up to date.
16. Trying to obtain a birth certificate before a death certificate. The death certificate will lead you to the birth certificate.
17. Not using a Research Calendar and keeping it up to date.
18. Going to the library and not having your charts up to date.
19. Ignoring spelling variations in names.
20. Doing primary research before secondary research. See what others have done first so you won't reinvent the wheel.
21. Reading only the index and not the book.
22. Not being familiar with and reading standard genealogy reference works.
23. Not documenting your research. Sources should be cited on the back of each document.
24. Not reviewing research findings and notes right after a research trip.
25. Not filing, organizing, and updating findings after research trips.
26. Accepting the information in census records as gospel.
27. Relying mainly on census research.
28. Getting on-line too soon.
29. Relying too heavily on one source. Leave no stone unturned and research any and all records.
30. Trying to trace slave ancestors prematurely.
31. Attending only conferences and lectures labeled "African American."
32. Assuming everyone with the same surname is related. Some surnames are rare in some communities and common in others.
33. Tracing only direct ancestors, not their brothers and sisters. These are your collateral lines or collateral ancestors (aunts, uncles, great-aunts, great-uncles, cousins, second cousins, etc.), and they have the same parents who are your direct ancestors.
34. Being impatient and lacking discipline.

Directory of Sources

National Archives and Records Administration Regions

National Archives I (Washington, DC)
7th & Pennsylvania Avenue
Washington, DC 20408
202-523-3285
E-mail: inquire@nara.gov.
comments@nara.gov.

National Archives II (College Park)
8610 Adelphi Road
College Park, MD 20740-6001
301-713-7230

Northeast Region (New York City)
201 Varick Street
New York, NY 10014-4811
212-337-1300
Fax: 212-337-1306
E-mail: archives@newyork.nara.gov

Northeast Region (Boston)
Frederick C. Murphy Federal Center
380 Trapelo Road
Waltham, MA 02452-6399
781-647-8104
Fax: 781-647-8088
E-mail: center@waltham.nara.gov

Northeast Region (Pittsfield)
10 Conte Drive
Pittsfield, MA 01201-8230
413-445-6885
Fax: 413-445-7305
E-mail: center@pittsfield.nara.gov

Mid-Atlantic Region (Philadelphia)
900 Market Street
Philadelphia, PA 19107-4292
215-597-3000
Fax: 215-597-2303
E-mail: archives@philarch.nara.gov

Great Lakes Region (Chicago)
7358 South Pulaski Road
Chicago, IL 60629-5898
773-581-7816
Fax: 312-353-1294
E-mail: archives@chicago.nara.gov

Central Plains Region (Kansas City)
2312 East Bannister Road
Kansas City, MO 64131-3011
816-926-6920
Fax: 816-926-6982
E-mail: center@kansascity.nara.gov

Rocky Mountain Region (Denver)
Building 48, Denver Federal Center
Denver, CO 80225-0307
Mailing address: P.O. Box 25307, Denver,
    CO 80225-0307
303-236-0804
Fax: 303-236-9297
E-mail: center@denver.nara.gov

Southeast Region (Atlanta)
1557 St. Joseph Avenue
East Point, GA 30344-2593
404/763-7474
Fax: 404-763-7059
E-mail: center@atlanta.nara.gov

Southwest Region (Fort Worth)
501 West Felix Street, Building 1
Fort Worth, TX 76115-3405
Mailing address: P.O. 6216, Fort Worth, TX
    76115-0216
817-334-5515
Fax: 817-334-5511
E-mail: center@ftworth.nara.gov

Pacific Region (Laguna Niguel)
24000 Avila Road—1st Floor, East Entrance
Laguna Niguel, CA 92677-3497
Mailing address: P.O. Box 6719, Laguna
    Niguel, CA 92607-6719
949-360-2641
Fax: 949-360-2624
E-mail: archives@laguna.nara.gov

Pacific Region (San Francisco)
1000 Commodore Drive
San Bruno, CA 94066-2350
650-876-9001
Fax: 650-876-0920
E-mail: archives@sanbruno.nara.gov

Pacific Alaska Region (Seattle)
6125 Sand Point Way NE
Seattle, WA 98115-7999
206-526-6501
Fax: 206-526-6575
E-mail: center@seattle.nara.gov

Pacific Alaska Region (Anchorage)
654 West Third Avenue
Anchorage, AK 99501-2145
907-271-2441
Fax: 907-271-2442
E-mail: archives@alaska.nara.gov

African American Genealogical Societies

Genealogical societies are organized groups of genealogists that meet regularly. Meetings usually consist of society business discussion and a speaker on a genealogical topic. Societies sometimes sponsor workshops and research trips. Some publish newsletters and journals. Newsletters can have upcoming events, book reviews, tips, techniques, and members' research stories. Journals publish more serious research that genealogical and historical society members have conducted. Joining a society is a good way to meet others who are tracing similar states, counties, and surnames, as well as to learn about methods and techniques from other genealogists.

The list below was assembled from currently available sources. However, P.O. box numbers and e-mail addresses often change as officers change. Therefore, addresses may not be current when you read this list. If your correspondence is "Returned to Sender," it does not mean the organization is no longer in existence. Try to contact the nearest genealogical library, public library, historical society, archive, or Federation of Genealogical Societies to see if the organization is still active and if there has been an address change.

Alabama
African Ancestored Family Studies
P.O. Box 4250
Anniston, AL 36204
E-mail: vnelson@tracks.cpxl.com

Afro-American Historical and Genealogical
Society (AAHGS)—Freedom Trail Chapter
220 Oak Drive
Lowndesboro, AL 36752

Arizona
Black Family History Society
415 East Grand Street
Phoenix, AZ 85004
E-mail: hbeck@inficad.com

AAHGS—Tucson Chapter
P.O. Box 58272
Tucson, AZ 85754

Arkansas
AAHGS—Arkansas Chapter
P.O. Box 4294
Little Rock, AR 72214
E-mail: TRTL0793@aol.com

California
California African American Genealogical
Society
P.O. Box 8442
Los Angeles, CA 90008-0442

African American Genealogical Society of
Northern California
P.O. Box 10942
Oakland, CA 94610-0942
E-mail: baobabtree@aagsnc.org
Web site: http://www.aagsnc.org

San Diego African American Genealogical
Research Group
P.O. Box 740240
San Diego, CA 92174-0240
E-mail: marvh@prodigy.net

Colorado
Denver Afro-American Genealogical Society
P.O. Box 40674
Denver, CO 80204-0674
E-mail: OscarH1934@aol.com

District of Columbia
D.C. Genealogical Society
2505 13th Street NW
Washington, DC 20009

Afro-American Historical and Genealogical
Society (AAHGS)
P.O. Box 73086
Washington, DC 20056-3086
Web site:
http://www.rootsweb.com/~mdaahgs

Florida
AAHGS—Central Florida Chapter
P.O. Box 780872
Orlando, FL 32878-0872
E-mail: LBChapman@juno.com

Georgia
AAHGS—Atlanta Chapter
Back in the Day
P.O. Box 162516
Atlanta, GA 30321-2516
E-mail: clcscott@Bigfoot.com

African American Family History
   Association, Inc.
P.O. Box 115268
Atlanta, GA 30310
E-mail: Etur459@aol.com

Illinois
AAHGS—Little Egypt Chapter
207 Lendview Drive
Carbondale, IL 62901

AAHGS—Patricia Liddell Researchers
   Chapter
P.O. Box 438652
Chicago, IL 60643-8652

Afro-American Genealogical and Historical
   Society of Chicago
P.O. Box 377651
Chicago, IL 60637-7651
E-mail: aaghschi@aol.com

Indiana
Afro-American Genealogical Group
c/o Willard Library
21 First Avenue
Evansville, IN 47710

Louisiana
Multicultural Genealogical Research Society
2118 Benefit Street
New Orleans, LA 70122

Maryland
AAHGS—Baltimore Chapter
P.O. Box 9366
Baltimore, MD 21229-3125

AAHGS—Central Maryland Chapter
P.O. Box 2774
Columbia, MD 21045

AAHGS—Prince George's County Chapter
P.O. Box 44772
Fort Washington, MD 20744

AAHGS—James Dent Walker Chapter
P.O. Box 1848
Germantown, MD 20875-1848

Massachusetts
AAHGS—New England Chapter
P.O. Box 3266
Saxonville, MA 01705-3266
E-mail: smith@baynetworks.com

Michigan
Fred Hart Williams Genealogical Society
c/o Detroit Public Library
5201 Woodward Avenue
Detroit, MI 48202

Missouri
AAHGS—MAGIC Chapter
P.O. Box 300972
Kansas City, MO 64139-0972

The African Historical Society
P.O. Box 4964
St. Louis, MO 63108-0964
E-mail: zulurobin@primary.net
Web site: http://www.geocities.com/athens/
olympus/8815

AAHGS—Landon Cheek Chapter
P.O. Box 23804
St. Louis, MO 63121-0804

New Jersey
AAHGS—New Jersey Chapter
785 Sterling Drive East
South Orange, NJ 07079

New York
AAHGS—Jean Sampson Scott Greater NY
Chapter
P.O. Box 022340
Brooklyn, NY 11201-0049

Buffalo Genealogical Society of the African
Diaspora
812 Tacoma Avenue
Buffalo, NY 14216
E-mail: SWalkerNY@aol.com

African American Genealogy Society of
Rochester
123 Wisconsin Street
Rochester, NY 14609
E-mail: Rici2@aol.com

North Carolina
African American Genealogical Interest
Group
7701 Michael Drive
Charlotte, NC 28215

AAHGS—North Carolina Piedmont-Triad
P.O. Box 36254
Greensboro, NC 27416

North Carolina Afro-American Historical
and Genealogical Society—defunct
P.O. Box 26785
Raleigh, NC 27611-6785

Ohio
African American Interest Group—
Ohio Genealogical Society
P.O. Box 18551
Cincinnati, OH 45839

African American Genealogical Society
Cleveland
P.O. Box 200382
Cleveland, OH 44120-9998

African American Genealogy Group of the
Miami Valley
c/o Xenia Community Public Library
76 East Market Street
Xenia, OH 45385-3109

African American Interest Group of the
Franklin County Genealogical Society
750 West Broad Street
Columbus, OH 43222-1417
Web site: http://www.coax.net/people/lwf/
acgig.htm

Pennsylvania
African American Genealogy Group
P.O. Box 1798
Philadelphia, PA 19150-1798
E-mail: EGSStackhouse@mail.biosis.org

AAHGS—Western Pennsylvania Chapter
P.O. Box 5707
Pittsburgh, PA 15208

Rhode Island
Rhode Island Black Heritage Society
202 Washington St.
Providence, RI 02903
E-mail: riblkhrtg@juno.com

South Carolina
AAHGS—Columbia Chapter
P.O. Box 8836
Columbia, SC 29202
E-mail: egaholness@aol.com

Tennessee
African American Genealogical and
    Historical Society
P.O. Box 171124
Nashville, TN 37217

Texas
African American Interest Group of the
    Dallas Genealogical Society
P.O. Box 12648
Dallas, TX 75225-0648

Tarrant County Black Historical and
    Genealogical Society
1150 East Rosedale
Fort Worth, TX 76104

AAHGS—Houston Chapter
P.O. Box 750877
Houston, TX 77275-0877

Afro-American Genealogical and Historical
    Society of San Antonio
P.O. Box 200784
San Antonio, TX 78220
E-mail: genea50@aol.com

Virginia
AAHGS—Hampton Rhodes Chapter
P.O. Box 2448
Newport News, VA 23609

AAHGS—Tidewater Chapter
P.O. Box 10522
Virginia Beach, VA 23450

Central Virginia African American
    Genalogical and Historical Society
P.O. Box 9452
Richmond, VA 23228
belschese@prodigy.net

Washington
Black Heritage Society of Washington State,
    Inc.
P.O. Box 22565
Seattle, WA 98122

Wisconsin
Afro-American Genealogical Society of
    Milwaukee
2620 West Center Street
Milwaukee, WI 53206
E-mail: canturic@execpc.com

National Genealogical Organizations

National Genealogical Society (NGS)
4527 Seventeenth Street N
Arlington, VA 22207-2399
703-525-0050
Fax: 703-525-0052
E-mail: membership@ngsgenealogy.org
Web site: http://www.ngsgenealogy.org
Journal: *National Genealogical Society
    Quarterly* (NGSQ)

Federation of Genealogical Societies (FGS)
P.O. Box 200940
Austin, TX 78720-0940
888-347-1500
Fax: 888-380-0500
E-mail: fgs-office@fgs.org
Web site: http://www.fgs.org/~fgs/
Newsletter: *The Forum*

Association of Professional Genealogists
    (APG)
P.O. Box 40393
Denver, CO 80204-0393
Fax: 303-456-8825
E-mail: apg-admin@genealogy.org
Web site: http://www.apgen.org
Journal: *Association of Professional Genealogists
    Quarterly* (APGQ)

Board for Certification of Genealogists
    (BCG)
P.O. Box 14291
Washington, DC 20044
Web site: http://www.genealogy.org/~bcg/
Newsletter: *On Board*

GENTECH
P.O. Box 140277
Irving, TX 75014-0277
Fax: 888-522-7313
Web site: http://www.gentech.org/~gentech/

Historical Associations

American Historical Association
400 A Street SE
Washington, DC 20003
202-544-2422
E-mail: aha@theaha.org
Web site: http://www.theaha.org/
Journal: *American Historical Review*
Annual conference: First week in January—
    different cities—3 days

Organization of American Historians
112 North Bryan Street
Bloomington, IN 47408-4199
812-855-7311
Fax: 821-855-0696
E-mail: oah@oah.org

Web site: http://www.indiana.edu/~oah/
Journal: *Journal of American History*
Annual conference: Last week in March—
    different cities—4 days

Southern Historical Association
History Department
University of Georgia
Athens, GA 30602-1602
706-542-8848
Fax: 713-285-5207
Web site: http://www.uga.edu/~sha
Journal: *Journal of Southern History*
Annual conference: Second week in
    November—different cities—4 days

Association for the Study of Afro-American
   Life and History
1407 14th Street NW
Washington, DC 20005
202-667-2822
Fax: 202-387-3802

E-mail: asalh@earthlink.net
Web site: http://www.artnoir.com/asalh/
Journal: *Journal of Negro History*
Annual conference: Third week in
   October—different cities—3 days

Genealogical Institutes and Conferences

Genealogical Institutes

National Institute on Genealogical Research
P.O. Box 14274
Washington, DC 20044-4274
Founded in 1950
Independent, private, nonprofit corpora-
   tion, incorporated in 1989
Third week in July—6 days
Federal records—intermediate to
   advanced
Research at National Archives
Total enrollment limited to 44 students
Hotel rooms available near National
   Archives

Institute of Genealogy and Historical
   Research
Samford University Library
Birmingham, AL 35229-7008
205-870-2846
Web site: http://www.samford.edu/schools/
   ighr/ighr.html
Founded in 1964
Co-sponsored by the Board for Certification
   of Genealogists
Third week in June—5 days
Seven courses—beginning to advanced—
   British research trip
Research at Samford University Library
Dorm rooms available

Salt Lake Institute of Genealogy
Utah Genealogical Association
P.O. Box 1144
Salt Lake City, UT 84110-1144
1-888-463-6842
Founded in 1996
Sponsored by the Utah Genealogical
   Association
Third week in January—5 days
Class size limited to 30
Eight courses—intermediate to advanced
Research at Family History Library
Special hotel rates

Genealogical Institute of Mid-America
Continuing Education
University of Illinois at Springfield
P.O. Box 19243
Springfield, IL 62794-9243
217-786-7464
Fax: 217-786-7279
E-mail: slackjulie@uis.edu
Founded in 1994
Sponsored by the Illinois Genealogical
   Society and University of Illinois
Third week in July—4 days
Four courses—intermediate to advanced
Research at University of Illinois at Spring-
   field Library
Dorm rooms available

Institute of Genealogical Studies
P.O. Box 25556
Dallas, TX 75225-5556
214-341-5166
E-mail: igs@cyberramp.net
Founded in 1993

Sponsored by the Dallas Genealogical
  Society
Last week in July
Six courses—intermediate to advanced
Research at Dallas Public Library
Special hotel rates

Genealogical Conferences

Afro-American Historical and Genealogical
  Society
  Last week in October—Washington, D.C.
Afro-American Genealogical & Historical
Society of Chicago
  October—Chicago
African-American Genealogical Society—
Cleveland
  October—Cleveland

Association of Professional Genealogists
(APG)
  First day of FGS conference—different
  states
Federation of Genealogical Societies (FGS)
  August or September—different states
GENTECH
  Last week in January—different states
National Genealogical Society (NGS)
  Second week in May—different states

Miscellaneous Addresses

Allen County Public Library
P.O. Box 2270
Fort Wayne, IN 46801
E-mail: mclegg@everest.acpl.lib.in.us

The Association for Gravestone Studies
278 Main Street, Suite 207
Greenfield, MA 01301
413-772-0836
E-mail: ags@javanet.com
Web site: http://www.berkshire.net/ags/
  index.shtml

Family History Library
35 West North Temple
Salt Lake City, UT 84150-3400
800-346-6044
http://www.familysearch.org

International Commission for the
  Accreditation of Professional
  Genealogists (ICAPGEN)
P.O. Box 1144
Salt Lake City, UT 84110
http://www.inforuga.org

National Archives Microfilm Rental
  Program
P.O. Box 30
Annapolis Junction, MD 20701-0030
301-604-3699

National Archives Trust Fund Board
  (NEDC)
P.O. Box 100793
Atlanta, GA 30384
(For Buying Census Microfilm)

Repeat Performance
2911 Crabapple Lane
Hobart, IN 46342
219-465-1234
Web site: http//www.audiotapes.com

U.S. Geological Survey
Branch of Geographic Names
523 National Center, Reston, VA 22092
703-648-4544

U.S. Railroad Retirement Board
Office of Public Affairs
844 North Rush Street
Chicago, IL 60611-2092
312-751-4776
Web site: http://www.rrb.gov

Genealogical and Archival Vendors

American Genealogical Lending Library
  (AGLL): *see* Heritage Quest

Ancestry.com (formerly Ancestry Inc.)
266 West Center Street, Bldg 2
Orem, UT 84057
1-800-ANCESTRY
Web site: http://www.ancestry.com

Appleton's Books & Genealogy
8700 Pineville-Matthews Road
Charlotte, NC 28226
704-341-2266
E-mail: catalogue.request@appletons.com

Betterway Books
1507 Dana Ave.
Cincinnati, OH 45220
1-800-289-0963

Broderbund Software
39500 Stevenson Place, Suite 204
Fremont, CA 94539
1-800-223-8941
Web site: http://www.familytreemaker.com

Century Photo Products & Accessories
P.O. Box 2393
Brea, CA 92622
1-800-767-0777
Web site: http://www.20thcenturydirect.com

Everton Publishers, Inc.
P.O. Box 368
Logan, UT 84323-0368
425-752-6022
1-800-443-6325
E-mail: order@everton.com
Web site: http://www.everton.com

Frontier Press
21 Railroad Avenue
Cooperstown, NY 13326
607-547-1956
E-mail: kgfrontier@aol.com

Genealogical Publishing Co.
1001 N. Calvert Street
Baltimore, MD 21202
1-800-296-6687
Web site: http://www.genealogybookshop.
  com

Hearthstone Books
5735-A Telegraph Road
Alexandria, VA 22303
703-960-0086
E-mail: info@hearthstonebooks.com
Web site: http://www.hearthstonebooks.com

Heritage Books, Inc.
1540-E Pointer Ridge Place
Bowie, MD 20716
1-800-398-7709
E-mail: heritagebooks@pipeline.com
Web site: http://www.heritagebooks.com

Heritage Quest
P.O. Box 329
Bountiful, UT 84011-0329
1-800-760-2455
Web site: http://www.HeritageQuest.com

Light Impressions
439 Monroe Avenue
P.O. Box 940
Rochester, NY 14603-0940
1-800-828-6216
Web site: http://www.lightimpressions.com

Scholarly Resources
104 Greenhill Ave.
Wilmington, DE 19805-1897
1-800-772-8937
E-mail: sales@scholarly.com
Web site: http://www.scholarly.com

University Products
517 Main Street, P.O. Box 101
Holyoke, MA 01041-0101
1-800-628-1912
Web site: http://www.universityproducts.
    com

Willow Bend and Family Line
65 E. Main St.
Westminster, VA 21157-5036
410-876-6101
E-mail: willowbend@mediasoft.net

Bibliography

Following are genealogical and historical references, including works cited in the text.

BEGINNING AFRICAN AMERICAN GENEALOGY

Linder, Bill. *Black Genealogy: Basic Steps to Research.* Technical Leaflet 135. Nashville: American Association for State and Local History, 1981.

Scott, Jean Sampson. *Beginning an Afro-American Genealogical Pursuit.* New York: Eppress Printers, 1985.

Thackery, David, and Deloris Woodtor. *Case Studies in Afro-American Genealogy.* Chicago: The Newberry Library, 1989.

Walker, James Dent. *Black Genealogy: How to Begin.* Athens: University of Georgia, 1977.

BEGINNING GENEALOGY

Allen, Desmond Walls. *First Steps in Genealogy: A Beginner's Guide to Researching Your Family History.* Cincinnati: Betterway Books, 1998.

Boy Scouts of America. *Genealogy.* Irving, Tex.: Boy Scouts of America, 1988.

Crandall, Ralph. *Shaking Your Family Tree: A Basic Guide to Tracing Your Family Genealogy.* Dublin, N.H.: Yankee Publishers, 1986.

Croom, Emily Anne. *Unpuzzling Your Past: A Basic Guide to Genealogy.* Whitehall, Va.: Betterway Publications, 1995.

Dollarhide, William. *Managing a Genealogical Research Project.* Rev. ed. Baltimore: Genealogical Publishing Co., 1991.

Ingalls, Kay, and Christine Rose. *Complete Idiot's Guide to Genealogy.* New York: Alpha Books, 1997.

Willard, Jim, and Terry, with Jane Wilson. *Ancestors: A Beginning Guide to Tracing Family History.* Boston: Houghton-Mifflin, 1997.

Wolfman, Ira. *Do People Grow on Family Trees?: Genealogy for Kids & Other Beginners: The Official Ellis Island Handbook.* New York: Workman Publishing, 1991.

BIOGRAPHIES

Bigelow, Barbara Carlisle. *Contemporary Black Biography.* Detroit: Gale Research, 1991–present (3 vols. per year).

Burkett, Randall K., Nancy Hall Burkett, and Henry Louis Gates, Jr., eds. *Black Biographical Dictionaries, 1790–1950.* Alexandria, Va.: Chadwyck-Healey, 1991.

———. *Black Biography, 1790–1950: A Cumulative Index.* Alexandria, Va.: Chadwyck-Healey, 1991 (3-vol. index to above biographical dictionaries).

Davis, Lenwood G. *The Black Family in the United States: A Selected Bibliography of Annotated Books, Articles and Dissertations on Black Families in America.* Westport, Conn.: Greenwood Press, 1978.

Dorman, P. L. *Biographical History of Colored People, Arkansas.* N.p., 193? (printer's copy in Beinecke Rare Book and Manuscript Library, Yale University).

Hewlett, Rene A., and J. Max Williams. *Negro Who's Who in California.* N.p., 1948.

Hine, Darlene Clark, ed. *Black Women in America: An Historical Encyclopedia.* 2 vols. Brooklyn, N.Y.: Carlson, 1993.

Logan, Rayford W., and Michael R. Winston. *Dictionary of American Negro Biography.* New York: W. W. Norton, 1982.

Litwack, Leon, and August Meier. *Black Leaders of the Nineteenth Century.* Chicago: University of Illinois Press, 1988.

Mather, Frank Lincoln. *Who's Who of the Colored Race: A General Biographical Dictionary of Men and Women of African Descent.* Vol 1. Chicago: Memento Edition, Half-Century Anniversary of Negro Freedom in U.S., 1915. Reprint, Detroit: Gale Research, 1976.

Mollison, W. E. *The Leading Afro-Americans of Vicksburg, Mississippi, Their Enterprises, Churches, Schools, Lodges, and Societies.* Vicksburg, Miss.: Biographica Publishing Co., 1908.

Mott, A. *Biographical Sketches and Interesting Anecdotes of Persons of Color.* New York: 1839.

Robinson, Wilhelmena S. *Historical Negro Biographies.* 2nd ed., rev. New York: Publishers Co., 1969.

Schubert, Frank N. *On the Trail of the Buffalo Soldier: Biographies of African-Americans in the U.S. Army, 1866–1917.* Wilmington, Del.: Scholarly Resources, 1994.

Simmons, William J. *Men of Mark: Eminent, Progressive and Rising.* Cleveland: G. M. Rewell & Co., 1887.

Smith, J. Clay Jr., and Thurgood Marshall. *Emancipation: The Making of the Black Lawyer, 1844–1944.* Philadelphia: University of Pennsylvania Press, 1993.

Smith, Jessie Carney, ed. *Notable Black American Women.* Detroit: Gale Research, 1996.

Spradling, Mary Mace, ed. *In Black and White: Afro-Americans in Print: A Guide to Africans and Americans Who Have Made Contributions to the United States of America.* 2nd ed. Kalamazoo, Mich.: Kalamazoo Public Library, 1976.

———. *In Black and White Supplement: A Guide to Magazine Articles, Newspaper Articles, and Books Concerning 6,700 Black Individuals and Groups.* 3rd ed. Detroit: Gale Research, 1985.

Thompson, John L. *History and Views of Colored Officers Training Camp for 1917 at Fort Des Moines, Iowa.* Des Moines: The Bystander, 1917.

Trotter, James M. *Music and Some Highly Musical People . . . Sketches of the Lives of Remarkable Musicians of the Colored Race.* Boston: Lee Shepard, and New York: C.T. Dillingham, 1878.

Who's Who Among Black Americans. Detroit: Gale Research and other publishers, 1977–present.

Who's Who in Colored America: A Biographical Dictionary of Notable Living Men and Women. Vols. 1–7, 1927–1950. New York: Who's Who in Colored America Corp. and various publishers.

Williams, Ethel L. *Biographical Directories of Negro Ministers.* New York: Scarecrow Press, 1965.

BLACK FAMILY HISTORIES AND GENEALOGIES

Brasfield, Curtis. "To My Daughter and the Heirs of Her Body: Slave Passages as Illustrated by the Latham-Smithwick Family." *National Genealogical Society Quarterly* 81 (Dec 1993): 270–282.

Cerny, Johnnie. "From Maria to Bill Cosby: A Case Study in Tracing Black Slave Ancestry." *National Genealogical Society Quarterly* 75:1 (March 1987): 5–14.

Clark-Lewis, Elizabeth. *Living In, Living Out: African American Domestics in Washington, D.C., 1910–1940.* Washington, D.C.: Smithsonian Institution Press, 1994.

Delaney, Sarah L., and Annie Elizabeth Delaney, with Amy Hill Hearth. *Having Our Say: The Delaney Sisters' First 100 Years.* New York: Kodansha, 1993.

Haizlip, Shirlee Taylor. *The Sweeter the Juice: A Family Memoir in Black and White.* New York: Simon & Schuster, 1994.

Haley, Alex. *Roots: The Saga of an American Family.* Garden City, N.Y.: Doubleday, 1976.

Jupiter, Del E. "Agustina and the Kelkers: A Spanish West Florida Line." *National Genealogical Society Quarterly* 80:4 (December 1992): 265–279.

————. *Agustina of Spanish West Florida and Her Descendants: With Related Families of Egan, Kelker, Palmer, and Taylor.* Franklin, N.C.: Genealogy Publishing Service, 1994.

————. "From Agustina to Ester: Analyzing a Slave Household for Child-Parent Relationships." *National Genealogical Society Quarterly.* 85:4 (December 1997): 245–275.

Lawson, Sandra K. *Generations Past: A Select List of Sources for Afro-American Genealogical Research.* Washington, D.C.: Library of Congress, 1988.

Madden, T. O. *We Were Always Free: The Maddens of Culpepper County, Virginia, a 200-Year Family History.* New York: W. W. Norton, 1992.

Mallory, Rudena Kramer. "An African-American Odyssey Through Multiple Surnames: Mortons, Tapps, and Englishes of Kansas and Missouri." *National Genealogical Society Quarterly* 85:1 (March 1997): 25–38.

Negro History Bulletin. Washington, D.C.: Association for the Study of Negro Life and History (32 family histories published between 1942 and 1979).

Redford, Dorothy Spruill, with Michael D'Orso. *Somerset Homecoming: Recovering a Lost Heritage.* New York: Doubleday, 1988 (original publisher); Chapel Hill, N.C.: University of North Carolina Press, 2000 (reprint edition).

Ruffin, C. Bernard III. "In Search of the Unappreciated Past: The Ruffin-Cormick Family of Virginia." *National Genealogical Society Quarterly* 81:2 (June 1993): 126–138.

Sewell, Rhonda B. "Writer Finds Her Tenacity in Ancestors: Family Has a Habit of Breaking Barriers." *Toledo Blade* (February 1, 1998): 1, 10–11.

Taulbert, Clifton. *Once Upon a Time When We Were Colored.* Tulsa, Okla.: Council Oak Books, 1989.

Walker, Juliet E. K. *Free Frank: A Black Pioneer on the Antebellum Frontier.* Lexington: University of Kentucky Press, 1983.

BLACK HISTORY—BEGINNING

Dennis, Denise. *Black History for Beginners.* New York: Writers and Readers Publishing, 1984.

Peoples Publishing Group. *In Our Own Image: An African American History.* Maywood, N.J.: Peoples Publishing Group, 1998.

Smead, Howard. *The Afro-Americans: The Peoples of North America.* New York: Chelsea House, 1989.

BLACK HISTORY—INTERMEDIATE

African Methodist Episcopal Church. *Christian Recorder.* Philadelphia: African Methodist Episcopal Church (weekly since 1854).

Aptheker, Herbert. *American Negro Slave Revolts.* New York: Columbia University Press, 1943. Reprint, New York: International Publishers, 1993.

Ashe, Arthur R. *A Hard Road to Glory: A History of the African-American Athlete 1619–1918.* 3 vols. New York: Warner Books, 1988.

Bennett, Lerone Jr. *Before the Mayflower: A History of Black America.* Rev. ed. Chicago: Johnson Publishing Co., 1962, 1993.

Bergman, Peter M., and Mort N. Bergman. *The Chronological History of the Negro in America.* New York: Munster Books, 1969.

Cowan, Tom, Jack Maguire, and Richard Newman. *Timelines of African-American History: 500 Years of Black Achievement.* New York: Perigee, 1994.

Davis, Lenwood G. *The Black Family in the United States.* Westport, Conn.: Greenwood Press, 1986.

Drake, St. Clair, and Horace Cayton. *Black Metropolis: A Study of Negro Life in a Northern City.* New York: Harcourt, Brace and Co., 1945. Reprint, Chicago: University of Chicago Press, 1993.

Ebony. *Ebony Pictorial History of Black America.* 4 vols. Chicago: Johnson Publishing Co., 1973.

Estell, Kenneth, ed. *The African American Almanac.* 6th ed. Detroit: Gale Research, 1994.

Franklin, John Hope. *From Slavery to Freedom: A History of Negro Americans.* 5th ed. New York: Knopf, 1979.

Gutman, Herbert G. *The Black Family from Slavery to Freedom.* New York: Vintage Books, 1976.

Harley, Sharon. *The Timetables of African-American History—A Chronology of the Most Important People and Events in African-American History.* New York: Simon & Schuster, 1995.

Hine, Darlene Clark, and Kathleen Thompson. *A Shining Thread of Hope: The History of Black Women in America.* New York: Broadway Books, 1998.

Low, W. Augustus, and Virgil A. Clift. *Encyclopedia of Black America.* New York: McGrawHill, 1981. Reprint, New York: Da Capo Press, 1984.

The National Association for the Advancement of Colored People: A Register of Its Records in the Library of Congress, Vol. I, 1909–1939. Washington, D.C.: Library of Congress, Manuscript Division, 1972.

Negro History Bulletin. Washington, D.C.: Association for the Study of Negro Life and History, 1937–present.

Newman, Richard, comp. *Black Access: A Bibliography of Afro-American Bibliographies.* Westport, Conn.: Greenwood Press, 1984.

Papers of the NAACP (431 reels of film with a printed guide). Bethesda, Md.: University Publications of America, 1990.

Plater, Michael A. *African American Entrepreneurship in Richmond, 1890–1940: The Story of R. C. Scott.* New York: Garland Publishing Co., 1996.

Porter, Dorothy B., comp. *The Negro in the United States: A Selected Bibliography.* Washington, D.C.: Library of Congress, 1970.

Rhea, H. W., ed. *Rhea's New Citizens' Directory of Chicago, Ill., and Suburban Towns, Also Other Towns and Cities.* Chicago: W. S. McCleland, 1908.

Salzman, Jack, David Lionel Smith, and Cornell West. *Encyclopedia of African-American Culture and History.* New York: Macmillian Library Reference USA, 1996.

Smith, Dwight L. *Afro-American History: A Bibliography.* Santa Barbara, Calif.: ABC-CLIO, 1974.

Smith, Jessie Carney, and Carrell Peterson Horton. *Historical Statistics of Black America.* Detroit: Gale Research, 1995.

Spears, Alan. *Black Chicago: The Making of a Ghetto, 1890–1920.* Chicago: University of Chicago Press, 1967.

Work, Monroe N. *Bibliography of the Negro in Africa and America.* New York: H. W. Wilson, 1928. Reprint, New York: Octagon Books, 1965 and 1970.

———. *Negro Year Book, an Annual Encyclopedia of the Negro.* Tuskegee Institute, Ala.: Negro Year Book Publishing Co., 1912–1938.

CEMETERIES

Baker, F. Joanne, and Daniel Farber. "Recording Cemetery Data." *Markers I: The Journal of the Association for Gravestone Studies* (1980). http://www. oklahoma.net/~davidm/recdcem.txt

Bell, Edward L. *Vestiges of Mortality & Remembrance: A Bibliography on the Historical Archaeology of Cemeteries.* Metuchen, N.J.: Scarecrow Press, 1994.

Callaway, Annette. "Cheatham Brings Life Back to Cemetery." *Citizens Journal* (Cass County, Tex.), July 8, 1996, p. 6.

———. "Valuable History Lesson Buried in Whittaker Cemetery: History of Slave Cemetery." *Citizens Journal* (Cass County, Tex.), July 8, 1996, p. 6.

Cheatham, Belzora. *History of Whittaker Memorial Cemetery.* Self-published, 1996. Author: 7948 S. Perry Avenue, Chicago, IL 60620-1147.

———. *Index to Whittaker Memorial Cemetery.* Self-published, 1995. Author: 7948 S. Perry Avenue; Chicago, IL 60620-1147.

Directory of United States Cemeteries. San Jose, Calif.: Cemetery Research, 1974.

Dunn, Lori. "Woman's Efforts Gain Recognition for Historic Cemetery." *Texarkana Gazette* (Sunday, August 4, 1996): 7A.

Farber, Jessie Lie. "Gravestone Rubbing for Beginners." The Association for Gravestone Studies. http://www.oklahoma.net/~davidm/graverub.txt

———. "A Technique for the Experienced Rubber." The Association for Gravestone Studies. http://www.oklahoma.net/~davidm/graverub.txt

Fenn, Elizabeth. "Honoring the Ancestors: Kongo Graves in the American South." *Southern Exposure* (September-October 1985): 42–47.

Finley, Elisabeth. "County Site Makes History." *Citizens Journal* (Cass County, Tex.), August 7, 1996, pp. 1–2.

———. "Marker Marks Gravesite of Slaves" *Cass County Sun* (Cass County, Tex.), August 7, 1996, pp. 1, 8.

Genealogical Institute. *How to Search a Cemetery.* Salt Lake City: Family History World, 1974.

Helsley, Alexia Jones. *Silent Cities: Cemeteries and Classrooms.* Columbia, S.C.: Department of Archives and History, 1997.

Howells, Mark. "Computerized Tombstones." *Ancestry* 16:5 (September-October 1998): 59–62.

International Cemetery Directory. Columbus, Ohio: American Cemetery Association, 1974.

Kahloula, Angelika Kruger. "Tributes in Stone and Lapidary Lapses: Commemorating Black People in Eighteenth and Nineteenth-Century America." *Journal of the Association of Gravestone Studies* 6 (1989): 32–100 (Lanhan, Md.: University Press of America).

Kot, Elizabeth Gorrell, and James Douglas Kot. *United States Cemetery Address Book.* Vallejo, Calif.: Indices Publishing, 1994.

Little, Ruth M. "Afro-American Gravemarkers in North Carolina." *Journal of the Association of Gravestone Studies* 6 (1989): 103–134 (Lanhan, Md.: University Press of America).

Malloy, Tom, and Brenda. "Slavery in Colonial Massachusetts as Seen Through Selected Gravestones." *Markers II: The Journal of the Association for Gravestone Studies* (1983): 112–141.

Mayer, Lance. "The Care of Old Cemeteries and Gravestones." *Markers 1: The Journal of the Association of Gravestone Studies* I (1979/80): 118–141.

Newman, John J. *Cemetery Transcribing: Preparations and Procedures.* Technical Leaflet 9. Nashville: American Association for State and Local History, 1971.

Nichols, Elaine. *The Last Miles of the Way: African American Homegoing Traditions, 1890–Present.* Columbia, S.C.: South Carolina State Museum, 1989.

Palmer, Ronald. "James Palmer and Other African American Civil War Soldiers Buried in Fayette County, Pennsylvania." *Journal of the Afro-American Historical and Genealogical Society* 15:2 (1996): 87–102.

Potter, Elisabeth Walton, and Beth M. Boland. *Guidelines for Evaluating and Registering Cemeteries and Burial Grounds.* National Register Bulletin 41. Washington, D.C.: U.S. Department of the Interior, National Park Service, Interagency Resources Division, National Register of Historic Places, 1992.

Sluby, Paul E. *Woodlawn Cemetery, Washington, D.C.: Brief History and Interments.* Washington, D.C.: Columbian Harmony Society, 1984. (Sluby has published records from many other cemeteries.)

Stemmons, John E., and E. Diane. *The Cemetery Record Compendium.* Logan, Utah: Everton Publishers, 1979.

Strangstad, Laynette. *A Graveyard Preservation Primer.* Walnut Creek, Calif.: AltaMira Press, 1995.

———. *Preservation of Historic Burying Grounds.* Information Series #76. Washington, D.C.: National Trust for Historic Preservation, 1993.

Stubblefield, Ruth. *Walker County, Texas, Black Cemeteries.* Huntsville: Walker County Genealogical Society, 1999.

Thompson, Sharyn. *A Bibliography for Historic Cemeteries Preservation in the Southern United States.* Tallahassee, Fla.: The Center for Historic Cemeteries Preservation (P.O. Box 6296), 1995.

Vlach, John. "Graveyards and Afro-American Art." *Southern Exposure* 5 (1977): 2–3.

Wright, Roberta, and Wilber Hughes. *Lay Down Body: Living History in African-American Cemeteries.* Detroit: Visible Ink., 1996.

CENSUS RESEARCH

Bohme, Frederick. *200 Years of Census Taking: Population and Housing Questions, 1790–1990.* Washington, D.C.: U.S. Department of Commerce, Bureau of the Census, 1989.

Bureau of the Census. *Twenty Censuses: Population and Housing Questions, 1790–1990.* Washington, D.C.: U.S. Department of Commerce, Bureau of the Census, 1979.

Dollarhide, William. *The Census Book: A Genealogist's Guide to Census Facts, Schedules and Indexes.* Bountiful, Utah: Heritage Quest, 1999.

Green, Kellee. "The Fourteenth Numbering of the People: The 1920 Federal Census." *Prologue* 23:2 (Summer 1991): 131–145.

National Archives and Records Administration. *Fast Facts About the 1920 Census.* General Information Leaflet 43. Washington, D.C.: National Archives and Records Administration, 1992.

———. *Using Census Records*. Washington, D.C.: National Archives and Records Administration, 1990.

National Archives Trust Fund Board. *The 1920 Federal Population Census: Catalogue of the National Archives Microfilm*. Washington, D.C.: National Archives and Records Administration, 1991.

Saldana, Richard H., ed. *A Practical Guide to the Mistakes Made in Census Indexes*. Bountiful, Utah: Precision Indexing, 1987.

Steuart, Bradley W., ed. *The Soundex Reference Guide*. 2nd ed. Bountiful, Utah: Precision Indexing, 1994.

COLLECTION GUIDES

Begley, Paul R., and Steven D. Tuttle. *South Carolina Department of Archives & History—African American Genealogical Research*. Columbia: South Carolina Department of Archives and History, 1991.

Detroit Public Library. *Sources for Black Genealogy in the Burton Historical Collection*. Detroit: The Burton Historical Collection, 1989.

Florida Department of State, Division of Library and Information Services. *The Black Experience: A Guide to Afro-American Resources in the Florida State Archives*. Tallahassee: Florida Department of State, 1988, 1991.

Hodge, Ruth, ed. *Guide to African American Resources at the Pennsylvania State Archives*. Harrisburg: Pennsylvania Historical and Museum Commission, 2000.

Jacobsen, Phoebe R. *Researching Black Families at the Maryland Hall of Records*. Annapolis, Md.: Maryland Hall of Records, Department of General Services, 1984.

McBride, David. *The Afro-American in Pennsylvania: A Critical Guide to Sources in the Pennsylvania State Archives*. Harrisburg: Pennsylvania Historical and Museum Commission, 1979.

Thackery, David. *Afro-American Family History at the Newberry Library: A Research Guide and Bibliography*. Chicago: The Newberry Library, 1988, 1993.

Witcher, Curt Bryan. *A Bibliography of Sources for Black Family History in the Allen County Public Library, Genealogy Department*. Fort Wayne, Ind.: Allen County Public Library, 1989.

ELECTRONIC GENEALOGY

Bonner, Laurie, and Steve. *Searching for Cyber-Roots*. Salt Lake City: Ancestry Inc., 1997.

Bourne, Delia Cothrum. *Bibliographic Sources for Genealogists Starring Worldcat from FirstSearch*. Audiotape of lecture presented at the Millennium Conference, Fort Wayne, Ind. (Tape #F-44).

Burroughs, Tony. "Using Word Processors to Transcribe Documents." *Genealogical Computing* 12:3 (January–March 1993): 25–26.

The Computer Genealogist Newsletter. Boston: New England Historic Genealogical Society (bimonthly). *Note:* In 2000 this newsletter folded into the new magazine *New England Ancestors*.

Genealogical Computing Newsletter. Salt Lake City: Ancestry Inc. (quarterly).

Helm, Matthew, and April Leigh Helm. *Genealogy Online for Dummies*. Foster City, Calif.: IDG Books Worldwide, 1998.

Howells, Cyndi. *Cyndi's List—The Book! A Comprehensive List of 40,000 Genealogy Sites on the Internet*. Baltimore: Genealogical Publishing Co., 1999.

———. *Netting Your Ancestors: Genealogical Research on the Internet*. Baltimore: Genealogical Publishing Co., 1997.

Kemp, Thomas Jay. *Virtual Roots: A Guide to Genealogy and Local History on the World Wide Web*. Wilmington, Del.: Scholarly Resources, 1997.

McClure, Rhonda. "Surfing for Genealogy?" *Genealogical Computing* 16:4 (Spring 1997): 52.

NGS/SIG Newsletter. Arlington, Va.: National Genealogical Society (bimonthly).

Nichols, Elizabeth L. *Understanding Genealogy in the Computer Age: Family Search.* Salt Lake City: Family History Educators, 1994.

Renick, Barbara, and Richard S. Wilson. *The Internet for Genealogists: A Beginner's Guide.* 3rd ed. LaHabra, Calif.: Computology, 1998.

Roberts, Ralph. *Genealogy via the Internet: Tracing Your Family Roots Quickly and Easily: Computerized Genealogy in Plain English.* Alexander, N.C.: Alexander Books, 1997.

Smith, Drew. "Looking for Quality." *Genealogical Computing* 16:4 (Spring 1997): 19–22.

Stoll, Clifford. *Silicon Snake Oil: Second Thoughts on the Information Highway.* New York: Doubleday, 1995.

EVIDENCE, DOCUMENTATION, AND CITING SOURCES

Board for Certification of Genealogists. *The BCG Application Guide.* Washington, D.C.: Board for Certification of Genealogists, 1999.

———. *The BCG Genealogical Standards Manual.* Washington, D.C.: Board for Certification of Genealogists, 2000.

Garner, Diane L., and Diane H. Smith. *The Complete Guide to Citing Government Documents: A Manual for Writers and Librarians.* Rev. ed. Bethesda, Md.: Congressional Information Service, 1993.

Lackey, Richard S. *Cite Your Sources: A Manual for Documenting Family Histories and Genealogical Records.* Jackson: University Press of Mississippi, 1980.

Mills, Elizabeth Shown. *Evidence: Citation and Analysis for the Family Historian.* Baltimore: Genealogical Publishing Co., 1997.

National Archives and Records Administration. *Citing Sources in the National Archives of the United States.* General Information Leaflet No. 17 (rev.). Washington, D.C.: National Archives and Records Administration, 1993.

———. *Using Records in the National Archives for Genealogical Research.* General Information Leaflet Number 5 (rev.). Washington, D.C.: National Archives and Records Administration, 1986.

National Society of the Daughters of the American Revolution. *Is That Lineage Right?* Washington, D.C.: National Society of the Daughters of the American Revolution, 1984.

Rubincam, Milton. *Pitfalls in Genealogical Research.* Salt Lake City: Ancestry Inc., 1987.

Stevenson, Noel. *Genealogical Evidence: A Guide to the Standard of Proof Relating to Pedigrees, Ancestry, Heirship and Family History.* Rev. ed. Laguna Hills, Calif.: Aegean Park Press, 1989.

White, Elizabeth Pearson. "Documentation in 1995." *Illinois State Genealogical Society Quarterly* 27:4 (1995): 234–241.

FUNERAL HOMES

Blue Book of Funeral Directors, 1982–1983. 26th ed. New York: The American Funeral Director, 1983 (annual).

Carlson, Lisa. *Caring for Your Own Dead.* Hinesburg, Vt.: Upper Access Publishers, 1987.

Cheatham, Belzora. *Funeral Programs/Obituaries of 579 African Americans.* Self-published, 1998. Author: 7948 S. Perry Avenue, Chicago, Ill. 60620-1147.

Horn, Miriam. "The Death Care Business." *U.S. News & World Report* (March 23, 1998): 50–58.

Plater, Michael A. *African American Entrepreneurship in Richmond, 1890–1940: The Story of R. C. Scott.* New York: Garland, 1996.

Ruffin, Rev. Bernard C. "Records of the Sellers Funeral Home in Chambersburg, Pennsylvania, Relating to the Black Families of Franklin County, 1866–1933." *Journal of the Afro-American Historical and Genealogical Society* 3:2 (Summer 1982): 73–83; 3:3 (Fall 1982): 106–116; 3:4 (Winter 1982): 166–182; 4:1 (Spring 1983): 32–34.

Sluby, Paul E., Sr., and Stanton L. Wormley. *Register of Burials of the Joseph F. Birch Funeral Home.* Washington, D.C.: Columbian Harmony Society, 1989.

GENEALOGY REFERENCE GUIDES

Bentley, Elizabeth Petty. *The Genealogist's Address Book.* 3rd ed. Baltimore: Genealogical Publishing Co., 1995. (Also available on CD-ROM from Ancestry.com)

Berry, Ellen Thomas, and David Allen Berry. *Our Quaker Ancestors: Finding Them in Quaker Records.* Baltimore: Genealogical Publishing Co., 1987.

Byers, Paula. *African American Genealogical Sourcebook.* Detroit: Gale Research, 1995.

Cerny, Johni, and Arlene Eakle. *The Source: A Guidebook of American Genealogy.* Salt Lake City: Ancestry Inc., 1984. Rev. ed., edited by Loretto D. Szucs and Sandra H. Luebking. Salt Lake City: Ancestry Inc., 1997.

Eichholz, Alice. *Ancestry's Red Book: American State, County, and Town Sources.* Rev. ed. Salt Lake City: Ancestry Inc., 1992.

Everton, George. *The Handy Book for Genealogists.* 9th ed. Logan, Utah: Everton Publishers, 1999.

Georgia Genealogical Society. "Georgia Genealogy in 1992: A Bibliography." *Georgia Genealogical Society Quarterly* 31:4 (1995): 218.

———. "Georgia Genealogy in 1991: A Bibliography." *Georgia Genealogical Society Quarterly* 30:4 (1994): 223.

———. "Georgia Genealogy in 1990: A Bibliography." *Georgia Genealogical Society Quarterly* 30:2 (1994): 74.

———. "Georgia Genealogy in 1989: A Bibliography." *Georgia Genealogical Society Quarterly.* 29:4 (1993): 220.

———. "Georgia Genealogy in 1988: A Bibliography." *Georgia Genealogical Society Quarterly* 26:4 (1990): 218.

Gifis, Steven H. *Law Dictionary.* Woodbury, N.Y.: Baron's Educational Series, 1975.

Greenwood, Val D. *The Researcher's Guide to American Genealogy.* 3rd ed. Baltimore: Genealogical Publishing Co., 2000.

Guide to Genealogical Research in the National Archives. Washington, D.C.: National Archives and Records Service, 1982.

Hinckley, Kathleen W. *Locating Lost Family Members and Friends: Modern Genealogical Research Techniques for Locating People of Your Past and Present.* Cincinnati, Oh.: Betterway Books, 1999.

Journal of the Afro-American Historical and Genealogical Society Quarterly. P.O. Box 73086, Washington, D.C. 20056-3086.

Kaufman, Betty R., ed. *Organizational Handbook: A Guide for the Organization and Management of Genealogical Societies.* Rev. ed. Salt Lake City: Federation of Genealogical Societies, 1992.

Leary, Helen F. M. *North Carolina Research: Genealogy and Local History.* Raleigh: North Carolina Genealogical Society, 1996.

Lipscomb, Anne S., and Kathleen S. Hutchinson. *Tracing Your Mississippi Ancestors.* Jackson: University Press of Mississippi, 1995.

Meyer, Mary Keysor. *Meyer's Directory of Genealogical Societies in the United States and Canada.* Mount Airy, Md.: Libra Publishing (the author), 1994.

Meyerink, Kory. *Genealogical Publications: A List of 50,000 Sources from the Library of Congress.* CD-ROM. Salt Lake City: Ancestry Inc., 1997.

———, ed. *Printed Sources: A Guide to Published Genealogical Records.* Salt Lake City: Ancestry Inc., 1998.

Reisinger, Joy. *Index to NGS and FGS Conferences and Syllabi.* Arlington, Va.: National Genealogical Society and Salt Lake City: Federation of Genealogical Societies, 1993.

Rose, Christine. *Nicknames: Past and Present.* San Jose, Calif.: Rose Family Association, 1998.

Rubincam, Milton, ed. *Genealogical Research: Methods and Sources.* Washington, D.C.: The American Society of Genealogists, 1980.

Schweitzer, George K. *South Carolina Genealogical Research.* Self-published, 1993. Author: 407 Ascot Court, Knoxville, TN 37923.

Stebbins, Luke. *The Genealogy of the Family of Mr. Samuel Stebbins, and Mrs. Hannah Stebbins, His Wife, from the Year 1707 to the Year 1771.* Boston: E. Watson, 1879.

Wheeler, Mary Bray, ed. *Directory of Historical Organizations in the United States and Canada.* Nashville: American Association for State and Local History, 1990.

GEOGRAPHY RESEARCH

Abate, Frank R. *American Places Dictionary: A Guide to 45,000 Populated Places, Natural Features, and Other Places in the United States.* 4 vols. Detroit: Omnigraphics, 1994.

———. *Omni Gazetteer of the United States.* 8 vols. Detroit: Omnigraphics, 1991.

Androit, John L., comp. and ed. *Township Atlas of the United States.* McLean, Va.: Androit Associates, 1979.

Bullinger's Postal and Shippers Guide for the United States and Canada. Westwood, N.J.: Bullinger's Guides (annual since 1897).

Columbia-Lippincott Gazetteer of the World. Morningside Heights, N.Y.: Columbia University Press and J. B. Lippincott Co., 1905 and 1952.

Cram, George Franklin. *Gazetteer of the United States, Showing Population of Every County, City, Town and Village According to the Census of 1890.* Chicago: George F. Cram, 1893. Reprinted as *American Place Names of Long Ago: A Republication of the Index to Cram's Unrivaled Atlas of the World, as Based on the Census of 1890,* with an introduction by Gilbert S. Bahn, Ph.D. Baltimore: Genealogical Publishing Co., 1998.

Gannett, Henry. *A Gazetteer of Virginia and West Virginia.* 1904. Reprint, Baltimore: Genealogical Publishing Co., 1975.

Long, John Hamilton, ed. *Historical Atlas and Chronology of County Boundaries, 1788–1980.* New York: Simon & Schuster, 1993.

The Map Catalogue. New York: Vantage Press, 1990.

Map Collections in the United States and Canada: A Directory. New York: Special Libraries Association, 1984.

Rand McNally Commercial Marketing Atlas and Marketing Guide. New York: Rand McNally and Co. (annual).

Sealock, Richard B., Margaret M. Sealock, and Margaret S. Powell. *Bibliography of Place-Name Literature, United States and Canada.* 3rd ed. Chicago: American Library Association, 1982.

Thorndale, William, and William Dollarhide. *Map Guide to the U.S. Federal Censuses, 1790–1920.* Baltimore, Md.: Genealogical Publishing Co., 1987.

United States Board on Geographic Names. *Report of the United States Board on Geographic Names, 1890–1891.* 52nd Congress, 1st Session, House of Representatives Document No. 16 (Serial Set 2949). Washington, D.C.: U.S. Government Printing Office, 1892 (also published by Thomas Corwin Mendenhall, 1892).

United States Board on Geographic Names. *Second Report of United States Board on Geographic Names, 1890–1899.* 56th Congress, 1st Session, House of Representatives Document No. 472 (Serial Set 3988). Washington, D.C.: U.S. Government Printing Office, 1900.

United States Postal Service. *United States Directory of Post Offices.* Washington, D.C.: U.S. Postal Service (annual).

United States War Department. *The Official Atlas of the Civil War.* New York: Thomas Yoseloff, 1958.

———. *Official Records of the Union and Confederate Armies in the War of the Rebellion* (known as "The *OR*"). 128 vols. Washington, D.C.: Government Printing Office, 1901.

Using Maps in Genealogy (formerly *Maps Can Help You Trace Your Family Tree: How to Use Maps in Genealogy,* August 1991). Washington, D.C.: U.S. Department of the Interior and the U.S. Geological Survey, September 1994.

Webster's Geographical Dictionary. Springfield, Mass.: G. & C. Merriam Co., 1957.

LIBRARIES

American Library Directory. New Providence, N.J.: R. R. Bowker (annual).

Burroughs, Tony. *Using the Family History Library for African-American Research.* Audiotape of lecture presented at the Federation of Genealogical Societies conference, Salt Lake City, September 2000 (Tape #S-172, Repeat Performance, phone 219-465-1234).

Cerny, Johni, and Wendy Elliott. *The Library: A Guide to the LDS Family History Library.* Salt Lake City: Ancestry Inc., 1988.

Child, Sargent B., and Dorothy P. Holmes. *Bibliography of Research Projects Reports: Checklist of Historical Records Survey Publications.* WPA Technical Series, Research and Records Bibliography No. 7. Washington, D.C.: Work Projects Administration, 1943. Reprint, Baltimore: Genealogical Publishing Co., 1969.

Clegg, Michael, ed. *Bibliography of Genealogical and Local History Periodicals with Union List of Major U.S. Collections.* Fort Wayne, Ind.: Allen County Public Library Foundation, 1990.

Corporation of the President of the Church of Jesus Christ of Latter-Day Saints. *Family History Library.* Salt Lake City: 1988.

———. *In a Granite Mountain.* Salt Lake City: 1988.

———. Library Services and Resources. Salt Lake City: 1994.

Dollarhide, William, and Ronald A. Bremer. *America's Best Genealogy Resource Centers.* Bountiful, Utah: Heritage Quest, 1998.

The Encyclopedia of Associations. Detroit: Gale Research (annual).

Filby, P. William. *Directory of American Libraries with Genealogy or Local History Collections.* Wilmington, Del.: Scholarly Resources, 1988.

Hefner, Loretta L. *The WPA Historical Records Survey: A Guide to the Unpublished Inventories, Indexes and Transcripts.* Chicago: The Society of American Archivists, 1980.

Henderson, Martha L., and Annette W. Curtis, comp. *Genealogy from the Heartland, 1998 Supplement: A Catalogue of Titles in the Mid-Continent Public Library Genealogy Circulating Collection.* Independence, Mo.: Mid-Continent Public Library in cooperation with the American Family Records Association and the Missouri State Genealogical Association, 1998.

———. *Genealogy from the Heartland, 1996 Supplement: A Catalogue of Titles in the Mid-Continent Public Library Genealogy Circulating Collection.* Independence, Mo.: Mid-Continent Public Library in cooperation with the American Family Records Association and the Missouri State Genealogical Association, 1996.

Henderson, Martha Meyers, and Kermit B. Karns, comp. *Genealogy from the Heartland, 1994 Supplement: A Catalogue of Titles in the Mid-Continent Public Library Genealogy Circulating Collection.* Independence,

Mo.: Mid-Continent Public Library in cooperation with the American Family Records Association and the Missouri State Genealogical Association, 1994.

Kaminkow, M. J. *A Complement to Genealogies in the Library of Congress.* Baltimore: Magna Carta Book Company, 1981.

Kitchens, John W., ed. *Tuskegee Institute Newspaper Clipping Files: 1899–1966.* Tuskegee, Ala.: Division of Behavioral Science Research, Carver Research Foundation, Tuskegee Institute, 1978.

Library of Congress. *National Union Catalogue, Pre-1956 Imprints: A Cumulative Author List Representing Library of Congress Printed Cards and Titles Reported by Other American Libraries.* London: Mansell, 1968–1981.

———. *New Serial Titles: A Union List of Serials Commencing Publication After December 31, 1949.* New York: R. R. Bowker, 1975.

———. Union List of Serials in the United States and Canada.

Library of Congress Cataloging Policy and Support Office. *Library of Congress Subject Headings.* 4 vols. Washington, D.C.: Cataloging Distribution Service, Library of Congress, 1997.

Mann, Thomas. *A Guide to Library Research Methods.* New York: Oxford University Press, 1987.

McDonald, Donna, ed. *Directory of Historical Societies and Agencies in the U.S. and Canada.* Nashville: American Association for State and Local History, 1990.

Meyers, Martha L., Kermit B. Karns, and Michael C. Henderson, comp. *Genealogy from the Heartland: A Catalogue of Titles in the Mid-Continent Public Library Genealogy Circulating Collection.* Independence, Mo.: Mid-Continent Public Library in cooperation with the American Family Records Association and the Missouri State Genealogical Association, 1992.

Mid-Continent Public Library, Genealogy and Local History Department. *Interlibrary Loan Sources: A Guide for Librarians and Genealogists.* Independence, Mo.: Mid-Continent Public Library, 1997.

Parker, J. Carlyle. *Going to Salt Lake City to Do Family History.* 2nd ed., rev. Turlock, Calif.: Marietta Publishing Company, 1993.

Roller, David C., and Robert W. Twyman. *The Encyclopedia of Southern History.* Baton Rouge: Louisiana State University Press, 1979.

Smith, Juliana Szucs. *The Ancestry Family Historian's Address Book.* Salt Lake City: Ancestry Inc., 1997.

Taylor, Marie. *Family History Library Bibliography of African American Sources.* Salt Lake City: Family History Library, 2000.

———, compiler. *African American Records Quick Guide* (No. 36367). Salt Lake City: Family History Library, 2000.

Titus, Edna Brown, ed. *Union List of Serials in the United States and Canada.* New York: H. W. Wilson, 1965.

Williams, Margo. "Using the LDS Family History Library in Building Your Genealogy." *Journal of the Afro-American Historical and Genealogical Society* 2:1 & 2 (Spring & Fall 1990): 23–32.

WPA. *Guide to Vital Statistics Records in Mississippi.* Vol. 1, Public Archives. Jackson: Mississippi Historical Records Survey, Service Division, Work Projects Administration, April 1942.

———. *Inventory of the County Archives of Georgia, No. 25. Chatham County (Savannah).* Savannah, Ga.: Historical Records Survey, Division of Women's and Professional Projects, Works Progress Administration, March 1938.

———. *Inventory of the County Archives of Mississippi, No. 22. Grenada County (Grenada).* Jackson: Mississippi Historical Records Survey, Division of Professional and Service Projects, Work Projects Administration, April 1940.

LOCAL HISTORY

Bracey, Susan L. *Life by the Rolling Roanoke: A History of Mecklenburg County, Virginia.* Richmond, Va.: Whittet and Shepperson, 1977.

Crumrine, Boyd, ed. *History of Washington County, Pennsylvania, with Biographical Sketches of Many of Its Pioneers and Prominent Men.* Harrisburg, Pa.: L. H. Everts & Co., 1882.

Ellis, Franklin, ed. *History of Fayette County, Pennsylvania.* Philadelphia, 1890.

———. *History of Fayette County, Pennsylvania.* Evansville, Ind.: Whippoorwill Publishing, reprint, 1986.

Filby, P. William. *Bibliography of American County Histories.* Baltimore: Genealogical Publishing Co., 1985.

Kaminkow, Marion J. *Local Histories in the Library of Congress: A Bibliography.* 5 vols. Baltimore: Magna Carta Book Co., 1975.

Peterson, Clarence Stewart. *Consolidated Bibliography of County Histories in Fifty States in 1961.* Baltimore: Genealogical Publishing Co., 1973.

OBITUARIES AND NEWSPAPERS

Abajian, James de T. *Blacks in Selected Newspapers, Censuses, and Other Sources: An Index to Names and Subjects.* Boston, Mass.: G. K. Hall, 1977.

———. *Blacks in Selected Newspapers, Censuses, and Other Sources: An Index to Names and Subjects. First Supplement.* 2 vols. Detroit: Gale Research, 1985.

Bryl, Susan, and Erwin K. Welsch, comps. *Black Periodicals and Newspapers: A Union List of Holdings in Libraries of the University of Wisconsin and the Library of the State Historical Society of Wisconsin.* Madison: Memorial Library, University of Wisconsin–Madison, 1975.

Burroughs, Tony. "Obituaries for African Americans." www.familytree maker.com/12_obits, February 5, 1997.

Danky, James P. *African-American Newspapers and Periodicals: A National Bibliography and Union List.* Cambridge, Mass.: Harvard University Press, 1999.

Gregory, Winifred, ed. *American Newspapers, 1821–1936: A Union List of Files Available in the United States and Canada.* New York: Wilson, 1937. Reprint, New York: Kraus Reprint, 1967.

Haendiges, Beth, ed. *Black Newspapers Index* (formerly *Index to Black Newspapers*). Ann Arbor, Mich.: University Microfilms, 1985–present.

Henritze, Barbara. *Bibliographic Checklist of African-American Newspapers.* Baltimore: Genealogical Publishing Co., 1995.

Husband, Lori. *Deaths in the Chicago Defender, 1910–1920.* Park Forest, Ill.: Self-published, 1990.

Index to Black Newspapers (now *Black Newspapers Index*). Wooster, Ohio: Bell and Howell Co., 1977–1984.

Jacobs, Donald. *Antebellum Black Newspapers: Indices to NY Freedom's Journal 1827–1829, The Rights of All 1829, Weekly Advocate 1837, and The Colored American 1837–1841,* Westport, Conn.: Greenwood Press, 1976.

Jarboe, Betty M. *Obituaries: A Guide to Sources.* 2nd ed. Boston: G. K. Hall, 1989.

Kaiser Index to Black Resources, 1948–1986. 5 vols. Brooklyn, N.Y.: Carlson Publishing, 1992.

Kitchens, John W., ed. *Tuskegee Institute Newspaper Clipping Files: 1899–1966.* Tuskegee, Ala.: Division of Behavioral Science Research, Carver Research Foundation, Tuskegee Institute, 1978.

Milner, Anita Cheek. *Newspaper Indexes: A Location and Subject Guide for Researchers.* 3 vols. Metuchen, N.J.: Scarecrow Press, 1977–1982.

Natanson, Nicholas, ed. *Index to the Hampton University Newspaper Clipping File.* New York: Chadwyck-Healy, 1990.

Library of Congress. *Negro Newspapers on Microfilm.* Washington, D.C.: Library of Congress, 1947.

———. *Newspapers in Microform, United States 1948–1972.* Washington, D.C.: Library of Congress, 1973.

Schomburg Center for Black Culture. *Index to the Schomburg Clipping File.* Alexandria, Va.: Chadwyck-Healy, 1986.

ORAL HISTORY

Baum, Willa K. *Oral History for the Local Historical Society.* Nashville: American Association for State and Local History, 1987.

———. *Transcribing and Editing Oral History.* Nashville: American Association for State and Local History, 1991.

Clark-Lewis, Elizabeth. "Oral History, Its Utilization in the Genealogical Research Process." *National Genealogical Society Quarterly* 67 (March 1979): 25–33.

Gluck, Sherna Berger, and Daphne Patai, eds. *Women's Words: The Feminist Practice of Oral History.* New York: Routledge, 1991.

Greene, Bob, and D. G. Fulford. *To Our Children's Children: Preserving Family Histories for Generations to Come.* New York: Doubleday, 1993.

Havlice, Patricia Pate. *Oral History: A Reference Guide and Annotated Bibliography.* Jefferson, N.C.: McFarland, 1985.

Ritchie, Donald A. *Doing Oral History.* New York: Twayne Publishers, 1995.

Strum, Duane and Pat. *Video Family History.* Salt Lake City: Ancestry Inc., 1989.

Wright, George C. "Oral History and the Search for the Black Past in Kentucky." *Oral History Review* 10 (1982): 73–91.

Wright, Giles R. "Oral History and the Writing of Afro-American History: The Great Migration Experience 1915–1930." *Journal of the Afro-American Historical and Genealogical Society* 10:1 (January 1989): 6–13.

Zimmerman, Bill. *How to Tape Instant Oral Biographies.* New York: Bantam Books, 1988.

PERIODICAL INDEXES

America: History and Life—A Guide to Periodical Literature. Part A, Article Abstracts; Part B, Index to Book Reviews; Part C, Bibliographies, Books, Dissertations, and Articles; Part D, Annual Index. Santa Barbara, Calif.: ABC-Clio (annual).

Analytical Guide and Indexes to the Colored American Magazine, 1900–1909. Westport, Conn.: Greenwood Press, 1974.

Biography Index. New York: H. W. Wilson (annual).

Buckway, G. Eileen. *Index to Texas Periodicals.* Salt Lake City: Family History Library, 1987.

Burroughs, Tony. "A Lazy Man's Way to Research." *National Genealogical Society Newsletter* 22 (May-June 1996): 66–67.

Business Periodicals Index. New York: H. W. Wilson (annual).

Humanities Index. New York: H. W. Wilson (annual).

Index to Legal Periodicals. New York: H. W. Wilson (annual).

Index to Periodical Articles by and About Negroes, 1960–1970. Boston: G. K. Hall, 1971.

Journal of Negro History: Index. New York: United Publishing Corp., 1970.

Newman, Richard. *Black Index: Afro-Americana in Selected Periodicals, 1907–1949.* New York: Garland Publishing Co., 1981.

Periodical Source Index (PERSI). Fort Wayne, Ind.: Allen County Public Library Foundation, 1847–1985 and 1986–1997 (annual). (1998–present on CD-ROM, Salt Lake City, Ancestry.com.)

Readers' Guide to Periodical Literature. New York: H. W. Wilson (annual).

Rodgers, Ellen Stanley, and George Ely Russell. *Genealogical Periodical Annual Index: Key to Genealogical Literature (GPAI)*. Bowie, Md.: Heritage Books (annual).

Sperry, Kip. *Index to Genealogical Periodical Literature, 1960–1977*. Gale Genealogy and Local History Series, Vol. 3. Detroit: Gale Research, 1978.

Swem, Earl Gregg. *Virginia Historical Index, 1934–36*. 2 vols. Reprint, Gloucester, Mass.: Peter Smith, 1985.

Trapp, Glenda K., and Michael L. Cook. *Kentucky Genealogical Index*. Evansville, Ind.: Cook Publications, 1985.

Walker, Barbara D. *Index to the Journal of the Afro-American Historical and Genealogical Society Quarterly: Issues of 1980–1990*. Bowie, Md.: Heritage Books, 1992.

Wile, Annadel N., ed. *Combined Retrospective Index to Journals in History, 1838–1974*. Washington, D.C.: Carrollton Press, 1977.

Writings on American History: A Subject Bibliography of Articles. Washington, D.C.: American Historical Association, Library of Congress, and National Historical Publications Commission, 1908–1990.

PHOTOGRAPHY

Frish-Ripley, Karen. *Unlocking the Secrets in Old Photographs*. Salt Lake City: Ancestry Inc., 1991.

Eastman Kodak Co. *Care & Identification of 19th-Century Photographic Prints*. G-2S. Rochester, N.Y.: Eastman Kodak Co., 1986.

———. *Conservation of Photographs*. F-40. Rochester, N.Y.: Eastman Kodak Co., 1985.

———. *Copying and Duplicating in Black-and-White and Color*. M-1. Rochester, N.Y.: Eastman Kodak Co., 1984.

Jones, Mary Ellen. "Photographing Tombstones: Equipment and Techniques, Technical Leaflet 92." *History News. American Association for State and Local History* 32:2 (February 1977).

Wilhelm, Henry. *The Permanence and Care of Color Photographs: Traditional and Digital Color Prints, Color Negatives, Slides, and Motion Pictures*. Grinnell, Iowa: Preservation Publishing Co., 1994.

PRESERVATION

Daniels, Mary. "Miracle Workers." *Chicago Tribune* (February 27, 1994), Sec. 15, pp. 1, 6–7.

Graeber, Laurel. "Ah, Memories: To preserve the priceless, rely on museum methods to mount photos, papers in acid-free holders." *Chicago Tribune* (October 31, 1993), Sec. 15, p. 11.

Levenstein, Mary Kerney. *Caring for Your Cherished Possessions: The Experts' Guide to Cleaning, Preserving and Protecting Your China, Silver, Furniture, Clothing, Paintings, and More*. New York: Crown Publishers, 1989.

Tuttle, Craig A. *An Ounce of Prevention: A Guide to the Care of Papers and Photographs*. Highland City, Fla.: Rainbow Books, 1994.

PUBLISHED AUTOBIOGRAPHIES

Andrew, William L. *To Tell a Free Story: The First Century of Afro-American Autobiography, 1760–1865*. Urbana: University of Illinois Press, 1986.

Brignano, Russell C. *Black Americans in Autobiography*. Durham, N.C.: Duke University Press, 1984.

Butterfield, Stephen. *Black Autobiography in America*. Amherst: University of Massachusetts Press, 1974.

Russell, James Solomon. *Adventure in Faith: An Autobiographic Story of St. Paul Normal and Industrial School, Lawrenceville, Virginia*. New York: Morehouse Publishing Co., 1936.

PUBLISHING YOUR FAMILY HISTORY

Finley, Carmen. *Creating a Winning Family History: A Guide to the NGS Family History Writing Contest*. Arlington, Va.: National Genealogical Society, ca. 1996.

"Genealogical Writer's Market, Part 1: The Five U.S. National Journals." *Association of Professional Genealogists Quarterly* 5 (Fall 1990): 60–62; and 6 (Summer 1993): 61–73.

Hatcher, Patricia Law. *Producing a Quality Family History*. Salt Lake City: Ancestry Inc., 1996.

Hatcher, Patricia Law, and John V. Wylie. "Indexing Family Histories." *National Genealogical Society Quarterly* 81 (June 1993): 85–98.

Henderson, Bill. *The Publish It Yourself Handbook*. Wainscott, New York: Pushcart Press, 1998.

Hughes, Ann Hege. "Publishing Genealogical Research Commercially and Privately." *Association of Professional Genealogists Quarterly* 5 (Fall 1990): 60–62.

Poynter, Dan. *How to Write, Print, and Sell Your Own Book*. Rev. ed. Santa Barbara, Calif.: Para Publishing, 1989.

Society of American Archivists. *Donating Your Personal or Family Papers to a Repository*. Chicago: Society of American Archivists, 1994.

PULLMAN PORTERS AND THE PULLMAN COMPANY

Arnesen, Eric. "Charting an Independent Course: African-American Railroad Workers in the World War I Era." In *Labor Histories: Class, Politics, and the Working-Class Experience*, by Eric Arnesen, Julie Greene, and Bruce Lauri. Urbana: University of Illinois Press, 1998.

Bates, Beth Thompkins. "The Brotherhood." *Chicago History* (fall 1996): 4–23.

Foner, Philip, and Ronald Lewis, eds. "The Brotherhood of Sleeping Car Porters and Other Black Unions in the Train Service." In *The Era of Post-War Prosperity and the Great Depression, 1920–1936*. Vol. 6 of *The Black Worker: A Documentary History from Colonial Times to the Present*. Philadelphia: Temple University Press, 1981.

———. "The Pullman Porters, The Railroad Brotherhoods, and The Black Worker, 1886–1902." *The Black Worker During the Era of the American Federation of Labor and the Railroad Brotherhoods*. Vol. 4 of *The Black Worker: A Documentary History from Colonial Times to the Present*. Philadelphia: Temple University Press, 1979.

Hall, H. N. "The Art of the Pullman Porter." *American Mercury* 23:91 (July 1931): 329–335.

Harris, William H. *Keeping the Faith: A. Philip Randolph, Milton Webster and the Brotherhood of Sleeping Car Porters, 1925–1937*. Urbana: University of Illinois Press, 1977.

Holderness, Herbert O. "Reminiscences of a Pullman Porter." *Pullman Porter Review* 4:1 (June 1916).

Howells, William Dean. *The Sleeping Car, A Farce*. Boston: J. R. Osgood and Co., 1883.

Husband, Joseph. *The Story of the Pullman Car*. Chicago: A. C. McClurg and Co., 1917. Reprint, New York: Arno Press, 1972.

Leyendecker, Liston Edgington. *The Palace Car Prince: A Biography of George Mortimer Pullman*. Niwot: University Press of Colorado, 1992.

Maiken, Peter T. *Night Trains: The Pullman System in the Golden Years of American Rail Travel*. Chicago: Lakme Press, 1989.

Mergen, Bernard. "The Pullman Porter from 'George' to Brotherhood." *The South Atlantic Quarterly* 74:2 (1974): 224–235.

Perata, David D. *Those Pullman Blues: An Oral History of the African American Railroad Attendant.* New York: Twayne Publishers, 1996.

Santino, Jack. *Miles of Smiles, Years of Struggle: Stories of Black Pullman Porters.* Champaign: University of Illinois Press, 1991.

Spero, Sterling, and Abram Harris. "The Pullman Porters." In *The Black Worker: The Negro and the Labor Movement.* New York: Columbia Press, 1930.

Stover, John F. *The Life and Decline of the American Railroad.* Chicago: University of Chicago Press, 1997.

White, John H. Jr. *The American Railroad Passenger Car.* Baltimore: John Hopkins University Press, 1978, 1985.

VITAL RECORDS

Allen, Desmond Walls. *Arkansas Death Record Index, 1914–1932.* Conway, Ark.: Research Associates, 1996.

————. *Arkansas Death Record Index, 1934–1940.* Conway, Ark.: Research Associates, 1996.

Bentley, Elizabeth Petty. *County Courthouse Book.* 2nd ed. Baltimore: Genealogical Publishing Co., 1995.

Billingsley, Carolyn Earle, and Desmond Walls Allen. *How to Get the Most Out of Death Certificates.* Bryant, Ark.: Research Associates, 1991.

Gaskin, Ina May. "Interview with Margaret Charles Smith." *Birth Gazette* 13:1 (Winter 1996): 6–8.

Ginzburg, Ralph. *100 Years of Lynchings.* New York: Lancer Books, 1969. Reprint, Baltimore: Black Classic Press, 1988.

Graninger, Elizabeth. "Granny-Midwives: Matriarchs of Birth in the African-American Community, 1600–1940." *Birth Gazette* 13:1 (Winter 1996): 9–13.

Grove, R. D. *Studies in Completeness of Birth Registration. Part I, Completeness of Birth Registration in the United States, December 1, 1939, to March 31, 1940.* Vital Statistics: Special Reports, Vol. 17, No. 18. Washington, D.C.: Government Printing Office, 1943.

Hodge, Robert A. *Birth Records, Fredericksburg, Virginia, A–Z (Colored), 1900–1940.* Fredericksburg, Va.: Self-published, 1988.

Jones, Iris Carter. "The Fight to Keep California Vital Records Open: Part I. Awareness and Action." *FGS Forum* 9:2 (Summer 1997): 11–13.

————. "The Fight to Keep California Vital Records Open: Part II. Lessons Learned and Pitfalls." *FGS Forum* 9:3 (Fall 1997): 6–8.

Kemp, Thomas J. *International Vital Records Handbook.* Baltimore: Genealogical Publishing Co., 1990.

Meitzler, Leland. *United States County Courthouse Address Book.* 3rd ed. Orting, Wash.: Heritage Quest, 1991.

North, S.N.D. *Marriage Laws in the United States, 1887–1906.* Conway, Ark.: Arkansas Research, 1993.

Ray, David Thornton. *Black Marriage Records, Hart County, Georgia: Vol. I, 1866–1923.* Hartwell, Ga.: Savannah River Valley Genealogical Society, 1994.

Rencher, David. "Records Preservation and Access: Make It Happen." *FGS Forum* 9:3 (Fall 1997): 3, 10.

Robinson, Sharon A. "A Historical Development of Midwifery in the Black Community: 1600–1940." *Journal of Nurse Midwifery* 29:4 (July-August 1984): 247–250.

Shapiro, S. "Development of Birth Registration and Birth Statistics in the United States." *Population Studies: A Quarterly Journal of Demography* 4 (1950): 86–111.

Tippie, Gwendolyn. *Afro-American Births of Adair thru Ballard County, Kentucky, 1852–1862.* The Author, 1980. (Tippie has published many similar records.)

Turner, Freda Reed. *Henry County, Georgia, 1821–1894: Marriages, Colored/Freedmen; Record of Sales, Inventory and Wills.* Roswell, Ga.: Wolfe Publishing, 1995.

U.S. Department of Health and Human Services. *Where to Write for Vital Records: Births, Deaths, Marriages, and Divorces.* Hyattsville, Md.: Public Health Service, National Center for Health Statistics, 1998.

WRITING AUTOBIOGRAPHIES

American Association of Retired Persons. *Reminisce* (D13186). AARP Fulfillment EE01086, 601 E Street NW, Washington, D.C. 20049.

Banks, Keith E. *How to Write Your Personal & Family History: A Resource Manual.* Bowie, Md.: Heritage Books, 1988.

Daniel, Lois. *How to Write Your Own Life Story: A Step by Step Guide for the Non-Professional Writer.* Chicago: Chicago Review Press, 1985.

Hartley, William. *Preparing a Personal History.* Salt Lake City: Primer Publications, 1976.

Hofmann, William J. *Life Writing: A Guide to Family Journals and Personal Memoirs.* New York: St. Martin's Press, 1982.

Ledoux, Dennis. *Turning Memories into Memoirs: A Handbook for Writing Life Stories.* Lisbon Falls, Maine: Soleil Press, 1993.

Levin, Beatrice. "Writing Your Personal Memoirs." *Ancestry Newsletter* 10:4 (July-August 1992): 1, 2–3.

Polking, Kirk. *Writing Family Histories and Memoirs.* Cincinnati: Betterway Books, 1995.

Reminisce: The Magazine That Brings Back the Good Times. Bi-monthly, P.O. Box 5294, Harlan, Iowa 51593-0794 ($16.98 annually).

WRITING YOUR FAMILY HISTORY

Banks, Keith E. *How to Write Your Personal and Family History: A Resource Manual.* Bowie, Md.: Heritage Books, 1988.

Beck, Stan. "Documenting Your Research." *Family Trails.* Reprinted in the White Bear Lake (Minn.) *Genealogical Society Newsletter* 2:11 (Sept 1980). Abstracted in *Creating a Winning Family History: A Guide to the NGS Family History Writing Contest,* by Carmen J. Finley. Arlington, Va.: National Genealogical Society, ca. 1996.

Carmack, Sharon Bartolo. *Placing Your Family in Historical Context.* Audiotape of lecture presented at the Federation of Genealogical Societies conference, Fort Wayne, Ind., 1991 (Tape #FW-39, Repeat Performance, phone 219-465-1234).

Colorado Genealogical Society. *Black Sheep Contest Entries.* Colorado Genealogical Society, Publications and Sales, P.O. Box 9218, Denver, Colo. 80209.

Costello, Margaret F., and Jane Fletcher Fiske. *Guidelines for Genealogical Writing: Style Guide for the New England Historical and Genealogical Register, with Suggestions for Genealogical Books.* Boston: New England Historic Genealogical Society, 1990.

Crane, Madilyn Coen. "Numbering Your Genealogy—Special Cases: Surname Changes, Step Relationships, and Adoptions." *National Genealogical Society Quarterly* 83:2 (June 1995): 85–95.

Curran, Joan Ferris. "Numbering Your Genealogy: Sound and Simple Systems." *National Genealogical Society Quarterly* 79 (1991): 181–93. Reproduced as Special Publication No. 59. Arlington, Va.: National Genealogical Society, 1992.

Felt, Thomas. *Researching, Writing, and Publishing Local History.* Nashville: American Association for State and Local History, 1976.

Franklin, Jon. *Writing for Story: Craft Secrets of Dramatic Nonfiction.* New York: Mentor Books, 1986.

Gerard, Philip. *Creative Nonfiction: Researching and Crafting Stories of Real Life.* Cincinnati: Story Press, 1996.

Goldrup, Lawrence. *Writing the Family Narrative.* Salt Lake City: Ancestry Inc., 1987.

————. *Writing the Family Narrative Workbook.* Salt Lake City: Ancestry Inc., 1993.

Kozachek, Thomas. *Guidelines for Authors of Compiled Genealogies.* Boston: Newberry Street Press, 1998.

Kyvig, David E. *Your Family History: A Handbook for Research and Writing.* Nashville: American Association for State and Local History, 1978.

Strum, Duane, and Pat. *Video Family History.* Salt Lake City: Ancestry Inc., 1989.

Warren, James W. *Still Unpublished After All These Years: Writing Your Family History in Small, Manageable Pieces.* Audiotape of lecture presented at the Federation of Genealogical Societies conference, Rochester, N.Y., August 1996 (Tape #RHF73, Repeat Performance, phone 219-465-1234).

Index